A HISTORY OF THE SOUTH

VOLUMES IN THE SERIES

Volume VI

THE GROWTH OF SOUTHERN NATIONALISM

1848–1861

A HISTORY

OF

THE SOUTH

Volume VI

EDITORS

WENDELL HOLMES STEPHENSON

E. MERTON COULTER

The Growth of
Southern
Nationalism
1848-1861

BY AVERY O. CRAVEN

LOUISIANA STATE UNIVERSITY PRESS

THE LITTLEFIELD FUND FOR SOUTHERN
HISTORY OF THE UNIVERSITY OF TEXAS

ISBN 0-8071-0006-4

Designed by Robert Josephy

SECOND PRINTING 1957
THIRD PRINTING 1962
FOURTH PRINTING 1964
FIFTH PRINTING 1968
SIXTH PRINTING 1973

PRINTED IN THE UNITED STATES OF AMERICA

PUBLISHERS' PREFACE

A HISTORY OF THE SOUTH is sponsored by Louisiana State University and the Trustees of the Littlefield Fund for Southern History at The University of Texas. More remotely, it is the outgrowth of the vision of Major George W. Littlefield, C.S.A., who established a fund at The University of Texas in 1914 for the collection of materials on Southern history and the publication of a "full and impartial study of the South and its part in American history." Trustees of the Littlefield Fund began preparations in 1937 for the writing of the history that Major Littlefield contemplated. Meanwhile, a plan had been conceived at Louisiana State University for a history of the South as a part of that institution's comprehensive program to promote interest, research, and writing in the field of Southern history.

As the two undertakings harmonized in essentials, the planning groups united to become joint sponsors of *A History of the South.* Wendell Holmes Stephenson, then professor of American history at Louisiana State University, and the late Charles W. Ramsdell, professor of American history at The University of Texas, were chosen to edit the series. They had been primarily interested in initiating the plans, and it was appropriate that they should be selected to edit the work. Upon the death of Professor Ramsdell in 1943, E. Merton Coulter, professor of history at the University of Georgia, was named his successor.

The Growth of Southern Nationalism, 1848–1861 was the sixth volume to be published. Nine of the ten volumes are now in print.

AUTHOR'S PREFACE

TO WRITE of the South in the years from 1848 to 1861 presents many difficulties not faced by those who write of other periods. By that time social-economic institutions and habits were pretty well established and most that was to characterize the region as a distinct unit in American life was more or less fixed. There would be a few changes in the state governments, in the educational systems, and in agriculture and industry in the next decade, but they would largely represent developments on foundations already well laid. Most that would occur would have to do with the relations of the section to the other states and to the Federal government. A civil war was coming on and the growth of Southern nationalism, which gives title to this volume, was largely the product of those relationships. This work of necessity, therefore, becomes more than just a history of the South. It is, to a degree, the story of the development of the sectional quarrel as seen through the evolution of Southern attitudes towards national events. It becomes an effort to explain how the American states drifted into civil war through the breakdown of the democratic process in government.

Since the coming of the Civil War involved both the South and the North, the author has been forced, at times, to cross Mason and Dixon's Line in order to make the story clear. Often what happened in the North and the reaction of Northern men to events determined Southern action and reaction. The sections were being drawn closer together and their interests more and more entwined. That was one of the great reasons for the increased friction and discord.

To write of the South's part in events that culminated in civil war invites immediately the charge of bias. Historians have made a fetish of objectivity, even though there is no such thing in cases where judgments and choices have to be made. All that any historian can say for his work is that he has been enough interested in discovering and presenting the truth that he has not consciously attempted to incriminate or to defend. A nation's tragedy is not something to distort. If it has lessons to teach, the facts, not the historian, should do the talking. Yet when an author has worked his way through a mass of materials dealing with events so complex and involved as those leading to civil war, he is under obligation to give his larger impressions of how such a tragedy came about. For that reason the concluding chapter of this book takes its present form. It is not intended to be a discussion of the *causes* of the Civil War. It is only an attempt to state a few general impressions as to how events got into such shape that they could not be handled by the democratic process. That some people cannot see the difference between such an effort and one attempting to state *causes*, the author from previous experiences well knows. He has, nevertheless, felt the obligation to try again. Only in that way can any benefit from the study of this central period in American history be gained.

The author has at all times felt the handicap of being required to cover certain phases of Southern life of which he knows all too little. Education and literature especially lie outside his fields of preparation. He has therefore been forced to lean heavily on others for information and his gratitude is in proportion. He owes much to librarians, archivists, and newspaper offices in both the South and the North. To his graduate students the debt is heaviest. Special thanks must go to Percy Rainwater, Madison Kuhn, Helen Cavanagh, Roger Van Bolt, Bernard Weisberger, Aaron Boom, Elsie Lewis, David Sparks, Luther Jackson, Godfrey Anderson, Richard Stalberg, Helen Greene, Norman Graebner, Jack Rabun, and E. B. Smith. Each of these has broken new ground, and all have had some part in making the writing of this book easier. The Committee on Research at the University of Chicago has provided funds for research assistance, and thereby lightened his load.

Would that it were possible to give adequate thanks to Gladys Hamilton, who has carefully checked the manuscript and typed it, both in preliminary and final form.

A. O. C.

Dune Acres, 1952.

CONTENTS

ILLUSTRATIONS

CHAPTER I

THE CONSCIOUS SECTION

THOMAS HART BENTON was disgusted. He was anxious to get on with the business of government. Bills were piling up, and measures essential to the general welfare awaited action. Yet here was John C. Calhoun introducing another set of resolutions dealing in abstractions and "leading to no result." They had no application whatsoever to matters in hand. They raised issues that had better not be raised. They only stirred men's passions and led to long and angry debate. There was simply no excuse for wasting Congress' time in asserting the abstract right of slaveholders to enter territories which they were not ready to enter, and of forcing members to commit themselves in regard to dangers only anticipated. To insist that an immediate adoption or rejection of such resolutions formed a "test question" to determine the fate of the Union was a rank absurdity.

So, with a bluntness that bordered on rudeness, Benton proposed to ignore the man and his abstractions. He allowed him to finish and then, with studied indifference, suggested that Congress get on with its real business. If anybody thought that *he* was going to lay aside the necessary business of the session to vote on such a string of abstractions he was badly mistaken.

Calhoun was stunned. All the great rules of life, he said, were abstractions. The Constitution was an abstraction. The Declaration of Independence was made on an abstraction. His resolutions had been moved in good faith, under a solemn conviction of what was due his constituents, due the whole South and the whole Union. He had expected that Benton, as a Southern man representing a slaveholding State, would have seen the importance of the move and would have lent his support.

1

Benton only added insult to injury by the curt remark that he would pursue his own course; that he knew what were abstractions and what was business; and that he was for "going on with the business of the session." He was not going to vote for abstractions involving no immediate problem while serious business was being delayed. Calhoun ought to know by this time that he, Benton, would never "leave public business to take up firebrands to set the world on fire." [1]

The date was February 19, 1847. For ten years or more, Calhoun had been struggling to stir the South to a realization of what was happening in the United States and what it meant to the Southern people. Great changes were under way. Southern interests and values were being threatened. Two drives, the success of either fatal to the Southern way of life, were well under way: the United States was becoming a consolidated nation and forgetting that it had been set up as a federation of sovereign states; and a powerful antislavery impulse had developed to insist that the holding of Negroes in bondage was not "a positive good."

Calhoun had pleaded in vain for Southern unity, for a Southern convention, for the forcing of issues upon the North before it was too late. Benton's reaction was only the latest evidence of his failure. Back in the 1830's he had struggled against the antislavery petitions of various kinds which had poured into Congress, and had attempted to secure support for a clear-cut statement that the intermeddling of the states or of their citizens or of Congress in an effort to abolish slavery in the District of Columbia or in any of the territories on the grounds that it was immoral or sinful "would be a direct and dangerous attack on the institutions of all the slaveholding States." He had, however, soon discovered that "the Senate

---

[1] *Cong. Globe*, 29 Cong., 2 Sess., 453–55; Thomas Hart Benton, *Thirty Years' View; or, A History of the Working of the American Government for Thirty Years, from 1820 to 1850* (New York, 1854–1856), II, 696–700. The story as related in the *Globe* differs slightly from that given by Benton. The version given in the text is that of the *Globe*. Benton's version is that when the resolutions were read, "Mr. Benton rose in his place, and called them 'firebrand'." To Calhoun's statement that he had counted on Benton's support, Benton says that he replied "that it was impossible that he [Calhoun] could have expected such a thing." Then Calhoun is reported as saying: "I shall know where to find the gentleman." Benton's answer, which he hoped history would record, was: "I shall be found in the right place—on the side of my country and the Union."

. . . [had] not elevated its view sufficiently to comprehend the extent and magnitude of the existing danger." Sadly he confessed that "It was, perhaps, his misfortune to look too much to the future, and to move against dangers at too great a distance." He had as a result been "involved . . . in many difficulties and exposed . . . to the imputation of unworthy motives." Yet it seemed to him that a man must see little of what was going on if he did not perceive that the minds of the rising generation at the North were being infused with a deadly poison and instilled with a bitter hatred for the other half of the Union.[2]

Calhoun was right. He did see farther ahead and more clearly than other men. He was also right in his belief that unless the sweep of consolidated nationalism and the drive against slavery were checked, either the South would be forced to alter its basic ways or the Union would have to be destroyed for their preservation. A new day was dawning. It had already come to much of western Europe and had there foretold the necessity of a new nationalism; of laborers who could be gathered and discarded with changing demands; of "backward" areas, as sources of raw materials and markets, reduced to colonial status; of capital and credit facilities of unlimited size; of new transportation agencies to link the increasingly interdependent peoples and regions together; and of new political and social doctrines to justify and alleviate new relationships. The future evidently belonged to the city and the factory, to finance and industrial capitalism. Already, as William H. Seward would soon be boasting, the North was catching stride with this new age. It was in step with "Progress." The South, he warned, must either peacefully yield its provincialism, its slavery, and its outgrown social values and catch up with the world, or yield them later in force and blood. Calhoun understood as much.[3]

The Southern problem was no longer one of resisting tariffs, checking homestead legislation, preventing the appropriation of public funds for local internal improvements. It was the far more serious one of retaining equal rights in the Union for the South

---

[2] Richard K. Crallé (ed.), *The Works of John C. Calhoun* (New York, 1851–1856), III, 153; *Cong. Globe*, 29 Cong., 2 Sess., 453–55.

[3] George E. Baker (ed.), *Works of William H. Seward* (New York, 1853), I, 66, 67, 74–75, 108, 87–88.

and preventing the destruction of her social-economic system. Most certainly the man who could see farther than his fellows had good reason to be alarmed.

The great changes that had taken place in the life of the American people in the past two decades were enough to justify all of Calhoun's fears. The northeastern corner of the nation had been completely altered by the coming of the factory and the factory town. The character of its commerce, its financial structure, and its agriculture had undergone near-revolutionary changes. Population centers had shifted as the fall line with its water power had become as important as the harbors, and the port of New York, because of its fortunate location, had assumed national leadership in matters of finance and trade. Country boys and girls in the region from Boston to Philadelphia had become factory workers. Foreign immigrants in growing numbers had begun to seek the land of opportunity and to change its character. Entrepreneurs and capitalists had appeared. A new group of merchants were piling up unheard-of wealth in domestic and foreign trade, and enterprising bankers were financing land speculations and internal improvements in the West and cotton planting and marketing in the South. Business had become national and international in its scope. To a man of Calhoun's insight, it was perfectly clear that unless checks were imposed, political consolidation would follow.[4]

Social ills and dislocations had been a part of these changes. Few old relationships between man and man had been untouched. The gulf between the rich and the poor had widened; capital and labor had begun their unending conflict; the ties between town and country had been strained; banks and bankers had come in for bitter condemnation. In New England, especially, the rural areas, never too prosperous, had suffered. The rise of the factory town had at first, in favored places, provided markets and encouraged specialization and improved methods. Vegetable gardening, dairying, and the raising of better breeds of sheep and cattle had brought new prosperity and had led to the investment of larger

[4] Robert G. Albion, *The Rise of New York Port* (New York, 1939); James T. Adams, *New England in the Republic, 1776–1850* (Boston, 1926).

4

capital in farming. The opening of the farther West and the rapid spread of railway lines, however, had soon brought disaster. Produce from better lands poured into New England markets, and cheap factory goods rendered household manufacturing, as a part of the old rural economy, unprofitable. Abandoned farms had appeared in every neighborhood, and the flow of population cityward and westward took the young people and left the older ones bitter and discouraged. Thus in rural areas as well as in urban, the living of the many was falling into the hands of the few. Something was wrong with the world, and the Puritan conscience had not been inclined to stand idly by and accept injustice and wrong without protest.[5]

Already, out of the ills of the new age, reform movements had been generated in the Old World and had touched the New. As organized expressions of discontent, these coincided with the deep social ferment that had already begun to stir, among Americans capable of disinterested thinking, in those regions where earlier approaches to social problems had proved inadequate. The old idea that good men alone made a good society and environment counted for little had lost its authority as workers yielded their independence and forces quite beyond individual control seemed to shape the destiny of persons and groups. Neither the old Christianity nor the old democracy had come to grips with changing conditions.

In the 1830's and 1840's there had burned through the rising industrial Northeast a consciousness of evils and an urge to set things right such as have seldom come to any people. The whole structure of society had been re-examined, wrongs pointed out, and remedies suggested. Men had asked how wealth was produced and why those who toiled received so small a share. A few had asked that property be redistributed; that public lands and public education be equally shared; that wars and intemperance be ended; that women be given their rights; and that the prisons and asylums

[5] *New England Farmer* (Boston), XI (March 27, 1833), 293; Percy W. Bidwell, "The Agricultural Revolution in New England," in *American Historical Review* (New York), XXVI (1920–1921), 683–702; Frederick J. Turner, *The United States, 1830–1850; The Nation and Its Sections* (New York, 1935), 39–91; Avery Craven, "The Abandoned Farms of New England," in American Historical Association, *Annual Report, 1922*, I (Washington, 1926), 353–54.

be rebuilt for new purposes. More and more, the reformers had turned their eyes southward and viewed Negro slavery as the greatest violation of Christian and democratic ideals. Gradually antislavery sentiment had become abolitionism and a growing band of Northern politicians had taken their stand against the further extension of slavery. A reform movement had become a crusade. If Calhoun had good reasons to fear the destruction of state rights in the changing order, he had even better reason to fear for the security of slavery itself.[6]

Northern threats to vital interests were bad enough in themselves, but what made matters worse was the situation within the South itself. The section was falling behind in population, in wealth, and in political strength. The census was against it. In the days ahead, it must accept the place of a permanent minority. The old alliance with the Northwest, which had served to check tariffs, to get rid of the national bank, and to prevent extravagant land and internal-improvement legislation, was weakening. The unity of the Democratic party, through which the South had wielded much political influence, was gone. Only the uncertain words and phrases of the Constitution now protected the section from unjust legislation and guaranteed her equality in the nation. The South would, indeed, be in bad shape if one day men should begin burning that document in contempt or should discover a "higher law."

It was, most certainly, a situation which demanded sectional consciousness and unity. Agreement on vital issues was essential. Only a united front and a firm insistence on the recognition and acceptance of Southern rights would offer any security for the future. Yet the South in the 1840's was only vaguely conscious of itself as a section, and incapable of united action. The great surge of nationalism and the realization of a manifest destiny which had swept over the American people had not passed it by. Southerners were acutely conscious of the nation's growth and its rising power. They took genuine pride in the swaggering boasts of its statesmen and the willingness of its President to look John Bull straight in the eye. They had not responded as a section to John C. Calhoun's efforts to become President in 1844 or in 1848. They had shown

6 Alice F. Tyler, *Freedom's Ferment* (Minneapolis, 1944).

considerably more patriotism and national interest in the Mexican War than had the men of the Northeast. There were no Charles Sumners in the South to call the American army "a *legalized band* of brigands, marauders, and banditti, [fighting] against the sanctions of civilization, justice, and humanity." Calhoun, himself, had been opposed to the war, but he would not have dared condemn a friend for voting supplies to the army or declared that "Rather than lend your hand to this wickedness you should have suffered the army of the United States to pass submissively through the Claudine Forks of Mexican power,—to perish, it might be, like the legions of Varas." [7]

The assumption that the only interest Southerners had in territorial expansion was the desire to spread slavery does them a great injustice. When Senator Henry S. Foote of Mississippi talked of "getting fairly and honestly the whole continent" and Senator Solomon W. Downs of Louisiana urged the same "for the spread of population," they were speaking the language of Western men and revealing a perfectly normal American trait. When Alexander H. Stephens opposed them both and would take no lands from Mexico, he spoke as a Whig, not as a Southerner. One need not read deeply into the history of this period to know that in spite of certain important features characteristic of the South as a whole, much of fear and hatred had yet to be added before Southern sectionalism would expand into Southern nationalism. [8]

It is difficult to say just what were the factors in the Southern background which contributed to the development of distinct sectional qualities. The vast region that stretched from Maryland to western Texas was anything but a physical entity. From ten to fifteen degrees of latitude separated its northern and southern borders. Some of its states faced the Atlantic, some the Gulf of Mexico; some were securely landlocked in the interior and faced in the direction their rivers flowed. Coastal plains were often sharply divided from the rolling uplands behind them by falls and rapids which marked the end of navigation for ocean-going crafts.

[7] Charles Sumner to Robert C. Winthrop, October 25, 1846, in *The Works of Charles Sumner* (Boston, 1870–1883), I, 321, 323.

[8] *Cong. Globe*, 30 Cong., 1 Sess., Appendix, 163.

7

Farther inland a great chain of mountains rolled south and west from Pennsylvania to Alabama, effectually dividing peoples and interests and gathering some Southerners to itself to become "contemporary ancestors" of a generation yet unborn. And farther westward still, Old Man River and the streams that joined it on the way southward bound those along its course into a kind of unity, but by that very fact divided them from their fellows beyond its sweep. Variation in rainfall from some seventy inches on the Allegheny watersheds to a few inches in the far Southwest added its part to the diversification of Southern ways of life. Certainly no well-informed student of geography would view the Southern world of 1848 as a single *physical* province.[9]

Nor had past social-political experiences on this physical terrain always worked to produce unity. The South was never more than a bundle of contrasting and conflicting interests, classes, and values. Virginians who lived along the coast below the fall line and South Carolinians who lived in and around Charleston differed sharply in their social-economic status from each other and even more from those who dwelt in the back country of either state. Political conflicts, first in colonial and then in national days, disturbed their relationships, shifting their capitals and changing their constitutions. The plainer folk who settled in North Carolina and Georgia never quite matched their neighbors in quality and were never, for long, permitted to forget that fact. The peoples of the Lower South and of Tennessee and Kentucky were Westerners, regardless of the fact that many of them on favored soils were early able to reproduce the way of life they had left behind in the older South. They were young in fact and in spirit. They had lost some things and added others by contact with the wilderness and in the hard struggle to transform it from simplicity to greater social-economic complexity. And they too had their internal divisions. There were at least three Tennessees, with Knoxville, Nashville, and Memphis at their centers; the Bluegrass region of Kentucky differed sharply from both the mountain area in the east and the rolling clay lands nearer to the Mississippi; Alabamians around

[9] Rupert B. Vance, *Human Geography of the South* (Chapel Hill, 1932), 20–39, 77–108; Hugh H. Bennett, *The Soils and Agriculture of the Southern States* (New York, 1921), 1–68.

Huntsville and those about Mobile were not alike in ways and needs, and neither group had much in common with the spreading cotton world that built Montgomery, Selma, and Eufaula; Mississippi had her Natchez and her Jackson as well as her lowly folk who lived on piney lands to the north or along the sandy stretches near the Gulf; Louisiana surpassed them all with her Acadians, her great sugar and cotton planters above the sprawling, cosmopolitan city of New Orleans, and her more primitive herdsmen on the plains that swept westward into Texas. Nor was there unity in Missouri, Arkansas, or Texas. They had planters and cattlemen and mountain folk to add confusion to their generally Western point of view. They were not always sure that they were an integral part of the conscious South.[10]

Yet, in spite of all these differences, great and small, there were certain forces that had always worked for a kind of unity among these divergent and scattered peoples. They did not operate uniformly on all men in all places, but in some fashion, subtle or with force, they helped to mold attitudes and to give, whether vaguely or positively, the feeling that those who lived in this poorly defined region were more or less alike in the values they held and the assumptions they made. They were Southerners. They were largely of the same racial stocks; they liked the same sort of food; they thought the same things were serious or funny; they had the same general notions of what was moral and what was immoral, what constituted success and what failure; they were a people close to the soil and some among them held slaves; they could, in other words, understand each other with reasonable certainty and count on one another's conduct and reactions to a reasonable degree.

The first of these forces was a climate somewhat more mellow, but often more violent, than that which other parts of the nation enjoyed. The South did not constitute a distinct climatic province, but it did have a longer growing season for its vegetation, more hot days, and more concentrated rainfall than did any other section. Tobacco, rice, cotton, and sugar found their homes here and monopolized the Southern fields to the same degree that

[10] Francis B. Simkins, *The South Old and New* (New York, 1947), 3–11, 53–72; Clement Eaton, *A History of the Old South* (New York, 1949), 1–25; Benjamin B. Kendrick and Alex M. Arnett, *The South Looks at Its Past* (Chapel Hill, 1935), 13–68.

corn and wheat did those of the North and West. Trees and flowers and weeds grew in abundance and created problems for men who would keep fields clean and appearances neat. A heavy rainfall and a blazing sun put unusual strain on houses and fences at the very time that they decreased the human inclination to keep them in repair. Sudden, violent storms added their part to the load which all of man's finished efforts had to bear, and filled unruly streams to destructive overflowing. Everything at times took a beating from violent weather or hurried on to tumble-downness under the more subtle blows of long, hot summer days or quick-changing winter ones. Where everything in nature grew in such abundance and everything that man builded tumbled down with such rapidity, a tattered, careless appearance easily came to fields and barns and houses and fences. Heat slowed action and speech as well, and men seemed to be lazier than they really were. Southern psychology took on the pattern of good-natured submission to that which could not profitably be resisted. White folks agreed with the old Negro who insisted that it does no good to hurry, for you run by more than you overtake.

But weather had other effects. Excessive rainfall, coming in concentrated showers, combined with harmful micro-organisms, which heat and moisture encouraged, to exhaust the soils quickly and to render their cultivation unprofitable. Poor methods and staple crops planted year after year in the same fields hurried the destruction, and slave labor in most places did little to check its course. The problem of establishing a sound agriculture was more difficult in the South than elsewhere, and the fact that this was, to a high degree, accomplished by 1860 reflects great credit on the intelligence of the planting class.

Architecture too showed the influence of weather. The double cabin with its "dog run" between rooms, and the more pretentious home with its high ceilings, spacious hallways, and numerous piazzas, verandas, and balconies, were concessions to weather rather than to inherited traditions. Comfort dictated space even though there is some truth in the comment that Thomas Jefferson was the first American to call art in to help protect himself from the weather.[11]

[11] Avery Craven, *Soil Exhaustion as a Factor in the Agricultural History of Vir-*

The fact that the South was and had always been a rural-agricultural section also tended to give its people something of a common outlook and common interests—not that there were no cities and towns, no mechanics, merchants, and professional men; but most Southern wealth came from her soils in crops and timber, and the great majority of her citizens were in some way tied to farming. They were, in other words, plain country folk, members of evangelical churches, neighborly, provincial, eager to own land, hospitable, proud, and independent. They had inherited the county system of local government and with it a strong bent toward politics and things military. The production of staple crops permitted the development of the plantation system and the wide use of slave labor. This in turn stratified the economic order to a degree and encouraged the spread of the English country-gentleman ideal, which had early taken firm hold in Tidewater Virginia, to the section as a whole. It expressed itself not only in social ways and values but in attitudes toward the state. It never quite shook off a homespun quality, but the notion that "planting is the only independent and really honorable occupation" was general, and caused lawyers and doctors and even preachers to aspire to broad acres and a house of classical design.

As producers of an agricultural surplus and as importers of most of the manufactured articles used, the planters of the South were, except in the "sugar bowl" of Louisiana, generally the opponents of protective tariffs. As slaveholders they early saw the advantage of government close at hand in county and state. As great property holders they might question the good in too much democracy and in the urgent drive for change which seemed, at times, to characterize life at the North. As producers of the nation's great exports, they might feel a closer bond between themselves and the ruling groups in European countries.

But the planters and their slaves did not constitute anything like a majority in the South. The men who farmed a modest number of acres with the help of their families and a slave or two, if any, far outnumbered their more fortunate neighbors. But, like

ginia and Maryland, 1606–1860, in University of Illinois Studies in the Social Sciences, XIII, No. 1 (Urbana, 1925), 56–71, 122–61; Vance, Human Geography of the South, 351–441.

their kind in other sections, they generally aspired to the ways of the larger men and granted them leadership in public affairs. They were provincial in their outlook, suspicious of different ways and values, loyal to friends, and inclined to violence against those who offended. They were thus Southern to the core and quick to resent outside interference and criticism. Living in a section where color and slavery went together, they prized their white skins with more than ordinary zeal. They were race conscious. In color, and hence in the one sense that really counted, they were the equals of all other Southerners. Farms could grow into plantations. Common men of ability could reach high place in Southern life. Rural democracy was as much a reality here as elsewhere in America. Calhoun, James H. Hammond, Albert Gallatin Brown, Foote, Jefferson Davis, and others proved it.[12]

There was, however, a third background factor that contributed to the making of Southern unity. To this warmer, wetter, rural-agricultural section had early come the Negro. First he labored in the fields and then gradually took on also the tasks of servant and artisan. In race and in station he differed widely from those who profited by his toil. He formed a great undigested bloc in the social order. By 1850 there were something over 3,400,000 Negroes, free and slave, in the South as against a white population of some 6,200,000. They thus constituted around 35 per cent of the total. Their very number gave them enormous significance; their personal qualities and their social status made them doubly important. Even as slaves they created a race question. Insurrections and fear of them, occasional lynchings, and harsh regulations to check the Negro from wandering, assembling, and learning to read and write, all stressed the social dangers involved and the vigilance required if this was to remain "a white man's country." And all through

---

12 Thomas J. Wertenbaker, *Patrician and Plebeian in Virginia* (Charlottesville, 1910); Minnie C. Boyd, *Alabama in the Fifties; A Social Study* (New York, 1931), 25–47, 214–41; Blanche H. Clark, *The Tennessee Yeomen, 1840–1860* (Nashville, 1942), 22–68, 108–40; Herbert Weaver, *Mississippi Farmers, 1850–1860* (Nashville, 1945), 47–62, 106–22; Frank L. Owsley, "The Pattern of Migration and Settlement on the Southern Frontier," in *Journal of Southern History* (Baton Rouge, Lexington), XI (1945), 147–76; Frank L. Owsley and Harriet C. Owsley, "The Economic Basis of Society in the Late Ante-Bellum South," *ibid.*, VI (1940), 24–45; Daniel R. Hundley, *Social Relations in Our Southern States* (New York, 1860), 7–76, 191–222.

the years close association in homes and on isolated farms and plantations wove the threads of black and white into a fantastic but enduring fabric of interdependence, affection, and understanding. The Negro learned to speak English or found it a part of his heritage. He acquired the economic skills demanded in kitchen, field, and workshop. He passed on his superstitions and folklore to white children and their elders, corrupted their pronunciation, tempered their values, and added to their happiness by his song and his sense of humor. He eased the drudgery of life for those he served by carrying it willingly or unwillingly on his own shoulders. He made a place for himself in Southern life and hearts that would outlive the institution under which he began his course in America. In ways too subtle to yield to words, he helped to make the South Southern.[13]

Such were the great background forces that had long operated in Southern life to give it a unique quality. Yet, powerful as they undoubtedly were, they had produced only a superficial unity among its people and had given little of agreement on important issues. Party lines still held firm between Whigs and Democrats. Low country and upcountry had not always agreed on policies having to do with tariffs, homesteads, and internal improvements. What was most disturbing was that the rise of the new West had completely upset old balances and had forced much of the section along ways quite at variance with old Southern patterns. Crowding the Indians before it, cotton had builded a great kingdom that reached from a few counties in southern Virginia down across the Piedmont and along the Gulf far out into Texas, Arkansas, and even up into the edges of Missouri. In 1834, for the first time, the newer states of the interior produced more cotton than those along the Atlantic Coast. Every year thereafter saw the margin increase and the economic-political advantage of the Southwest grow in proportion. While the rate of population increase in the Old South remained low, it shot upward in every corner where cotton would grow.[14] The population of Georgia grew from 516,823 in 1830 to 906,185

[13] John H. Franklin, *From Slavery to Freedom* (New York, 1947), 184–238.
[14] Frederick J. Turner, *The Rise of the New West, 1819–1829* (New York, 1906), 67–95.

13

in 1850. That of Tennessee increased from 681,904 to over a million. The growth in Mississippi and Alabama was even more spectacular, the population of the former rising from 136,621 to 606,526, and of the latter from 309,517 to 771,623. Louisiana added 300,000 to her population in the same period and Arkansas nearly 180,000. The bales of cotton, which poured out into a hungry market, meanwhile rose from 870,415 to 2,796,706 and the number of slaves increased in proportion. A great new South had come into being.

This western South was a richer one. At its front, in earlier days, had moved the trapper and trader, the cattleman, the gold seeker, and the restless pioneer farmer. Life was simple and crude, but society advanced rapidly as Indians were removed and the fields filled with cotton. At all times it revealed typical Western attitudes towards Indians, the public lands, and the law. "Flush times" and overspeculation, debts and bankruptcy alternated. It hurried. It wasted. It stressed both freedom and equality. Yet the break was never complete, for the ends toward which men aspired were those which had already been reached in Tidewater Virginia or in and around Charleston. Representatives in Congress might vote as Western men on land, internal improvement, and expansion measures, but on questions that had to do with the basic structure of society they usually fell back in line with men from the Old South.

In other words, the Western movement in the South had been primarily the expansion of old forms and values into a new geographic basin—the reproduction of old patterns in a raw region from frontier beginnings. A Western temper and outlook had been added, but nowhere was there a sharp, serious break that invalidated old approaches and old assumptions. There was never any reason for questioning the soundness of the political order as it had evolved under the Constitution. There was no reason for doubting the satisfactory character of a social system in which those who succeeded widened their acres, enlarged their laboring force, and went on with an agricultural effort. There was no reason for rejecting the fact that some men were by birth or attainment worthy of designation as "gentlemen," and others, for like reasons, properly known as "poor whites." Nor were there many who, like Washington and Jefferson in an earlier day, dealt in abstractions

14

and seriously questioned the goodness of slavery or who maintained a place in the estimation of neighbors if they did. The good society was still the stable society. Upon sin, as understood by any good Methodist, Baptist, or Presbyterian, all respectable persons would be inclined to frown. Temperance societies might exist; opposition to dueling could be permitted even if not quite respected; but any suggestion that accepted practices and institutions be fundamentally changed might be expected to meet effective resistance. The Cotton Kingdom had simply taken over leadership from the Old South and given a more aggressive, a more positive quality to its voice in national affairs. It had strengthened the old Southern-Western alliance in politics through common Western attitudes and Mississippi River trade. It had thereby prolonged the dominance of the Democratic party and Southern influence in its affairs.[15]

But the spread of cotton to the Lower South had done something more. It had assigned a new and lesser role in the South itself to the older Atlantic Coast states. Since early national days much of this region had been in difficulty. Tobacco, which had built and shaped the life of Maryland and Virginia, had lost its once dominant place and had become merely one of the specialized crops in a region of general farming, vegetable gardening, and fruit raising. Adjustments in production had been difficult, and losses from depleted lands and emigration, heavy. The rice planters of coastal South Carolina had also suffered intensely. Nature had set quite definite limits to the spread of rice cultivation, and markets had not developed satisfactorily even for this limited production. The growing of cotton in the upcountry and its marketing through Charleston had given some early relief, but the sweep of that staple to the farther West had brought ruinous competition with richer, cheaper soils, the harvest of which went out from Mobile and New Orleans.

As a result of these shifts, a halting had come over the older states. Lands had fallen in value. A steady stream of slaves had run from Eastern fields to meet the labor needs of Western planters. Political leadership, as has been said, had gone with economic strength,

[15] Avery Craven, "The 'Turner Theories' and the South," in *Journal of Southern History*, V (1939), 291–314.

and men from Tennessee, Kentucky, and the Gulf States now spoke for the South and occupied the important offices. As the economic life of the old tobacco region became more like that of its neighbors to the North, some of its politicians allied themselves with those from New York and Pennsylvania. Some fell in behind John C. Calhoun, as he spoke for minority rights through emphasis on state rights and strict construction. Councils were thus divided and relative position sacrificed. Virginia and Maryland, to a degree, lost step with the Lower South without sharing greatly in the growing benefits of the North.

South Carolina, meanwhile, heard men like William Gregg proclaim the virtues of manufactures, praise the thrift and progressiveness of industrial New England, and saw her political leaders forced out of line with both their Northern and their Southern party colleagues. Often they stood alone. Troubled and uncertain, the aging Calhoun had been forced to seek refuge behind the Constitution and the intentions of the "Founding Fathers." [16]

Of equal importance was the fact that under these changing conditions North Carolina, Tennessee, Kentucky, and Missouri half turned around, away from the Lower South. The term "Border States" was often used to describe a fact that was becoming all too apparent. These states were not cotton states. Even though some of them found minor profits from cotton and major profits from the horses, mules, hemp, foodstuffs, and surplus slaves which they marketed on cotton plantations, they were rapidly developing interests of their own. Their ways were largely those of general and specialized farmers. Towns of more than local importance had sprung up within their borders. Trade ran north as well as south, and slavery not only had its critics in the Border States but played a lesser part in their economy.

Criticism of slavery at home was not a new thing. It was significant in the two decades before 1850 because of the full rounded character of the attack and because it coincided with the development of an organized abolition movement in the North. It was

[16] Craven, *Soil Exhaustion . . . of Virginia and Maryland,* 122–61; Charles H. Ambler, *Sectionalism in Virginia from 1776 to 1861* (Chicago, 1910), 219–50; Duncan C. Heyward, *Seed from Madagascar* (Chapel Hill, 1937), 3–89; James H. Easterby (ed.), *The South Carolina Rice Plantation as Revealed in the Papers of Robert F. W. Allston* (Chicago, 1945), 1–49.

quite marked in North Carolina and Georgia, but, even in South Carolina, it was noticeable enough to produce a rather elaborate defense of the institution and to receive some attention in the state legislature.[17] In Virginia it broke into the open and in the Constitutional Convention of 1829–1830, and in the legislative debates of 1832, reached a climax. The occasion was strikingly like that which the nation as a whole would face in 1860. Through growth and expansion the state had become divided into two rather distinct sections. The older East, with a slave-plantation economy, had, by maintaining a restricted franchise, counting three fifths of its slaves as population, and manipulating representation, kept a strict control over the government in spite of the fact that a majority of the population now lived in the nearly nonslaveholding, farming West. It had resisted all demands for reform as well as for adequate funds to build internal improvements and provide for public education. Not until 1829 did it reluctantly yield to the pressure for a constitutional convention.

When that body began its deliberations, it soon became clear that Eastern opposition to change grew out of a fear that slave property would be taxed or even abolished. As one speaker said in regard to franchise reform: "I am satisfied, if no such thing as slavery existed, that the people of our Atlantic border would meet their brethren of the West upon the basis of a majority of the free white population." Another warned: "Let it be once openly avowed . . . that the price which Western people must pay for the protection of your slaves, is the surrender of their power in the government, and you render that property hateful to them in the extreme, and hold out to them the strongest of all possible temptations to make constant war upon it." Thus slavery became the symbol of all differences and all strife. It raised the issue of minority rights, of property rights, against the action of numerical majorities; it symbolized the difference between a "progressive" order that would promote manufacturing, build internal improvements, encourage free public education, and develop a society of free farm-

[17] Guion G. Johnson, *Ante-Bellum North Carolina* (Chapel Hill, 1937), 560–72; Theodore D. Jervey, *The Slave Trade* (Columbia, S.C., 1925), 21–34; Chauncey S. Boucher, *The Nullification Controversy in South Carolina* (Chicago, 1916), 107, n. 3; Ulrich B. Phillips, *Georgia and State Rights*, in American Historical Association, *Annual Report*, 1901, II (Washington, 1902), 155–59.

ers, and one that favored the few with their "peculiar property" and their aristocratic ways. That forced a frank and open consideration of the merits and the lack of them in slavery itself.[18]

For the next five years, while Calhoun pronounced slavery "a positive good," Virginians debated the question. Slavery found its defenders, but there was usually something of apology or resignation in their statements. Only gradually, and not for some time, did they approximate Calhoun's position. The attack, on the other hand, was sharp and unqualified. Slavery was "a blighting, withering curse" that robbed the soils, drove away the white laborers, turned aside the foreign immigrant, and debased the morals. It was "a mildew which . . . blighted in its course every region it . . . touched, from the creation of the world." It was responsible for Virginia's decline among the states; it exercised a "most pernicious influence upon the manners, habits and character, of those among whom it . . . [existed]"; it produced illiteracy and stifled enterprise; it robbed the lesser whites of their chance to labor and to prosper; it debased a whole race; divided its families; deprived it of self-interest; held down that "innate longing for liberty" which burned in the "poorest tattered negro" as well as in the white man. Nothing which Northern abolitionists would charge against slavery was lacking.[19]

Even ten years later Virginians would listen quietly to James and Lucretia Mott, when they spoke "plainly" about the "peculiar institution," and they would not get greatly excited when Henry Ruffner, in 1847, insisted that slavery was injurious to the public welfare and offered plans for its abolition. The state produced no outstanding antislavery leaders so vigorous as Cassius M. Clay or Robert J. Breckinridge, who throughout the 1840's kept Kentucky in an uproar, but the character of slavery in Virginia was being drastically altered and attitudes were definitely moderate. Calhoun was aware of this, as he was of the existence of a Free-Soil party in Louisiana, the Quaker opposition in North Carolina, and the

[18] Ambler, *Sectionalism in Virginia*, 137–74; *Proceedings and Debates of the Virginia State Convention of 1829–30* (Richmond, 1830), 63, 149, 282–83, 858, 389; William A. Schaper, "Sectionalism and Representation in South Carolina," in American Historical Association, *Annual Report*, 1900, I (Washington, 1901), 237–463.

[19] Joseph C. Robert, *The Road from Monticello* (Durham, 1941), 64, 65, 70, 85–86, 94.

German indifference in Texas and Missouri. Complete unity in support of slavery as a positive good was seemingly as difficult to achieve as was opposition to a growing national consciousness.[20]

Calhoun's efforts to create a solid South by an appeal based on the fact of common interests had thus not met with wide response. He had been something of a voice crying in the wilderness. Talk of danger to abstract rights did not stir the masses nor counteract the pride taken in national growth and economic prosperity. Better reason for unity would have to be found.

Unfortunately, such reasons had already made their appearance. The South, as a section, was beginning to face other conscious sections, whose demands and attitudes could not be ignored. These sections had begun to stress the fact that all the Southern states held slaves and to make that fact responsible for all Southern attitudes and interests. They had begun to talk of a "Slave Power." Regardless of Southern feelings concerning slavery and regardless of whether slavery determined their opinions on territorial expansion or economic measures, men of the Northeast and soon those of the Northwest began to assume that all Southerners were slaveholders and that they voted and acted in certain ways because of that fact.

A new force began to operate—operate both to make Southerners conscious of slavery and its place in their lives as Calhoun had not been able to do and to give them a unity they had not known before. They too began to magnify and distort the slavery interest, and soon to make its welfare the test of sectional rights and equality. The Texas question, the Oregon question, the Mexican War, and now the matter of the organization of new territories all began to have a slavery slant. A symbol of Southern values—political, social, and economic—had been created. The force inherent in a great humanitarian, democratic crusade was now added to normal sectional rivalries, and the equally powerful force inherent in the defense of an accepted social order was drawn about Southern positions. If there had been indifference and division before, there

[20] Anna D. Hallowell, *James and Lucretia Mott* (Boston, 1884), 235–37; Ambler, *Sectionalism in Virginia*, 244–45; J. Winston Coleman, Jr., *Slavery Times in Kentucky* (Chapel Hill, 1940), 290–325.

19

was unity of a new degree and character in opposition to such a measure as the Wilmot Proviso. A fight for equality and the preservation of a way of life was something quite different from a response to an abstraction.

CHAPTER II

REALIGNMENT OF SECTIONS

THE most alarming feature of developments in the 1840's was the growing cleavage between the Northwest and the South. These regions had long been tied together both physically and socially. Like the blood vessels of a human body, the Ohio–Mississippi River system had helped to bind the whole interior of the continent into organic unity. The streams that drained every state in the Old Northwest except Michigan rose well back in the interior and flowed southward, and the rivers of Kentucky and Tennessee, sometimes after strange wanderings, turned northward, also to empty their waters into the Ohio. Missouri, southeastern Iowa, and Minnesota were tied in from the west as the Mississippi gathered to itself the total flood and bore it on to the Gulf.

These rivers early had become the highways along which population moved. By way of the Watauga, the Nolichucky, the Clinch; down the New and the Kanawha; through mountain gaps to the Kentucky, the Cumberland, and the Tennessee, ever reaching for the Ohio itself, the tall, angular men of the Piedmont South had pushed their way from the Carolinas and Virginia into the hilly, wooded sections of the great Northwest and made them their own. Until 1850 these men and their descendants exerted the predominant influence on the social and political ways of the section. From the kind of food they ate to the patterns worked into the quilts on their beds, they revealed their origins and the kinship they bore to the friends and neighbors they had left behind. Southern-born men were responsible for the county type of local government set up, for the prevalence of Quaker, Methodist, Baptist, and Presbyterian churches, and for the region's corn and hog economy.

Southern-born men made both the effort to perpetuate some kind of forced labor for Negroes and the effort to prevent it. They were the men who, in different Northwestern states, denied the franchise to Negroes, drew up "black codes" for their regulation, and, even as late as 1848, forbade them to enter their territory. But they were also the men who published the first antislavery periodicals in the nation and laid the foundations of the underground railroad.[1]

Nor did these immigrants to the Ohio Valley in its broadest extent differ from their fellow upland Southerners who turned south and west to carry cotton along the Gulf. That too was a movement of pioneers on to a frontier.[2] It revealed all the characteristics of a typical American westward movement. There were distinct stages in the advance. Trappers and traders led the way, and well before the Revolution great quantities of furs and skins found their way to market through Richmond and Charleston. Restless farmers followed the trappers' wake and crowded the Indians into bloody resistance but inevitable retreat. On the southern frontier the national policy of Indian removal to "permanent" reservations beyond the Mississippi was developed. In the battles against these Indians and the accomplishment of their removal from potential cotton fields Andrew Jackson won the undying affection of Western men.

There were cattle days on the Georgia frontier and later in Mississippi Territory—roundups and brandings, cowboys "mounted on low built, shaggy, but muscular and hardy horses . . . and armed with raw hide whips . . . and sometimes with a catching rope or lasso. . . . They scour[ed] the woods . . . sometimes driving a herd of a thousand heads to the pen." [3]

The mining rush was also present. A recent writer has told of the "gold fever" which raged in North Carolina in 1825. Travelers "heard scarce anything . . . except gold"; of "bankrupts . . . restored to affluence, and paupers turned to nabobs." "The pros-

---

[1] Avery Craven, "The Advance of Civilization into the Middle West in the Period of Settlement," in Dixon R. Fox (ed.), *Sources of Culture in the Middle West* (New York, 1934), 39–71.

[2] Craven, " 'Turner Theories' and the South," *loc. cit.,* 291–314; Verner W. Crane, *The Southern Frontier, 1670–1732* (Philadelphia, 1929), 108–36.

[3] J. F. H. Claiborne, "A Trip Through the Piney Woods," in *Publications of the Mississippi Historical Society* (Oxford), IX (1906), 521.

pector" became "a distinct race," and the population around the mines "agonized under the increased and increasing fever for gold." Prospectors rushed from diggings to diggings, boom towns rose and fell, and "the state of morals" became "deplorably bad." Mining days in North Carolina, Georgia, and Alabama differed little in character and temper from those on other frontiers.[4]

The agricultural advance was also typical. The more or less unstable pioneer in the vanguard came as a rule from the Piedmont region, where he had been farming. He made a clearing but moved easily when fresher soils lured or when some more substantial emigrant offered a profit from the sale of his land. He raised his own food; his womenfolk made the family clothing; he had a small amount of livestock, and he might or might not raise a little cotton to sell to the outside world. If he had a slave or two, they were more nearly a part of his family than a separate working force. The more fortunate or more energetic might "make," as the saying was—enlarge their holdings and, planting cotton, become planters after the accepted Southern pattern. On the other hand, they might be still on the move when Texas offered its opportunities.[5]

With hard times dogging the steps of planters in the older Atlantic coastal region and slaves becoming a burden to their owners, some planters early joined the trek to the new cotton kingdom to be. When the future was well assured, still others moved out with their establishments complete, purchased lands from those who had pioneered, and added a bit of maturity in capital, labor, and management to the economy of the region. They corresponded to the "timber barons" and the "cattle kings" of other frontiers, and they conformed to the free, individualistic, democratic social customs of their lesser neighbors, or they found themselves disliked and isolated.[6]

In spirit and temper too the Lower South was strictly Western. "Everyone was over-optimistic." Speculation drove land prices and rates of interest to unheard-of levels. A New Orleans newspaper

[4] Quoted in Fletcher M. Green, "Gold Mining: A Forgotten Industry of Ante-Bellum North Carolina," in *North Carolina Historical Review* (Raleigh), XIV (1937), 1–19, 135–55; see especially 10, 17.

[5] Thomas P. Abernethy, *The Formative Period in Alabama, 1815–1828* (Montgomery, 1922), 24–32, 57–72.

[6] Susan D. Smedes, *A Southern Planter* (London, 1889), 27–39.

described the period after 1835 as one in which the people were "drunk with success. . . . The poor man of yesterday was worth his thousands today; the beggar of the morning retired to his straw pallet at night, burdened with the cares of a fortune acquired between the rising and the setting of the sun." [7] A visitor to the Louisiana metropolis in 1833 wrote: "There is a hurry, a 'rush' among all classes of people here, that I have not seen in so great a degree, elsewhere. It looks almost like intrusion to detain any one upon matters unconnected with ordinary business-pursuits." [8]

It was a personal world in which men settled their differences by direct methods and in which "gun-toting" was widely practiced. A Natchez citizen unblushingly complained of a sprained wrist and a dislocated thumb resulting from a hard fought battle with Daniel Hickey, "whose Eyes by the Bye I completely closed." [9] An Alabama paper listed the fines for fist fights at from five to ten dollars, fights with sticks at twice as much, those with dirks at from twenty to thirty dollars, and those with bowie knives or pistols at from thirty to fifty dollars.[10] Reuben Davis admitted that the people of his neighborhood "drank hard, swore freely, and were utterly reckless of consequences when their passions were aroused," but he insisted that they were sober, reverent, and industrious. His version of the Mississippian's creed is as good a statement of the frontiersman's social attitudes as can be found for any West: "A man ought to fear God, and mind his own business. He should be respectful and courteous to all women; he should love his friends and hate his enemies. He should eat when he was hungry, drink when he was thirsty, dance when he was merry, vote for the candidate he liked best, and knock down any man who questioned his right to these privileges." [11]

Religious expression was also of the frontier brand. The itinerant preacher usually pioneered the way for the different evangelical

---

[7] New Orleans *Daily True Delta*, February 6, 1850.

[8] Dwight L. Dumond (ed.), *Letters of James Gillespie Birney, 1831–1857* (New York, 1938), I, 69.

[9] Quoted in Charles S. Sydnor, *A Gentleman of the Old Natchez Region: Benjamin L. C. Wailes* (Durham, 1938), 6.

[10] Boyd, *Alabama in the Fifties*, 197.

[11] Reuben Davis, *Recollections of Mississippi and Mississippians* (Boston, 1889), 18–19.

denominations. The wanderings and deeds of a Lorenzo Dow in Mississippi differed little in essential detail from those of a Peter Cartwright in Illinois. Both of these men would have agreed with the Georgian who a few years earlier insisted that "larnin' " made preachers "proud and worldly" and that Westerners wanted "none of your new-fangled, high-flying preaching." Camp meetings flourished, and men and women "got religion" after desperate struggles with the Lord and an undue amount of noise. A contemporary description of how Methodism won its way would apply to all other denominations: "It lodged roughly, and it fared scantily. It tramped up muddy ridges, it swam or forded rivers to the waist; it slept on leaves or raw deer-skin, and pillowed its head on saddle-bags; it bivouacked among wolves or Indians . . . *but it throve.*" [12]

To these common ties of blood and experiences between the men of the Northwest and the South were soon added those of trade. In early days stock and some other agricultural products had found a way back through the mountain gaps to the planters of the Old South. Now flatboats loaded with the produce of Northern farms floated down the smaller streams to the main thoroughfares that led to New Orleans and the rising cotton kingdom. As early as 1825, from the upper portion of the Mississippi Valley, there had come to New Orleans "a hundred forty thousand barrels of flour, half that amount of corn, sixteen thousand barrels of pork, thirty thousand barrels of whiskey, and eighteen thousand hogsheads of tobacco." [13]

Even with the building of canals and railroads, which linked the Northwest with eastern seaboard cities, trade still flourished with the South. In 1844, for instance, "of nearly a million and a half bushels of corn exported," 90 per cent went South; of nearly eight hundred thousand barrels of pork and bacon, 81 per cent went South; and of a hundred thousand barrels of whisky some 95 per cent followed the same course. Only the bulk of wheat and wool found its way eastward.

[12] John D. Wade, *Augustus Baldwin Longstreet; A Study of the Development of Culture in the South* (New York, 1924), 64; William M. Wightman, *Life of William Capers, D.D.* (Nashville, 1858), 471–72.

[13] Albert L. Kohlmeier, *The Old Northwest as the Keystone of the Arch of American Federal Union* (Bloomington, Ind., 1938), 4, 54–55.

It is, therefore, not surprising that up to the middle of the forties the "Mississippi Valley" as a whole was in general agreement on the larger national issues or that these farmers were also on the best of terms with those of the older South. The newer regions, in particular, favored liberal land policies for settlers, and men, both North and South, talked of the "natural right" to a share in the national domain. Senator John McKinley of Alabama, in 1830, spoke as enthusiastically for the squatters on the public lands as did Henry H. Sibley of Minnesota in 1852. Both refused to consider them "violators of the law" or "trespassers" but insisted that they were "meritorious individuals" who pioneered settlement and opened the wilderness to profits both for individuals and the government.[14] Northwest and Southwest alike denounced the speculator, and both produced ardent advocates of homestead legislation and votes in Congress for its passage. On the other hand, the representatives of the older settlements of Ohio, Kentucky, and Tennessee stood together in opposition to the moves to reduce the price of lands in their neighborhoods. All spoke as Westerners and, in spite of local differences, generally accepted the position taken by Albert Gallatin Brown of Mississippi in support of "land to the landless and homes to the homeless."

Nor did the upper and lower parts of the great valley differ as regions on the protective tariff issue. Democrats in both favored tariffs for revenue only, while Whigs, regardless of region, followed Henry Clay in support of protection. In the Northwest the Ohio Valley was usually the Democratic stronghold, but in the late thirties and early forties, the wheat growers of the Lakes region, in their drive to break the English corn laws and to open markets for their growing surplus, were free traders almost as ardent as the cotton producers in the Lower South.[15] Even the stanch antislavery leaders of the region quickly saw the advantage to be gained for their cause by association with British antislavery lead-

[14] New York *Weekly Tribune*, July 27, 1847; St. Anthony (Minn.) *Express*, February 28, 1852; *Cong. Debates*, 21 Cong., 1 Sess., 415, 505; *American State Papers* (Washington, 1832–1861), *Public Lands*, V, 8, 435; IV, 529.

[15] Thomas P. Martin, "Free Trade and the Oregon Question, 1842–1846," in Arthur H. Cole, A. L. Dunham, and N. S. B. Gras (eds.), *Facts and Factors in Economic History* (Cambridge, Mass., 1932), 480.

ers and joined their voices in support of free trade and more liberal land legislation.

The expansionist urge which brought the annexation of Texas and the demand for Oregon up to 54 degrees and 40 minutes found its main strength in a West that knew no division into North and South. Enthusiasm for the Mexican War was generally more intense here and volunteering to fight its battles more popular than in other parts of the nation but showed little variation from Indiana and Illinois to Mississippi and Louisiana. In spite of differences that may have been on the increase, the Valley, up to the outbreak of the Mexican War, showed few signs of serious cleavage.

Nor had John C. Calhoun, who now spoke more directly for the Old South, lost hopes of forming a close political alliance between the West and the South as a whole on which he might ride to the presidency. He urged the Western states to claim the public lands within their borders on grounds of state rights and offered, over and over again, his bill for the cession of lands to the states. He was willing to go so far in accepting a moderately protective tariff, in 1842, that even Robert Barnwell Rhett drew back in surprise. At the Memphis Convention of 1845, called to promote Western trade and internal improvements, he urged the right of the Federal government to take any steps necessary to increase the "safety and facility of commerce" on the Mississippi River. He frankly confessed the hope that this would remove all causes for alliance between the Northeast and the West.[16]

The election of James K. Polk in 1844 had left much bitterness in its train and had intensified personal and group differences already existing. The twelve years of party rule under Andrew Jackson and Martin Van Buren had brought a sharp split in Democratic ranks. Jackson had quarreled with Calhoun, who had, in turn, made use of the nullification controversy and the question of receiving antislavery petitions in Congress to organize Southern resentment into a working bloc. Van Buren's efforts to establish the

16 John C. Calhoun to James E. Calhoun, July 2, 1846, in J. Franklin Jameson (ed.), *Correspondence of John C. Calhoun*, American Historical Association, *Annual Report, 1899*, II (Washington, 1900), 698.

Independent Treasury and his decided leanings towards the Loco-foco element in the party had alienated others and had led to the Whig victory in 1840. Calhoun had, in the meantime, returned to the fold but had done so with the very clear idea of engrafting a Southern position on the party and of winning the nomination for himself in 1844. Benton, Francis P. Blair, and others of the old Jackson group were as determined to renominate Van Buren and kept a firm hold on party machinery for that purpose. Calhoun was pushed aside, but the introduction of the Texas annexation issue into the campaign and Van Buren's refusal to accept it as a pressing measure led to his downfall and the quick turning to Polk as the man best suited to carry the party to victory on an expansionist program.[17] He was strictly a "dark horse" candidate. His platform, favoring the annexation of Texas and the settlement of the Oregon boundary, represented the demands of the aggressive element.

Calhoun secured revenge for his failure by accepting the post of Secretary of State under President John Tyler and twisting the annexation of Texas into a step absolutely necessary for the protection of slavery. Both he and President Tyler accepted Polk's election in November as an ultimatum for immediate action and forthwith pressed annexation to completion. Van Buren, Benton, and Blair, on the other hand, could only sulk and complain. They gave Polk little support in his campaign. They were quite ready to criticize his administration at every opportunity.

Polk in office did not improve the situation by seeming to favor the New York group opposed to Van Buren in his appointments. His blunt dismissal of Blair and his *Globe* as the administration organ hurt even more. The ready acceptance of war with Mexico and the termination of the agreement for joint occupation of Oregon with England widened the opposition and gave it a sectional quality. In New England, upper New York, and Ohio the Mexican War, which had developed over Texas boundary differences, was viewed by many as a war of conquest and an effort to find new fields for the expansion of slavery. Opposition was open and ugly. Determination to check the further spread of slavery was widely expressed. Joshua R. Giddings, in Congress, took the

[17] Avery Craven, *The Coming of the Civil War* (New York, 1942), 187-99.

lead but many Old Jacksonian Democrats began to show decided sympathy. Political parties were beginning to feel the stress and strain of the new day.

The impact of these events on the West was sharp and immediate. Ohio Whigs of strong antislavery convictions early expressed their fears and resentments. In May, 1844, Giddings called attention to the balance and rivalry between North and South, which had produced a deadlock in legislation. "But so equally balanced has been the political power," he said, ". . . that for five years past our lake commerce has been entirely abandoned; and such were the defects of the tariff, that for many years our revenues were unequal to the support of the government." He insisted that the annexation of Texas was urged "most obviously to enhance the price of human flesh in our slave-breeding States." He was convinced that the addition of Texas strength to the South would place the control of the "policy and destiny of this nation" in their hands.[18]

"Are the liberty-loving Democrats of Pennsylvania ready to give up the tariff?" he asked. "Are the farmers of the West, of Ohio, Indiana, and Illinois, prepared to give up the sale of their beef, pork, and flour, in order to increase the profits of those who raise children for sale, and deal in the bodies of women? Are the free states prepared to suspend their harbor and river improvements for the purpose of establishing this slave-trade with Texas, and to perpetuate slavery therein?"

To Giddings, slavery had become the symbol of an interest hostile to his own. "Our Tariff," he said, "is as much an antislavery measure as the rejection of Texas. So is the subject of internal improvements and the distribution of the proceeds of the public Lands. The advocates of perpetual slavery oppose all of them, they regard them as opposed to the interests of slavery." He was soon convinced that the Northern people had "literally" become the " 'hewers of wood and the drawers of water' to the slave-holding South."[19]

[18] *Cong. Globe,* 28 Cong., 1 Sess., Appendix, 705; 29 Cong., 1 Sess., Appendix, 72–74, 826–29; Joshua R. Giddings, *Speeches in Congress* (Boston, 1853), 98.

[19] Joshua R. Giddings to Oran Follett, November 18, 1844, in "Selections from the Follett Papers," III, *Quarterly Publication of the Historical and Philosophical Society of Ohio* (Cincinnati), X (1915), 20; *Cong. Globe,* 29 Cong., 1 Sess., Appendix, 826–29.

So when Texas had been annexed and the Oregon boundary compromised, he talked of the Northern states being driven "to the alternative of abjectly surrendering up their political rights" or "of resuming their sovereignty as States." He was certain that Polk, as a slaveholder, had betrayed the Northern Democrats on Oregon and had violated the Constitutional "compact of 1787" in annexing Texas. He was sure of his Constitutional position, because the legislatures of several Northern states had passed resolutions "declaring that Congress possessed no constitutional power to annex a foreign government to this Union." With "the voice of these sovereign States to support" his position, he was as confident as South Carolina had been in the nullification days.

Senator Thomas Corwin, of the same state and the same party, viewed the war with Mexico as "wanton, unprovoked, *unnecessary,* and therefore, unjust." He saw it shot through with the slavery issue, and announced the "deeply-rooted determination" of men in the nonslaveholding states, from all parties, to check the further spread of that institution. He also recognized the perfectly natural determination of Southern men to carry their slaves into any territory won in part by the spending of their blood and treasure. Territory acquired by conquest from Mexico would, therefore, bring North and South into "collision on a point where neither . . . [would] yield." The "fires of internal war" would be lit; "the sister States of this Union" would be hurled "into the bottomless gulf of civil strife." As a patriot he would have none of it! [20]

That some Southerners did not approve of the war with Mexico and were not in favor of seizing Mexican territory did not alter the case when there were others, especially in the Lower South, ready for the conquest and seizure not only of all Mexico but of Central America as well. The free North, said Giddings, was about to be "politically bound, hand and foot, and surrendered to the rule and government of a slave-holding oligarchy."

But it was Polk's handling of the Oregon question which stirred the Northwest most deeply. Hard times in the 1840's and the ever-present problem of satisfactory markets had engendered an emigration fever and brought dreams of rich markets to be found in far-

[20] *Cong. Globe,* 29 Cong., 2 Sess., Appendix, 213, 218.

off China and other lands of the East. The platform on which Polk had come into office asserted our "clear and unquestionable" title to "the whole of the territory of Oregon" and declared the "reoccupation of Oregon and the reannexation of Texas" to be "great American measures." So, with Texas annexed and its boundaries maintained at the cost of a war, men of the Northwest reasonably understood that the granting of Polk's request for permission to notify England of the termination of joint occupation opened the way for some positive step in that direction. The delay in granting the request and the sharp opposition by Southern leaders to it had already raised suspicion of bad faith. Polk's stated willingness to submit to Congress any British offer of compromise on the 49 degree line and the perfectly clear linking of compromise with the reduction of the tariff incensed men of the Ohio Valley. Senator Edward A. Hannegan of Indiana spoke of the report "that for Oregon we can get free trade" and declared that as much as he loved free trade, it would never "be bought by me by the territory of my country." "A new and most profitable market" for Western wheat "for a surrender of ports and harbors on the Pacific" was not to be considered. He reminded his fellow congressmen that "Texas and Oregon were born at the same instant, nursed and cradled in the same cradle—the Baltimore Convention." He noted that there had not been "a moment's hesitation, until Texas was admitted; but the moment she was admitted, the peculiar friends of Texas turned, and were doing all they could to strangle Oregon!" [21]

John Wentworth, Congressman and editor of the Chicago *Daily Democrat*, wanted to know from Southerners what had occurred since "the adjournment of the last Congress to make our title [to Oregon] good to only forty-nine degrees, when it was good to fifty-four degrees and forty minutes when the House passed the bill, at the last session?" He noted further that "Already have certain politicians and papers begun to predict the South, having used the West to get Texas, would now abandon it, and go against Oregon?" Stephen A. Douglas was equally sarcastic. He charged that "every little question" possible was seized upon "to postpone and prevent action" on Oregon; that men were terrified by it where they

[21] *Cong. Globe*, 29 Cong., 1 Sess., 460, 110.

"had met the Texas question boldly and without shrinking, last year." So harsh was the criticism of these Western men that Calhoun felt impelled to explain his position by saying that Texas was a Western gain and that a difference in method was all that he had ever desired.[22]

The effects, however, had already become apparent. Polk was soon recording in his diary that "Messrs. Hannegan, Semple, and Atchison have lashed themselves into a passion because two thirds of the Senate advised the acceptance of the Brittish [sic] proposition for the adjustment of the Oregon question" and were voting with the Whigs on other measures. "Their course is that of spoiled children," he added.[23]

Discussion of the tariff, which preceded the act of 1846, again aroused Western anger. Prices of all Western produce were low that year and surpluses great. The proposed tax on tea and coffee especially aroused feelings. Jacob Brinkerhoff of Ohio called it "a *sectional* tax"—one that was "wrong, unequal and unjust." All Western people—all free laborers—used tea and coffee, whereas "three million slave laborers" scarcely used them at all. "[You] ask us for a war tax upon tea and coffee to make Southern conquests," he concluded, "while Northern territory is given away by empires." [24]

The fact that the Walker tariff finally passed the Senate only by the aid of the two new Texas members was not overlooked. Its sectional implications were too obvious.

Presidential veto of a river and harbor bill, which was primarily intended to aid shipping on the Great Lakes and other Western waters, was the final proof that Polk's administration, under Southern influence, was determined to thwart every Northwestern interest.

The "Democracy prefers to pay money for blowing out brains, rather than blowing up & getting round rocks, that impede the progress of the most efficient civilizer of our Barberous [sic] race —commerce," charged Corwin. "The lives and property of the

22 *Ibid.*, 205–206, 662 (John Wentworth), 125 (Stephen A. Douglas), Appendix, 475–76 (Calhoun).
23 Milo M. Quaife (ed.), *The Diary of James K. Polk* (Chicago, 1910), I, 486–87.
24 *Cong. Globe*, 29 Cong., 1 Sess., Appendix, 784–85.

freemen of the North, her free laborers, sailors, and those passing to and fro on her great Lakes and Rivers," echoed the Chicago *Daily Journal,* "are of no concern to the government. They live and labor in a portion of the country which is out of the pale of its care and protection. The lives of an hundred or two of hardy mariners, and a few millions of property are of no consequence in the eye of James K. Polk, when weighed against a Virginia abstraction, or that idol of the South, negro slavery." [25]

Everything added up to studied neglect, if not hostility. Slavery ruled and slavery cared only for its own interests. "Is it not strange that enlightened men of the South cannot be persuaded that our Lakes are something more than goose ponds?" asked the Chicago *Democrat.* "If we were *blessed* with the *glorious* institution of *slavery* this comprehension would not be so difficult!" Then the warning: "But let them beware! Let them take heed how they trifle with the West." "Hereafter the West must be respected, and her commerce must be protected as well as that of other portions of the Union; and the iron rod wielded over her by Southern despots must be broken. The Constitution was intended for the great West as well as for the South." [26] "We must have these improvements," said Brinkerhoff, "and I tell you . . . we will have them, veto or no veto." "If no measures for the protection and improvement of anything North or West are to be suffered by our Southern masters," added the Chicago *Daily Journal,* "if we are to be downtrodden, and all our cherished interests crushed by them, a signal revolution will eventually ensue." [27]

The Western answer was, indeed, not long in coming. On a hot August evening in 1846, David Wilmot, representative in Congress from a somewhat backward district in Pennsylvania, moved an amendment to an appropriation bill under consideration, to the effect that slavery should be forever prohibited in any territory acquired from Mexico. His proposal was to extend the Jeffersonian prohibition in the Northwest Ordinance to all such territory.

The reactions to this proposal were violent and destined to be

[25] "Selections from the William Greene Papers," I, in *Quarterly Publication of the Historical and Philosophical Society of Ohio,* XIII (1918), 15; Chicago *Daily Journal,* August 19, 1846.

[26] *Weekly Chicago Democrat,* September 15, 1846; July 11, 1847.

[27] Chicago *Daily Journal,* April 19, 1846.

33

enduring throughout the ensuing years. The proviso was quickly rejected, but it had so completely expressed the feelings and impulses of Northern and Western men that it became their answer to every Southern demand which seemed to carry a sectional import. Wilmot had not acted alone. Brinkerhoff and other Western men had worked closely with him, and one of them would certainly have introduced a like proviso if Wilmot had not done so. The point is that the North, and especially the Northwest, felt itself abused and neglected. Southern influence, now symbolized by slavery, seemed to dominate, and Southern demands were granted while those of the North were neglected. The time had come to right the balance in national and party affairs. Resolutions in support poured in from Northern states, and speakers on the floors of Congress let it be known that there would be no further admission of slaveholding states to the Union and no further extension of slavery into any territory.[28]

Calhoun, as has been seen, answered this uprising with a series of resolutions pointing out the grave danger to Southern interests in a move which would soon reduce his section to "a helpless minority" in all the affairs of government. He noted that the territories belonged "to the several States of this Union," and were held "as their joint and common property." He denied the right of Congress to pass any law or to do any act which discriminated between the states of the union or by which any one of them was denied full and equal opportunity to migrate to the territories "with their property." The Wilmot Proviso was thus a violation of the Constitution, a flagrant effort to weaken the South.[29]

Others joined in Calhoun's protest and a few began to talk of the necessity for secession from the Union if such unfair and unsound procedures were permitted. The Richmond *Enquirer* spoke of the tocsin, "the firebell at night," which was sounding in Southern ears. "The madmen of the North and Northwest," it said, "have, we fear, cast the die, and numbered the days of this glorious Union." South Carolina meetings suggested that their representatives withdraw from Congress and come home. Robert Toombs of Georgia let it be known that "The South would remain in the Union on a ground of perfect equality . . . or they would not

[28] *Cong. Globe*, 29 Cong., 2 Sess., 453.　　　[29] *Ibid.*, 453–55.

stay at all." Early the next year the Virginia legislature passed resolutions supporting Calhoun's position, threatening opposition to the last extremity; and the governor of Mississippi declared that the South would resist even to secession and civil war.[30]

Calhoun had, by his attitude toward Oregon, lost his hold on the West and all hope of its further support. The South, for the same reason, had lost an ally and the Democratic party more of its unity. Whereas it had seemed that Calhoun's efforts to unite South and West were about to succeed, now he was forced back to the near-hopeless task of securing a unified Southern bloc. He had, moreover, only the Constitution with which to protect his section. The Northwest was gone and with it all chances of the Democratic nomination of 1848. And what was more important, the Northwest was bitter and angry. It blamed Southern men and their influence with the administration for their plight. They were placing the blame for Southern and Democratic attitudes on slavery. The term "slave power" began to slip naturally into their talk. They were not yet ready to ally themselves with the Northeast. They were, however, well on their way towards an independent course that no longer took Southern friendships and support for granted.

[30] Richmond *Enquirer,* February 18, 1847; Raleigh *North Carolina Standard,* March 8, 1847; Philip M. Hamer, *The Secession Movement in South Carolina, 1847–1852* (Allentown, Pa., 1918), for county resolutions; James B. Ranck, *Albert Gallatin Brown, Radical Southern Nationalist* (New York, 1937), 48–56; Ulrich B. Phillips, *The Life of Robert Toombs* (New York, 1913), 41–43.

CHAPTER III

PRELUDE TO CRISIS

THE last year of Polk's administration was a stormy one. The Mexican War dragged on with increased bickering on the part both of generals and of politicians. Tempers grew shorter and debates longer as personal and sectional interests clashed. Two facts were perfectly clear. The war would end in victory, and with victory new territory would be acquired from the defeated Mexicans. That could only mean the prolongation and the intensifying of the struggle over the expansion of slavery, which was rapidly becoming the symbol of all sectional, interest, and party rivalries.

The Congress that met in the winter of 1846–1847 was, therefore, marked by acrimonious debate and harsh criticism of the administration. The rift within the Democratic party widened. Sectional antagonisms deepened. Southern assertions of the Constitutional right to carry slaves into any new territory were matched by equally emphatic denials of that right by Northern representatives. Moderates, sensing the troubles ahead, began to question the wisdom of acquiring any new lands. War weariness added emphasis to all positions.

Under such conditions, every matter related to the conduct of the war, immediate or remote, sooner or later produced statements that indicated the growing seriousness of the situation. Men became blunt and offensive. Cornelius Darragh of Pennsylvania declared himself "quite sick of leaving boundary questions to be settled by Mr. Polk," who "had eaten his own words" on Oregon. He "was utterly opposed to the acquisition of one foot of Mexican territory, if our possession carried with it the existence of slavery

36

there." [1] Charles Hudson of Massachusetts warned "that dismembering one republic may rupture another," because "There are thousands upon thousands in the northern section of this Union (and I allude to no fanatics, but to sober, deliberate, and substantial men, men who have the good of the country at heart) who would resist, by every means in their power, the establishment of slavery in these Mexican provinces, if they should be annexed to the United States." Success in war would thus "be more dangerous to us than defeat." [2] Giddings of Ohio went even further. He questioned the truth of Polk's statements as to the beginning of the war, spoke of his "specious misrepresentation of facts," and insisted that Mexico be abandoned "at once." His colleague, Daniel R. Tilden, served notice that "We have paid the last dollar, and fought the last battle, in the cause of oppression." [3]

Southern Democrats, on the other hand, defended both the President and the war. Isaac E. Morse of Louisiana denied that the war was unpopular and Thomas H. Bayly of Virginia argued long and vigorously in defense of Polk's actions and the right of a victorious nation to seize territory as indemnity for losses.[4] Henry W. Hilliard of Alabama reminded his hearers that the question was not one of war or peace, but one of finishing a war already in progress. He warned Preston King of New York that "he was treading on dangerous ground" when he avowed the North's intention to keep slavery forever out of lands taken from Mexico. If this was the Northern intention, he would tell the gentleman that "this Union could only stand on those compromises which he [Hilliard] regarded in their sacred obligation as second only to the Constitution." If the North followed this course, "the South . . . would rend the bonds of this Union, as Samson burst the withes that bound him." [5]

While Martin Grover of New York scoffed at the idea that the safety of the Union was endangered by the determination of Northern men to prevent slavery from ever going "where it is now unknown," and insisted that this did not interfere with a single Con-

[1] *Cong. Globe*, 29 Cong., 2 Sess., 22.   [2] *Ibid.*, 51–52.

[3] *Ibid.*, Appendix, 47–52, 172. See also Thomas Corwin's charge that the President sought war and forced it on Mexico. *Ibid.*, 213. Joseph M. Root was equally severe. *Cong. Globe*, 29 Cong., 2 Sess., 332.

[4] *Cong. Globe*, 29 Cong., 2 Sess., 62, 73–76.   [5] *Ibid.*, 119–20.

stitutional right, Stephens of Georgia, in a much less emotional strain, warned against testing the strength of the Union "by running against that rock upon which Mr. Jefferson predicted we should be finally wrecked." His colleague Toombs was equally certain that Southern rights in the territories could not be trifled with, but he was not for the addition of any new territory. "We had territory enough," he said. "Let us improve what we had; let us cover it with an industrious, enterprising population, who should spread over its mountains and its valleys till the wilderness was subdued and covered with waving harvests." And to him, that included the slaveholders with their slaves—men who had helped win that territory "by their arms." To drive them out might prove a much more difficult task than driving out the Mexicans.[6]

James A. Seddon of Virginia was a bit more personal. Preston King's move to exclude slavery from all territory which we "might acquire by arms" was simply "reckless agitation." It was "as offensive" as it was "grossly unconstitutional . . . sustained by a long argument . . . not less arrogant and presumptuous than fallacious and untrue." Rather than submit to it, "The Union would and must be first sacrificed." He challenged the assertion that the presence of slaves in a territory checked the entrance of free labor. He pointed to the South itself, where the free white workers overwhelmingly outnumbered the slaves. He called the Northern contention an insult to every white man in the South. Robert W. Roberts of Mississippi was even more emphatic than Seddon. Answering the threat to bar the slaveholders from conquered territory, he spoke of the "sickly, morbid philanthropy" which would rob the South of its "indefeasible right" yet open the territories to "The canting Abolitionist, who secretly and stealthily, openly and fiendishly, overleaps the barriers of the Constitution, . . . scatters fire-brands, arrows, and death among you, envelops your house in flames, and murders your wife and children before your eyes." When "the benefits, privileges, and protection" for which the Union was formed were no longer granted "in exact and equal proportions to all the States," what was left that was worthy of Southern regard?[7]

The more practical issue of relative political strength involved

[6] *Ibid.*, 137, 142, Appendix, 354.   [7] *Ibid.*, Appendix, 76–80, 134–36.

in the question of permitting slavery in new territories was generally avoided but cropped out at intervals. Robert Barnwell Rhett of South Carolina boldly declared: "Political power, the power of the different sections of the Union, seeking the mastery, is undoubtedly a strong element in the proposed exclusion of slavery from our territory. If a portion of our territory is settled by the southern States, twenty-eight thousand white inhabitants may create a State—the rest of the seventy thousand required for a Representative in Congress being made up of slaves—three-fifths of whom are counted in representation. . . . Now, it is designed to impede the growth of the southern States, in political power, by excluding them from our territories. The North is to grow indefinitely, and all our territories are to be kept open to their special enjoyment and aggrandizement." [8]

This, said Rhett, would determine the character of the constituency of the future states and of the nation, and reduce the South to an impotent minority. It was all unconstitutional. It would lead to a dissolution of the Union.

George Rathbun of New York was just as frank. He had figured out that by its three-fifths representation of slaves, the South gained some twenty-three members in Congress. With this vote they had "turned the scale upon every important question that had divided this country in the last forty years." By it they had ruled the nation. Out of fifty-seven years, Northern men had filled the presidency only twelve years and a single month. For forty years out of that same period, the Secretary of State had been a Southerner. It was the same with the speakership, the officers in the army and the navy. He, therefore, opposed slavery in the territories because slaves gave "representation and political power." He was willing to submit a proposition to the effect that if the South would agree to amend the Constitution so as to exclude the representation of slaves, then he was willing that Southerners should be permitted to go into any territory and take their slaves with them. It was a question of "the pursuit of power."

David S. Kaufman of Texas was quick to seize the opportunity. Here was "conclusive evidence" that in some cases, at least, the *"opposition to slavery . . . was purely a question of federal and*

[8] *Ibid.*, 246.

39

political power." Slavery was being objected to "not because it was a sin; not at all; but simply because *it was to the South an element of political power."* The people of the nation should observe this fact.[9]

And that this opposition was but the first step in an all-out war against slavery everywhere was made perfectly clear by Congressman Columbus Delano of Ohio: "Never, never shall you extend your institution of slavery one inch beyond its present limits. Go on, if you will. Conquer Mexico, and add the territory, but we will make it *free;* if not with the politicians we have now, the people of the North will bury these, and send honest men in their places. If you will drive on this bloody war of conquest to annexation, we will establish a cordon of free States that shall surround you; and then we will light up the fires of liberty on every side, until they melt your present chains, and render all your people *free.* This is no idle boast; and it is time for you to determine whether, in view of this fact, you will push on this war." [10]

Southern reaction to the Wilmot Proviso outside of Congress developed slowly. At first the move to limit the spread of slavery attracted little attention. Not until the Northern press and legislatures began to express their earnest approval was there much of interest. Calhoun's resolutions sounded a more direct alarm, and from that time forward resistance spread with increasing intensity. The Virginia legislature led off with a series of resolutions which denied Federal control over slavery and asserted the equal rights of slaveholders in the territories. They pledged determined resistance "at all hazards and to the last extremity." The Alabama Democratic convention adopted these resolutions and added a pledge to withhold votes from any citizen for the office of President of the United States who had not publicly avowed his opposition to the measure. The Raleigh *Register* suggested that it was "time for party distinctions to sleep, and for the South to present a united front." Reaction in the Old North State was, however, sporadic, even though one Democratic paper talked of disunion and civil war "as sure as God lives in Heaven," if the Proviso was passed. The Governor of Mississippi, in reply to the Virginia resolutions, spoke in like manner,

9 *Cong. Globe,* 29 Cong., 2 Sess., 364–65, Appendix, 152.
10 *Ibid.,* Appendix, 281.

declaring that the South would resist even to secession and civil war. In Georgia the state Democratic convention pledged itself not to vote for any Presidential candidate "who did not 'unequivocally declare his opposition to the Principles and Provisions of the Wilmot Proviso,' " asserted the right of slavery to enter all territories, and refused to accept any Proviso legislation as binding. Even the Whigs in convention condemned the Proviso as "unjust and unconstitutional." The legislature of Texas, already revealing normal Southern attitudes, let it be known that it would "never submit to a usurpation of power which robbed the state of its rights." [11]

South Carolina, meanwhile, was content to let others take the lead. The press of the state quickly came to the support of Virginia's resolutions, and a meeting in Charleston, at which Calhoun was the speaker, adopted them verbatim with a declaration that submission to the Proviso "would be unwise, dangerous, dishonorable, and debasing." Calhoun's suggestions for the formation of a Southern party and for a newspaper in Washington to defend slavery against aggressions were noticed but not acted upon. Other local meetings echoed their approval, and even the men of the upper districts followed Calhoun's lead. The unity of the state as well as its willingness to follow the lead of others were notable exceptions to the usual rule.[12]

The South thus approached the meeting of Congress in the winter of 1847–1848 and the Presidential campaign of the following summer in an alert, defensive mood. For the first time in its history, the section as a whole was ready to consider secession seriously as a practical remedy for grievances. The nation was about to face its most serious crisis.

Polk's message to the Thirtieth Congress conveyed the information "that the Mexican Government and people . . . [had evi-

[11] Henry T. Shanks, *The Secession Movement in Virginia, 1847–1861* (Richmond, 1934), 22–23; Clarence P. Denman, *The Secession Movement in Alabama* (Montgomery, 1933), 1–13; Raleigh *Register*, February 26, 1847; J. Carlyle Sitterson, *The Secession Movement in North Carolina* (Chapel Hill, 1939), 39–40; Cleo C. Hearon, *Mississippi and the Compromise of 1850* (Oxford, Miss., 1913), 23–24; Richard H. Shryock, *Georgia and the Union in 1850* (Durham, 1926), 141–43.

[12] Lillian A. Kibler, *Benjamin F. Perry, South Carolina Unionist* (Durham, 1946), 220–22; Charleston *Mercury*, March 10, 1847.

dently] misconstrued or misunderstood our forbearance and our objects in desiring to conclude an amicable adjustment of the existing differences between the two countries." Their commissioners proposed to negotiate "as if Mexico were the victorious, and not the vanquished, party." More men and more money were, therefore, necessary. It might also be wise to begin to consider the early establishment of territorial governments for New Mexico and California—regions we would certainly have to take as compensation for our expenditures. With the slavery issue already holding back the organization of Oregon, the latter suggestion promised as little of peace on the domestic front as had been secured on the foreign border.[13]

With war weariness increasingly evident, the Thirtieth Congress began its work. Sectional feelings flared up at once when Rhett of South Carolina took a bold stand against the efforts of Samuel F. Vinton of Ohio to forward internal improvements, and colleagues on both sides joined in to express their prejudices. Polk's veto of "an act to provide for continuing certain works in the Territory of Wisconsin" served only to intensify feelings and to prolong debate. It did, however, set the stage for the more serious issues revolving about the President's war policies. Calhoun led off with resolutions denouncing the conquest of Mexico and the holding of it as a province or attempting to incorporate it into the Union. This, he said, was a departure from the settled policy of our government. He was convinced that there were some who had this in mind. He would force them into the open. A few days later, to crowded galleries, he demanded the withdrawal of American troops from the interior of Mexico and an open renunciation of territorial ambitions. Any addition of inhabited territory would endanger our republican system, and a continuation of war would threaten our liberties by a mad increase of officeholders and office seekers. It was time to call a halt. As Senator John M. Clayton put it, the Constitution was for "the establishment of justice, not for aggrandizement or plunder." [14]

In the House Andrew Steward of Pennsylvania charged Polk

---

[13] James D. Richardson (comp.), *A Compilation of the Messages and Papers of the Presidents, 1789–1902* (Washington, 1903), IV, 532–67; see especially 546.

[14] *Cong. Globe*, 30 Cong., 1 Sess., 27–28 (Robert Barnwell Rhett), 53, 96–100 (Calhoun).

with having torn down "the great Democratic column which Washington, and Jefferson, and Madison, and Monroe, had, by their joint labors, built up," and having replaced them with "a column of military glory." Polk had exchanged peace for bloody war, internal improvement and protective tariffs for waste and excessive taxation. For the war and for all the ills that had followed, "the President alone" was responsible.[15]

Reverdy Johnson of Maryland insisted that the President was the sole author of the war and upon his hands rested "the blood which . . . crimsoned its many glorious battle-fields." "The war was unnecessarily and unconstitutionally commenced by the President," said Joseph M. Root of Ohio. And as to seizing Mexican territory, we should take it all. If we were determined to turn robbers, we should "take the gain as well as the guilt of robbery." [16]

Abraham Lincoln, serving his first session in Congress, added his bit by suggesting that "Polk was lost—that he did not know where he was—that he did not know what to do . . . —that he was most completely bewildered." He even implied that Polk's conscience was bothering him! Stephens of Georgia thought it ought to bother him, for "the principle of waging war against a neighboring people to compel them to sell their country, is not only dishonorable, but disgraceful and infamous." [17]

Washington Barrow of Tennessee summed up the opposition in the House by saying: "We have passed upon this President a rebuke which will continue to blister his name so long as he lives upon this earth, and will affix a stain upon his remembrance while history endures." Foote, in the Senate, spoke of the "scurrilous reproach" that had been "indulged [in] towards the President" and listed words and phrases he had heard used—"falsehood," "dishonesty," "robbery," "pillage," "murder," "hypocrisy," "violation of the Constitution," and "the usurping of powers." "Now," said Foote, "if the President be half as guilty, as he is accused by honorable Senators of being, he ought, for the honor of the country, to be immediately impeached." [18]

---

[15] *Ibid.,* 141–43.   [16] *Ibid.,* Appendix, 66 (Reverdy Johnson), 394–96 (Root).

[17] *Cong. Globe,* 30 Cong., 1 Sess., 156 (Abraham Lincoln), Appendix, 163 (Alexander H. Stephens).

[18] *Cong. Globe,* 30 Cong., 1 Sess., 225 (Washington Barrow), 217–18 (Henry S. Foote).

Though rebuked, the President was not without defenders. Downs of Louisiana declared that he could not assent to a single one of Calhoun's opinions. The war did not commence by the act of the President. It "could not have been avoided." Thomas L. Clingman of North Carolina ventured the assertion "that out of the State of South Carolina . . . Mr. Calhoun was not sustained in any one State of this Union by five per cent. of the population. In fact, his strength at the South was about as great as that of the abolitionists at the North. His violence or denunciation was food for the abolitionists, just as their fanaticism gave him materials to work with. The South, generally, had not chosen him to defend her." Morse, also from Louisiana, charged the Whig opposition to nothing but politics. "Have you no great question that you can go into the next Presidential canvass with?" he asked. "Are you, while condemning the war, about to rally around the hero whom it has made distinguished, as your standard-bearer?" Senators Hopkins L. Turney of Tennessee and Douglas of Illinois repeated the charge of playing politics, defended Polk, and asked for "indemnity for the past and security for the future." Howell Cobb of Georgia went the whole way, asserting that Polk had throughout been actuated by the highest and purest motives and that his conduct had been wise, judicious, and statesmanlike.[19]

Late in February, the bitter debates in Congress came to an abrupt ending with the news that a treaty of peace had been signed, some three weeks earlier, between Mexican commissioners and Nicholas P. Trist. It was a strange and embarrassing situation. Trist, who had been sent along with the invading army to carry the olive branch and secure an early peace, had soon fallen into disfavor with the President and had been officially recalled more than three months previously. He was, therefore, now only an individual American citizen acting in a private capacity. Even the language he employed in submitting his treaty was anything but respectful and diplomatic. Polk was furious. He had already confided to his diary that Trist was "a very base man"—"destitute of honour or principle." Yet he had to admit that the terms of the treaty were

[19] Quaife (ed.), *Diary of James K. Polk*, III, 320; *Cong. Globe*, 30 Cong., 1 Sess., Appendix, 140 (Solomon W. Downs), 46 (Thomas L. Clingman), 149–52, 202, 227, 231 (Isaac E. Morse, Hopkins L. Turney, Douglas, Howell Cobb).

within the instructions which Trist had been originally given, and he also knew how bitter the opposition to the war had become. Reluctantly he conceded that if the "Treaty is one that can be accepted, it should not be rejected on account of his [Trist's] bad conduct." A majority of the Cabinet thought likewise. The treaty was, therefore, submitted, amid cheers and jeers, to the Senate of the United States. By its ratification the question of territorial organization, now hopelessly tangled with that of slavery extension, ceased to be abstract and became acutely concrete.[20]

With a Presidential campaign getting under way, Congress was reluctant to take positive action on the troublesome territorial questions. Polk, however, was not one to neglect his duty. On May 29, in a special message, he urged a territorial government for Oregon and followed this, on July 6, with another in which he asked for "the immediate establishment of territorial governments, and the extension of our laws" over New Mexico and upper California. Roger S. Baldwin of Connecticut and Arthur P. Bagby of Alabama had already, in resolutions, served notice that the slavery issue would "ride insolently" over any efforts in these directions.[21]

In fact, as Benton said, "the real business of the country, the pressing, urgent, crying business of the country" was being stopped and defeated by the constant thrusting forward of the slavery issue. "We read in Holy Writ," he said, "that a certain people were cursed by the plague of frogs, and that the plague was everywhere. You could not look upon the table but there were frogs, you could not sit down at the banquet but there were frogs, you could not go to the bridal couch and lift the sheets but there were frogs!" And so it now was with slavery. "We can see nothing, touch nothing, have no measures proposed, without having this pestilence thrust before us. Here it is, this black question, forever on the table, on the nuptial couch, everywhere!" [22]

Consequently every mention of Oregon, New Mexico, or California brought strife. Southerners did not hope for the extension of "the peculiar institution" to Oregon, and many were anxious to extend the Missouri Compromise line to the Pacific, yet they were

---

[20] Quaife (ed.), *Diary of James K. Polk*, III, 345.
[21] *Cong. Globe*, 30 Cong., 1 Sess., 387, 241, 617. [22] *Ibid.*, Appendix, 686.

45

unwilling to yield what they considered a Constitutional right. There was also much doubt as to whether slavery would go either to New Mexico or to California, but only a few Northern men, such as Douglas and James Buchanan, were willing to take the risk by any concessions. Senator Clayton of Delaware tried to secure a compromise by which Oregon would be free: California and New Mexico would be organized with a prohibition of action for or against slavery by the territorial legislature, and all issues having to do with the legality of slavery in the territories would be settled in the local and Federal courts. But even this failed, and only the organization of Oregon, accomplished with the aid of Benton of Missouri and Sam Houston of Texas, came out of all the strife and deepening sectional hostility of another Congress.[23]

The question of fugitive slaves also added its part to the growing tension. Giddings on numerous occasions upheld the right of the slave to escape his bondage by the use of "any means God had given him." Since liberty was an inalienable right, any man who attempted to interfere with that right did it at his own peril. He was willing to say that slaves "possessed before the universal world and before God himself the right to free themselves by any means God has put into the[ir] power." He insisted that a fugitive slave who might kill his master on Ohio soil defending his freedom would not be hanged. He later expressed the hope that this information would penetrate to the slaves across the Ohio. John G. Palfrey of Massachusetts boasted that there were three or four hundred colored people in New Bedford who had "emancipated themselves . . . by 'praying with their heels.'" He praised their accomplishments under freedom and declared them equal to those of the whites. When, in April, 1848, the schooner *Pearl* was captured with seventy or eighty fugitives from the District of Columbia on board, Giddings was quick to contact the captain. A mob formed, and its threat to a Congressman became the subject of bitter debate.[24]

"They have kept up the agitation here to dispose the slaves to run away," roared Bayly; "they have raised funds to aid him in escaping; they have succeeded in exciting a feeling in the non-

[23] *Cong. Globe,* 30 Cong., 1 Sess., 542–48, 617–19, 1002–1005.
[24] *Ibid.,* 654, 609–10.

46

slaveholding States, which makes it dangerous for any man to aid a master in asserting his legal and constitutional rights; they have passed laws nullifying the Constitution, and making the recapture of a fugitive slave impossible." Abraham W. Venable of North Carolina was even more bitter. "He loved the Union," he said, "but love it as he did, he hailed dissolution with pleasure and joy, if they were continually to be taunted by fanatics and hypocrites —if their wives and little ones were to be assassinated and destroyed by intermeddling men with hearts black as hell." Frederick P. Stanton of Tennessee merely noted that those who held " 'that there is no moral wrong in the violation of positive law, to aid the escape of slaves from their owners,' could not complain if slaveholders, whose rights . . . [were] involved, should hang the offenders upon the first tree." [25]

The Presidential election of 1848 clearly revealed the political effects of all that had been said and done in the past four years. Both Democrats and Whigs were badly disrupted by personal and sectional conflicts. Polk, for services rendered, deserved renomination by his party. The problems he had been forced to face, however, had left too few friends and too many enemies. He did not want the office, and, besides, Presidents no longer succeeded themselves. Calhoun, on the other hand, had not quite been able to form his Southern bloc, but he had most certainly eliminated himself as a Presidential candidate. Van Buren and Blair, as old Jacksonian Democrats, were close to open rebellion—a step Van Buren was soon to take. Benton had gone his independent way, and it had cost him not only national standing but impending ruin at home in Missouri. Wilmot Proviso sentiment had increased rapidly throughout the North, and the Democratic party there had borne the brunt of its disruptive force. Southern Democrats, in turn, had struck back with equal determination. A sharp line of cleavage between those who supported the administration and those who would assert the rights of the states at all costs had been increasingly apparent. Some men spoke of their differences in terms of union versus secession.

The Whigs were better off only because they had been out of

25 *Ibid.*, 661 (Thomas H. Bayly), 657 (Frederick P. Stanton).

power and because Democratic disruption gave them a golden opportunity to win an election. Of course, they could not win with either of their great party leaders, Henry Clay or Daniel Webster. They would have to find a dark horse and run him on a meaningless platform. But they had done it once before, and shrewd leaders, like William H. Seward and Thurlow Weed, Truman Smith and John J. Crittenden, Toombs and Stephens, had already laid their plans.[26] The Mexican War had produced a hero. He was also, due to a great victory after a large body of troops had been removed from his command, something of a martyr to administration dealings. He had never voted, and his son-in-law asserted that he was a Jeffersonian Democrat; but that did not matter. General Zachary Taylor was angry with Polk and, while quite certain that he himself was unfitted for the office, was willing to accept the nomination by the Whigs if it was offered to him on a nonpartisan basis. He was also willing to accept it from any Democrats who wished to offer it on the same terms.

The stage was thus set. When the Democratic convention met in Baltimore, rival delegations from New York appeared; and when a rule was passed requiring all delegates to support any candidate nominated, the Barnburner–Wilmot Proviso faction walked out to launch a new Free-Soil party expressive of the new spirit abroad in the land. William L. Yancey of Alabama also bolted when the "platform" which he had brought from his state convention against support for any candidate not opposed to Federal interference with slavery in the territories was rejected. Those who remained chose Lewis Cass of Michigan as their candidate on a platform as devoid of deep convictions on pressing issues as was their leader. The Whigs, with a greater show of harmony, met in Philadelphia to accept the nomination of General Taylor, as their master politicians had already planned. He was Southern born and a slaveholder. His claim to leadership lay in military deeds, and his political asset was mere availability. But he was popular just now, which enabled the party to dispense entirely with a declaration of principles in a platform. That was a real advantage.

Neither party nominee was entirely satisfactory to all those who

[26] Holman Hamilton, *Zachary Taylor, Soldier in the White House* (Indianapolis, 1951), 52–75, 98–116.

48

usually voted "the ticket." Calhoun urged South Carolina Democrats to remain neutral and to "rally a great Southern republican party." Disgruntled Georgia voters broke ranks and revolt spread south and west. It was soon apparent that Cass could never muster the Democratic strength of the South. Western Democrats were equally unhappy. Cass had not given wholehearted support to river and harbor improvements, and his well-known popular-sovereignty ideas on slavery in the territories lost votes in Michigan, Indiana, and Wisconsin. The real difficulty, however, was in New York, where sullen Barnburners led the move to launch a new party and to call ex-President Martin Van Buren to its head. Because support was purely sectional, a platform based on principle and expressive of urgent economic needs for those on their way into modern America could be offered. It began with a resolve "to maintain the rights of free labor against the aggressions of the slave power, and to secure free soil for a free people," moved on to a charge that the candidates of both major parties had been nominated "under slaveholding dictation," and then boldly asserted that "the proviso of Jefferson" in the Northwest Ordinance "clearly show[ed] that it was the settled policy of the nation not to extend, nationalize, or encourage, but to limit, localize, and discourage slavery."

With principles stated, it turned to more mundane affairs. "Freedom and established institutions" were asked for Oregon, New Mexico and California. Cheaper postage, lower government expenditures, river and harbor improvements, free lands to actual settlers, and a tariff adequate to meet the expenses of Federal government were urged as necessary steps to a more democratic order in the United States. The deep unrest of North and West was beginning to find political voice. Ideals and economic needs had been fused for the service of a sectional political party. The move was heavy with meaning for the future.[27]

The Whigs too had their troubles. Ardent followers of Henry Clay yielded reluctantly. Some talked of treachery and double-dealing. A few were ready to nominate their hero as an independent candidate. Clay himself spoke of Taylor as "the merest military man ever offered to the American people for that office," and

[27] Edward Stanwood, *A History of the Presidency* (Boston, 1901), 226–43.

49

bluntly refused to take any part in the campaign. A few Southern leaders, such as John M. Berrien of Georgia, James T. Morehead of North Carolina, C. C. Langdon of Alabama, and John M. Botts of Virginia, stood by Clay to the last, and throughout the campaign Whigs "unreconciled to the defeat of their leader . . . were to be found in considerable numbers in almost every southern state." It was in the North, however, that the greatest dissatisfaction was to be found. There many had sworn never to vote again for a man from the slaveholding states. They would bolt the party rather than do so. Henry Wilson of Massachusetts declared that he would do everything in his power to defeat Taylor. Giddings bolted with the statement "Sooner shall this right arm fall from its socket and my tongue cleave to the roof of my mouth than I will vote for Zach Taylor for President." Whigs who had supported the Wilmot Proviso in Ohio and Indiana were especially upset. A Cleveland newspaper expressed their feelings towards Taylor, saying: "And this is the cup offered by slaveholders for us to drink. We loathe the sight. We will neither touch, taste, nor handle the unclean thing." [28]

Party ties were, indeed, weakening and sectional attitudes taking their place. Most Southerners saw Taylor's nomination as a victory for their section, and Crittenden, Toombs, and Stephens made the most of it in their appeal. That a majority of Southerners felt the same way was clearly revealed when the popular vote was recorded. In spite of population increases, seven Southern states gave Cass fewer votes than they had given Polk four years earlier, and two more gave nearly the same to each. On the other hand, the vote for Taylor was larger in every Southern state than had been the vote for Clay in the preceding election. Two states, Georgia and Louisiana, shifted from the Democratic to the Whig column. As one Southern Democrat wrote to another, "The rank and file have rebelled by regiments." Said another, "We have lost hundreds of votes, solely on the ground that Gen. Cass was a Northerner and Gen. Taylor a Southern man." [29]

[28] Glyndon G. Van Deusen, *The Life of Henry Clay* (Boston, 1937), 392–93; Arthur C. Cole, *The Whig Party in the South* (Washington, 1913), 130; William H. Bennet to Caleb B. Smith, February 8, 1848; E. W. McGoughy to Smith, March 15, 1848, in Caleb Smith Papers (Division of Manuscripts, Library of Congress); Cleveland *American*, May 26, 1847.

[29] James F. Cooper to Cobb, Dahl[onega, Ga.], November 11, 1848, in Ulrich B.

The Democratic split in New York and desertions in the farther Northwest sealed the fate of Cass and made Zachary Taylor, in
spite of all the damage he had done to his cause by letter writing,
President of the United States. Leaders in both parties were
alarmed. Men were beginning to show themselves better Northerners and Southerners than party men.[30]

The campaign and election had only widened party and sectional rifts. The Whigs had won because Taylor's position on
slavery extension was vague enough to serve the purposes of politicians in both sections. Congressman John L. Robinson of Indiana
said that everyone knew that this was the case. Taylor's views were
either withheld or expressed in such language as to permit opposite
interpretations. Pure deception had won votes enough to defeat
Cass. The "fact that Taylor was a southern man, owning a large
number of slaves," and thus was identified in feelings and interest
with the South had canceled the issues which usually separated
the major parties there and given Taylor the advantage. Yet at the
very same time Northern men were being told, even by such leaders as Corwin, that the Taylor and Millard Fillmore ticket was the
true Free-Soil ticket—far more so than was that of Martin Van
Buren. Therefore, said Robinson, in spite of the fact that up to the
present he had voted against the Wilmot Proviso, from now on he
"should give no such vote." [31]

A member of the Whig state committee in Ohio, meanwhile,
told of how his efforts with men who had once been "reliable
Whigs" had been "repulsed with insult" and how many Whigs
had become "incorrigible fanaticky—mad men upon the subject
of electing a slaveholding President." It was this which soon permitted a combination of Democrats and Free-Soilers to send Salmon
P. Chase to the Senate. The same combination in Indiana, designated by a local leader as "the locofocos & the disappointed of *all*
factions," swelled the Cass vote and enabled such a stanch antislavery man as George W. Julian to enter Congress. As another In-

Phillips (ed.), *The Correspondence of Robert Toombs, Alexander H. Stephens, and
Howell Cobb*, American Historical Association, *Annual Report*, 1911, II (Washington,
1913), 137; Raleigh *North Carolina Standard*, November 15, 1848.

[30] Brainerd Dyer, *Zachary Taylor* (Baton Rouge, 1946), 271–301; Hamilton, *Zachary
Taylor*, 117–33.

[31] *Cong. Globe,* 30 Cong., 2 Sess., 54–55.

diana party leader put it, "Because the Whigs have elected a *Southern* President," many now argue that "every Democrat should turn free-soiler." John Wentworth, out in Chicago, merely noted that the Union was still ruled by the capitalists of the South with their slave representation and that they would not be satisfied until slavery had been carried into every territory.[32]

Southern reactions, in certain quarters, were equally disturbing. South Carolina was again in the lead. There, in the summer of 1848, both Calhoun and Rhett had spoken of the need for decisive action to secure Southern rights in the territories and to "save the South." Calhoun urged "a great Southern republican party, based on principles"—one with which "we can command our terms and control the North." If this failed, the section would at least be "as well prepared for the struggle as the North." "Though the Union is dear to us," he concluded, "our honor and our liberty are dearer." Rhett too wanted Southern unity, but he thought that a Southern convention was impossible and that a more practical method was for the states to instruct their representatives in Congress to leave their seats and return home should "Abolition in any of its forms prevail in the legislation of Congress." If others refused, South Carolina should act alone.

With the election over, each man sought to inaugurate his movement. Calhoun's followers sent a circular to the other states proposing a convention. Rhett urged the South Carolina legislature to implement his plan. Calhoun, however, "chanced" to visit the legislature when it met and, therefore, had his way. Resolutions were passed to the effect "that South Carolina was prepared to coöperate with her sister states in resisting the Wilmot Proviso at any and every hazard." Calhoun, thus reinforced, proceeded to Washington determined to achieve among the Southern delegates in Congress that unity of which he had so long dreamed.[33]

Excitement also spread to North Carolina, where a state-rights Whig introduced resolutions declaring the territories to be common property and denying the constitutionality of discrimination which deprived the citizens of any state of full and equal rights

[32] James A. Lazall to Smith, December 20, 1848, in Smith Papers; Chicago *Democrat*, November 14, December 1, 1848.

[33] Laura A. White, *Robert Barnwell Rhett; Father of Secession* (New York, 1931), 98–99.

therein. As amended and adopted, these resolutions denounced the aggressions on slavery by reckless Northern politicians, called the effort to exclude the slave trade from the District of Columbia an act of "gross injustice and wrong," advocated the extension of the Missouri Compromise line to the Pacific, and asserted the devoted attachment of North Carolina citizens to the Union. In Virginia, where both Whigs and Democrats had early been outspoken against the hated Wilmot Proviso, the Whigs now drew back. They did not wish to embarrass the administration. Slavery could not exist in the territories, they said, and, anyway, Taylor would quiet the excitement. Democrats, however, were still skeptical. The governor's message spoke of the "necessary and inevitable dissolution of this 'glorious Union' if Wilmot Proviso efforts persisted," and young John B. Floyd presented resolutions not only declaring such acts unconstitutional but also instructing the governor to convene the legislature in extra session if necessary. Both in North Carolina and in Virginia debate on these resolutions went on steadily while the members of Congress gathered for the final session under the Polk administration.[34]

Feelings in Georgia and in a few corners of the Lower South were also tense. The results of the election were scarcely known when one Democratic editor wrote: "*The Whigs in our streets are even now preparing excuses* for Gen. Taylor, in the event that he 'holds his hand' when 'the Proviso' is presented to him. The *party* will uphold him in it." Toombs urged calmness and stressed the fact that the South had no practical interest in the southwestern territories. That only increased the doubts that many had begun to feel regarding Taylor's position. Democratic journals in Augusta, Macon, Milledgeville, and Columbus, which had temporarily restrained their sympathy for Calhoun's Southern movement, now came out openly in its favor. South Carolina's circular suggesting a convention met with approval in Mississippi, and Florida soon pledged herself to join the other slaveholding states in whatever measures of defense the highest wisdom of all might devise.[35]

Meanwhile, Congress had begun its work. Polk in his last an-

[34] Sitterson, *Secession Movement in North Carolina*, 44–47; Richmond *Enquirer*, December 25, 1848; Richmond *Whig*, December 5, 1848.

[35] John Forsyth to Cobb, November 10, 1848, in Phillips (ed.), *Correspondence of Toombs, Stephens, and Cobb*, 136.

nual message insisted that it was "our solemn duty to provide, with the least practicable delay, for New Mexico and California, regularly organized territorial governments." Everyone, he said, knew why this had not been done in the last session. Yet how irrational it was, with such prospects for greatness and prosperity ahead of us, to permit "the agitation of a domestic question" to thwart these ends "and to endanger by internal strifes, geographical divisions, and heated contests for political power . . . the harmony of the glorious Union of our confederated States." He hoped that members would approach "the only domestic question which seriously threatens, or probably ever can threaten, to disturb the harmony and successful operation of our system," in a spirit of compromise and mutual concessions. The question of slavery in these territories was believed to be "rather abstract than practical"; yet all should remember that these lands had been won by the efforts of both sections and should therefore respect the equal rights of others.[36]

It was a serious, statesmanlike message with practical suggestions as to different ways in which the problem might be handled; yet it fell on deaf ears. The efforts of Douglas to organize the whole region into a single unit, admit it as a state, and leave the slavery question to the people met with little favor. His amended proposition to admit California, and to organize New Mexico as a territory, was even more flatly rejected by Southern supporters. A petition from citizens in New Mexico asking for a "speedy organization" and expressing a desire to exclude slavery was condemned by Calhoun as an insult—an act of "insolence"—and the efforts of Palfrey, Giddings, and Daniel Gott to end the slave trade in the District of Columbia brought back all the bitterness and uncompromising attitudes of the previous session. Root added what Southerners thought was insult to injury by asking that the Committee on Territories be instructed to report, "with as little delay as practicable," a bill providing territorial governments for New Mexico and California "and excluding slavery therefrom."

Slavery was again elbowing "all other business" out of Congress. It was again, as William Sawyer of Ohio said, "appropriating to its own use the time which properly . . . [belonged] to the peo-

[36] Cong. Globe, 30 Cong., 2 Sess., 5.

ple—the white people—the people who constitute[d] this great nation." "From morning to night, day after day, and week after week," he protested, "nothing can get a hearing that will not afford an opportunity to lug in something about negro slavery. It is negro in the morning—the poor negro at noon—and at night again this same negro is thrust in upon us. . . . I beg gentlemen to remember there are some white people in this country, and these white people are entitled to some consideration. . . . Yet, a stranger . . . listening to the debates on this floor . . . would very naturally suppose that Congress was instituted mainly for the benefit of negroes." [37]

Here were the things for which Calhoun and his friends had been waiting. Amid great excitement a call went out for a caucus of all Southern Congressmen. Some eighty members from both parties attended. Most Democrats were ready for strong action, but many Whigs, such as Toombs and Stephens, went for the purpose of checking any radical moves. Calhoun took the lead, and from a committee of which he was the chairman came a strong address directed to the people of the South. Moderates objected to it as impolitic and too threatening. Whigs saw danger in it to the incoming administration. As Toombs wrote to his friend Crittenden: "This Southern movement is a bold strike to disorganize the Southern Whigs and either to destroy Genl. Taylor in advance or compel him to throw himself in the hands of a large section of the democracy at the South." The address was, therefore, returned to committee and an effort made to substitute a much milder one drawn by Senator Berrien. In the end, however, the Calhoun address, slightly modified in one section, was adopted and sent out to the nation over the signatures of forty-eight members.[38]

This so-called Southern Address recounted the aggressions and encroachments of the North upon Constitutional rights: interference with the recovery of runaway slaves, "systematic agitation" against slavery itself, refusal of equal rights in the territories, and moves to check slavery in the District of Columbia. All threatened "with destruction the greatest and most vital of all the interests

[37] *Ibid.*, Appendix, 80.
[38] Robert Toombs to John J. Crittenden, January 3, 1849, in Phillips (ed.), *Correspondence of Toombs, Stephens, and Cobb,* 139.

and institutions of the South." Security was gone. Emancipation was a real threat. A race war impended. The South was being reduced to an impotent minority at the mercy of a fanatical majority. The people of the South must realize their situation and prepare for action.[39]

The effect of the Address on the South was not all that Calhoun might have wished. More moderate addresses by Berrien and Cobb had some effect, yet the real trouble lay deeper. The people were not yet greatly alarmed. A few papers in Mississippi and South Carolina talked of this as a genuine ultimatum the rejection of which should lead to secession, but the great majority were willing to await General Taylor and the new Whig administration.

While Congress rounded out its final days, more real and more pressing matters were occurring in faraway California. There on January 24, 1848, James W. Marshall found some flakes of gold in the tailrace of a sawmill which he and John A. Sutter were erecting some fifty miles northeast of Sutter's Fort. Soon other deposits were discovered in the neighborhood, and a new era, both for California and for the nation, opened. News of the find at first spread slowly, but by May the local rush was on and the news was sweeping eastward. Reports that individuals were washing out from twenty to one hundred dollars worth of gold in a day meant much to footloose Americans who moved easily, in the hope of bettering their fortunes. In California "peace and quiet vanished. To all appearances men seemed to have gone insane, or to have suddenly lost some of their five senses; they were apparently living in a dream." By fall the new and richer frontier had caught the attention of the whole nation and turned the more sober American westward movement into a mad rush which quickly transformed California from the rather vague "territory acquired from Mexico" into a strange new El Dorado toward which thousands were making their way. The matter of government, of territorial organization, which some had viewed up to now as something of an abstraction, suddenly became a practical, burning issue.

[39] Crallé (ed.), *Works of John C. Calhoun,* VI, 285-313.

CHAPTER IV

THE FIRST CRISIS—1850

W HEN James K. Polk heard of Zachary Taylor's election to the presidency, he viewed it as something
"deeply to be regretted." "Without political information and without experience in civil life," he wrote, "he is wholly
unqualified for the station." This opinion was seemingly confirmed
when, on the way to the inauguration ceremonies, Taylor suddenly turned to Polk and expressed the opinion that California and
Oregon were too distant to become members of the Union, and
that it would be better for them to be an independent government.
"He is . . . uneducated, exceedingly ignorant of public affairs,
and, I should judge, of very ordinary capacity," was Polk's blunt
and disturbed comment.[1]

The choosing of a weak cabinet, and a quick yielding to the influence of William H. Seward, soon spread distrust to wider quarters. The Southern Whigs had rallied their strength in the late
election by assuming that Taylor would support their interests. A
few had even been willing to make some concessions where only
an abstract principle seemed to be involved, because they believed
that Taylor would give adequate protection in all practical cases.
Most of them ignored the fact that Northern Whigs were supporting Taylor for exactly opposite reasons. Now, however, many were
in a position to be more realistic. As a result, two factions
quickly made their appearance: those who stood loyally behind
the new administration and excused the President's unpopular
acts on grounds of inexperience, and those who placed Southern
rights first and Taylor second. Southern Democrats, on the other
hand, in spite of many votes given to the General, had been quick

[1] Quaife (ed.), *Diary of James K. Polk*, IV, 184, 876.

57

to question Taylor's real value to their section. They had, moreover, been the chief backers of Calhoun's Southern Address and represented themselves as the real defenders of Southern rights. They stood ready to criticize and to make political capital either of hesitation or of unfriendly action. The situation was a delicate one, taking on added importance because of the local elections to be held in the autumn of 1849 and the pressing problems which the new territories would offer to the Congress when it met in early December.

With little understanding of political risks involved and, perhaps, with little regard for them, Taylor quickly revealed his plans. Before he had been a month in office, he sent his friend, Congressman Thomas Butler King of Georgia, to California to express his desire that the people form a "constitution and government, and petition Congress for admission as a state." It was not important, as he saw it, whether the first steps came from Congress or from the people themselves. The important thing was to get a government where it was needed. This plan probably originated with Secretary of State Clayton. He had, early in the Thirtieth Congress, suggested to Crittenden that the way out of the sectional difficulties arising from slavery extension was "to skip the territorial stage and organize states . . . with such constitutions as they adopted." Crittenden now urged him to carry out this plan in dealing with California, and received in reply assurance that Clayton had been *"wide awake"* on the subject; that the suggested plan would be carried out as Crittenden wished; and that California would be admitted—"free and Whig!" [2]

Regardless of whose plan it was, King did his work well, and on September 1 a little band of Californians, under the call of General Bennett Riley, met in Monterey to begin the work of framing a constitution. In six weeks the task was finished. A constitution based on those of Iowa and New York and *forever prohibiting slavery* was offered to the voters of the territory. By early December it had been adopted and state and Federal officials elected. Taylor could inform Congress when it met that California's application for admission to the Union would shortly arrive.

The President also took steps to secure action in New Mexico.

[2] Dyer, *Zachary Taylor*, 370–71; Hamilton, *Zachary Taylor*, 175–80.

In November he instructed Lieutenant Colonel George A. McCall, about to leave for that territory, to tell the people that they need not await Congressional action before establishing a government. "It is their right to appear before Congress and ask admission into the Union," he said. The purpose was clear. Taylor wished to avoid a renewal of the old slavery conflict at any price. He was not proving himself to be the ardent defender of slavery that Southern supporters had hoped. His speech in August, at Mercer, Pennsylvania, in which he declared that the "people of the North need have no apprehension of the further extension of slavery," confirmed their worst fears.[3]

These developments gave new vigor to the Southern movement which the Virginia resolutions and Calhoun's Address had launched. At first it seemed that its only real strength lay in South Carolina and Mississippi. Even Calhoun's most ardent followers did not expect Virginia to live up to her own threats. As Richard K. Crallé wrote: "In short, Sir, should the Wilmot Proviso be passed, nay, should Congress next proceed to abolish Slavery in the District, and the trade between the States, I am compelled to say, with feelings of deep mortification, that Virginia, after a few patriotic groans, will submit." Herschel V. Johnson was equally pessimistic regarding Georgia. The Democratic state convention had not dared to touch the Calhoun Address. "It would have torn us to atoms," he said. The Virginia resolutions had been adopted, but the people of the South were not "properly awake to the danger," nor "thoroughly nerved to united resistance."[4]

Yet damage had been done. Both Whigs and Democrats were feeling the strain. Although the Calhoun Address had not stirred "any popular excitement" it had, at least, everywhere prepared men's minds for any emergency that might arise. One Georgia elector frankly admitted that "the Northern democracy" had fought its last battle for Southern rights, and an Alabama leader informed Cobb that his state was *gone, 'hook and line'* to the Calhoun forces. Some Whigs too, as in Virginia, were willing to

---

[3] Quoted in Dyer, *Zachary Taylor*, 373. See also Hamilton, *Zachary Taylor*, 225.
[4] Crallé to Calhoun, July 25, 1849, in Jameson (ed.), *Correspondence of John C. Calhoun*, 1200; Herschel V. Johnson to Calhoun, July 20, 1849, *ibid.*, 1198.

support the Southern movement both by resolutions and by votes. Stephens told of a great effort in the interior of his state to "create excitement and agitation on the slave question," and Toombs was forced to explain Taylor's mistakes by the fact that he was "in a new position" surrounded by "strangers whose aims and objects . . . [were] not known to him." A few of the more pessimistic were already suggesting that the whole North was "becoming ultra anti-slavery and the whole South ultra pro-slavery." They were of the opinion that the existing political parties were doomed. Could the Southern Democracy depend upon the "Hunker democracy" of the North when they were everywhere merging into the Barn-burners? Could the Whigs survive the attempt to carry out any positive program? There was but one answer, said Henry L. Benning: "Old associations, old pledges, old hopes, perhaps convictions, . . . [might] for awhile keep a few old leaders of the Northern democracy in their old position on the slavery questions; but the body and the present leaders of the party . . . [were] gone, gone forever." The "wish to keep up the unity of the Democratic party . . . [was] now vain." Not only could it not protect slavery, it could not even "protect itself from annihilation, except by falling in with the anti-slavery current!" The Whigs, he thought, were in the same situation if not a worse one, and in some Southern states they were already "hopelessly split up" between those who retained a fading hope in Taylor and those who saw the necessity of taking a positive stand regardless of party. Neither group had anything in common with Northern Whigs. "Surely . . . it . . . [could] be but a little time, whether so soon as next Congress or not, before, owing to the causes now at work, the North and the South must stand face to face in hostile attitude." [5]

Taylor's moves in California and New Mexico thus supplied the Southern movement with a driving force that up to now it had lacked. Hard times, with cotton falling as low as four and a half cents a pound, added their part. In Virginia, where the Con-

[5] Hopkins Holsey to Cobb, February 13, 1849, in Phillips (ed.), *Correspondence of Toombs, Stephens, and Cobb,* 151; George S. Houston to Cobb, June 26, 1849, *ibid.,* 166; Stephens to George W. Crawford, March 2, 1849, *ibid.,* 155; Toombs to Mrs. Chapman Coleman, June 22, 1849, *ibid.,* 165; Henry L. Benning to Cobb, July 1, 1849, *ibid.,* 169–70; Thomas W. Thomas to Cobb, August 19, 1849, *ibid.,* 174; Shanks, *Secession Movement in Virginia,* 26–27.

gressional elections had already shown the willingness of Democrats and Southern Rights Whigs to work together, the Richmond
Enquirer on October 19 bluntly asserted that California should
not be admitted because she was too large and because she had
not gone through the territorial stage. Soon it was urging Southern
Congressmen to make their fight on the California issue, and to
check the abolitionists at the threshold. Whig papers still supported Taylor but admitted that the antislavery clause in the
California bill of rights was unwise. It could only be justified as a
step toward ending sectional conflict.

The shift in North Carolina, where elections came in the
autumn, was even more marked. Democrats made the protection
of Southern rights the major issue, and local meetings resolved
to support no man who did not believe "that the Wilmot Proviso
was directly at variance with the spirit and intention of the
Constitution." Editors begged for unity on such a platform, and
by July even the most conservative of Whig newspapers were
agreeing that the South would resist any encroachment on Constitutional rights "with all the force and power the God of nature
had given." Venable, who had spoken so firmly in the last Congress, frankly asked those who did not prefer disunion to accepting
the Wilmot Proviso or the abolition of slavery in the District of
Columbia not to vote for him. He was re-elected by an increased
majority. The Whigs elected six of the nine members of Congress,
but their majorities were greatly reduced in spite of such statements by outstanding leaders as that of Edward Stanly that he
would oppose the Proviso and abolition in all its forms. The discussions of the campaign, in spite of some sharp differences,
"served to get the subject of slavery in the territories before the
people as never before." Southern Rights Whigs became as outspoken as the Democrats. The *North Carolina Standard* spoke for
both when it said: "We warn you, in the presence of the civilized
world, and with all the solemnity which such an occasion can inspire, that if you fasten that Proviso upon us, with the evils which
it certainly foreshadows, you must make up your minds, and that
speedily, to undo the deed and repair the wrong, or we separate
forever." [6]

[6] Sitterson, *Secession Movement in North Carolina,* 49–53; Raleigh *North Carolina*

In Georgia both parties were badly divided, as had been her representatives in Congress over the Southern Address. Efforts at harmony, therefore, kept expression moderate. George W. Towns, the Democratic candidate for governor, was clearly more of a Southern Rights man than his opponent, Edward Y. Hill, yet both professed to be "sound" on issues. Towns did advocate "resistance at every hazard" if the Wilmot Proviso was passed, but did not push matters to an open break with Cobb and his North Georgia supporters. His election, therefore, indicated only a general drift towards the Southern position and not a willingness to assume leadership.

In Kentucky and Tennessee the Democratic candidates, who took Southern ground, were victorious. The Wilmot Proviso was an issue in both campaigns, and while disunion was not suggested as a remedy, the press in both states viewed Democratic success as an indication of public approval of the Southern position, and a rebuke to Whig indifference.[7]

These developments in the various states, while revealing a consciousness of danger, had produced little but conditional threats. Internal divisions and state interests stood in the way of a sectional response. Reactions had been defensive, not aggressive. Men were not yet quite certain as to what course they should take, even though quite certain as to their position on the issue presented.

The only real centers of active opposition were in South Carolina and Mississippi. In the first of these, local committees of safety and correspondence had been at work ever since the Southern Address was issued. In May delegates from twenty-nine district and parish committees had met in Columbia and issued a series of resolutions expressing alarm at the peril which was hanging "over the institutions and sovereign rights of the slaveholding states" as a result of the "unconstitutional and mischievous" actions of the people of the North. A willingness to take "firm, united and concerted action" with the other Southern states was expressed, a Central State Committee of Vigilance and Safety set up, and a call made upon the governor to convene the legislature for the con-

---

Standard, October 20, 1849; Shryock, *Georgia and the Union in 1850,* pp. 178–216; Savannah *Republican,* November 8, 19, 1848; January 1, 1849.

[7] New York *Semi-Weekly Tribune,* August 1, 18, 1849.

sideration of the mode and measure of redress in the event of the passage of the Wilmot Proviso legislation. Governor Whitemarsh B. Seabrook set about immediately to secure some measure of preparedness on the part of the state militia; suspicious characters were hurried out of communities; and in one place, at least, the reading of the Southern Address was substituted, on the Fourth of July program, for the Declaration of Independence. The people of South Carolina seemed ready to act independently of old party lines and for a Southern convention and a Southern ultimatum. Yet no one dared to propose specific action, so great was the fear of the jealousy of South Carolina leadership.[8]

The state of Mississippi soon removed the difficulty. As early as February 10, 1849, the *Mississippi Free Trader* had been urging a Southern convention. "The time for talking or threatening is past," it said. "We must lay down our platform broadly and openly, and say to our Northern brethren, 'thus far and no farther.'" Democrats and Whigs alike responded, and a group of forty-five leading citizens of both parties issued a call for a meeting to be held in Jackson on May 7. The object, as set forth in the call, was to consider the course being pursued by Northern legislatures and representatives in Congress in regard to the slavery issue in its various aspects, and to ascertain the state's attitude toward co-operation with other states to arrest these encroachments. The address which emanated from this meeting asserted the separate sovereignty of each state and the intent of the Federal Constitution to leave the protection of property to the states. It roundly condemned Northern attitudes toward the Constitution and toward slavery, approved the course of Mississippi Congressmen in regard to the Southern Address, and recommended a second meeting of broader scope to be held at Jackson in October.[9]

Both the Democrats and the Whigs, in their conventions, approved of this meeting. Both asserted their loyalty to the Union. Both defended the rights of slavery in the territories and urged Congressional protection. Democrats on the whole, however, were

[8] Hamer, *Secession Movement in South Carolina*, 32–37; Chauncey S. Boucher, "The Secession and Co-operation Movement in South Carolina, 1848 to 1852," in Washington University *Studies* (St. Louis), V, No. 2 (1918), 81–83.

[9] Natchez *Mississippi Free Trader*, May 16, 1849; Natchez *Weekly Courier*, May 15, 1849.

inclined to go further in their emotional appeal and to be more threatening than the Whigs. They eagerly sought Calhoun's advice as to the steps to be taken. They corresponded with the leaders in other states. They were ready when the convention met in October to give it not only local but sectional importance.[10]

The convention, in turn, acted from the beginning as though it spoke for the whole South. With Chief Justice William L. Sharkey presiding, a committee was at once put to work drawing up resolutions setting forth the reasons for the Southern movement and the steps necessary for resistance. Northern determination to destroy slavery, they said, was clearly revealed in the efforts made through press, pulpit, and ballot box. It grew year by year. Submission and resistance were the alternatives. Congress had no right to exclude slavery from the territories. The states were sovereign, and the Federal government had only its delegated powers. The institution of slavery had been left by the Constitution under the control of the states. Nor had Congress been given any power to abolish slavery in the District of Columbia, to prohibit the slave trade between the several states, or to check the entrance of slavery into the territories. The Wilmot Proviso was, therefore, "an unjust and insulting discrimination." To pass it or to pass any law abolishing slavery in the District of Columbia would be such a breach of the Federal compact as to make it the duty of the slaveholding states "to take care of their own safety, and to treat the non-holding states as enemies to the slaveholding States and their domestic institutions." The legislature was then requested to pass laws encouraging slaveholders, with their slaves, to emigrate to the new territories, and a call issued for a great convention of all slaveholding states to be held at Nashville, Tennessee, on the first Monday in June next, "to devise and adopt some mode of resistance to these aggressions." The committee then asked the convention to appoint to this meeting twelve delegates and an equal number of alternatives—"being double the number of Senators and Representatives in Congress"—and to request the other slaveholding states to do the same. Steps were then taken to organize the state by counties and to secure a gen-

[10] Natchez *Mississippi Free Trader,* June 27, 1849; Natchez *Weekly Courier,* July 24, 1849.

eral state convention in case Congress should, in the meantime, enact any of the hated legislation.[11]

Thus was a working program given the Southern movement. All that Calhoun and his South Carolina followers had wanted was provided without the hindering factors of jealousy and distrust. Some, perhaps, hoped that it even had opened the way for "the assailed States" to provide, "in the last resort, for their separate welfare by the formation of a compact and a union that . . . [would] afford protection to their liberties and rights."

At the North, the determination to check the spread of slavery and to remove its stain from the national capital had also deepened throughout the summer. A generation long exposed to anti-slavery propaganda was now on the stage. The percentage of outright abolitionists was not large, but the sentiment against slavery extension was overwhelming. The belief that the "slave power" was preventing the passage of legislation necessary for the well-being and development of the Northwest was now widespread and contributed to the same end. Taylor's friendly attitude gave added confidence. Newspapers, especially those with Whig affiliations, assumed advanced ground against any yielding. Horace Greeley's *Tribune*, which was rapidly becoming the "political bible" of a growing constituency, took the lead. The New York *Evening Post*, the Albany *Evening Journal*, and the Springfield *Republican*, however, were not far behind. All accepted the moral implication of the struggle and felt the obligation to the democratic dogma.

Aggressive attitudes were not confined to Whigs. Coalitions between Democrats and Free-Soilers went on in Vermont and Massachusetts, Wisconsin and Ohio. In Massachusetts the state Democratic convention declared itself opposed to slavery "in every form and color" and in favor of freedom everywhere. It pledged the party to use every Constitutional means possible to check its expansion and boldly announced that such sentiments were so universally held at the North that they belonged to no party. The Chicago *Democrat* sullenly remarked that the only way to satisfy the slaveholding states was to "shut one's eyes . . . until slavery is

[11] Natchez *Mississippi Free Trader*, October 10, 1849.

extended in all the territories of the United States and free labor is entirely degraded there." It insisted that the Wilmot Proviso was necessary to satisfy the North and that it in no way affected the South.[12]

Such was the national temper when Congress assembled in December, 1849. Conflict and confusion developed in the House of Representatives at once, and the democratic process seemed on the verge of breaking completely down. Democrats and Whigs were nearly equal in numbers, and the balance of power rested with a handful of Free-Soil men. The attempt to elect a speaker and organize for action resulted in a deadlock. The candidates selected by party caucus, Cobb of Georgia by the Democrats and Robert C. Winthrop of Massachusetts by the Whigs, received 103 and 96 votes respectively. The remainder of the votes were scattered among nine other persons, whose totals ranged from one to eight. No one could muster a majority. Day after day the voting continued. As many as five ballots were taken on a single day with the inconsequential shifting of only a few votes. A week went by. The Whigs stood stanchly by Winthrop, whose total remained stationary after a few slight gains. The Democrats, however, early began to shift about in search of another candidate. Emery D. Potter of Ohio and William A. Richardson of Illinois began to replace Cobb, and then a definite shift began to William J. Brown of Indiana, whose voting record on the Texas issue had been satisfactory to the South. On the eighth day, after seven ballots, his total reached 109, and on the next, 112. The Whig vote now scattered, but the Free-Soil element still manipulated their votes to prevent a majority and an election. Confusion reigned. Time after time the House reporter commented that he could not hear the speakers, and much misunderstanding developed between members for the same reason. Proposals for settlement, even by the drawing of lots, were offered. Others spoke of the disgust that the people of the nation felt at the disgraceful scene. Root of Ohio tried to be humorous. Edward Stanly of North Carolina spoke of Free-Soilism and Wilmot Provisoism as "tomfoolery." Root was on his feet again at once. Stanly may have expressed the

[12] Chicago *Democrat*, September 11, 1849.

feelings of a Southern Whig, but if Northern Whigs uttered such sentiments, political graves in that section would be as thickly spread as graves in a village where the cholera had swept.

As Brown's votes increased, suddenly a rumor spread that he had made certain commitments to Giddings and his Free-Soilers. An explanation was demanded. Brown tried to explain. He had received a letter and he had answered it. He had conferred with these men. The question had been as to whether, if elected, his committee appointments would represent every section of the Union. He had only promised that much. He did say, however, "that if a proposition were made, by way of amendment to a Territorial bill, to extend slavery, he, as a Representative from a free district, could not vote for it." [13]

Southern men sprang to their feet to regret and to withdraw their votes. Disorder reigned. Brown's efforts to explain were futile. Wilmot, under questioning, admitted that his understanding with Brown was that a majority of the committees which Brown would appoint, if elected, would be "fair Northern men"—men who represented the sentiment "that slavery shall go no further." The noise and confusion increased. The House adjourned for the day without taking another vote.

That night plans matured but tempers did not improve. The next day various plans, including one of continuous voting, were introduced for the solution of difficulties. They resulted only in more violent debate. At length Richard K. Meade of Virginia took the floor. Bluntly he went to the point. If the organization of the House was to be followed by the abolition of slavery in the District or by the prohibition of slavery in the territories, he trusted that his eyes had rested upon the last Speaker of the House of Representatives. If these measures passed, there would be "but one determination at the South—one solemn resolve to defend their homes and maintain their honor."

Root replied with the equally blunt remark that "if dissolution *must* come, why, the sooner the better. Let it come before the House was organized." William Duer of New York followed with a harsh charge of disunionist sentiment against Meade. "It is false," cried Meade. "You are a liar, sir," retorted Duer. Meade rushed

[13] *Cong. Globe*, 31 Cong., 1 Sess., 21.

towards him. "Indescribable confusion followed—threats, violent gesticulations, calls to order, and demands for adjournment were mingled together. The House was like a heaving billow. The clerk called to order, but there was none to heed him." [14]

When order was at length partially restored, Toombs of Georgia secured the floor. His course until now had been that of a conservative Union Whig. Now as he spoke, his eyes glowed "like coals of fire," and his sentences rattled "like volleys of musketry." "A great sectional question lies at the foundation of all these troubles," he said. The "Free Soilers" had by a "discreditable trick" attempted to gain an advantage. The interests of the South were in danger. He "was unwilling to surrender the great power of the Speaker's chair without obtaining security for the future." Power to the North now meant power to oppress. Eulogies upon the Union would not intimidate. In spite of "as much attachment to the Union . . . under the Constitution of our fathers, as any freeman ought to have," he did not "hesitate to avow before this House and the country, and in the presence of the living God, that if by your legislation you seek to drive us from the territories of California and New Mexico, purchased by the common blood and treasure of the whole people, and to abolish slavery in this District, thereby attempting to fix a national degradation upon half the States of this Confederacy, *I am for disunion;* and if my physical courage be equal to the maintenance of my convictions of right and duty, I will devote all I am and all I have on earth to its consummation."

Bursts of loud applause greeted these words. The blunt facing of disunion sobered members. Edward D. Baker of Illinois spoke earnestly of love of Union and denied the wish of the great body of Northern men to raise the question of disunion or "to excite unreasonable agitation." The spirit deepened as Alexander H. Stephens also expressed his devotion to "the glorious compact formed by our fathers of the revolutionary struggle," then added: "But I tell the gentleman . . . and I tell this House—whether he believes it or not, and whether the people of the North believe it or not—that the day in which aggression is consummated upon any sec-

[14] *Ibid.,* 27.

tion of the country, much and deeply as I regret it, this Union is dissolved." [15]

Debate was suspended for continuous voting. On December 23 Cobb of Georgia was made speaker by a plurality vote. The House was then organized.

The Senate, meanwhile, assembled and adjourned day after day. On one occasion, at least, they too felt the press of the slavery fury. A resolution was offered at one of their brief sessions to permit the Reverend Theobald Mathew, a visitor from Ireland, to sit within the bar of the Senate. Southerners objected on the grounds of opinions he had expressed some years previously, hostile to slavery, and the question of hospitality quickly degenerated into attack and defense of the troublesome institution. Tempers, however, were better than in the House. Even a set of strong pro-slavery resolutions from the Missouri General Assembly presented by Senator David R. Atchison brought only a mild rejoinder from his colleague, Benton. Vermont's usual resolves against slavery produced a few outbursts, but there were Southern Senators who upheld the right to have them printed. The significant fact, however, was that everyone was conscious of strained relations, and that all roads led directly to the one great issue. Salmon P. Chase seized the opportunity offered by the Vermont resolutions to inform his hearers that threats of disunion would have no effect on the people of Ohio; Jeremiah Clemens from Alabama answered him with a recital of Northern abuses. "We do not intend to stand still and have our throats cut," he said. "The Union is valuable only for the privileges it confers and the rights it secures." The North intended to destroy slavery everywhere, he charged, and no people would stand idly by and see nearly a billion dollars worth of property threatened. If the South waged an incessant campaign against factories and their white slaves, would the North remain calm? No, it was time to resist, for "concessions never yet satisfied fanaticism." [16]

Others joined in the debate without adding much other than emotion, while, at the other end of the Capitol, the members of the House of Representatives continued voting and quarreling over the election of their lesser officials. It was soon apparent that

[15] *Ibid.*, 28–29.   [16] *Ibid.*, 120–23, 133, Appendix, 52–54.

unless something was done to clear the air and to reach some reasonable understanding, not only would the Thirty-first Congress fail to do constructive work but the Union itself would be definitely endangered. "The Southern members are more determined and bold than I ever saw them," wrote Calhoun. "Many avow themselves to be disunionists, and a still greater number admit, that there is little hope of any remedy short of it." [17] Clingman of North Carolina, after a trip through the North, declared that Southerners had no idea of "the force and extent of the present anti-slavery movement." The popular mind had been completely poisoned. Such an intense degree of "feeling and prejudice" had been created against the South that, in some places, they viewed all Southerners "as being so coarse and ruffianly in manner that a lady would not trust herself in such a presence." [18]

As passions mounted and many began to despair of the Union, Henry Clay developed a plan. He had returned to the Senate after his party, on the verge of success, had pushed him aside for the more popular Zachary Taylor. Age and illness had taken heavy toll of the once virile body but had not erased the genial smile nor destroyed the charm of personality that drew men to him. "His cheeks were a bit hollow now, his nose had a pinched look, and his head was bald on the top." Ambition for high place had weakened, and he had early begged to be relieved of arduous duties. But his love of the Union was as intense as ever. He was, moreover, now in a better position to work with those other great figures of the past, Webster, Benton, Cass, and Calhoun, who like himself had felt the softening influence of recurring political disappointment and the forgiving mellowness of old age. On the evening of January 21, "his lungs wracked by a cruel cough," he braved the stormy weather and, without appointment, knocked on Webster's door. For an hour he outlined his plan and received assurance of Webster's support. Eight days later he "rose in the Senate chamber and began his last great struggle to save the Union that he loved." [19]

"Mr. President," he began, "I hold in my hand a series of reso-

[17] Calhoun to Andrew P. Calhoun, January 12, 1850, in Jameson (ed.), *Correspondence of John C. Calhoun*, 780.
[18] *Cong. Globe*, 31 Cong., 1 Sess., 201.
[19] Van Deusen, *Life of Henry Clay*, 395–401.

lutions which I desire to submit to the consideration of this body."
Their object, he explained, was an "amicable arrangement of all
questions in controversy between the free and the slave States, growing out of the subject of slavery." Then followed the proposals to
admit California without Congressional action on slavery; to organize the remaining territory secured from Mexico without provision for or against the admission of slavery; to compensate Texas
for a boundary settlement; to abolish the slave trade in the District of Columbia with security for slavery itself as long as it existed
in Maryland or until her people and those of the District should
accept compensation for abolition; and to enact a new and effective
fugitive-slave law.[20]

These resolutions brought quick objection from Southern members, but, by strenuous effort, Clay was able to check debate until
he was ready to speak. A week went by in which Brown of Mississippi delivered one of the most threatening speeches of the session.
He warned that the South was in earnest. He boasted of its strength.
He announced boldly that his section had calculated the value of
the Union. The North must choose between respect for Southern
rights and dissolution. Interests that could not be relinquished
were involved.[21]

Brown's purpose was unquestionably to influence Clay, who arose
on February 5 to defend his proposals. The Senate chamber was
crowded. The doors had to be shut and the halls and anterooms
cleared. A roar of applause greeted him. He looked weak and
exhausted. His first words were those of anxiety. Passion and intemperance were dividing our distracted country. The Union was
in danger. His plea was for moderation, for patriotism. Each side
must yield something. Neither extreme could serve. That was why
he had offered his compromise. Then one by one, throughout this
day and the next, he took up his resolutions and begged for
thoughtful consideration. Was the Wilmot Proviso necessary in
California or New Mexico? The Californians had already chosen
freedom, and nature had barred slavery elsewhere. The boundaries
suggested for Texas were fair and adequate and the assumption
of her debts compensated for any losses. To end the slave trade in
the District of Columbia was only to end what most men agreed

[20] *Cong. Globe*, 31 Cong., 1 Sess., 244-47.   [21] *Ibid.*, 257-61.

was a shocking spectacle. And as to a new fugitive-slave law, it was simple justice to the South, which had "just and serious cause" for complaint.

Here was concession to balance concession. Only in the case of California, which had decided for itself, was nothing given in return. The appeal was to reason, to the past where mutual accommodation had made progress possible. Disunion would solve no problems. Secession was not a right and would mean a bloody civil war; separation would bring only bitter, costly rivalry. The dangers were too great even to contemplate. Pause "at the edge of the precipice," he pleaded, "before the fearful and disastrous leap is taken in the yawning abyss below, which will inevitably lead to certain and irretrievable destruction." [22]

Response to Clay's fervent appeal was not immediately favorable. Speaker Cobb called it a "great speech" but thought "no good . . . [would] result from it." It would, in fact, "have a bad effect on the public mind of the north" by appearing to express "southern sentiment." It had not abated the excitement. Stephens was equally pessimistic. He could see "very little prospect of future peace and quiet in the public mind" upon the subject. There was "too much demagogism and too little statesmanship" involved. Thomas J. Rusk of Texas called the proposal regarding the boundary of his state the unceremonious usurping of territory as "a peace-offering to a spirit of encroachment on the constitutional rights of one-half of this Union." Foote flatly denied the right of Congress to abolish slavery in the District, while James M. Mason of Virginia and Jefferson Davis of Mississippi quickly rejected the idea of any compromise on the Constitutional right of slavery to enter the territories. President Taylor, meanwhile, held his Whig forces intact and would have none of Clay's proposals.[23]

The events of the next few days were equally discouraging. A petition from a group of Pennsylvania and Delaware citizens, asking for "the immediate and peaceful dissolution" of the Union, again raised the whole question of how to deal with such extreme documents and offered the opportunity for continued statement

[22] *Ibid.*, Appendix, 115–27.
[23] Cobb to Mrs. Cobb, February 9, 1850, in Phillips (ed.), *Correspondence of Toombs, Stephens, and Cobb*, 183–84; *Cong. Globe*, 31 Cong., 1 Sess., 247–50.

of sectional positions. Few showed any inclination to tolerate or to compromise. Few could keep away from the slavery issue.[24]

Then on February 13 Jefferson Davis opened the great debate on Clay's resolutions. He spoke of the indifference of those who represented the majority to the gathering storm and labeled Clay's proposals a concession to that "aggressive majority." Evidently it was a case "of conquest on the one side, or submission on the other" to sectional domination. It was no longer "the clamor of a noisy fanaticism, but the steady advance of a self-sustaining power to the goal of unlimited supremacy." The North was determined to deny to slavery its Constitutional rights for the sole purpose of gaining political power. Under such conditions it might even be better for the preservation of the Union if the North was given a majority in one house and the South in the other. No section should have the power to trample upon the rights of the other.

As to slavery in the territories, neither the Federal nor the territorial governments had a right to prohibit it. The Mexican law did not do so. He could, therefore, nowhere find any concession to the South in Clay's proposals. He would be willing to accept the Missouri Compromise line because it represented mutual concessions. He could not accept the checking of slavery in the territories on any other grounds. Slavery as it existed in the United States was not an evil. It had rescued the Negro from the barbarian masters of benighted Africa and had brought him where civilization could elevate and dignify his nature. History and the Bible both justified it. A moral issue was not involved. Slavery would benefit California. Nature had not excluded it there. Anyway, the South only asked the right to give it an equal chance.

He closed with a sharp shifting of all blame for difficulties to Northern agitation against slavery—the effort to degrade his people in the eyes of Christendom. It was this that was sowing the seeds of disunion. It was this that had put the South on the defensive. It was this that had steeled the South, in the spirit of the barons of England against King John, to resolve to defend their rights as the only sure way to preserve the Union.[25]

It was not a great speech. It was partisan and intemperate. It served mainly to state the position of those who were in no mood

[24] *Cong. Globe,* 31 Cong., 1 Sess., 414.   [25] *Ibid.,* Appendix, 149–57.

to compromise. It expressed the temper of a younger element from the Lower South that matched the younger group from the North which the recent combination of Free-Soilers and Democrats had thrown forward.

The real spokesman of Southern opposition, however, was not Jefferson Davis. Davis was a late-comer. The man who had toiled through the heat of the day, year in and year out, for Southern rights and Southern unity, alone could claim that distinction. He was now an old man. Ambition for high place was gone. The shadow of death was already on his face. His intense devotion to minority rights, and his sincere belief that national unity was impossible unless the Constitution, as the fathers had intended, was respected, was as strong as ever. John C. Calhoun had won and still held the right, by tradition, to speak for the South.

Calhoun's situation was a tragic one, but he did not know it. Possessed of a mind more keen and better disciplined than that of any other man of his generation, he had been forced by circumstances and choice into a position from which he had to defend slavery when all the rest of the Christian world was leaving it behind; he had to defend the political rights of the locality when all the forces of modern technology and business were producing interdependence and the need for centralized efficiency; he had to uphold strict construction of the Constitution when the forward sweep of the whole modern social-economic order demanded a broader view; he had to speak for an agricultural interest and way of life just as industry and the city were about to take over; he was forced to be a voice out of the past while he yet lived because he was more logical and more consistent and more native than those on whose side were both numbers and "progress."

Calhoun had been too ill to hear Clay's speech or to attend the regular sessions of the Senate. This day he had tottered up the steps of the Capitol and to his place, a mere shadow of a man swathed in blankets. He sat quietly, his eyes half closed, until Clay's resolutions came up for discussion. He then arose, stated his inability to speak, and asked that his friend Senator Mason read the "sentiments" which he had "reduced to writing." [26]

26 Crallé (ed.), *Works of John C. Calhoun*, IV, 542–73; *Cong. Globe*, 31 Cong., 1 Sess., 451–55; Charles M. Wiltse, *John C. Calhoun, Sectionalist, 1840–1850* (Indianapolis, 1951), 458–65.

"I have, Senators, believed from the first that the agitation of the subject of slavery would, if not prevented by some timely and effective measure, end in disunion." The stinging words caught and held the audience. Calhoun sat motionless. Not a change passed over his face. Mason read on: The agitation had been permitted to proceed. The question of the preservation of the Union had now to be faced. The trouble, said Calhoun, was the almost universal discontent which pervaded the Southern states and the belief that they could not, consistently with honor and safety, remain in the Union. This could be traced only to the long-continued agitation of the slave question and the destruction of that equilibrium between the sections in the government which existed when the Constitution was ratified. The South had fallen behind because it had steadily yielded territory to the free section—in the Northwest Ordinance, the Missouri Compromise, and the Oregon settlement. The result was a majority of states and of population in the North, which, in turn, meant Northern domination, the exclusion of the South from the territories, an unfair revenue and disbursement system, and an enormous increase of the central government's powers.

These issues would not be so serious if no question of vital importance to the minority section existed. But slavery was vital to Southern interests and the North was hostile to its existence. Its radicals held slavery to be a sin and a crime. Their number was on the increase; from a fanatical few they had grown to a size which could influence both of the major parties. How could their progress be checked? How could complete abolition of slavery be prevented?

On the answer to these questions rested the fate of the nation. Already the chords of union were snapping. The Methodist and the Baptist churches had already divided. Political ties would come next. Eulogies of the glorious past would not serve. Clay's proposals would not save the Union. The President's efforts to bring California in would not do it. There was, in fact, but one way, and that was "by a full and final settlement, on the principle of justice, of all questions at issue between the two sections." The South had no compromises to offer. It asked for simple justice, nothing less. It wanted its Constitutional rights. And to Calhoun that meant equality in the territories, the faithful return of all fugitive slaves, the ending of all agitation of the slave question, and amendments to the Constitution which would restore to the South the power of protecting itself it possessed when the Constitution was first made. California was the test question.

Calhoun had made his demands. His hands, at least, were freed of further responsibility. His assumption that slavery would have existed everywhere unless restricted was most certainly open to serious question. Just how all discussion of slavery could be prevented in a democracy, he did not make clear. Yet that he was correct as to what was necessary to save his South should have been clear to all. That what he demanded from the North was absolutely impossible should have been equally clear. Yet either few saw or, if they did, were able to act.

Three days later Daniel Webster spoke.[27] Like Clay, he had reached the point where he could speak as an American, not just "as a Massachusetts man, nor as a northern man." He had become something of a symbol of nationalism, the man who was always expected to utter the final word on loyalty to the Union. He represented the "wise, moderate, patriotic, and healing counsels" which yet remained in the Senate. He spoke "out of a solicitous and anxious heart for the restoration to the country" of quiet and harmony. Briefly he reviewed the immediate reasons for strife, and the history of the slavery controversy between North and South. Both sections had voted to check the slave trade, and both had favored the freedom clause in the Northwest Ordinance. Since that time Northern opposition had grown in intensity; cotton had fixed slavery more firmly on the South and given her political dominance. Time, however, had shifted the balance. The North was now in the ascendancy. That change was not due, as Calhoun had said, to Southern surrenders. Northern votes had helped to acquire Louisiana and Texas, both vast slave areas. It was just a case of the North's being in step with progress; nature, not Northern votes, would make New Mexico and California free. The Wilmot Proviso was not necessary. It would only reaffirm "an ordinance of nature," re-enact "the will of God."

On the matter of fugitive slaves, however, the South had a just grievance, as did the North on the unfair contrasting of free labor

27 *Cong. Globe,* 31 Cong., 1 Sess., Appendix, 269–76.

with slavery and on treatment of free Negroes who chanced to be aboard Northern ships entering Southern ports.

But none of these things justified talk of secession. Nor was there such a thing as peaceful secession. No one could draw a satisfactory line between North and South, or make a fair distribution of property. The Mississippi River could not be cut into two parts. Instead of looking into such "caverns of darkness," let men "enjoy the fresh air of liberty and union" and dwell on the boundless prospects of the future.

It was a conciliatory speech which met quick response. New England antislavery leaders were furious. Webster had betrayed his section. They called him a "Benedict Arnold," a man whose honor was dead. His was a brazen bid for the presidency. One spoke of the "meanness of the lion turned spaniel in his fawning on the masters whose hands he was licking"; another called it "a break from his own principles and from the principles of New England, . . . a terrible mistake." Southerners, on the other hand, realized that a turning point had been reached. Compromise was now a possibility. Shortly after Webster had spoken, a Virginian noted that "Our politicians have gone over to the compromises." Toombs, about the same time, assured a friend that "We have a tolerable prospect for a proper settlement of the slavery question" and implied that it would be along the compromise lines "backed by Webster." "The phantom of disunion is retiring before an awakened, healthful public interest," said the New Orleans *Daily Crescent*. "There is now no mistaking the evidence which comes to us from every quarter of the country. The sentiment of *'liberty and union, one and inseparable,'* is at length thoroughly aroused in the capitol of the nation, and is springing up, with giant force, from the body of the people in every portion of the country." Conservative Northerners generally felt the same way. A few saw that Webster had only asked for patience and forbearance while time, ever on the side of the North, brought its inevitable results.[28]

28 Worcester (Mass.) *Spy*, March 18, 1850; Dedham (Mass.) *Gazette*, March 16, 1850; Boston *Liberator*, February 1, 1850. The writer is indebted to Mr. Godfrey Anderson, one of his graduate students, for a study of New England reactions. See his study, "The Slavery Issue as a Factor in Massachusetts Politics from the Compromise of 1850 to the Outbreak of the Civil War" (Ph.D. dissertation, University of Chicago, 1944); New Orleans *Daily Crescent*, March 27, 1850; J. R. Tucker to James H. Hammond,

A better spirit had, indeed, begun to develop, but it did not end the debate or bring immediate action. Only four days after Webster's effort, Berrien of Georgia took issue with Clay on most of his proposals but was willing to leave Constitutional differences to the Supreme Court. Horace Mann almost immediately restored much of the waning bitterness by charging the whole difficulty to Southern members. He boasted of being an abolitionist. To spread slavery was to cast aside "with scorn, not only the teachings of Christianity, but the clearest principles of natural religion and of natural law." It was to sink to the Dark Ages. The abolitionist would only abolish a thing which destroyed "the inalienable, indefeasible, indestructible rights of man." He would grant every man the right to carry legitimate property to all territories. But men and women were not property. To call them such and to base discrimination on refusal to spread slavery was a trick for which any "juggler or mountebank" would be hissed off the stage in any respectable village. Yes, when you reached the boundary line between a slave state and a free state, you reached the boundary line of slavery itself. The civilized world was against the South, and if it seceded, its runaway slaves would be welcomed in the North; it would surrender its claim to all national property; it would be subject to even greater antislavery agitation. A devastating civil war would follow. Slave insurrections would be inevitable, for "The state of slavery is always a state of war." But because of "the character of slavery, . . . under a full sense of responsibility to country and to God," he was willing to say, "better disunion, better a civil or a servile war—better anything that God in his providence shall send, than an extension of the boundaries of slavery." [29]

Others followed without adding much to what had already been said. The significance of a speech came to depend entirely on the importance of the individual who made it. Consequently, when William H. Seward spoke, few were present to listen, but his words meant much for the future.[30] He represented the younger Northern element and the new day; he was close to President

March 26, 1850, in James H. Hammond Papers (Division of Manuscripts, Library of Congress); Toombs to Linton Stephens, March 22, 1850, in Phillips (ed.), *Correspondence of Toombs, Stephens, and Cobb,* 188.

[29] *Cong. Globe,* 31 Cong., 1 Sess., Appendix, 218–24.   [30] *Ibid.,* 260–69.

Taylor. Quickly he brushed aside the objections to admitting California, pointed the glories possible for a united nation, and then stated his opposition to all compromises proposed on the question of slavery. Human freedom was not something to be bartered about. And besides, Clay's proposals did not offer equality of advantage. To admit California under any system of her own choosing was just plain necessity. To grant the South what Calhoun demanded was to give a minority equality of power with a clear majority—a majority of states, a majority of population, and majorities in both houses of Congress. It would be a return to the Articles of Confederation.

The South had lost and would continue to lose equality with the North. The progress of free population, augmented by emigration from Europe, could not be checked, nor slave-state stagnation altered. No fugitive-slave law could be enforced when men believed it "unjust, unconstitutional and immoral," and when all mankind, except in the South, considered "hospitality to the refugee" a virtue. "We [of the North] are not slave-holders," he said. "We cannot, in our judgment, be either true Christians or real freemen, if we impose on another a chain that we defy all human power to fasten on ourselves." He could accept neither "peace for slavery" in the District of Columbia nor the spread of slavery to the territories. The spirit of the people of the free states was set upon a spring that rose with the pressure upon it. Pressed too hard, it would recoil with a force that would not leave a single hesitating member in Congress.

With compromise of principles rejected, Seward then turned to the question of Southern rights. The states were not parties to the Constitution as states, he said; "it is the Constitution of the people of the United States."

"But even if the States continue as States, they surrendered their equality as States, and submitted themselves to the sway of the numerical majority." The United States was not just "a joint stock association." It was "a political state," an "organized society, whose end . . . [was] government." The fact that some states had slaves and some were free was incidental and had no effect on the larger fact of an organic whole. The idea of equality guaranteed between states as such had no Constitutional basis.

79

And as to slavery, it was "only a temporary, accidental, partial, and incongruous" affair even in the slave states, while freedom was "perpetual, organic, universal." We had no right to spread slavery to the territories. We had only a stewardship there, and "the Constitution devotes the domain to union, to justice, to defence, to welfare, and to liberty." There was, indeed, "a higher law than the Constitution, which regulates our authority over the domain, and devotes it to the same noble purposes." No Christian peoples free to choose could spread slavery. Even if climate had checked its spread, the Wilmot Proviso should be applied in order to make freedom certain.

As to the threats to dissolve the Union, Seward did not take them seriously. This was not, in fact, a conflict of parties; it was, he said, "the agony of distracted parties—a convulsion resulting from the too narrow foundations of both and of all parties— foundations laid in compromises of natural justice and of human liberty. A question—a moral question, transcending the too narrow creeds of parties—had arisen; the public conscience expands with it, and the green withes of party associations give way, and break, and fall off from it. No, sir; it is not the State that is dying of the fever of party spirit; it is merely a paralysis of parties— premonitory, however, of their restoration, with new elements of health and vigor, to be imbibed from that spirit of the age which is so justly called Progress."

Here was the whole matter in a nutshell. The race was between slavery and Progress—between backwardness and freedom. And the dice were loaded on the side of progress. The slave states had been steadily losing power and would continue to do so as long as they had any to lose. "Slavery must give way," said Seward, give way "to the salutary instructions of economy, and to the ripening influence of humanity." Emancipation was inevitable. The only question was "whether it be peaceful or violent," and that depended on whether it be hastened or hindered. The Union would stand if slavery, "under the steady, peaceful action of moral, social, and political causes," were gradually and voluntarily removed, or it would fall when civil war would force "complete and immediate emancipation."

Seward had met the issue squarely and uncompromisingly. He

had expounded the doctrine of consolidated nationalism and the supremacy of a numerical majority that knew nothing of special state or sectional rights for those who held slaves. He had foreseen the end of slavery because it had no place in the modern world. He had thrust the moral issue forward and proclaimed the obligations of Americans to face it. An "irrepressible conflict" with everything Constitutional, political, economic, social, and moral which Davis and Calhoun had defended was emphatically declared and the certainty of victory announced.

Seward's bold statements disturbed friends and foes alike but sank deep into the receptive soil of Northern opinion. They unquestionably played a part in forcing conservatives to realize that some concerted effort was now necessary—that the expression of extreme opinion, however sound, only made compromise more difficult. In response to that realization a group from the West and the South, under the leadership of Senator Douglas, now agreed to press for the admission of California, the organization of New Mexico and Utah without the exclusion of slavery, and the defeat of any effort to abolish slavery in the District. On March 13 and 14 Douglas spoke for this group and for the people of the Mississippi Valley, whose mission, he said, was to do justice to all sections and to preserve the Union inviolate.[31] He accepted the idea that nature had decided the issue against slavery in the Southwest and defended the doctrine of noninterference and decision by the people. He denied the existence of sectional rights, as such, to any share of the territories. It was no violation of Southern rights to prohibit slavery or of Northern rights to let the people decide for themselves. Calhoun was wrong in saying that legislation had robbed the South in the Northwest Ordinance. Slavery had existed there until the people themselves rejected it. That proved that national laws forced on a people were dead letters; the only real force was the will of the people themselves. Nor had the Missouri Compromise and the Oregon bill done anything but re-enact what nature and the will of the actual settlers themselves decided. That

---

[31] *Ibid.*, 364–75. For the story of Southern determination to oppose Zachary Taylor's efforts to admit California and Douglas' moves for a compromise, see Alexander H. Stephens, *A Constitutional View of the Late War Between the States* . . . (Philadelphia, 1868–1870), II, 201–205.

was the only sound policy for the future. And it would give freedom, for slavery was on the decline. It was weakening all along the border and could never go into the vast territory between the Mississippi and the Pacific. The issue, as debated, was an abstraction. It was time to get down to reality and move ahead.

Cass held much the same opinions, and even Benton agreed as to the inability of slavery to enter either New Mexico or California. Robert M. T. Hunter of Virginia and George E. Badger of North Carolina repeated the Southern arguments and threats. Others joined their voices to the confusion, but, somehow, the crest had been passed. The strain had weakened. John Bell aided the drift by adding resolutions to those of Clay, and Foote, acting with Douglas, secured a committee of thirteen to handle all proposals. Only President Taylor and the extreme Southerners held back—Taylor largely because of personal jealousy of Clay; the Southerners because they saw nothing to be gained by compromise.

Suddenly the scene shifted. On the last day of March news spread over Washington that Calhoun was dead. The central figure in Southern resistance was gone. Everyone knew that without his leadership the growing cleavage in Southern ranks was bound to widen.

Then on July 4 President Taylor was stricken after exposure to the hot sun at a patriotic celebration and a few days later followed Calhoun off the stage. In more friendly hands, compromise was now possible. Perhaps, as Senator Daniel S. Dickinson had said, the question which had delayed all "public business" while men engaged in the expression of "abstract views" could now move toward settlement.

CHAPTER V

COMPROMISE AND THE SOUTH

WHILE the great national debates developed in Congress, the people of the South were facing the same issues, as Whigs and Democrats, as loyal Southerners and patriotic Americans. They had been deeply stirred by the developments of the past year, and the growth of sectional consciousness had been marked. Party lines had weakened. Calhoun's constant warning that issues must be forced to a settlement and that some definite guarantees must be secured had begun, at last, to take effect. While Congress attempted to organize and while issues were taking shape in December and January, Southern opinion, as expressed in the newspapers, public meetings, and private correspondence, was decidedly aggressive. Democrats, as a rule, took the lead, but Whigs too were tense and, in some quarters, equally ready for action. It was a Whig paper in conservative North Carolina that warned "the fanatics" of the North that "the sentiment at the South is assuming a sterner character than heretofore" and that "unless there is a reform, and that speedily, there will be found an immense majority in all the Southern States, who will very readily entertain a proposition for disunion." [1]

Under such conditions, Mississippi's call for a Southern convention met with favor. Even those who sensed danger in the move were inclined to hold their tongues. The more radical were willing to think of the possibility of secession and a Southern confederacy coming out of the Nashville meeting.

Virginians had been less excited until now than were the peo-

[1] Wilmington (N.C.) *Commercial*, quoted in Raleigh *North Carolina Standard*, January 16, 1850.

83

ple in most of the other Southern states. The continued agitation of the Wilmot Proviso in Congress and talk of abolishing slavery in the District of Columbia, however, brought sharp reactions. "If we submit now," asked the Richmond *Whig,* "what can we expect hereafter? Can we have any security for the observance of any of the guaranties of the constitution?" The *Enquirer* was even more emphatic. The destiny of the Union depended on the settlement of present issues. "The Union of the old thirteen states" could not stand unless "the guarantees of the Constitution for the safety of the South in the possession and undisturbed enjoyment of its slave property" were observed. The Nashville convention, said the editor, offered the best means for saving the Union by preserving Southern rights.[2]

Extremists like Edmund Ruffin, M. R. H. Garnett, Mason, and Beverly Tucker, meanwhile, fanned the flames with radical talk, and on January 2 J. H. Claiborne responded with resolutions, offered in the House of Delegates, calling for a committee on Federal affairs. As amended, they also provided for the appointment of delegates to the Nashville convention.[3]

Governor Floyd supported this move and told the legislature that "the time has already passed for the discussion of the question between us; no human reason or eloquence can stop the headlong career of injury and wrong which the North is pursuing towards us." The legislature, however, altered the original resolutions, merely "recommending" state action in case of the passage of unfavorable legislation, and the appointment of delegates to Nashville by local district conventions. The popular response to this action was, at the time, unanimous enough to cause the *Enquirer* to announce that "The two great political parties have ceased to exist in the Southern States so far as the present slavery issue is concerned. . . . With united voices . . . they proclaim . . . the preservation of the Union, if we can, the preservation of our rights if we cannot." [4]

In North Carolina for the first time a concerted movement

---

[2] Richmond *Whig,* December 21, 1849; Richmond *Enquirer,* October 16, December 25, 1849; January 10, 1850.

[3] Shanks, *Secession Movement in Virginia,* 30–31.

[4] Richmond *Enquirer,* January 15, 1850; Virginia *Acts,* 1849–1850, pp. 233, 234.

backed by both parties developed. Led by the *North Carolina Standard*, the press generally demanded a check on Northern action and favored a positive stand in defense of Southern rights. The state Democratic convention, while insisting on its devotion to the Union, announced its determination "to resist all palpable violations of the Constitution, and all attempts to wield this government by a mere sectional majority, to the injury and degradation of the Southern people." The Whigs were nearly as emphatic, declaring themselves to be "staunch Union men so long as there was no undue interference with slavery and no longer." As to the Nashville convention, the Democrats, again with the *North Carolina Standard* leading, urged the sending of delegates. A few Whigs agreed, and fewer expressed objections even if they had them. The idea, however, was not disunion. It was rather to prove that the state was in earnest and willing to act with her neighbors for self-protection.[5]

Opinion in Georgia, which had been somewhat uncertain until the legislature met in November, 1849, soon began to stiffen. Governor Towns accepted his election as a mandate to resist further Northern "aggressions," and his first message called for immediate action. He urged that the state take a firm stand against the anti-slavery movement and asked that he be authorized to call a convention to consider measures proper for "safety and preservation" in case the Wilmot Proviso or kindred measures were passed by Congress. Both houses of the legislature responded with resolutions definitely more radical in character than any before presented to those bodies. For the first time, the possibility of secession was given formal expression. For the first time, Whigs were as extreme as Democrats. The only serious disagreement that developed in granting the governor's request for the power to call a convention and in providing for the election of delegates to Nashville arose over the question as to whether the admission of California as a state should be included in the reasons for action. Many Georgians evidently agreed with John B. Lamar that "If the matter can not

[5] Raleigh *North Carolina Standard,* June 19, 1850; Herbert D. Pegg, "The Whig Party in North Carolina, 1834–1861" (Ph.D. dissertation, University of North Carolina, 1932), 320, quoted in Sitterson, *Secession Movement in North Carolina,* 56; *ibid.,* 57–63.

be settled without the degradation of exclusion of us by Congress from all the new territory and without abolition in the Dist., then the sooner the Union is dissolved the better." [6]

Few expressions of this extreme type were heard in Alabama. Editors talked of the necessity of convincing the North that the South was in earnest, and Governor Henry W. Collier suggested that the legislature might " 'announce the ultimatum' " of the state on issues. That body, however, failed either to pass such resolutions or to provide for representation at Nashville. Members, meeting in extralegal session, later did select delegates but made it perfectly clear that disunion was not the purpose. Many, however, agreed with the Mobile *Daily Register* that Northern politicians could push issues "to the catastrophe of a dissolution of the Union." [7]

Men in Louisiana were of like mind. They agreed that Northern radicals were "menacing both the South and slavery," but they were not ready for disunion. The New Orleans *True Delta,* therefore, suggested that Southern representatives in Congress should walk out whenever an attempt was made to introduce the Wilmot Proviso or any act to abolish slavery in the District. And if "fanatics and trading politicians of the North" forced the alternative of "subjection . . . to Northern domination or a dissolution of the Union," which God forbid, then there could be little doubt "in any honest Southern breast which alternative" the people would choose. Governor Isaac Johnson, meanwhile, suggested that the state be represented at Nashville, but the press generally was cautious. The *Daily Crescent* (Whig) thought Louisiana should be represented in order to hold radicals in check and to influence "the well-meaning men" of the North by "a calm and decided course." The *Bee* took the same position, denounced Calhoun's assertion that dissolution was inevitable, and let it be known that South Carolina opinion did not hold in Louisiana. [8]

6 Shryock, *Georgia and the Union in 1850,* pp. 218–32; John B. Lamar to Cobb, February 7, 1850, in Phillips (ed.), *Correspondence of Toombs, Stephens, and Cobb,* 183.

7 Denman, *Secession Movement in Alabama,* 23–26; Montgomery *Advertiser and State Gazette,* December 18, 1849; Mobile *Daily Register,* January 9, February 2, 1850.

8 New Orleans *True Delta,* December 30, 1849; New Orleans *Daily Crescent,* February 23, 1850; New Orleans *Bee,* February 8, 21, 1850.

The legislature of Tennessee, meanwhile, by a strict party vote, resolved that the state would not submit to the passage of the Wilmot Proviso but withheld its judgment in regard to California. It did not recognize the call for a Southern convention, and the press divided along strict party lines in attitudes. The Nashville *Union* (Democratic) stanchly defended the convention as a move "to preserve the Union" by checking "Northern fanatics from destroying it" and roundly denounced the Whig press for its false charges. The *Republican Banner and Nashville Whig* loudly proclaimed the *unity* of the South against *disunion,* forecast the correction of all ills before a convention could meet, and let it be known, for outside consumption, that Tennessee frowned upon the move which threatened to desecrate her capital city. Parson William G. Brownlow, with characteristic force, warned his fellow Whigs to "have neither lot nor part in this nefarious enterprise." "And those who attend this *Hartford* Convention at Nashville, in search of *political salvation,*" he said, "will find when it is too late . . . that they have found POLITICAL DAMNATION!" [9]

Opinion in Arkansas was slow in developing. Communication facilities were bad and news traveled slowly. Not until January, 1850, did the *Arkansas Banner* take notice of the "fearful state of affairs in Washington City" and suggest the sending of representatives to Nashville. Its rival, the *Arkansas State Democrat,* strongly opposed the suggestion, and there was little response until Congressman Robert W. Johnson issued an "Address to the People of Arkansas" in which he asserted that "the Union of the Northern and Southern States, under a Common Government for a period beyond this Congress is a matter that may be seriously questioned." He urged the sending of delegates to the Southern convention, at which "The South will present to the world one united brotherhood and will move in one column under a banner,—Equality or Independence, Our Rights Under the Constitution Within or Without the Union."

This address stirred some debate on issues but no united action. "Our people do not believe that the time has yet come when

[9] Nashville *Union,* February 27, 1850; *Republican Banner and Nashville Whig,* January 28, February 14, 1850; Knoxville *Whig and Independent Journal,* March 2, 1850.

they are called upon to assist in dismembering the Confederacy," said the *State Gazette and Democrat.* "It is the universal sentiment that the Union must be preserved and the universal belief that it cannot be dissolved." Whig journals took the same position, and the *Southern Shield* declared the Nashville convention unwise, unconstitutional, and "revolutionary in character." Johnson, nevertheless, continued his efforts, and the debate became violent and personal. It showed in the main, however, that public opinion was definitely on the side of union and compromise. Arkansas had too much need of Federal aid in dealing with Indians, roads, and mail service to be talking about disunion.[10]

The situation in Florida was equally confused. The state was young, and the influence of her public men unusually strong. Both of her Senators were opposed to the Compromise, but her lone member of the House, while denying the right of Congress to prohibit the spread of slavery, had joined the Whigs in opposing the acquisition of any territory from Mexico. Senator David L. Yulee had taken a particularly strong stand against the Compromise measures. He had insisted that either slavery or the Union must be abolished and had favored a Constitutional amendment as the only means of protecting the South. He now joined with Representative Edward C. Cabell in a letter to Governor Thomas Brown urging him to support the Nashville convention and to appoint delegates to it.

Governor Brown, however, was of a different mind. In his inaugural of the preceding year he had denounced Southern demagogues and now questioned either the wisdom or the constitutionality of a Southern convention. He bluntly denied his right to appoint delegates and suggested that the time for revolution had not arrived. Local bipartisan meetings, however, did choose delegates, and Whigs as well as Democrats talked of defending Southern rights to the last extremity. Brown himself was ready to defend the sovereignty of the state.[11]

[10] Elsie M. Lewis, "From Nationalism to Disunion: A Study of the Secession Movement in Arkansas, 1850–1861" (Ph.D. dissertation, University of Chicago, 1946); Little Rock *Arkansas Banner*, January 1, 18, 1850; Little Rock *State Gazette and Democrat*, March 1, 1850; Helena (Ark.) *Southern Shield*, March 2, 1850.

[11] Dorothy Dodd, "The Secession Movement in Florida, 1850–1861," in *Florida Historical Quarterly* (Jacksonville, Gainesville, Tallahassee), XII (1933–1934), 3–9.

With Kentucky moderate in attitude and Texas primarily interested in maintaining her boundary claims, the centers of most aggressive opposition remained in Mississippi and South Carolina.[12] In the former, Governor Joseph W. Matthews denied the constitutionality of the Wilmot Proviso, insisted that Northern refusal to abide by the terms of the Missouri Compromise had opened all territories to slavery, and expressed his conviction that unless the South maintained its position "with unyielding firmness" the days of "this glorious Union . . . [were] numbered." He wanted a convention called whenever any action, including the admission of California, was taken by Congress. His successor, John A. Quitman, contented himself with a firm assertion of state rights and a harsh denunciation of Northern "fanaticism." But he too thought that the "ties that bind us together" were being "deliberately" severed.

The legislature expressed like fears and determination and backed them by the appropriation of $220,000 to defray the expenses of delegates to Nashville and to permit "the adoption of necessary measures for protecting the constitutional and sovereign rights of the states" in case of the passage of the threatened legislation. Whigs and Democrats divided on the question of California, but neither showed any inclination to recede from the positions taken and demands made in the October convention.[13]

South Carolina, as usual, was well in advance of her sister states. When her legislature met in early December, Governor Seabrook "hailed with satisfaction" the proposed Nashville convention and suggested that he be given power to call the legislature into special session or to issue writs for a state convention should the Wilmot Proviso or similar legislation be enacted. He also asked for funds to improve and arm the militia efficiently. The legislature, in complete agreement, provided for the election of delegates to Nashville, granted the right to call a special session of the legislature under the conditions suggested, but appropriated only a small sum for the purchase of arms. Its action met with general approval. For once the moderate Charleston *Courier* and the more radical *Mercury* were in complete accord. Both agreed that the time had come

[12] See analysis in Augusta *Daily Chronicle and Sentinel*, January 16, 1850.
[13] Hearon, *Mississippi and the Compromise of 1850*, pp. 78–87.

for a united South "to uphold her institutions, her rights and her sacred honor." Some newspapers still demanded secession, "the sooner the better," but the calm of confidence had generally taken the place of excited appeal. The district and parish meetings to choose delegates to Nashville revealed a calm, determined spirit bent on the protection of Southern rights as they understood them or a dissolution of the existing union. They understood and accepted the issue as "submission" or "disunion." [14]

Reports of what was occurring in Washington had played a very definite part in producing the attitudes and steps taken in the Southern states up to this time. The moves toward compromise and settlement of issues which Clay launched in February, and which Webster and others so eloquently defended in the weeks following, also quickly made themselves felt back in the states. Whigs who had never unanimously supported Southern action were quick to see the advantage to their party in new assertions of loyalty and in rugged opposition to radical steps. Conservative Democrats were equally anxious for the opportunity to hold back. The talk of disunion which had become so open in certain quarters was not to their liking. It hurt them politically in states where the parties were almost equally divided.

Clay's proposals and Webster's speech were, therefore, hailed with genuine enthusiasm. "Let the illustrious Senator from Kentucky be congratulated upon this the greatest epoch of his public life," said the Augusta *Daily Chronicle and Sentinel*. "He has stood forth in the noblest characteristics of his nature. The American people listen to him with respectful attention. He is above the range of the cloudy atmosphere of factions, and he speaks from the blue empyrean of a composed mind, in a manner worthy of the great *Consulares* of the Republic." The editor was certain that the distracting question which had excited so much sectional animosity was "on a fair way for a harmonious adjustment." [15] The Lynchburg *Virginian* pronounced Clay's compromises "satisfactory," and Parson Brownlow rapturously announced that "while there was one

[14] Hamer, *Secession Movement in South Carolina*, 45–48; Harold S. Schultz, *Nationalism and Sectionalism in South Carolina, 1852–1860* (Durham, 1950), 3–25.

[15] Augusta (Ga.) *Daily Chronicle and Sentinel*, February 5, March 5, 1850.

gleam of the ancient glory of Greece remaining—while there is a decent regard for Liberty still lingering on the shores of America —while there remains . . . clouds to float in the sky, birds to wing their way through the air, and boughs to battle with the blast, will the name of HENRY CLAY be honored! Than whom God never created a nobler patriot,—HENRY CLAY!" [16]

Webster came in for equal praise. The New Orleans *Daily Delta* called his speech a "God-send." "It is the midday sun breaking through the clouds that have hung for forty days and nights over the ark of the Constitution. It is the trident of old Neptune, calming the excited sea and soothing the raging billows." [17] Its neighbor the *Daily Crescent* saw "the phantom of disunion" retiring before an awakened public opinion. There was no mistaking the evidence. "The sentiment of 'liberty and union, one and inseparable,' . . . [was] at length thoroughly aroused in the capitol of the nation and . . . [was] springing up, with giant force, from the body of the people in every portion of the country. . . . The tide of disunion . . . [was] rolling back; the Union . . . [was] safe." [18] The Augusta *Daily Chronicle and Sentinel* found language inadequate to express its "high gratification" on reading this "noble contribution to harmony, conciliation and fraternal feeling." It was the greatest effort of a great man.[19] Nor was enthusiasm entirely confined to Whig editors. The Richmond *Enquirer* called it "a masterly production,"—a move "not to make concessions (for the South ask[ed] none) but to do justice to the aggrieved South," and the Augusta *Daily Constitutionalist* hailed it as "a noble and patriotic speech . . . , highly conciliatory to the South and containing a thorough repudiation of the Wilmot Proviso." True, Webster had not declared it unconstitutional, and the reception his speech had received in the North clearly revealed that this was but "a little rill" of conservatism in the "swelling tide" of Northern antislavery fanaticism.[20]

Whigs, however, knew that the turning had begun. Calhoun's

[16] Knoxville *Whig and Independent Journal*, March 2, 1850; April 2, 1851.
[17] New Orleans *Daily Delta*, March 16, 1850.
[18] New Orleans *Daily Crescent*, March 27, 1850.
[19] Augusta *Daily Chronicle and Sentinel*, March 10, 1850.
[20] Richmond *Enquirer*, March 13, 1850; Augusta (Ga.) *Daily Constitutionalist*, March 21, 1850.

speech had been a bit too gloomy even for Democrats, and neither Foote nor Davis had attracted much attention outside his own state. Opposition to the Nashville convention, therefore, became more bold and open. Some began to say that such a meeting was no longer necessary. It should be abandoned. "One week ago," said the New Orleans *Daily Crescent* on February 23, "we thought that the Convention would certainly be held . . . as proposed; and that it might be important to send to it as delegates from this state men of comprehensive patriotism, enlarged statesmanship and eminent ability. . . . We are now of a different opinion. . . . We have doubts as to whether there will be a convention." Its neighbor, the New Orleans *Bee,* was of the opinion that "the extreme probability of an early and honorable settlement of existing difficulties . . . [had] united to destroy whatever of popularity the scheme . . . [might] once have enjoyed." The Augusta *Chronicle and Sentinel* found a like attitude in Georgia and "the necessity for a Convention seriously questioned." A Richmond editor thought that all that was now necessary for "the sun of tomorrow" to rise on "a land smiling in peace and harmony" was for all public men to be animated by "the calm, conservative, moderate and patriotic spirit" of the Whig leaders in Washington.[21]

The charge, now made openly, that the Nashville convention was planned as a secession move put the Southern Democrats definitely on the defensive. Realizing that the great majority were weary of strife and inclined to grasp at any move that offered peace, editors desperately reminded their readers of the continued hostility to slavery and the need for holding firm. Southern unity was still a necessity. "You cannot close your eyes upon the fact that a feeling of determined hostility towards the institution of slavery prevails generally in the non-slaveholding States of the Union," warned the Richmond *Enquirer.* "Abolitionism never sleeps," it added. The proposed convention was, therefore, still needed as a means of centering "serious attention" upon pressing problems. Yet it should be clearly understood that there were "no disunionists at the South." When the Nashville convention was "denounced as a movement to dissolve the Union,—it . . . [amounted] to

21 New Orleans *Bee,* April 5, 1850; Richmond *Republican and General Advertiser,* May 13, 1850; Savannah *News,* March 12, 1850.

nothing but a pretext for a deserting of the South and her interests in the hour of danger." [22]

Soon Democrats were insisting that the convention was just "a friendly Southern meeting" for the purpose of consulting "as to the best means of allaying the agitation, which . . . [was] continually imperilling the friendly relations of these States, and seriously affecting the peace and prosperity of the South." It had no disunion purpose. One editor spoke of the sly campaign, originating in the North, which "by innuendoes, sneers and whispered doubts, and at last by open and vociferous assertions" had attempted to picture the convention as "having in view nothing less than the dismemberment of the Union." This he flatly denied and asserted its purpose as one of adopting "measures by which that Union . . . [might] be preserved." [23]

The charge of playing politics was also raised and denied. Whigs pretended to believe that the whole business was an effort to discredit President Taylor; Democrats insisted that party had nothing to do with it. The effect, however, was to raise doubts, and more than one local meeting resolved to choose delegates only if all political partisanship were eliminated.[24]

The hostility of Tennessee was another hindering factor. Her legislature refused to recognize the convention, and the Whig press early urged the people "to frown upon it as it deserves." The *Republican Banner and Nashville Whig* charged "a treasonable purpose in the Convention" and suggested that Tennessee "tell the plotters to assemble elsewhere." It urged the state to maintain its honor by refusing the use of the state capitol for such meetings. The Democratic press attempted to refute the charge of disunion and insisted that the object of the convention was "to preserve the Union, by adopting efficient measures to prevent Northern fanatics from destroying it." But the Democrats were clearly on the defensive, and their strictly negative efforts only encouraged outsiders to hope with Edward Stanly that "the citizens of Nashville . . . [would] drive every traitor of them into the Cumberland River." [25]

[22] Richmond *Enquirer*, March 26, April 16, 17, 1850.

[23] New Orleans *Delta*, March 12, 1850; Natchez *Mississippi Free Trader*, March 6, 1850; Mobile *Daily Register*, March 4, 1850.

[24] Montgomery *Advertiser and State Gazette*, March 6, April 13, 1850.

[25] Raleigh *North Carolina Standard*, March 27, 1850.

Interest in the convention, therefore, lagged. Outside of Mississippi and South Carolina there was little interest in the selection of delegates. In some states the reaction was so marked that Democrats were reduced to urging the sending of delegates for the sole purpose of checking radical action. More than half the Virginia counties refused to choose their delegates; only six of the fourteen finally chosen were willing to attend. In Alabama Henry W. Hilliard questioned the right of the legislature to appoint delegates, and county conventions made it clear that delegates were being sent to preserve, not to dissolve, the Union. The people of North Carolina and Louisiana failed to take any action, and the April election in Georgia was so much a farce that even the Democrats admitted that the movement was dead and buried.

Governor Brown of Florida, as has been said, refused to use his influence to have delegates appointed and suggested that the South turn to the Supreme Court for redress. By mid-April Mississippi Whigs were emboldened to question the authority of a meeting as unrepresentative as this one promised to be, and Judge Sharkey was frankly prophesying that "the convention movement would result in a total failure." Democrats, however, kept up the pressure and cited Northern reactions to Webster's and Seward's speeches as showing the importance of united action by the Southern states. South Carolinians, meanwhile, were still insisting that "The hour of [the South's] independence or of her submission was now at hand," and trusting "that the Nashville convention . . . [would] take a noble and fearless course." [26]

Representing opinion so divided and uncertain, and composed of delegates with such wavering support, the convention which opened on June 3 in the unfriendly atmosphere of Nashville was doomed to failure. Only nine of the slaveholding states were represented. Some sent only a handful of delegates, and the credentials of many of these were without weight. Mississippi, for instance, had

[26] Richmond *Enquirer*, March 19, April 16, 1850; Richmond *Whig*, May 10, 1850; Huntsville (Ala.) *Southern Advocate*, May 29, 1850; Huntsville *Democrat*, May 2, 1850; Sitterson, *Secession Movement in North Carolina*, 57–63; Horace Montgomery, *Cracker Parties* (Baton Rouge, 1950), 21–23; Hearon, *Mississippi and the Compromise of 1850*, pp. 117–28; Sumter (S.C.) *Black River Watchman*, May 1, 1850; New York *Herald*, April 5, 1850.

the full number of delegates fixed by her October convention, but while every Democrat appointed by the legislature appeared, only three Whigs were present. Nor were all the delegates particularly notable for their prominence in Southern affairs. The South Carolina delegation was outstanding. It contained such men as the venerable Langdon Cheves, Hammond, Rhett, and Francis W. Pickens. Judge Sharkey headed the Mississippians, with Governor Matthews, Judge Alexander M. Clayton, and John J. McRae as capable assistants. Beverly Tucker, Willoughby Newton, and William O. Goode, of the small Virginia delegation, were all capable men but were not as yet in agreement as to the steps to be taken. Alabama sent a full delegation, but only John A. Campbell and Benjamin Fitzpatrick were known outside their own communities. General James P. Henderson, S. G. Roane, and J. Powell were the sole representatives of Texas and Arkansas, and Henry L. Benning and Charles J. McDonald provided most of the talent in the little group of eight Democrats and three Whigs which Georgia had been able to get together after much difficulty. Florida sent five delegates, none of great distinction, and Tennessee, with more than a hundred official members, created a conservative atmosphere from the very beginning.[27]

Judge Sharkey was elected president. His address to the convention was an earnest appeal for harmony and the enactment of courageous but conservative measures. He made it clear, however, that the preservation of the Union in its original purity was the sole purpose of the gathering. A committee composed of two members from each state then set to work to draw up resolutions and an address to the people.

After all the storm and fury of the past months, the thirteen resolutions adopted by the convention appear quite tame and inoffensive. They repeated the Southern claim of equal rights in the territories for slaveholders and the duty of Congress to recognize and protect slave property. In the only section at all belligerent in tone, they declared "That slave-holding States cannot and will not submit to the enactment by Congress of any law imposing onerous conditions or restraints upon the rights of masters to remove with their

[27] *Republican Banner and Nashville Whig*, June 5, 6, 1850.

property into the Territories of the United States, or to any law making discriminations in favor of the proprietors of other property against them."

And if a dominant majority refused to recognize Southern rights as here asserted, then it was the duty of the Federal government to divide the territories between the North and the South. The extension of the Missouri Compromise line to the Pacific would be a satisfactory settlement. It would end a conflict which, if continued, must rend the nation asunder.

The "Address to the People of the Southern States," written by Robert Barnwell Rhett, was a considerably stronger document. It began with a review of Northern aggressions on Southern rights and the increasing hostility to slavery; it then took up each item of Clay's compromise proposals and denounced it as unfair and unsatisfactory to the South. Californians had no right to form a government and to prohibit slavery. That territory belonged to the United States, not to a few individuals. If Congress admitted her, it was as if Congress itself had enacted the Wilmot Proviso. To take territory away from Texas and give it to New Mexico was nothing more than a scheme to enable that territory to follow the example of California and wrest more slave territory from the South. And as to abolishing the slave trade in the District of Columbia, that would imply a power over slavery which Maryland and Virginia had never intended to yield. If Congress could liberate a slave because he was *brought into the District,* the next step would be to liberate him because he *was in the District.* Nor was it worth while to pass a new fugitive-slave law. It could not be enforced. And besides, no bill would give to the South anything that it was not already entitled to. It would only lead to Congress legislating between the master and the slave in a state, and that was fraught with even greater danger.

The possibility of compromise, however, was not ignored. The South had already proposed either the extension of the Missouri Compromise line or the submission of Southern rights to court decision. In spite of the fact that both had been rejected, it was still willing to accept 36 degrees 30 minutes as a satisfactory partition line between the quarreling sections.

Debate on the resolutions and the Address gave opportunity for speechmaking and brought from conservatives expressions of devotion to the Union "without sacrifice of rights and honor," and from radicals, such as Beverly Tucker, assurance that delay meant degradation to the South and the postponement of a peaceful and prosperous independence. But outside the convention, neither attracted much attention. The membership of the convention was not representative enough, and the eyes of the people were on Washington, not on Nashville. That being the case, the convention did the only thing possible. Since it could not devise measures to meet acts not yet adopted, it adjourned, agreeing to reassemble after the adjournment of Congress if its demands had not been met.[28]

That the convention had been a failure few could deny. Even Hammond thought its only value lay in the fact that some Southerners had met in harmony and had *"agreed to meet again."* The *National Era* expressed the other extreme: "Its proceedings have excited little interest. It was an abortion and is not worth a word of comment." [29] Neither judgment was sound. The Nashville convention was not the forerunner of a series of successful Southern political gatherings. The idea, in fact, had been born with Calhoun. It was his great objective, preached in and out of season ever since nullification days. It belonged to his program of forcing the slavery issue by aggressive action, and driving the North to guarantees by the show of a solid front. The program was to die with him. The new leadership would abandon the idea of the Southern convention. But, on the other hand, the convention was worthy of notice. Its radical members went home encouraged to fight against all compromise and openly to preach secession. There was no reason

[28] *Resolutions, Address, and Journal of Proceedings of the Southern Convention, held at Nashville, Tennessee, June 3d to 12th, Inclusive, in the year 1850* (Nashville, 1850); *Condensed proceedings of the Southern convention, held at Nashville, Tennessee, June, 1850* (Jackson, Miss., 1850); *Resolutions and address, adopted by the Southern convention. Held at Nashville, Tennessee, June 3d to 12th inclusive, in the Year 1850* (Nashville, 1850); Dallas T. Herndon, "The Nashville Convention of 1850," *Transactions of the Alabama Historical Society*, 1904 (Montgomery), V (1906), 214–18; St. George L. Sioussat, "Tennessee, the Compromise of 1850, and the Nashville Convention," in *Mississippi Valley Historical Review* (Cedar Rapids), II (1915–1916), 332–36.
[29] Hammond to William Gilmore Simms, June 16, September 30, 1850, in Hammond Papers (University of North Carolina Library, Chapel Hill); Washington *National Era*, June 20, 1850; Charleston *Mercury*, June 15, 17, 20, 1850.

longer to be restrained. They had gone along with the moderates and failure had been the reward. Now they knew their friends and the course ahead was clear. Rhett, falling back into "the sophomoric rhetoric of 1828," foretold " 'the beginning of a Revolution,' the 'grand Drama of the dissolution of the Union.' " He was willing, he said, to be a traitor in the "cause of liberty." He wanted his state to strike for her independence and "instead of shrinking" to "pant for the trial" which would isolate her "in this great conflict." Others were not quite so bold, but Quitman in Mississippi, Henderson in Texas, and McDonald, Walter T. Colquitt, and Andrew H. Dawson in Georgia all spoke their minds and helped to forward the Southern Rights associations which now sprang up all over the South.[30]

The outcome of the Nashville convention, however, had its most important effects on the course of events in Washington. The compromise measures had not been having an easy time. There the Committee of Thirteen of the Senate had submitted three bills in the early part of May—one providing for the admission of California, the organization of Utah and New Mexico, and the settlement of the Texas boundary; a second dealing with fugitive slaves; and a third prohibiting the slave trade in the District of Columbia. The first of these was what President Taylor called "the omnibus." It represented a combination of separate bills which Southerners had demanded as a check on Taylor's possible veto of other items after California's admission. To it was now added, over Clay's opposition, a clause prohibiting territorial legislatures from acting on the subject of slavery.[31]

In the face of Taylor's opposition and of wide Southern hostility, the passage of these acts was doubtful. Many believed that the whole program had been set up in this fashion in order to ensure its defeat. Clemens of Alabama and Yulee of Florida thought the South was getting the worst of the bargain. They would have none of it. Houston of Texas was quick to repel any encroachment on the borders of his state. "I am for compromise with my whole heart," he said, "unless it is proposed to compromise our honor and

---

[30] White, *Robert Barnwell Rhett*, 108–10; Huntsville (Ala.) *Democrat*, June 20, 1850; Shryock, *Georgia and the Union in 1850*, pp. 273–89.

[31] *Cong. Globe*, 31 Cong., 1 Sess., 944–48, Appendix, 571, 1410.

safety." Restricting the Texas boundary evidently came within this category. John P. Hale of New Hampshire, on the other hand, viewed the whole proposal as a flagrant yielding to the interests of the South. Why Southerners should object to its provisions was beyond his comprehension. If this report did not satisfy them, what could they possibly want? The territories were being turned into a "slave pasture," and nowhere was there any obstruction to the spread of slavery. The fugitive bill was even worse. If Southerners asked more than was here being offered them, "Let them put this report down," he cried, "and then let us go home and tell the country we have exhausted the cup of concession. . . . These gentlemen . . . never mean to be satisfied and never will be." [32]

The real problem, however, was one of securing President Taylor's support. Clay spoke of his "anxious desire" to co-operate with "the Executive branch" and was careful to control his words so as not to give offense. Taylor was silent. The administration newspaper, the *Republic,* was seemingly friendly.

The debates in Congress, however, were for a time bitter enough to bring back all the violent charges and threats that had first induced Clay to offer his compromise. Then they seemed to soften. On May 13 Clay himself spoke of the way in which "the minds of men" had moderated. Everywhere passion had given place to reason, he said. The proposals offered by the committee represented a fair balancing of claims and if submitted to the people of the United States, nine tenths would favor their adoption.[33]

The calm, however, was only temporary. Taylor had not the slightest notion of yielding. His stubborn opposition and the quick removal of the *Republic* editor soon drove Clay to an open declaration of war to the finish. Stung by the attacks of the *Republic* under its new editor, he arose on May 21 and opened a vigorous assault on the President's program. The very life of the nation was at stake. The body politic could not be preserved "unless this agitation, this destruction, this exasperation" going on between the sections should cease. There were five wounds, "open and bleeding" and "threatening the well-being, if not the existence, of the body politic." And what did Taylor propose? He would try to stanch only one of them by the admission of California. He would leave the

[32] *Cong. Globe,* 31 Cong., 1 Sess., 950–55.   [33] *Ibid.,* Appendix, 567–73.

99

others "to harass and exasperate the country." That was not Clay's conception of duty.

Clay closed by pointing out the impossibility of establishing an equilibrium of power between the two sections and appealed to the South to accept the present guarantees of the Constitution as "reasonable security" against the growing majority at the North. To "oppose the immutable and irrevocable laws of population and of nature . . . [was] equivalent to a demand for the severance of the Union." "We must be reconciled to the condition which is inevitable," he warned.[34]

To accept the fate of a permanent minority and trust the future to those who were talking about a higher law than the Constitution was not very reassuring to Southerners. To have his statesmanship so harshly condemned was not something Taylor could accept with good humor. Clay had called for a show of hands.

With what grace the more positive Southerners would accept the inevitable was revealed by Robert Toombs in the debate over the admission of California. He denied the charge of opposing admission because California had excluded slavery. The great principle was whether the South had a right to equal participation in the territories of the United States. "I claim the right for her to enter them all with her property and security to enjoy it," he said. "She will divide with you . . . but the right to enter all or divide I shall never surrender. In my judgement, this right, involving, as it does, political equality, is worth a thousand such Unions as we have, even if they each were a thousand times more valuable than this. Deprive us of this right and appropriate this common property to yourselves, it is then your government, not mine. Then I am its enemy, and I will then, if I can, bring my children and my constituents to the altar of liberty, and like Hamilcar, I would swear them eternal hostility to your foul domination." [35]

Taylor showed his reactions to Clay's speech through an editorial appearing in the *Republic* on May 27. He was hurt and he was indignant. The editor needed more than four columns to describe Clay's unjust and domineering conduct. He made it clear that all good Whigs would stand loyally by Taylor. And Taylor had not the slightest notion of yielding an inch.[36]

---

[34] *Cong. Globe*, 31 Cong., 1 Sess., 612–16, 1091.   [35] *Ibid.*, 1216.
[36] Hamilton, *Zachary Taylor*, 336–37.

News of what had happened at the Nashville convention strengthened the hands of those who labored for compromise. Tension
lessened almost at once. The ultimate passage of legislation along
the general lines of Clay's proposals was practically assured. Taylor's position, moreover, was now weakened by two unfortunate occurrences. Already embarrassed by the incompetency of his Cabinet, he now had to face a scandal. It grew out of a generous settlement by the Treasury of the so-called Galpin claims, for which
George W. Crawford, Secretary of War, was the attorney. The
claims went back to certain debts which two Southern Indian tribes
owed to George Galpin and other traders before the American
Revolution, and which, it was now claimed, should be assumed by
the United States government. Payment with interest, in which
Crawford would share, suggested official influence if not corruption
and resulted in a Congressional investigation and much unfavorable publicity for the whole administration.[37]

Taylor's second difficulty came from his efforts in New Mexico.
There under his encouragement a convention met in May and
drew up a constitution excluding slavery. This immediately precipitated a conflict with Texas, whose claims to that region had already
been vigorously asserted. Her governor, therefore, called a special
session of the legislature, while the press broke into violent protest
and volunteer companies prepared to do battle for the rights of their
state. Southerners everywhere rose to the defense of Texas, and a
group of Whigs in Congress sent a delegation to warn Taylor that
if he persisted in his present course, they would be driven to open
resistance. Taylor stood his ground. Stephens talked of impeachment. Taylor responded with threats of hanging rebels now as he
had hung "spies and deserters in Mexico!" [38]

It was brave but foolish talk which only reacted unfavorably on
the compromise struggle and still further divided the Whig party.
Things looked more gloomy than ever. A renewal of uncompromising strife seemed imminent as both sides laid their plans. Then suddenly all was changed by the death of President Taylor. Millard
Fillmore, friend of compromise, became President. Progress toward
a settlement began again.[39]

The real difficulty all along had been over the question of dealing

[37] *Cong. Globe,* 31 Cong., 1 Sess., Appendix, 546–56.
[38] Hamilton, *Zachary Taylor,* 374–79.   [39] *Ibid.,* 388–92.

with California, New Mexico, and the Texas boundary as a unity in the "omnibus bill." Benton had insisted that the combined issues could never be passed, and Douglas had largely agreed. Their opponents, nevertheless, had held for unity both because they felt that the Texas boundary and the New Mexico issues would be carried by California's admission, and because the combination checked action and gave bargaining strength. Now under the new conditions created by the failure of the Nashville convention and by President Taylor's death, Douglas was able to secure the removal of the clause prohibiting the territorial legislatures from acting upon the subject of slavery. Then in order to render the bill more acceptable, a caucus decided to substitute for the Texas boundary provisions an amendment to refer the whole question to a commission composed of representatives from both Texas and the United States. Dawson of Georgia managed to attach to this a proviso that the New Mexico act should not go into effect east of the Rio Grande until Texas approved. James A. Pearce of Maryland objected to this as a tacit recognition of the Texas claim, and since the chair ruled that the amendment and the proviso could not be separated, he moved to strike out both. This carried, and against the intentions of everyone concerned the Texas boundary issue was thus eliminated from the omnibus. That wrecked the whole combination, threw the Texas votes for compromise, and left only the provision for the organization of Utah as part of the original. The enemies of the omnibus were jubilant. The five issues would have to be dealt with separately. Clay and his supporters had been defeated.[40]

The celebration, however, was short-lived. Opponents had not reckoned with the driving force of Stephen A. Douglas. While Clay, worn out by his efforts, withdrew to Newport for a rest, Douglas, with Fillmore's backing, framed new separate bills providing for California's admission, the drawing of the present Texas boundary with the payment of ten million dollars as indemnity, the organization of New Mexico, a new fugitive-slave law, and the prohibition of the slave trade in the District of Columbia. With a bloc of thirteen Democrats and four Whigs supporting nearly all the measures, enough votes were slowly secured, now from the North, now from the South, to carry each measure and by September 16 to complete

[40] *Cong. Globe,* 31 Cong., 1 Sess., 1481–82, 1490–91, Appendix, 1447–91.

the program. The House, after some stormy sessions, concurred in each case, and the final acts went out for the judgment of the people of the nation.[41]

Southern opinion on the Compromise divided along lines already drawn by the Nashville convention. In Virginia, where the Richmond *Enquirer* had viewed Clay's resolutions as a complete surrender to the North, and even the Richmond *Whig* had seen the compromise as all on one side, there was a general feeling that it should be accepted as a necessity rather than as a fair adjustment. It was not what was desired, said the *Enquirer,* but it was the best that could be gotten. But this acceptance had one condition attached. John R. Thompson expressed it in the *Southern Literary Messenger* in this fashion: "We say to the people of the North then not as alarmists, but as those who love the Union of our fathers, in no spirit of menace but rather in that of expostulation, that in our judgment *the continued existence of the United States as one nation, depends upon the full and faithful execution of the Fugitive Slave Bill.*" [42]

North Carolina's acceptance was also conditional. Whigs as a rule followed Stanly in his wholehearted approval, but the radical wing of the Democratic party was not happy. "We cannot stay in the Union any longer with such dishonor attached to the terms of our remaining," said the Charlotte *Hornet's Nest.*[43] "The South has been vanquished in the struggle," admitted the *North Carolina Standard,* "and thus, as the circle of fire approaches us on all sides, red with the wrath of Fanaticism born in hell, we are commanded on pain of treason, to be silent." Before accepting the command, however, it warned the North to "Let this question of slavery alone —take it out and keep it out of Congress; and respect and enforce the Fugitive Slave Law as it stands. If not, WE LEAVE YOU! Before God and man . . . if you fail in this simple act of justice, THE BONDS WILL BE DISSOLVED!" Meetings in Charlotte and in Wilmington took a like attitude, and the opinion that peace

[41] George F. Milton, *The Eve of Conflict; Stephen A. Douglas and the Needless War* (Boston, 1934), 72–78.

[42] Richmond *Enquirer*, October 15, September 10, 1850; *Southern Literary Messenger* (Richmond), XVI (1850), 697.

[43] Quoted in Sumter *Black River Watchman*, September 21, 1850.

and union depended on Northern observance of the terms of the fugitive-slave act was widely expressed.[44]

Georgia's reaction was important for the South as a whole. The state was making rapid progress along all lines and the other Southern states had begun to look to her for sound leadership. Her governor, moreover, was pledged to call a state convention if California was admitted. Her resistance was then expected to launch the wider Southern movement. With this in mind, her representatives, returning from Nashville, had been busy creating the impression that Clay's proposals were an insult to the South, and both Rhett and Yancey had visited Georgia to speak at Southern Rights meetings. Henry L. Benning had even been talking of the "United States South." The *Georgia Telegraph* was advocating "secession, . . . resistance, open unqualified resistance," and the Columbia *Sentinel* had abandoned the Union "as an engine of infamous oppression." It too was for "secession, open, unqualified, naked secession." [45]

The Whigs, on the other hand, had given stanch support to compromise and had met the radical moves with Union meetings of their own. They had been greatly encouraged by the support which Stephens, Toombs, and Cobb had given in Congress. They were, therefore, ready when on September 23 Governor Towns issued his proclamation calling for the election of a convention.

"In this hour of danger," read the governor's appeal, "when your institutions are in jeopardy—your feelings wantonly outraged; your social organization derided; and the Federal Constitution violated by a series of aggressive measures, all tending to the consummation of one object, the abolition of slavery . . . it well becomes you to assemble, to deliberate, and counsel together for your mutual protection and safety." [46]

It was a bold appeal, but even the doughty governor understood

[44] Raleigh *North Carolina Standard*, November 13, 1850; Raleigh *Register*, November 13, 1850; Salisbury (N.C.) *Carolina Watchman*, November 14, 1850.

[45] Washington *Southern Press*, August 23, 1850; Savannah *Georgian*, August 23, 24, 1850; Sumter *Black River Watchman*, October 19, 1850; Shryock, *Georgia and the Union in 1850*, pp. 272–89. Milledgeville (Ga.) *Federal Union*, July 10, August 20, 1850, cited in Montgomery, *Cracker Parties*, 25, reports two dozen county meetings against the Compromise.

[46] *Debates and Proceedings of the Georgia Convention*, 1850, pp. 27–28; Columbia *South Carolinian*, September 26, 1850.

that his state was not ready for open resistance. Sadly he informed the anxious governor of South Carolina "that probably nineteen twentieths of the old state rights group" were "submissionists." The odds were fearful and his efforts were "cheerless and discouraging." The campaign which followed proved him correct. The election on November 25 was a veritable landslide, the Union majority being the greatest that one party had ever rolled up in the state. The convention, when it met, was in the hands of unionists and was willing to go no further than to issue an "Exposition and Resolutions," soon known as the Georgia Platform, which declared that Georgia could "consistently with her honor" accept the Compromise measures. Acceptance, however, was again conditional. As the fourth resolution put it:

"The state of Georgia, will and ought to resist even (as a last resort) to a disruption of every tie that binds her to the Union, any action of Congress upon the subject of slavery in the District of Columbia, or in places subject to the jurisdiction of Congress, incompatible with the safety, and domestic tranquility, the rights and honor of the slave holding states, or any refusal to admit as a state any territory hereafter applying, because of the existence of slavery therein, or any act, prohibiting the introduction of slaves into the territories of Utah and New Mexico, or any act repealing or materially modifying the laws now in force for the recovery of fugitive slaves." [47]

The people of Alabama were badly divided in their opinions of the Compromise measures. The majority, however, were seemingly willing to accept them as the best that could be secured. In January they organized a Union party and passed resolutions favoring the Compromise and denying the right of secession. Yancey led the opposition. To him it was a case of Congress "calmly and deliberately" consummating "this great fraud upon the South." "Submission or secession" were the only alternatives. He was for action, and action could best be found in the formation of Southern Rights clubs. J. J.

---

[47] Governor George W. Towns to Governor Whitemarsh Seabrook of South Carolina, September 25, 1850, in Whitemarsh Seabrook Manuscripts (Division of Manuscripts, Library of Congress); Augusta *Daily Chronicle and Sentinel,* November 24, 1850; Savannah *Republican,* December 17, 1850; *Debates and Proceedings of the Georgia Convention,* 1850, pp. 5–9.

Seibels of the powerful Montgomery *Advertiser* joined the movement but was convinced that what Georgia did would determine the course of events in Alabama. The equally influential Mobile *Register,* also Democratic, insisted that three fourths of the people of the state were already against the Southern Rights party and that Georgia's action would not matter. Radical groups at Eufaula, Montgomery, and Selma, however, kept the idea of secession alive, especially if other states took that step. In February a convention was called, and a Southern Rights party was launched to combat the idea of "tame submission" to the "hostile" Compromise.[48]

Governor Collier, meanwhile, had remained neutral. He would neither approve nor disapprove of the Compromise. He did suggest a few changes. Furthermore, he was opposed to any Southern convention until the people demanded it. Such attempts at straddling proved popular, and he was re-elected in August by a large majority. The legislature, elected with him, was Unionist almost two to one. The party also carried five of the seven Congressional districts. Alabama was definitely for giving compromise a trial.

With its commerce linked to the whole Mississippi Valley and its sugar industry protected by tariff legislation, Louisiana took little interest in talk of secession. The finality of the Compromise was from the first widely and heartily advocated. Both Whigs and Democrats endorsed it and only a small faction under Senator Pierre Soulé opposed it. The New Orleans *Picayune* suggested that most of those in this group were Carolina emigrants who still read the Calhoun press.[49]

The people of Texas were also surprisingly quiet. After all of her representatives in Congress and her legislature had accepted the boundary settlement contained in one of the Compromise measures, opposition in that state largely subsided. Only Louis T. Wigfall was unhappy. Others were of the opinion that ten million dollars covered a multitude of sins. The *National Intelligencer* on

[48] Lewy Dorman, *Party Politics in Alabama from 1850 through 1860* (Wetumpka, 1935), 43–55; Mobile *Daily Register*, February 18, 1851; Denman, *Secession Movement in Alabama,* 56–64.

[49] Melvin J. White, "Louisiana and the Secession Movement of the Early Fifties," in *Proceedings of the Mississippi Valley Historical Association* (Cedar Rapids), VIII (1916), 278–88; New Orleans *Picayune*, August 9, 1850.

October 1 reported the Compromise well received. "No excitement of a dangerous nature," said another, "now exists west of the Mississippi River." [50]

A state election to choose a Congressman and members of the legislature put the Compromise measures before the people of Florida early in October. The Whigs generally took their position in support of the Compromise and renominated Edward Cabell for representative on the basis of his voting record. The Democrats brought forward Major John Beard, who announced that he would resist the measures to the last extremity and preferred the dissolution of the Union to their adoption. Such extreme statements brought the charge of disloyalty against the party and clouded the issue to a degree. The Democratic press did its best to clear the air, but the damage had been done and Cabell was re-elected by a narrow margin. The Democrats, however, gained a majority in the legislature, and Southern Rights associations began to be formed widely throughout the state. The Madison Association took as its motto "Equality in the Union or Independence out of it." Others declared that the repeal of the Fugitive Slave Law would mean separation. Governor Brown supported this position and asserted that a repudiation of that act would "leave us no alternative compatible with national unity." He requested of the legislature the authority to call a convention to devise a remedy in case of such an emergency. The Legislative Committee on Federal Relations, meanwhile, presented a "well-reasoned statement" on the legal right of secession.[51]

Sentiment in Arkansas was definitely in favor of the Compromise. Senator Solon Boreland had come home in June and had taken no part in the work of passing the various measures. He had, however, both criticised some of the bills and proclaimed his ardent love of the Union. Senator William K. Sebastian, on the other hand, had remained at his post, said nothing, and voted for each measure. Only Congressman Johnson had opposed every step that was taken. He now announced that he would not be a candidate for re-election. "If the people of Arkansas are satisfied with less than their clear

[50] Washington *National Intelligencer,* October 1, 1850.
[51] Dodd, "Secession Movement in Florida," *loc. cit.,* 3–19.

constitutional rights and equality in the acquired territories," he said, "I have not spoken for them or truly represented their will." [52]

Johnson's political influence in Arkansas, however, was still strong, and the state elections quickly revealed a sharp split in Democratic ranks. The new governor, John S. Roane, in his message to the legislature asserted the sovereignty of the state and his firm belief that the Compromise had violated its rights. He was careful to say that he was no disunionist, but "rather than yield and concede the power of the General Government to enforce obedience to her unjust laws at the point of a bayonet, . . . [he] would say dissolve the Union."

Radicals in the legislature were quick to seize the opportunity to introduce resolutions critical of the Compromise, but their efforts only stirred the expression of equally strong opinion in its favor. Local meetings showed the same division, but internal issues and personalities were so important in almost every man's position that little could be told about attitudes toward the Compromise itself. Even the call for Johnson to re-enter the race for Congress and his success in late summer meant little more than personal popularity and family power.[53]

Since there had been at no time any question as to the favorable attitude entertained toward compromise in Tennessee and Kentucky, the fate of the Southern Rights movement ultimately depended on what happened in Mississippi and South Carolina. The Mississippi delegation in Congress had sharply divided on the Compromise issues. Senator Foote had been quick to refute Calhoun's assertion that California was the final test case between the sections, and he had played a decisive part in the formation of the Committee of Thirteen. From that time forward, he had been a leading figure in pushing compromise. Slight, nervous, energetic, and quick-tempered, he had supplied much of the irritation which at times threatened to wreck progress. But he had also rallied Southern support and shared credit with Douglas for final success. Davis and Brown, on the other hand, had seen little but Southern submission in Clay's program and had opposed it to the very end. Con-

[52] Little Rock *Arkansas State Gazette and Democrat,* October 14, 1850.
[53] Lewis, "From Nationalism to Disunion," 151–68.

stituents back in Mississippi had reflected the attitudes of their leaders, and party lines had early begun to fade.[54]

The *Mississippi Free Trader* called Foote a "parrotty quibbler," an "endless explainer and talker" who had at last gotten into his true company—"the party of the 'Whig free-soilers.' " It demanded the recall of Mississippi's Senators and Representatives and the presentation of "secession or submission" to a state convention. It was convinced that if the South submitted to the terms of the Compromise, it was doomed. Within six years slavery would be abolished and the section would know a fate worse than that of Jamaica and Martinique. "Either we must submit to *disgrace,* and soon to ABOLITION, with all its horrors, or we must . . . prevent it . . . by *Secession,*" growled the Woodville *Republican.* Governor Quitman, in full agreement, issued a call for a special session of the legislature and prepared to press for a convention "fully empowered to take into consideration . . . federal relations, and to change or annul them." [55]

Southern Rights and Union groups, meanwhile, organized, discussed the right of secession, and the nature of Federal relationships. By the time the legislature assembled, issues were well drawn and sides taken. Governor Quitman submitted a long and carefully prepared message which condemned the Compromise measures and advised steps toward resistance. He urged the calling of a convention and stressed the idea of co-operation with other states. He suggested that an effort be made to obtain from California concessions south of 36° 30′ and advanced the opinion that if some guarantees were not now secured, aggressions would increase year by year until the South would be forced to secession. He thought that committees of safety should be set up in each state and that these committees should then co-operate with each other in the interest of Southern safety.[56]

[54] *Cong. Globe,* 31 Cong., 1 Sess., 247, 257–61, 323–24, 355, 366, Appendix, 149–57 (speeches of Brown, Foote, and Jefferson Davis); Ranck, *Albert Gallatin Brown,* 65–83; Hearon, *Mississippi and the Compromise of 1850,* pp. 109–13 (Foote).

[55] Natchez *Mississippi Free Trader,* August 31, 1850.

[56] *Ibid.,* September 25, 1850 ("We see but two ways, secession or submission"); John A. Quitman to J. J. M'Rae, September 28, 1850, in J. F. H. Claiborne, *Life and Correspondence of John A. Quitman* (New York, 1860), II, 44–46; Quitman's message to the legislature, November 18, 1850, *ibid.,* 46–51; Quitman to Col. John S. Preston (for secession), March 29, 1851, *ibid.,* 123–27.

The Unionists countered with a meeting held in Jackson while the legislature was in session. They organized a "Union party," denounced the governor's proposals, and "acquiesce[d] in the enactments of the late session of Congress, but warned the outside world that interference by congressional legislation with the institution of slavery in the states," the prohibition of slavery in any territory, or the repeal of the Fugitive Slave Law or refusal to enforce it, would justify a resort to measures of resistance.

The legislature, however, was unmoved. It supported resistance to the Compromise and issued the call for a convention to devise and put into effect "the best means of redress for the past," and to obtain "certain security for the future." That action brought the necessity for two new parties to a climax and sent them into a bitter campaign to secure a majority of the delegates. At first their forces seemed about equal, but as the other Southern states took their positions, the Southern Rights party lost strength. Georgia's action was especially valuable to the Union party, and the extreme expressions of opinion that came from South Carolina aided it almost as much. It was soon apparent that in spite of Quitman's efforts, Mississippi would not blindly follow his lead.[57]

The final test came in the election of state officials and members of the convention. The Southern Rights party named Quitman as its candidate for governor, and the Union party named Foote. Since the tide was now running clearly toward acceptance of the Compromise, some Southern Rights men tried to prevent Quitman's nomination, and even he was forced to deny the charge of being a disunionist. The line, however, seemed to be clearly drawn, and the campaign was waged largely on the issue of union versus secession. It was a violent affair. Extreme charges were hurled back and forth. A series of debates between the candidates ended in a fist fight. Foote, however, proved the better campaigner, and in September Union candidates for the convention were elected in all but eighteen counties. Chagrined at the outcome, Quitman resigned as the candidate of his party for governor, and Jefferson Davis was named in his place. It was, however, too late to recover lost ground, and in November Foote was the victor, although by a smaller

[57] Natchez *Semi-weekly Courier,* October 15, 1850; New York *Semi-weekly Tribune,* December 7, 1850; Vicksburg *Whig,* November 27, 1850.

majority than that given Union candidates for the convention.

When the convention met on November 10, it declared that the people of Mississippi, "whilst they do not entirely approve, will abide by . . . [the Compromise] as a permanent adjustment of this sectional controversy, so long as the same, in all its features, shall be faithfully adhered to and enforced." It also resolved that "the asserted right of secession from the Union on the part of a State or States is utterly unsanctioned by the Federal Constitution." That brought the matter to a close for the moment and left South Carolina to stand alone.[58]

The passage of the Compromise measures had served only to increase an already active disunion movement in South Carolina. Whigs and Democrats alike considered the argument ended and the time for action at hand. "No earthly power can save this Confederacy from dissolution," said the *Mercury*. "We must give up the Union or give up slavery," echoed the *Spartan*. To all of which Edward Bryan added: "Give us SLAVERY or give us death." [59]

Francis Lieber reported that "ultimate disunion" was "the universal cry and disposition," and he was impressed by "the intense religious fervor" which characterized the movement. Richard Yeadon declared it to be his "thorough conviction" that Charleston was "wholly alienated from the Union & that a long list of Union-regarding citizens" could "not be found within her limits." It was not a case, he said, of disunion if there were further Northern aggressions, but one of disunion rather than "submission to the late compromise." Since the government of the United States had become "an abolition machine, whose main employment" was "to forge manacles for the South," it was time to resist "the plundering and insulting bill of Henry Clay." [60]

[58] Quitman to Governor John H. Means (South Carolina), May 25, 1851, in Claiborne, *Life and Correspondence of John A. Quitman*, II, 135–36: "Every other Southern state, except Mississippi, has bowed her neck to the yoke or silently submitted. Nowhere but in Mississippi has even any authoritative step been taken to meet you in a Southern congress. . . .

"Experience has fully demonstrated that united action can not be had; the frontier slave states are even now indicating a disposition to cling to the Union at the hazard of their slave institutions." See also Hearon, *Mississippi and the Compromise of 1850*, pp. 203–20.

[59] Hamer, *Secession Movement in South Carolina*, 66.

[60] Francis Lieber to George S. Hilliard, December 8, 13, 1850, in Francis Lieber

Determined as were the South Carolina leaders, they still clung to the old Calhoun idea of co-operation with the other Southern states. They realized, furthermore, that South Carolina's effort at leadership would damage the whole movement. Wisdom was on the side of letting others act while South Carolina stood pledged to follow. In keeping with this idea, Governor Seabrook opened a correspondence with the governors of other states, suggesting that they take the lead and pledging South Carolina to be early at their side. One by one they failed him and, in the end, forced the issue of submission or separate state action. "Where is Virginia, whose Legislature was to light up the fires of resistance on the passage of the Wilmot Proviso, or any kindred measure," asked a writer in the Charleston *Mercury*. "Alas! She fulminated against the name not the substance" and left her sons to blush and taunt her with the subterfuge. "Where is Texas? Ten millions of dollars have stilled the indignation of the men of San Jacinto, and gold is there, as everywhere nowadays, the *King*. And lastly, where is Georgia? God grant that the voice of freedom may hush the mewlings of her submissionists, and that she may take the lead which her talent and strength, and the hopes of the whole South, have assigned to her." But Georgia, alas, was also to fail the cause, and Mississippi too.[61]

The second meeting of the Nashville convention was even more disheartening. Many of its members did not return. Only seven states were irregularly represented. Langdon Cheves tried to carry the South Carolina attitude into action but quickly discovered a new conciliatory temper that had not been present at the June meeting. The resolutions that came out of the brief session admitted that all the anticipated evils had been realized but recommended only that the Southern states stay out of national political conventions until their rights were secured and that another Southern convention be held at a later date.[62]

These developments left South Carolina without hope of outside

Papers (Huntington Library, San Marino, Calif.); Richard Yeadon to Benjamin F. Perry, January 6, 1851, in Benjamin F. Perry Papers (Alabama State Department of Archives and History, Montgomery.)

[61] Charleston *Mercury*, October 1, 1850; Boucher, "Secession and Co-operation Movement in South Carolina," in Washington University *Studies*, V, No. 2 (1918), 101.

[62] Herndon, "Nashville Convention of 1850," in *Transactions of the Alabama Historical Society*, 1904, V (1906), 227–34.

support. She was, moreover, divided within herself. Rhett and his followers in the Southern Rights associations were ready to act singlehandedly if necessary. The Charleston *Mercury* expressed their attitude when it asked:

"Are we ready, people of Carolina, to stand alone in defense of rights far more precious than life or gold? Or are we too, only waiting the keynote of submission from others, to swell the false and pitiable cry of 'peace, peace,' ourselves? . . . What! is it come to this, that the State whose talk of chivalry has passed into a proverb —whose creed of State Sovereignty has been proclaimed for half a century, henceforth looks for redress in the courage and swords of others? . . . History, honor, and our own consistency force upon us what some may think the terrible alternative of *separate state action.*" [63]

There were others, however, who believed that South Carolina should act only in co-operation with the other Southern states. Secession was neither wise nor justified. Singlehanded action was pure folly. Under the leadership of Joel R. Poinsett, James L. Petigru, and William Grayson in the east, and Benjamin F. Perry and Waddy Thompson in the west, they now spoke out openly for the Union and in opposition to separate state action. Even ex-Governors James Hamilton and James H. Hammond advised caution in the face of the fact that no other state considered the Compromise measures sufficient cause for a dissolution of the Union. [64]

When the legislature met in November, Governor Seabrook recommended economic and military preparation and suggested that the time had come "to resume the exercise of the powers of self protection." An atmosphere of disunion prevailed, but there was no agreement as to the proper action to be taken. Radicals demanded a convention to take the state out of the Union. Conservatives opposed this and talked of another convention of all the Southern states. In the end, they compromised and provided both for a state convention and for the election of delegates to a Southern convention to meet at Montgomery, Alabama, on January 2, 1852.

[63] Charleston *Mercury*, October 1, 1850.

[64] Lieber to Hilliard, January 29, 1851, in Lieber Papers; Kibler, *Benjamin F. Perry*, 243–52; Nathaniel W. Stephenson, "Southern Nationalism in South Carolina in 1851," in *American Historical Review* (New York), XXXVI (1930–1931), 314–35.

They then elected Rhett to fill Calhoun's seat in the Senate.[65]

Strangely enough, the election of delegates to the state convention created little interest. Petigru wrote of the "great apathy in the public mind," and Lieber said he now found tens and hundreds who thought separate state secession would be folly, whereas a few months ago he found but one. The vote was light but the separate secessionists had a majority. Confident of their position, they called a great meeting of the Southern Rights associations early in May to announce to the world their intention to relieve South Carolina, "with or without the co-operation of the other Southern states," from "the wrongs and aggressions" which the Northern states and the Federal government had inflicted. That was a blunder. Reaction set in at once. Opposition strength grew rapidly. Perry's *Southern Patriot,* ably backed by James L. Orr and Thompson, rallied the west while William C. Preston, Judge John B. O'Neall, Poinsett, Senator Andrew P. Butler, and their friends carried on the fight along the coast. By the end of May, Lieber was writing: "Our secession is dead, at least fast dying." When, a little later, the news of Mississippi action reached the state, Perry bluntly told the disunionists to "hang up their fiddles." It would be a long time before they would ever hear their "favorite tune played successfully in the United States." [66]

He was right. The co-operationists elected their candidates to the "never-to-be-held" Montgomery convention in six of the seven Congressional districts. The state convention, elected as a secession body, found, when it met in May, 1852, its task to be one of healing the breach between state groups, not one of leaving the Union. It resolved that South Carolina had ample reasons for "dissolving at once all political connection with her co-states" but that she refrained from doing so only "from considerations of expediency."

South Carolina too had yielded. "The fact stares us in the face," said the *Black River Watchman,* "that we have submitted to wrongs which we solemnly—and wisely—resolved a free people could never submit to, without a loss of honor and of self respect. . . . We have

[65] South Carolina *House Journal,* 1850, pp. 279–80; South Carolina *Senate Journal,* 1850, p. 202.

[66] Sumter *Black River Watchman,* August 2, 1851; James Petigru to Lieber, February 11, 1851; Lieber to Daniel Webster, February 13, 1851; Lieber to Hilliard, May 31, 1851, in Lieber Papers; Kibler, *Benjamin F. Perry,* 262–77.

submitted, ingloriously submitted! . . . *The age of Chivalry is gone!* We live in an age of speculators, of calculating traders and narrow reasoners, who would never venture one blow for honor or independence, if that effort brought hazard or danger." [67]

The movement for Southern rights had collapsed. A crisis that at one time seemed about to wreck the Union had been passed. Through compromise the democratic process had been preserved. But it was a compromise dealing with concrete cases, not with principles or values. The conditions that had produced the crisis, and the interests and ideals that lay back of contending groups, were still there. Most of them had to do with, or had now been related to, things that men will not compromise. Even some of the terms of the compromises made could not be accepted without damage to consciences. Perhaps it was as a Georgia editor said: "The elements of that controversy are yet alive and they are destined to outlive the government. There is a feud between North and South which may be smothered, but never overcome." [68]

[67] Sumter *Black River Watchman,* November 8, 1851.
[68] Columbus (Ga.) *Sentinel,* quoted in Charleston *Mercury,* January 23, 1851.

CHAPTER VI

THE AFTERMATH

AS ONE looks back on the conflict that had reached its climax in the Compromise of 1850, certain things, important for the future, stand out in alarming fashion. To begin with, the crisis itself had been precipitated by factors quite normal to the development of national life. They were incidental to the growth and expansion of the young nation toward maturity in a given geographic setting and in a peculiar age. That the United States should have rounded out its boundaries and added new territories, even by conquest, was not surprising. Manifest destiny was in the air. A steady forward sweep of population and the organization of territory after territory had been and would be, in the future, a normal part of American life. Nor was the rapid growth of population a temporary thing in areas where the industrial revolution and its handmaids, commerce and general farming, predominated. That was a normal occurrence all over the Western world. Urban-industrial forces were overshadowing the rural-agricultural on all sides. And with the changes had gone the demand for a more consolidated nationalism and a rapid increase of those agencies of communication and business which a greater interdependence of persons and regions required. The age of finance and industrial capitalism was dawning.

The conflict between North and South in 1850 had thus grown out of certain very basic developments which would increase rather than decline in the years ahead. The tendency of the slavery issue to "elbow" all other business aside and become tangled with almost every measure presented was ample evidence of this fact.

Of equally alarming significance was the fact that the American political system under the Constitution was not a fixed, completed thing, but one that was growing and evolving in the tug and press of national growth and the conflict of interests. The rights of states, of minorities, of sections, of interests were not agreed upon by all, but were being determined by executives, judges, the members of Congress, and necessity. Conflict was inherent in the process. Nor did men agree on what was good and what was bad in social-economic institutions. The word "democracy" meant different things to different people and in different regions. The sprawling, crowding young giant of a nation was growing too rapidly for clothing of any sort long to fit.

Calhoun had sensed the drift and what it meant to his section back in the early thirties. A region that was primarily agricultural was destined to be a permanent minority. A people who held slaves were certain to meet criticism and condemnation. He had, therefore, sought to secure a permanent understanding of just what kind of a government we had. Was it a confederated system or was it a consolidated union? He insisted that the fathers had intended the first of these. He had also attempted to establish both the moral and the legal standing of slavery. He called it a positive good. He declared that its status had been fixed by the Constitution and that the Federal government had no right to interfere with it in the states where it existed but owed to it all the protection granted to any other property in the territories. He evolved theories of government for the protection of minorities both as states and as sections and seized every occasion to force the acceptance of his positions and to secure guarantees for his interests.[1]

That constant pressing of issues on the basis of principles was fatal to his cause. It strengthened the position of those who differed, by permitting principles to be met by principles when the political and moral drift of the age was against everything which he advocated. He lost ground, as did his section, at every clash of opinion —an intellectual fact that was in complete accord with the physical facts of growth. Slavery was not to be a part of the modern age. Neither was "state rights." [2]

A third fact, sometimes overlooked because of the clash of principles, was that back of all that had happened lay a struggle for

[1] Crallé (ed.), *Works of John C. Calhoun*, II, 197–262, 465–90, 625–33.
[2] Benton, *Thirty Years' View*, II, 134–43.

power. The strength to shape the policies of a political party and to influence legislation in Congress was necessary both in the protection of rights and for the carrying forward of what men called "progress." Land policies, tariff policies, internal-improvement policies—these and much else were involved in the admission of new states and in the settlement of new territories. "Slavery" and "freedom" had become symbols of two sets of interests and values. Traditional party affiliations were weakening. The old balances in Congress were passing. Even the protection given by the Constitution was being endangered by the uneven growth of population. The "higher law" doctrine was bad enough; numerical strength sufficient to amend that instrument to the advantage or disadvantage of conflicting interests was even worse.

Regardless of what lay back of developments, however, the significant thing about the sectional struggle of the late 1840's was that the Northern position was more and more shaped in the form of opposition to a great moral evil. Slavery was wrong. Its spread should be checked for reasons of both Christianity and democracy. It was an impediment to progress and hence to the fulfillment of the national destiny. The Southern position, on the other hand, was one of defending and securing Constitutional rights. Slavery had to be defended in the abstract as did the theory of state rights, but this was incidental to the right of an equal share in the territories and in national life.

The importance of the Compromise of 1850 was, therefore, the fact that in spite of the growing tendency, first apparent in Calhoun and the abolitionists, to reduce the whole conflict to one of abstract principles, *right* versus *rights,* Clay and his fellow statesmen had been able temporarily to push aside the abstract covering and to get back to the concrete issues involved. As long as the conflict was phrased as one between the right and wrong of slavery and the right of the South to share equally in national life and expansion, there could be little rational discussion and no compromise. As long as it involved the fundamental character of our form of government and the basic structure of society, no yielding was possible. Men fight and give their lives for such things; they do not compromise them. But these same men could argue sanely about California, the Texas border, and even the Fugitive Slave Law. They could make compromises. The democratic process could function. The nation need not be destroyed. Men could yield without feeling that they had made "a permanent or a fatal surrender of their vital interests." The statesman was still an important agent whose rational discussions were to be listened to and whose compromises could be accepted.

Yet in spite of success in getting around difficulties at this time, two things had been made perfectly clear. The first was that the South, as a section, was already a minority and would remain so. Its influence in both of the major parties had weakened; the balance both in the House and in the Senate would henceforth be against it. The section had only theory and abstract principles with which to oppose stubborn facts. It was doomed to fall back on these with increasing regularity.

The second fact, equally clear, was that slavery had reached its limits of expansion. Whether nature had set its boundaries or not made no difference. The people of the North had made up their minds that it should not expand, and they had, and would continue to have, the strength to enforce their will. The words "not one foot farther" and "not one inch farther" had run through the debates and through the Northern press like the repeated call of the whip-poorwill. Constitutional rights, or any other kind of rights, did not matter. Neither states, nor sections, nor any other kind of minority could stand in the way of nationalism and majority rule. A new age had the right to emerge. There was a "higher law" to which men owed allegiance.

Since all of this was so clear and since so many Southern leaders had announced the alternatives as submission or revolt, the question arises immediately as to why the Southern movement collapsed so completely in 1850–1851.

The answer to that question is not a simple one. The excitement and the determination had certainly been real; the threat to national unity had been serious even though few favored secession. The very feeling of relief that swept the country was proof enough. Francis Lieber, who had watched developments closely in South Carolina, warned his Northern friends that they did not "properly estimate the danger" which had been passed through. It was a case where fuel had long been accumulating and where a single match might have started a conflagration. "We have been saved," he cried. "The match, the torch, the powder horn, has been wrested out of the hands of daring fools and maniac demagogues and you owe a *Te Deum Laudamus* as much as we do. I sing it as Carolinian, as American, as man, as historian—I sing it from my soul as a friend of mankind and a Christian. I thank Thee, O Lord!" [3]

The quick acceptance of compromise by the majority, therefore, seems to suggest that most Southern people were thoroughly loyal and had been forced into extreme positions against their wills. On the practical issues, most of them were reasonable and willing to meet others halfway. They did, however, want their equal rights as partners in national life, and if given no choice between yielding their rights and leaving the Union, there were many who were willing to push the issue to the point where a decision might have been necessary.

It was fortunate under such conditions that there was little in the economic situation to produce dissatisfaction. The section was prosperous. Cotton was bringing thirteen cents a pound. There was plenty to live on and debts were not troubling. As one Alabama planter said:

"Disunion will not give us a better price for cotton—will not increase the value of slave property—will not render them more secure—will not diminish taxation—but will be likely under the best imaginable state of affairs, to double taxation, diminish the price of our staple, and reduce the value of negroes and land, fifty per cent. I am willing to die in the last ditch for my just rights, if it becomes necessary, but have no desire to involve my own interests and those of my section in irretrievable ruin, merely for the benefit of those who have nothing to lose but everything to gain by revolution; and who hope to ride the storm to place and power." [4]

Travelers spoke of the indifference of the masses to the crisis and of the satisfaction with present conditions which shut their eyes to future dangers. The masses were certainly not throwing up their caps and shouting for the dissolution of the Union. Furthermore, most of them knew that California had made her own choice of

---

[3] Lieber to Hilliard, October 18, 1851, in Lieber Papers.

[4] Montgomery *Alabama Journal,* July 23, 1850, quoted in Dorman, *Party Politics in Alabama,* 64.

freedom, and that physical conditions were not favorable to slavery in New Mexico. Only a very few persons, and most of these in the Border States, were troubled by the escape of their slaves north-ward.[5]

Such conditions formed a favorable background for compromise, but they did not preclude the possibility of extreme action if the issue had remained in the form of a blunt denial of Southern rights. What really saved the day was, on the one hand, the lingering loyalty of men to their old political parties and confidence in their onetime leaders and, on the other, the sharp cleavage in the ranks of each major party itself. James A. Seddon called it "the cursed Bonds of party."

For a short time the Southern movement had begun to assume a nonpartisan character. Whigs and Democrats alike gave it support. But when Clay and Webster took their stand and lesser leaders such as Stanly, Stephens, and Toombs came to the support of compro-mise, Southern Whigs quickly drew back. So sharp was the reaction that talk of secession was generally abandoned throughout the sec-tion and emphasis shifted largely to Southern rights. The efforts of Foote, Douglas, Benton, Cobb, Bayly, and other Democrats for compromise had a like effect on the more conservative men of their party. Before long the swing was strong enough to make conditional acceptance of the Compromise according to the Georgia Platform rather good Democratic doctrine. In a few places extremists held out, and fusion groups were formed to oppose them. But even in such cases a break with the national party organization was seldom advocated.

Strangely enough, the Whigs who had supported the Compro-mise and the Union with the greatest loyalty were to suffer most from the recent strife. Victory in 1848 with Taylor had not proved a party blessing. His open reliance on Seward, who was frankly hostile to slavery, and his break with Clay and Webster over the Compromise measures had played havoc with party unity. Whigs might, with some justice, claim major credit for the Compromise and for checking the disunion drive at the South, yet they were now little more than scattered local factions. Loyalty to a central body was largely gone. Yet they were still Whigs.

[5] Craven, *Coming of the Civil War*, 269–71.

The breaks in Democratic ranks, on the other hand, remained surprisingly local in character and seldom affected national loyalties. Southern factions fought among themselves and some deserted, yet their bitterness was more against each other than toward the party as such. It would be a long time before all wounds would heal, but few would prove fatal.

These facts, however, do not alter the general conclusion that the democratic process was saved in 1850 largely because of the strength of national political party ties and response to party leadership. Politics had taken the emphasis off of principles. The contest in many states had remained a Whig versus Democratic affair. In many instances, the nearly equal strength of parties and the memories of earlier struggles tended to stress party loyalty and to check the drift to extremes. Even where fusion parties had appeared, they were usually thought of as temporary affairs. Both parties tried to profit by appeal to traditional loyalties and hatreds. Both made some concessions for the sake of unity. Both, however, came out of the struggle somewhat battered and confused. Much reconstructing would have to be done. Much forgiving would be in order. The success or failure in restoring the two-party system would have much to do with the success or failure of the democratic process in the years ahead. The party developments of the next decade would, therefore, be of paramount importance. The course of political developments would hold the fate of the Union.

The struggle over the Compromise left the South divided and uncertain. Party lines in many places had been broken; personal strife had been common. Issues had not been settled in a way to produce universal confidence. Everything depended on whether agreements, admittedly unpopular, would be lived up to by a section that few Southerners trusted. Only one thing was certain. Most men were weary of strife. They wanted things to work out well, and the wishful thinking was enough to go on for the present.

The result was a rather sharp conservative reaction in most of the Southern states. How much they wanted peace was quickly revealed by their rather mild reactions to Northern condemnation of the Fugitive Slave Law. When one remembers the repeated and positive assertions that *"the continued existence of the United*

States, as one nation, depends upon the full and faithful execution of the Fugitive Slave Bill," and then notes that open defiance and the use of force to resist the return of fugitives in Boston and elsewhere brought only further words and talk of boycotting or taxing Northern goods, it becomes apparent that the storm had blown itself out. Most men in the South were ready to give the Union a further trial.[6]

In Virginia there was talk both of taxing and of boycotting Northern goods, and the Southern Rights associations, organized in the beginning to resist Northern aggressions, soon became centers of agitation for Southern economic independence. There was much talk of encouraging manufacturers, securing direct steamship connections with Europe, and buying only from Southern merchants. As excitement over the Compromise died down and the political parties began re-forming their lines, the question of the legal right of a state to secede was raised as a kind of face-saving device. The Democrats generally upheld such an abstract right as a basis on which its divided forces might be reunited. The Whigs, as a rule, denied such a right. The Richmond *Enquirer* offered Virginia's ratification ordinance and her resolutions of 1798–1799 as support for such a doctrine, and John Caskie, the Democratic candidate for Congress in the Richmond district, bluntly declared his belief in the "great constitutional doctrine of the right of a state to secede, in case of a fundamental violation of the articles of the federal compact." The Richmond *Whig,* on the other hand, denied that such a legal right existed. "No government," it contended, "is ever so suicidal as to provide for its own demolition." John M. Botts, the Whig candidate who opposed Caskie, declared "peaceful secession" to be "one of the most ridiculous, abstract humbugs ever talked about upon earth." [7]

Both parties, nevertheless, accepted the Compromise, and interest for the time being shifted to the problem of reforming the state

[6] Richmond *Enquirer,* November 12, 1850; *Southern Literary Messenger,* XVI (1850), 697.

[7] *Proceedings and Addresses of the Central Southern Rights Association to the Citizens of Virginia, adopted January 10, 1851* (Richmond, 1851); Arthur C. Cole, "The South and the Right of Secession in the Early Fifties," in *Mississippi Valley Historical Review,* I (1914–1915), 376–99; Richmond *Enquirer,* November 19, 26, 1850; Richmond *Whig,* November 22, 29, 1850.

constitution. The retirement of Thomas Ritchie, who had kept the Democrats safe for the Compromise, and the rivalry which soon developed between the Hunter state-rights group and young Henry Wise weakened the party but did not prevent it from uniting for the national election of 1852. Their success, however, was as much due to the failure of the Whigs to achieve unity as to their own strength, and to the all too apparent fact that the Whigs, as a national party, were doomed. Furthermore, Virginia was entering a new era of prosperity. New forces were turning her more and more into a border state. The Compromise struggle had forced many to realize that fact.

The North Carolina situation was much the same. In spite of the fact that there were still some objections to the Compromise, the majority found it satisfactory if honestly enforced. On the question of secession, however, there was sharp disagreement. No sooner had the legislature met than resolutions were introduced to the effect that "although we love the Union of the States . . . we nevertheless regard the right to secede from it as a right . . . which the people of North Carolina have never surrendered." These resolutions were toned down under Whig pressure and ultimately rejected, but the Democratic press, now and then supported by a Whig editor, continued to defend the doctrine throughout the following year. To uphold the right of secession was "the best means of preserving the Union and the only means of preventing a Civil War," said the Wilmington *Commercial*. Since no state could have been forced into the Union, no state could be prevented from going out of it, argued the *North Carolina Standard*. Its editor was certain that if the Fugitive Slave Law was repealed "millions of Southern men . . . [would] go about dissolving this Union as in the performance of a sacred duty." [8]

A few Southern Rights associations were formed and most of them supported the right of secession, but enthusiasm was never high. North Carolinians, like the Virginians, were eager for peace and quiet. The advantage was everywhere with those who wanted the agitation ended. Charging that insistence on the right to secede

---

[8] Sitterson, *Secession Movement in North Carolina*, 74–75; Raleigh *North Carolina Standard*, May 3, June 18, 21, August 6, May 3, 1851; Wilmington *Commercial*, December 4, 1850.

was only preparation for action, Whig leaders seized the initiative, called the whole idea a "great political humbug," and, in one case at least, declared that "the Federal Government has the power to coerce a sovereign State, or half a dozen Southern States." Edward Stanly, who had been the most active unionist in the North Carolina delegation in Congress, "not only denied the right of secession but even pledged his support to the national government in keeping an unruly state in the Union." With the feeling growing on all sides that the Compromise should be accepted as a final settlement, the Democrats could only deny that they were "agitators and disunionists." There was a difference between insisting on secession as a right and urging disunion. Some even went as far as to proclaim themselves the best of Union men because they upheld the only principles by which it could be preserved. Others merely admitted that the cause for secession, at this time, was not sufficient. They were thus able to hold their party together for the election of 1852. The fact that the vast majority of Democrats in the free states were believed to be sound on the Fugitive Slave Law made their task a bit easier than that of the Whigs. It was perfectly clear, however, that the existence of a large nonslaveholding element in the state had prevented any wide acceptance of the extreme Southern position and had left the state's future course about as uncertain as that of Virginia.[9]

The Georgia situation was more complicated. The break there had been sharper and had resulted in a new political alignment that some thought would be permanent. Compromise Whigs and Democrats had launched the Union party and had forced their opponents, largely under Democratic leadership, to become a Southern Rights party. As such, they had come out of the convention which produced the Georgia Platform, and as such they entered the campaign for the election of a governor and legislature in 1851.

Because the Union party contained both Whigs and Democrats, its spokesmen had not, as a rule, taken extreme ground. The Whig element generally denied the Constitutional right of secession but accepted it as a revolutionary right under oppression. The Augusta *Chronicle and Sentinel* scoffed at the idea that "any dissenting

---

[9] Sitterson, *Secession Movement in North Carolina*, 85–86; Cole, "South and the Right of Secession in the Early Fifties," *loc. cit.*, 393.

125

State" had the "exclusive right to judge without responsibility to the other States." Such claims, it asserted, were "as unfounded and absurd" as the old Federal doctrine. Anarchy would be the result.[10]

The Democratic element, on the other hand, upheld the abstract "sovereign right." "No political party at the South," said the Augusta *Constitutionalist,* "has yet dared to proclaim as a tenet of its creed that a State has not the right to secede." Cobb, as the party's candidate for governor, was forced to straddle the issue by admitting the right but insisting that action under it depended on the justice of the cause and "the power and ability to maintain the decision." As to South Carolina, however, all agreed that her course was "madness,—utter lunacy." So by insisting that "it would be a criminal blunder" to suppose that the danger which had threatened the peace and quiet of the country "had been entirely overcome and destroyed," the Union party was still able to maintain its solidarity for one more local campaign.[11]

Many Democrats, in the meantime, had seen the mistake of extreme positions and now began to deny that their group had ever favored secession. Some editors dropped the name "Southern-rights" and reassumed that of "Democratic." The Augusta *Daily Constitutionalist* made it clear that it had never considered "secession the only alternative to submission," but it did insist that most of the Union meetings in the North had been inspired by the radical Southern threat. Too much "submission, tame submission" now would only cause "a wild shout of triumph and fiendish rejoicing" to go up from the abolition hosts of the North. Perhaps, after all, "the disunionists per se" were the only class in the South which was taking "a long-sighted view" of things. At any rate, since almost everyone now accepted the Compromise and supported the Georgia Platform, the struggle was over and men had best return to their regular party folds.[12]

With an invitation to all former Democrats to co-operate, the party asserted the Constitutional right of a state to secede and nominated Charles J. McDonald for the governorship. The campaign

[10] Augusta *Chronicle and Sentinel,* August 26, 1851.
[11] Milledgeville (Ga.) *Southern Recorder,* August 19, 1851; Augusta *Chronicle and Sentinel,* September 20, 1851; Shryock, *Georgia and the Union in 1850,* pp. 343–62.
[12] Augusta *Daily Constitutionalist,* October 19, November 27, 1850.

which followed was a bitter one, but Cobb carried all but twenty-one of the ninety-five counties in the state and had a popular majority of 18,000 votes. The Union party had again demonstrated its strength. Its leaders, however, were anything but complacent. A national election was drawing near. What effect would this have on its divergent elements? Where would a purely local party fit into the national picture? The Democrats, in spite of a sound defeat at home, were meanwhile moving rapidly towards co-operation with their national party. As Stephens noted in late November: "Two months ago *no party* at the North with them was sound enough to be *trusted*. Now they are ready to go into a party caucus with the *National Democracy* without any inquiry into the past or any assurance for the future. We shall have more trouble from them in getting a purgation of the North than from any other quarter." "An effort is making to unite the Democracy of the South with *Hale,* and *Giddings,* and *Seward,* and Allen, and such other choice spirits who . . . proclaim that the Democratic and Freesoil parties of the North are one," wailed the Augusta *Chronicle and Sentinel.*[13]

The Union leaders could only denounce such folly and contradict the growing impression that the Northern Democrats were sound on the Compromise and on slavery. They were all too conscious of the fact that regardless of Northern Democratic attitudes, the Northern Whigs were far worse. The antislavery element was in control. Webster and his kind had been repudiated. There was but one safe thing to do. The Georgia Union party must be expanded into a new national party.[14]

For a short time local editors urged the move and party leaders felt out attitudes in Washington. Frantically they strove to hold back the Democrats. "We speak [to Southern Democrats], not to the demagogues and leaders who are seeking to associate you once more with the national Democracy, who have shown themselves

[13] Stephens to Cobb, November 26, 1851, in Phillips (ed.), *Correspondence of Toombs, Stephens, and Cobb,* 265; Augusta *Chronicle and Sentinel,* December 4, 1851.

[14] Toombs to Absalom H. Chappell and others, February 15, 1851, in Phillips (ed.), *Correspondence of Toombs, Stephens, and Cobb,* 227–29. "We believe that the people of Georgia signified their acquiescence in the late compromise measures *mainly because they relied upon the National Democracy to carry them honestly and faithfully out.*" John E. Ward and Henry R. Jackson to Cobb, February 28, 1852, *ibid.,* 286.

ready and willing to sacrifile [sic] the South and her institutions," pleaded the Augusta *Chronicle and Sentinel.* "Are you willing to form any such alliance? Had you not rather as patriots and good citizens, shake off all old party associations, and rally around the Stars and Stripes of this glorious Union, with your conservative brethren of the North, East, West and South, whether Whigs or Democrats—no matter what their previous politics—to save and perpetuate the institutions of our fathers?" It was the duty of such men to stand "shoulder to shoulder," to "sink or swim, survive or perish in a common effort to preserve the Union and the Constitution." [15]

The effort, however, was in vain. Before long some were convinced that a new party based on "a single idea" was "impractical for the present." It was better for Union men to "blend themselves with one or the other party, control it, and help select sound, able, patriotic candidates." Co-operation within the Union party gradually weakened, and an open break developed when the Union Democrats insisted on sending a delegation to the national party convention at Baltimore. The Southern Rights Democrats had, in the meantime, selected their own delegates, and the convention wisely admitted both groups. In this way the party was again united behind its nominee, Franklin Pierce. The Union Whigs were thereby hopelessly stranded. Some reluctantly drifted back into the party fold and supported Winfield Scott, but others, more resolute, rejected the party nominee and cast their votes, in 1852, for Daniel Webster, who by election day was in his grave.[16]

The Georgia conservatives, in spite of a sound majority, had lost the leadership. Cobb, Stephens, and Toombs, only recently so powerful in national councils and in state affairs, found themselves fighting for survival. Georgia's place in the South and in the nation

---

[15] Augusta *Chronicle and Sentinel,* December 4, 1851; January 24, 1852.

[16] See William Hope Hull to Cobb, February 14, 1852, in Phillips (ed.), *Correspondence of Toombs, Stephens, and Cobb,* 280–82: "The question will then arise, 'Where are we to go?' I am now satisfied from the course things are taking that a Union party . . . is out of the question. We cannot become Whigs—that is absurd —then we must be Democrats. If the Whigs would go with us and be Democrats it would be all well. We would keep up our Union organization and could govern the policy of Georgia and act in full fellowship with the National Democracy. But I suppose the Whigs will break off."

had been seriously altered. Only the undeserving Democratic party had profited.[17]

The triumph of the Union party had been as decisive in Alabama as in Georgia. It had not only elected the governor and a majority of the legislators; it had also carried five of the seven Congressional districts. The open threat of secession had definitely weakened the opposition. "In comparison with the American Union," said the Pickens *Republican,* "the institution of slavery is not worth a goat." "When Mr. Yancey, and others, hoisted the banner of Secession," complained the *Alabama Beacon,* "we foresaw . . . that the *Cause of the South* would thereby be injured in the State. And the ultra doctrines . . . have tended not only to paralyze the efforts of the friends of the South who occupied conservative ground, but to cause many of the Union men to take stronger grounds in favor of the Union, than they otherwise would have done." The Mobile *Daily Advertiser* told its readers that if the right of secession was conceded, the "national government would be but a rope of sand." Only the right of revolution existed. There could be no peaceful withdrawal from the Union, because the President had to "see the laws executed" even by the force of arms. Secessionists who had called upon the South to unite had only succeeded in producing the sharpest of divisions.[18]

The radicals, however, were not dismayed. "Why should we not secede?" asked the Montgomery *Atlas.* "If the Union has failed to answer the purpose for which it was created—if it has been so perverted as to operate as a curse instead of a blessing upon the Southern section—if it only serves to aggrandize the North at the expense of the South— . . . we ask why . . . the South should not secede." [19]

Under Yancey's urging, Southern Rights associations sprang up in radical counties. Their resolutions let it be known that "if we fail in the Union" to redress the wrongs of the South and to restore

[17] "We have now to contend with our enemies *in* the organization of the democratic party instead of *out* of it," was Cobb's sad comment. Cobb to John B. Lamar, September 18, 1852, *ibid.,* 321.
[18] Pickens (Miss.) *Republican,* quoted in the Eufaula (Ala.) *Spirit of the South,* May 20, 1850; Greensboro *Alabama Beacon,* August 16, 1851; Mobile *Daily Advertiser,* November 1, 1850; July 2, 1851; Montgomery *Advertiser,* October 16, 1851.
[19] Quoted in Charleston *Mercury,* May 16, 1851.

the Constitution to its original objects, "then we boldly avow as our object, the Independence and the equality of the Southern States." "There is no intermediate step between submission, under the guilded garb of 'acquiescence' and secession," said another. "If the North, having power, refuses longer to abide by the contract contained in the Constitution, let us not continue a Union where safety depends on the power to annoy, but like our gallant ancestors . . . let us seek new safe guards." [20]

The mistake in urging secession was so apparent in the crushing defeat at the polls in 1851 that the Southern Rights Democrats quickly dropped opposition to the Compromise and ceased to talk about secession. In November they issued an appeal to reorganize the party and announced that the causes which recently divided its members no longer existed. Both the Union Democrats and the extreme Southern Rights elements held back for a time, but the fact that the Northern Democrats seemed to be sound on the slavery issue, and the necessity for party regularity if national benefits were to be secured, soon brought most of them into line.

The Whigs, on the other hand, had no national force to aid them. Their only hope lay in the continuation of the Union party. They did their best to create distrust of the Democrats with the old secession charge, but after some success in controlling the legislature, they gradually lost ground. In self-defense the Whigs were forced to reorganize. One group made a final effort to revitalize the Union forces by a reorganization under the name of Southern Rights Union party. The response, however, was weak, and by January, 1852, the legislature was completely under the control of the old Democrats and, by November, able to carry the state overwhelmingly for Pierce.[21]

A small group of die-hard Democrats refused to make the journey with the majority and nominated and voted for George M. Troup of Georgia for President and John A. Quitman of Mississippi for Vice-President. The Whigs, making "the last tonic spasmodic

20 Eufaula *Spirit of the South,* October 15, 22, 1850; February 18, April 1, 1851; Mobile *Alabama Tribune,* March 27, 1851; Mobile *Daily Register,* March 21, 1851.
21 Dorman, *Party Politics in Alabama,* 65–73, gives an excellent account of party developments.

efforts of an effete party, whose grave yawned before them," could not agree on support for Winfield Scott, and only hurried the dissolution of their party. Politics in Alabama had also turned a corner. Out of defeat the Democrats, still with a Southern Rights tinge, had emerged as victors.[22]

The Compromise struggle in Mississippi had been particularly bitter. The call for the Nashville convention had originated there, and Whigs and Democrats had, in the beginning, moved along together. Differences, however, had soon developed, and personal and sectional lines, as well as those of party, had become apparent. The *Mississippi Free Trader,* representing the lesser property interests of the state, stanchly upheld the right of secession and was ready to apply it "against the wrongs . . . inflicted on the South." "We honestly believe," it said, "that the struggle for Southern rights and the preservation of slavery must be made now, or forever hereafter let the South hang her head in shame." It charged that nearly every Whig editor and the great mass of the teachers, preachers, and merchants in the state were Yankees or of Yankee origin. How many of the "largest slave-holders" were not "Northern men, Foreigners or dyed in the wool Federalists," it asked. These "interested Yankees who have come among us" were the ones who favored the Compromise and were opposed to the holding of another Southern congress to decide "whether through injustice and wrong" the South had been "driven to the last extreme." [23]

More moderate Democrats, however, denied that they were disunionists. "We abhor the term Disunionist," said the Woodville *Republican.* "Who will dare accuse us of the South of a desire to break our compact solemnly entered into? . . . And, on the other hand, who supposes that we will submit, for peace's sake, to the demands of insatiable passions in others?" "We love the Union," it insisted, "but when an irresponsible Faction has gained the ascendancy, and tramples . . . [the] Constitution under foot, . . . we hold it to be our duty to resist the encroachment and the injuries done; and if to resist, a withdrawal from the power of such a Union be proper and necessary, as we hold it to be, we have the right and

<hr>

22 Montgomery *Advertiser,* February 17, 1852.
23 Natchez *Mississippi Free Trader,* September 25, 28, 1850; April 9, 1851.

if we do our duty must secede." What was wanted was a guarantee against the "intolerable oppressions" which would force such action.[24]

The wide acceptance of the Compromise and the failure of other states to act soon suggested a further retreat. In February, 1851, Jacob Thompson declared that "All hope of resistance to the late measure which passed Congress, to any satisfactory end, is gone." Secession alone was "impracticable." The Woodville *Republican* also capitulated. "For the sake of peace, harmony and Union," it said, "we are willing in common with the mass of the Southern people, to acquiesce in the late adjustment." Quitman was more hopeful, but even he admitted that any unanimity among the Southern states was "not to be expected." He was to learn in the election of delegates to the state convention in September that Mississippi itself could not be counted on. Union candidates were chosen in all but eighteen counties, and together their majority was more than seven thousand votes. When they met in November, following Foote's victory over Davis for governor, they quickly removed all doubts as to the state's position. In a series of resolutions representing the "deliberate judgement" of the people, they expressed their willingness to abide by the Compromise "as a permanent adjustment of this sectional controversy, so long as the same, in all its features, shall be faithfully adhered to and enforced." They then declared it to be their opinion that "the asserted right of secession from the Union on the part of a State or States" is "utterly unsanctioned by the Federal Constitution, which was framed to 'establish' not to destroy the Union of the States." Secession, it added, was nothing but "civil revolution." [25]

Division within the parties themselves had reduced the struggle in Mississippi largely to a local affair and had taken men's minds away from the abstract principles involved. As one editor bitterly remarked: "The great question before us and the whole South is

[24] Woodville (Miss.) *Republican,* September 4, October 22, 1850; Yazoo City (Miss.) *Yazoo Democrat,* April 30, 1851.

[25] Woodville *Republican,* February 4, 1851, quoted in Natchez *Courier,* February 13, 1851; Natchez *Mississippi Free Trader,* March 27, June 25, 1851; Quitman to Preston, March 29, 1851, in Claiborne, *Life and Correspondence of John A. Quitman,* II, 123–27; Davis, *Recollections of Mississippi and Mississippians,* 317–18; *Journal of the Convention of the State of Mississippi, 1851* (Jackson, 1851).

not the Compromise,—the Compromise is a mere drop in the ocean hardly worth mentioning. The true issue for us to settle is whether anti-slavery shall triumph or not." That was unquestionably the case, but with a national election coming up, the politicians saw their problem as one of getting their parties back in order. Here, as elsewhere, the Democrats had the advantage. Men like Albert Gallatin Brown had only to declare "the Southern movement . . . dead" and to resume their places in the national organization. Whigs could only indulge in the vain hope that the Union party might somehow continue to exist.[26]

The reaction in favor of compromise had developed earlier in Louisiana than elsewhere. Its social-economic ties with the nation were of necessity strong. The Mississippi Valley fed her commerce, the tariffs protected her sugar, and the great sprawling city of New Orleans, whose trade reached far into the interior, was ever more cosmopolitan than Southern. Louisiana politics were, as a result, always complex. Planter and merchant, city and country, rich and poor, formed strange combinations in the Whig and Democratic parties, which were often more interested in local control than in any Southern movement. The state's government had long been in the hands of the few, but the Constitutional convention of 1845 had produced a remarkably democratic document. It had abridged the legislature's power, increased local elective offices, checked special charters, and done away with all property tests for voters and public officials. Merchants and large slaveholders had been very unhappy about these changes and were, therefore, much more interested in a new convention and in restoring "government by gentlemen" than in disrupting the nation. The party situation played into their hands. The fact that Senator Soulé opposed the Compromise while his colleague, Senator Downs, approved it, kept the Democrats divided and permitted the Whigs, who favored both the Compromise and a revision of the state constitution, to sweep the election in November and to control the convention of 1852.[27]

The Democrats thus learned their lesson. In spite of the fact that Soulé favored Stephen A. Douglas as the Presidential candidate and

26 Woodville *Republican*, May 13, 1851.

27 Roger W. Shugg, *Origins of Class Struggle in Louisiana . . . 1840–1875* (University, La., 1939), 125–45.

John Slidell was committed to Buchanan, they quickly fell in behind Pierce and William R. King, talked harmony and good will, and spoke of the excellent chance offered for controlling the state in the years ahead. The reward came in November. The Democrats carried the state, whereas the Whigs, who had defeated them at home, went to pieces on the national level.

Whether there had ever been a genuine Southern Rights movement in Arkansas, it is hard to say. True, the report of the House Committee on Federal Relations in December, 1850, spoke of the national feet "placed upon the necks of the prostrate states," asserted the right of the citizens of Arkansas "to expect a distribution" of the territories which would allow them to emigrate there with their slaves, and expressed a willingness to "act with the majority of the slave holding states." These resolutions, however, were overwhelmingly defeated in the house and carried in the senate only after long and acrimonious debate. Even Robert Johnson, on re-entering politics, maintained that he had been and still was "the truest and best friend of the Union." Since the Compromise measures were now the law of the land, he did "not propose disunion as the remedy." "I do not propose secession," he said; "I want the South to expect continued aggression and expecting it, I want her to unite and prepare herself, in a spirit of Union among ourselves to repel and forever to arrest it."

His candidacy, however, disrupted the Democratic party and gave the Whigs opportunity to deny the right of secession, and even to question the need for slavery expansion. Yet the cry of "Union or Disunion," which some tried to raise, had little meaning, and the chief result of the struggle in Arkansas was simply to widen the gap between the Johnson faction of the Democratic party and those who were weary of the "family" rule. The effects would be felt to the outbreak of the Civil War.[28]

In Florida, after the October election, in which the Congressional seat went to a Whig and a majority in the legislature to the Democrats, opinion remained divided. Southern Rights associations appeared in various places with resolutions demanding a strict obedi-

[28] Lewis, "From Nationalism to Disunion," 151–97; Little Rock *Arkansas Democratic Banner*, June 17, 1851; Helena *Southern Shield*, June 28, 1851; Little Rock *Arkansas Whig*, June 5, 1851.

ence to the fugitive-slave act as the price of continued union, and
with assertions of the legality of secession. Yet in March the Democratic legislature refused to re-elect David Yulee to the Senate, pre-
sumably because of his conduct in the Compromise struggle, and
sent the more moderate Stephen R. Mallory in his stead. The national election of 1852 still further revealed the confusion. The
Whig delegation to the national convention vigorously supported
the nomination of Millard Fillmore and the finality of the Compromise. When Scott was nominated, the party was split wide open, and
even Edward Cabell refused his support. The Democrats, meanwhile, had distributed their nominations between factions and,
while voting down a resolution recognizing the finality of the Compromise, entered a sharp protest against further agitation of the
slavery issue. In November they swept the state for Pierce. Florida
was ready to drift with the Southern current.[29]

The Whigs as the dominant party in Tennessee paid a heavy
price for the part they had played in the Compromise struggle.
John Bell's support of President Taylor had not everywhere been
popular, and close association of Whigs with antislavery men, such
as William H. Seward, became increasingly harder to explain. Bell
had tried to smooth matters with an open letter to the people of
Tennessee in which he condemned both Northern attacks on
slavery and "excess party spirit." The effort, however, had not been
particularly successful, and during the early part of 1851 he was
contemplating the formation of a new conservative Union party
which would attract moderates from all parties. The time, however, was not ripe. Men were unwilling to yield old names. Bell was
soon forced to abandon the idea and to bend his efforts towards
healing the breach in the existing organization.

In spite of serious divisions, the Whigs were able in 1851 to
keep control of the executive and legislative branches of the state
government, but the margin was close enough to raise doubts concerning the Presidential election of 1852. Anticipating trouble,
the legislature in February, 1852, adopted resolutions condemning
the abolitionists, expressing deep devotion to the Union, and pro-

[29] Dodd, "Secession Movement in Florida," *loc. cit.*, 3–19; Arthur W. Thompson,
"Political Nativism in Florida, 1848–1860: A Phase of Anti-Secessionism," in *Journal
of Southern History*, XV (1949), 39–42.

135

nouncing the Compromise the final word on the slavery controversy. Members, however, could not agree on Presidential candidates, and Scott's nomination brought quick revolt. A few even
expressed a preference for Pierce over Scott, and some voted for
Webster even after his death. The party, however, carried the state
for Scott, but almost immediately went to pieces. In the state elections of 1854 the Democrats elected Andrew Johnson governor and
secured a majority in the state senate. Well might the Democrats
gleefully announce the demise of "Whiggery" in Tennessee.[30]

South Carolina had been the last of the Southern states to accept the Compromise. The decision to do so had not been made on
the basis of loyalty to the Union but rather because of the refusal
of the majority to act without the co-operation of the other Southern states. As the Sumter *Banner* said:

"It may be taken as a fixed fact that the people of South Carolina
do not now love this Union. So far from it, their dislike, their de-
testation of it is rapidly increasing in its intensity. They have felt
the Union to have been the instrument of inflicting wrongs upon
them which if perpetrated by one independent people upon another would have caused the earth to flow with blood."

The majority, however, had seen the folly of South Carolina setting herself up as a "free and independent nation" and seeking an
alliance with Great Britain. Conservatives had labeled such proposals "unreasonable," "asinine," "wicked." "Single isolated secession," said one, was "the greatest humbug of the age, prolific as it
. . . [was] in humbugs." Yet this same writer favored a Southern
confederacy and spoke of the "general dissatisfaction with the acts
of the Federal Government." He was certain, nevertheless, that "the
ultras" had "overdone the matter" and that a sharp reaction was
bound to occur.[31]

The reaction was, indeed, a drastic one. "The State Rights party
—the Separate State Actionists—was utterly shattered" by the strug-

[30] Joseph H. Parks, *John Bell of Tennessee* (Baton Rouge, 1950), 261–77; Joseph H.
Parks, "John Bell and the Compromise of 1850," in *Journal of Southern History*, IX
(1943), 328–56.

[31] Sumter (S.C.) *Banner*, January 29, 1851; Lieber to Hilliard, May ?, 1851 (Huntington Library); W. S. Pettigrew to James C. Johnston, December 12, 1850, in Pettigrew Papers (University of North Carolina Library); W. W. Boyce to Perry, March
17, 1851, in Perry Papers.

gle. Bitter and disappointed, Robert Barnwell Rhett, their leader, retired from his position as United States Senator. Editors spoke of "the complete apathy" exhibited by the people. Some turned against the other Southern states that had deserted South Carolina. One of them shamed Virginia, "once so prompt to avenge insult and wrong, once so jealous of . . . liberty," now descended "from the heights where the history of the past had enthroned her, and crushed at the feet of power, heedless of many wrongs . . . and . . . blind to the dangers which are dimly visible in the future." The Charleston *Evening News* even wondered whether South Carolina's position could be defined. "What is her policy?" it asked. "Sullen apathy or compromise and spoils? Is she Union? No. Is she disunion? No. Her leaders—who are they?—Let her undefined position, her unaroused apathy, her unformed hopes, her purposeless action answer." Only on one point were all agreed: They wanted to forget the futile, unhappy past. They were weary and numb and confused. "Poised for the leap" into secession, the state had been dragged from the brink by sheer fright. Men were emotionally exhausted. They now sank into political indifference.[32]

When ultimately "mere lassitude began to end," a group of younger men under the leadership of James L. Orr and Benjamin F. Perry began to turn from the old, discredited issues and to seek new ones. They urged South Carolina to give up her old ways and to catch stride with the new forces that were stirring the nation. They would abandon the policy of isolation which had been followed since nullification. Instead of a mere "alliance" with the Democratic party, they would take their place in its national councils. They would play a part in fixing its policies. They would stop protesting, begin co-operating with the Northern as well as the Southern states, and cease to "stand apart" far in advance of their neighbors.[33]

The appeal was strictly national. But there was a local side as well which the reformers had to consider. South Carolina had

[32] Sumter *Black River Watchman*, April 5, 1851; Laura A. White, "The National Democrats in South Carolina, 1852 to 1860," in *South Atlantic Quarterly* (Durham), XXVIII (1929), 370–89; Charleston *Evening News*, August 23, 1854; John N. Williams to Perry, April 1, 1851, in Perry Papers.

[33] Charleston *Weekly News and Gazette*, September 6, 1855; April 24, May 12, 1856; Kibler, *Benjamin F. Perry*, 302–309.

lagged far behind the democratic trends of the day. "The property qualifications for membership in the legislature, the election of presidential electors and of the Governor by the legislature . . . , the basis of representation in the lower house of the legislature— half taxation, half population—worse still, the arbitrary apportionment for the Senate (one member to each of the districts and parishes) which gave permanent control to the low country parishes over the greater white population . . . of the back country, the concentration of power in the . . . legislature with relatively little local self-government, the prestige of wealth and family that made office holding the prescriptive right of a small group of planters—all formed a system more consciously aristocratic than could be found elsewhere in the United States." [34]

As a necessary step to bringing the old regime to an end, a democratic electoral reform had to be combined with the move toward national co-operation. This involved a conflict between the coastal areas and the upcountry, but it also involved a struggle between the old aristocracy and the more numerous yeomanry. In a way also the line ran between the radical group in the late struggle and the more conservative element. That added a quality of bitterness to an already strained atmosphere. Old party ties in South Carolina would suffer even more than in the other Southern states.

The reformers, however, were undismayed. With something of their former zeal they opposed the *Mercury*'s efforts to keep the state out of the Presidential campaign of 1852. In spite of denunciations of their group as a "spoils party," Orr and the co-operationist leaders in Charleston gave Pierce their support, sent Josiah J. Evans to the Senate to take Rhett's place, and in 1853 elected Preston S. Brooks to the House. Meanwhile, in the legislature, they urged the election of presidential electors by the people, agitated for a public school system, and preached the diversification of the state's economic life by the establishment of manufactures and the building of railroads.[35] Orr completely repudiated the traditional

[34] White, "National Democrats in South Carolina, 1852 to 1860," *loc. cit.*, 374.

[35] Schultz, *Nationalism and Sectionalism in South Carolina*, 21–25, 49–51. "By the fall of 1852 the attention of most citizens of the state was directed towards agriculture, the banking system, railroad construction, the public schools, and foreign trade." James L. Orr to the South Carolina Institute, in Charleston *Courier*, April 18, 1855; Cincinnati *Daily Enquirer*, June 1–7, 1856; Chauncey S. Boucher, "South Carolina

Southern attitude toward the "Yankee" and the "shop-keeper" and made it perfectly clear that his fight was for a new South Carolina. Progress was slow, and the opposition, with tradition on its side, strong and increasingly aggressive. By 1856, however, the National Democrats were able to hold a state convention and send delegates to the national convention in Cincinnati. There Orr played a conspicuous part in the effort to nominate Stephen A. Douglas, and the delegates were able to convey an impression of devotion to the Union strong enough to cause Charleston to be named as the meeting place in 1860.

The parishes of the coast took no part in the movement. They viewed it as a revolution—a renunciation of all the past. South Carolina was descending "from her proud eminence" and would henceforth "be swayed by the same mob spirit, the same tyranny of the majority as the Northern democracies."

Men from the upcountry agreed with this. But to them it meant that the "past dream . . . [was] over and that now . . . [South Carolina was] arousing herself like a strong man after sleep." [36]

The one thing which stands out in this brief survey of the years immediately following the Compromise of 1850 is the permanent damage done to the old political parties. Both Democrats and Whigs had been badly divided in every Southern state. Men had not only broken with their old associates; they had fought against them with a bitterness possible only in fraternal strife. The breach had been temporarily healed in most cases, but party loyalty and party harmony would not again, before 1860, be what it had once been. Many men had joined a new party, a party which would have been made permanent if that had been possible. They returned reluctantly to the old folds, expecting to give and to take hard blows. Party solidarity would henceforth be a brittle thing. It would be easy next time to change sides. It would be just as easy to distrust those at your side. [37]

and the South on the Eve of Secession, 1852 to 1860," in Washington University *Studies, Humanistic Series* (St. Louis), VI, No. 2 (1919), [79]–144.

[36] Charleston *Courier*, January 7, 15, 1856; Columbia *South Carolinian*, August 26, 1852; Charleston *Mercury*, December 18, 1852.

[37] John H. Lumpkin to Cobb, February 16, 1851, in Phillips (ed.), *Correspondence*

The national political damage was even more grave. In these troubled years the party was the one remaining tie which held men of different localities and differing interests together for larger national purposes. For the sake of party and the rewards of party victory, men were willing to yield a part of their demands, even a part of their convictions. Most party men were even willing to avoid troublesome issues and to tolerate difference of opinion. They had denounced "abstractions," bargained behind the scenes, and compromised on interests. Now something had happened. Sectional opinions and sectional interests had been allowed to enter and to destroy the confidence of men from different corners of the Union in each other. The matter of "right and rights" had divided North and South as sections, and men had felt a stronger pull than the political party was able to exert. They had acted not as Democrats and Whigs but as Northerners and Southerners. They had lost faith in their fellow party members. Northern and Southern Whigs were unable to present a united front in 1852 and after that date went rapidly to pieces as a national party. Robert Toombs expressed a general Southern opinion when he said: "We can never have peace and security with Seward, Greely and Co. in the ascendant in our national counsels, and we had better purchase them by the destruction of the Whig party than of the Union. If the Whig party is incapable of rising to the same standard of nationality as the motley crew which opposes it under the name of the Democracy, it is entitled to no resurrection. It will have none." [38]

The Democrats had suffered less, due in large measure to the fact that their party traditions were older and stronger. Yet ties had been loosened, and leaders, North and South, had very different ideas as to the future course of the party. Democrats had constituted the backbone of the Southern Rights movement, and they now returned to the national organization with the definite idea of making it serve their ends. They would make certain that it remained *right* on the slavery issue. Southern Whigs, who now joined the party, did so for the same reason. By 1860 opponents would

of Toombs, Stephens, and Cobb, 229–30; Cobb to John B. Lamar, September 18, 1852, *ibid.,* 320–21.

[38] Toombs to Crittenden, December 15, 1852, *ibid.,* 322.

charge that the Democratic party was little more than a tool of the "slave power."

This did not mean, however, that Southern Democrats were united in feelings or purposes. As one Georgian wrote: "Tell Mr. Ritchie that the Democratic party . . . are divided, and that the Union Democrats can never expect to act with the disunionists again." The hatreds engendered in the late struggle would "only end with life." [39]

Northern Democrats also had ideas about the future. The Compromise struggle had greatly strengthened the Free-Soil element in the party and had crowded the old Jacksonian Democrats further aside. Salmon P. Chase, in Ohio, had already warned what he called "the Old Line Democracy" that they must "take decided anti slavery ground" and not "lag behind the people." "Defeat will follow the adoption of the stationary policy as surely as day follows night," he said. "If the Democracy wishes to succeed let them act boldly—declare openly for freedom." [40] The New York Barnburners were equally determined and, for the sake of free soil, were willing to risk party solidarity. Factional bitterness had become stronger than dislike of Whigs. Conditions in Massachusetts were little better, while in the Northwest dislike of the Fugitive Slave Law and bitterness over the failure to secure liberal land and internal-improvement legislation were as common among Democrats as among Whigs. Toombs was right when he asserted that the Democratic party was nothing more than "a motley crew." Increasingly now, reference was made to the "Southern Democrats," to "Northwest Democrats," to "Administration Democrats," and to "Northern Democrats with Southern principles." The party had weathered this storm, but another one might wreck the weakened party of Jefferson and Jackson and with it bring to an end the successful working of the democratic process.

[39] Lumpkin to Cobb, February 16, 1851, *ibid.*, 230; Hull to Cobb, August 16, 1853, *ibid.*, 335.
[40] Salmon P. Chase to E. S. Hamlin, December 21, 1849, in *Diary and Correspondence of Salmon P. Chase,* American Historical Association, *Annual Report,* 1902, II (Washington, 1903), 193.

CHAPTER VII

COMPROMISE ON TRIAL

WHETHER the Compromise of 1850 presaged a new era of peace and harmony for the nation was a matter on which there was considerable difference of opinion. President Pierce expressed the fervent hope that "no sectional or ambitious or fanatical excitement . . . [would] again threaten the durability of our institutions or obscure the light of our prosperity." A Columbus, Georgia, editor, however, insisted that "There is a feud between North and South which may be smothered, but never overcome. They are at issue upon principles as dear and lasting as life itself. Reason as we may, or humbug as we choose, there is no denying the fact that the institutions of the South are the cause of this sectional controversy, and never until these institutions are destroyed, or there is an end to the opposition of the North to their existence, can there be any lasting and genuine settlement between the parties. We may purchase, as we have done in this instance, a temporary exemption from wrong by a course of compromise and concession; but we had as soon think of extirpating a malady by attacking its symptoms as to hope for a final adjustment of our difficulties. The evil is, Northern interference with the Southern institutions, an interference that is legalized by and grows out of our political connection with our enemies. . . . Does any man of common intelligence at the South entertain the remotest idea that our brethren will ever become more tolerant of our institutions? Will they ever cease their war upon them? . . . Let no Southern man be deceived: a momentary quiet has hushed the voice of agitation; but there is no peace. There can be none as long as slaveholders and abolitionists live under a common government." [1]

Henry L. Benning was equally pessimistic. He was certain that nothing the South could do, "short of general emancipation, would satisfy the North." After the defeat of 1852 he expected the scattering Northern Whigs to join the Free-Soil groups and form a strictly sectional party. The Democrats, he thought, would make one more successful effort in 1856—"a grand Union Rally"—and then go to pieces as had the Whigs. [2]

Others were more hopeful. Cobb regarded the late Compromise measures as a recognition of "those great constitutional principles" for which the South had always contended, and he expected it to be "a final disposition of past issues." Perry agreed, and rejoiced that South Carolina's energies were "no longer wasted on a fruitless wrangle over Federal politics." In January, 1851, a group of Congressmen signed a pledge not to support for office any man "who is not known to be opposed to the disturbance of the settlement, and to the renewal, in any form, of agitation upon the subject of slavery." Thirty-four of these were from the slave states. Stephen A. Douglas, one of the signers, announced that he had "determined never to make another speech on the slavery question." "Let us cease agitating," he added, "stop the debate, and drop the subject. If we do this, the Compromise will be recognized as a final settlement." Even William H. Seward took the position that the Compromise measures "were the law of the land; that whatever in them was irrepealable no one would be mad enough 'to attempt to repeal.' " [3]

The optimists, however, had overlooked two things: They did not understand all that had happened to the Democratic party in the recent struggle, and they completely ignored the disturbed consciences of Northern men. As to the first of these, it must be remem-

---

[1] Columbus *Sentinel,* quoted in Charleston *Mercury,* January 23, 1851; also quoted in Phillips, *Life of Robert Toombs,* 101–102.

[2] Benning to Cobb, September 2, 1852, in Phillips (ed.), *Correspondence of Toombs, Stephens, and Cobb,* 319.

[3] *Union Celebration in Macon, Georgia, on the Anniversary of Washington's Birthday, February 22, 1851* (Macon, 1851), 4–7; Kibler, *Benjamin F. Perry,* 280; James Ford Rhodes, *History of the United States, 1850–1896* (New York, 1893–1919), I, 207.

bered that the Southern Rights Democrats were the ones who had kept control of the party organization in all of the Southern states and who had led the movement for co-operation with the national party in 1852. The Union Democrats, who had opposed secession and favored the Compromise, were the bolters and the ones who had now, more or less reluctantly, drifted back to the fold. As John Forsyth, Jr., boasted, "the Southern rightists controlled . . . every state Democratic organization from Virginia to Louisiana." In the North, moreover, party control was still largely in the hands of the old Polk machine, many of whose members had done little to forward the Compromise measures. This meant that the national Democratic party owed little to the Compromise or to the men who had carried it through. Party spokesmen must of necessity pay lip service to it, but the spoils of office would have to favor its opponents. Yet, in spite of this, the party could ill afford to ignore Douglas and his loyal followers, who had rendered yeoman service in passing the Compromise measures, or to reject a goodly group of Jacksonian Democrats who had followed Van Buren in revolt in 1848, but who now came back when young John Van Buren failed to show competent leadership. Thus not only in the South but in the North as well, the party was far more seriously shattered than the victory of 1852 indicated. The party had no vital program nor outstanding leader to whom all factions gave support. An element in revolt or ready to revolt existed in nearly every state, and the demand for local and regional favors was outrunning the party's ability to satisfy. Men had been talking harmony and the finality of conflict when everything pointed in the opposite direction. Whig weakness, not Democratic unity, had given victory in 1852, and the very work of ruling might prove enough to destroy the few remaining shreds of party unity.[4]

President Pierce, a definitely weak person to begin with, was thus caught in an impossible situation. His party had triumphed on a platform which pledged the administration to "abide by, and adhere to, a faithful execution of the acts known as the 'compromise'

[4] Hopkins Holsey, "The political elements at the South are now in a perfect state of chaos," quoted in Montgomery, *Cracker Parties*, 64. See also *ibid.*, 91, and Helen I. Greene, "Politics in Georgia, 1853–54: The Ordeal of Howell Cobb, in *Georgia Historical Quarterly* (Savannah), XXX (1946), 185–211.

measures," yet his obligations were largely to those who had done little to pass them. The dilemma was revealed at once when he came to the appointment of cabinet members. Howell Cobb, who had led the fight in Georgia and whose example had helped to turn the tide in other Southern states, was ignored; Douglas, to whom the Compromise measures owed so much, was passed by; Francis Preston Blair's plea for his son Montgomery went unheeded; and the New York Barnburner faction was represented only by William L. Marcy, who until recently had been allied with the Hunkers.

In their stead were men who had either opposed the Compromise or had little to do with it—Jefferson Davis, James Guthrie, Caleb Cushing, James Campbell, James C. Dobbin, and Robert McClelland. As one ardent Democrat wrote: "The President seems to have determined to avow and act upon the principles of the Compromise Union men, and distribute the patronage among the fire-eaters and free-soilers." Blair, "cut to the very soul" because there was not "a single chief of the old Jackson party" recognized, bluntly told Pierce that he had filled his cabinet with enemies who would either rule or ruin him. Southerners were less outspoken, but few Compromise men could understand why Davis or Dobbin should have been selected. This blunt ignoring of Union Democrats, one of them wrote, would, before the "close of this administration prove a fatal mistake." [5]

That the Democrats were headed for trouble was soon apparent. In January, 1854, an observer noted: "Over everything there seems to hang a cloud which, whether it portends coming storm or whether it is soon to give way to 'bright skies' I am not the seer to foretell, and if I hope for the best I almost fear the worst. You have seen by the votes in Congress that the Democratic party has thus far kept together in refusing to join in an attempt to break up the Administration. . . . They have come on here determined to give the Adm. an honest support so long as it is true to democratic measures—but in so doing they do not consider themselves obli-

[5] George W. Jones to Cobb, May 19, 1853, in Phillips (ed.), Correspondence of Toombs, Stephens, and Cobb, 327; Francis P. Blair to Martin Van Buren, February 24, 1853, in Martin Van Buren Papers (Division of Manuscripts, Library of Congress); Robert P. Brooks, "Howell Cobb and the Crisis of 1850," in Mississippi Valley Historical Review, IV (1917–1918), 279–98.

gated to endorse the blunders of the Administration or the ethics of the Washington Union. They have no more love for John Van Buren, his adherents, and their heresies than they had when these gentlemen were plotting treason openly against the party and the interests of the Union. . . . There is not that healthy state of feeling here that I wish there was—there is not that eagerness to defend the Administration policy which is so necessary to Administration success." [6]

The second factor which raised doubts as to the degree of "finality" achieved by the Compromise had to do with Northern reactions to the new Fugitive Slave Law. Southerners had said specifically that their continued loyalty depended on its enforcement. It was the one measure in the Compromise on which there was to be no yielding. It had to be *final*.

From the antislavery point of view, however, it was the one measure whose acceptance was impossible. "When rulers have inverted their function and enacted wickedness into a law which treads down the inalienable rights of man to such a degree as this," said Theodore Parker, "then I know no ruler but God, no law but natural Justice." He would tear this "hateful statute of kidnappers to shivers [and] trample it underneath . . . [his] feet" in the name of all law and in the name of God. He scoffed at the idea that the people would keep such a law. "Come, come," he wrote at another time, "we know better. Men of New England know better than this. We know that we ought not to keep a wicked law, and that it must not be kept when the law of God forbids." If he were a fugitive slave, he declared, he would kill the man who attempted his capture "with as little compunction as . . . [he] would drive a mosquito from . . . [his] face." [7]

Samuel J. May voiced similar convictions, and even Robert Rantoul, Jr., who had been elected to fill Webster's unexpired term, placed man's "God-given liberty . . . above the Union, and above the Constitution, and above the works of men." Ralph Waldo Emerson's reactions were equally intense. He called it a "filthy law" which he would not obey and which he advised his neighbors to

6 Colin M. Ingersoll to Cobb, January 20, 1854, in Phillips (ed.), *Correspondence of Toombs, Stephens, and Cobb*, 339–40.

7 Henry S. Commager, *Theodore Parker* (Boston, 1936), 207.

"break on the earliest occasion," "a law which no man can obey or abet . . . without loss of self-respect and forfeiture of the name of a gentleman." [8]

It was, however, on Christian grounds that most men based their objections. The editor of the *Trumpet and Universalist Magazine* of Boston, after surveying reactions in the religious press, reported that "the new law,—the fugitive slave law, unlike any other we have before had, has created a new sore . . . it has roused a spirit in New England, which has scarcely been paralleled since the times of 1770 and 1775. . . . The Clergy of all denominations, in the North, are using their influence to show the people the odiousness of the law . . . ; they are making the blood of the people boil with indignation in regard to this matter. Men who have never interfered with the subject of slavery, are aroused on this subject."

An antislavery meeting in Dedham, Massachusetts, resolved that every man found arguing in defense of a law "so undeniably anti-Christian" or "counselling obedience to it" should be "marked and treated as a moral leper, branded as a traitor, and pronounced unfit to occupy any station of trust, emolument, or honor in the gift of the people." The Board of Managers of the Massachusetts Anti-Slavery Society called on the "Followers of Christ, the Redeemer" to prove "the sincerity of . . . [their] religious profession" by refusing to obey "an immoral and irreligious statute, whether it be constitutional or otherwise. . . . This law is to be denounced, resisted, disobeyed at all hazards. Its enforcement on Massachusetts soil must be rendered impossible. . . . Bear in mind that laws which are contrary to public opinion are dead, though living on the statute books." "This is the question," said the Worcester *Spy*, "Shall man, legislating under the inspiration of the devil, be obeyed, or shall the pure, the holy, the omnipotent God? . . . Congress has made the law. . . . We claim the right to disobey it; a right guaranteed to us by a higher law than the Constitution." The Reverend Charles Beecher of Newark, New Jersey, brought the argument to a climax by insisting that "The men that refuse

---

[8] James E. Cabot, *A Memoir of Ralph Waldo Emerson* (Boston, 1887), II, 578; Samuel J. May, *Some Recollections of Our Antislavery Conflict* (Boston, 1869), 361–62; *Memoirs, Speeches and Writings of Robert Rantoul, Jr.* (Boston, 1854), 743.

obedience to such laws are the only defenders of law." *"Disobey This Law,"* he cried, and "if you have ever dreamed of obeying it, repent before God, and ask his forgiveness." [9]

Reactions among antislavery men in the Northwest were positive if not quite so extreme. The Quincy (Illinois) *Whig* was surprised "that the great men of this country should suffer themselves to be so far deceived as to think this troublesome question finally settled by the passage of the Compromise measures through Congress." Instead of peace, it continued, the fugitive-slave bill would "create an excitement ten fold greater than any this country has ever before witnessed." "It is a violation of our most cherished sentiments and feelings," it said, "an outrage to humanity." All the great names in Washington could not make such a bill "palatable to over one-fourth of the population of these United States." A meeting at Ottawa, Illinois, resolved "that no legislative enactment can make it wrong to aid in the escape of fugitive slaves from bondage," while a Detroit meeting expressed its "disapprobation" of a law which broke down the safeguards "thrown around private rights." [10]

A Ravenna, Ohio, assembly went much further. It resolved that any man accepting an office which involved enforcement of the act would prove himself to "be a man utterly heartless and devoid of humanity." How could men expect to escape the vengeance of Heaven, it asked, if they did not "trample the law in the dust and indignantly frown upon its execution." A group in the neighboring city of Columbus announced that anyone aiding in the enforcement of the law, "whether as a magistrate, officer or citizen . . . is an enemy of the human race, a criminal of the deepest dye, fit only for treason, stratagem and spoils, and to be branded with Benedict Arnold and Judas Iscariot." Chicago's common council

[9] Worcester *Spy*, September 25, 1850; Boston *Liberator*, October 4, 1850; May 2, 1851; *Trumpet and Universalist Magazine* (Boston), XXIII, No. 19 (October, 1850), 74; Joshua R. Giddings to George W. Julian, February 21, 1852, in Giddings-Julian Papers (Division of Manuscripts, Library of Congress); *The Duty of Disobedience to Wicked Laws: A Sermon on the Fugitive Slave Law by Charles Beecher, Newark, N.J.* (Newark, 1851).

[10] Quincy (Ill.) *Whig*, October 29, 1850; Chicago *Watchman of the Prairies*, February 5, June 11, 1850; Detroit *Tribune*, October 15, 1850; Sandusky (Ohio) *Daily Sanduskian*, February 26, 1850. The writer is indebted to Professor Helen Cavanagh for calling his attention to some of these references.

made its contribution by declaring that the act violated the Constitution and the laws of God; that its authors were traitors; that Chicago's citizens and officers of the law should refuse aid in its enforcement.[11]

Opposition, moreover, did not end with words. In Lancaster, Pennsylvania, a master was killed and his son badly wounded in an attempt to recover two fugitives. In another Pennsylvania case, the master recovered his slaves only after a two-month delay, during which time he and a companion were thrown into jail for causing a riot. His costs were $1,450. In Detroit a runaway Negro was reclaimed only after a military force had been called to disperse a mob, and in Chicago an equally threatening crowd waited impatiently until a Federal commissioner discharged a Negro being held as a fugitive.[12]

But it was in Boston and upper New York that resistance reached its most dramatic heights. Late in October, 1850, a Boston Vigilance Committee under the leadership of Samuel Gridley Howe and Theodore Parker completely foiled the attempts of one Hughes, jailer of Macon, Georgia, to recover the fugitives William and Ellen Craft. On charges of defamation of character, Hughes was arrested, his carriage windows broken by a mob, and he so badly frightened by Parker's threats that he fled the city while the Crafts, armed with a veritable arsenal, hurried off to England.

A few months later the same group engineered the escape of the slave Shadrach, who was about to be returned to the South. This was accomplished by a mob which seized the prisoner and carried him off in their midst with wild cheering. In upper New York, meanwhile, a mob, urged on by Gerrit Smith and the Reverend Samuel J. May, seized a fugitive from the custody of a United States deputy marshal who had brought him before the commissioners of a Federal circuit court, and hurried him across the Canadian border to freedom.[13]

The interesting thing about these deeds was the air of righteous-

[11] Boston *Liberator*, April 11, 1851; New York *Tribune*, October 23, 1850; Chicago *Western Citizen*, December 30, 1850.

[12] Augusta *Chronicle and Sentinel*, September 23, 1851; New York *Tribune*, June 14, September 17, October 4, 1851; Rhodes, *History of the United States*, I, 208–209.

[13] Commager, *Theodore Parker*, 214–20; Ralph V. Harlow, *Gerrit Smith, Philanthropist and Reformer* (New York, 1939), 289–98.

ness with which they were performed. Of the Shadrach rescue Parker said: "The noblest deed done in Boston since the destruction of the tea in 1773." Judge Benjamin Curtis, who had attempted to enforce the law, was denounced as a public enemy, and the deputy marshal who had made the upper New York arrest was himself arrested and tried for kidnapping. What had begun as a defensive movement against unwise legislation was rapidly developing into an aggressive moral crusade which would bring men as unfitted for practical politics as Charles Sumner into the Senate of the United States.

To the emotional strength of this movement a new force was now added. On June 5, 1851, there appeared in the *National Era,* a rather obscure religious magazine, the first installment of a "story" by "Mrs. H. B. Stowe." It was entitled *Uncle Tom's Cabin; or, Life Among the Lowly.* Week after week, with only an occasional interruption, the chapters appeared. What had been planned as a series of short sketches to be completed in three months grew into a lengthy novel and ran for nearly a year. What had long been standard items were quickly crowded aside, and the deep emotional response of readers told author and editor that Uncle Tom was destined to reach a wider audience. Before the story was more than a third written, a contract to publish in book form had been signed.

The first printing of five thousand copies, which appeared in March, 1852, lasted but two days. Orders piled up. New editions were crowded from the press. In three weeks twenty thousand copies had been sold. By the end of the year the figures had passed three hundred thousand, and eight power presses were running night and day to keep up with the demand. An English edition met with equal success, and translations were soon spreading the work of this quiet little college professor's wife to the far corners of the Western world.[14]

The explanation of this remarkable literary achievement is not difficult. Mrs. Stowe knew little about slavery from personal observation. She even pleaded her ignorance of the Southern plantation in a request for information addressed to Frederick Douglass. But in this day of sectional conflict, a knowledge of facts regarding slavery was not essential. Mrs. Stowe did know what was far more

14 Boston *Liberator,* April 9, 1852.

important. She knew what the abolitionists thought slavery was like, and she knew human nature. She was acquainted at firsthand with poverty and suffering. She understood what it felt like to be domineered over by "superiors." She had been reared in the Beecher family. She had, moreover, grasped the deep religious-moral stirring of an age when, through the rise of the factory system and the new rich, the living of the many was passing into the hands of the few. She did not know the South, but she did know the North and the great new Western world that had already been devouring the works of Charles Dickens. So completely did she understand her public and what it wanted that at times she seemed honestly to believe that God, Himself, had written these pages by means of her hand.[15]

The importance of *Uncle Tom's Cabin* lies in the fact that in Uncle Tom, in Simon Legree, in Topsy, and in Little Eva, Ophelia, and George Harris, the restless, apprehensive, morally confused North had been supplied with concrete stereotypes with which to clarify and simplify its thinking. Too many men had been trying to hold a personal view of slavery as an evil and a legal view which accepted its existence. Too many had viewed it from afar and felt little of responsibility. Too many still dealt in abstractions and distorted it one way or the other. A growing number disliked the whole business, the abolitionist as well as the institution itself. The late Compromise struggle had disturbed men, but it had not greatly sharpened their convictions. There was too much confusion about. Old simple relationships in most lines were being upset. The gulf between capital and labor, between town and country, between rich and poor, was everywhere widening. Situations needed to be dramatized before new thought patterns could emerge.

Here in this rather simple novel was the tragedy of the broken family, the injustice of exploitation, the denial of freedom, the helplessness of frail humanity under the poundings of fate, the nearly perfect Christian loving his enemies and doing good to those who persecuted. Here was deep human appeal, slavery made concrete and personal, moral values vindicated, and enough of sentimental romanticism added to reach the most obtuse mind. Slavery

[15] Harriet Beecher Stowe to "My Lord," January 20, 1853, Harper Collection (Huntington Library).

was no longer something far off and impersonal. It was no longer an abstraction about which decent men could be indifferent. Uncle Tom brought it close and made it a matter about which one could get excited.

These developments did not at first widely disturb the Southern people. The reaction against extremes in the Compromise struggle had been too great. They were tired of agitation. There was too much friction at home. They did not, therefore, show much enthusiasm over the Southern appointments to the cabinet or great resentment because of Southerners neglected. The politicians, on their part, were too intent on restoring some sort of order and harmony within their ranks to bother much about national situations. The great mass of the people seemed indifferent. Northern resistance to the fugitive-slave act should, in the light of earlier pronouncements, have reopened the whole sectional struggle. Obedience to that act had been the one absolute requirement which Southern men had set as the price of peace. As the *Carolina Watchman* had said: "The Fugitive Slave law must be executed, or we are ready to sever every tie that binds this Union." The only result, however, was a few violent editorials in newspapers which brought little or no response from their readers.[16]

The Mobile *Daily Register* stated that Boston's action had produced "an intense excitement throughout the South," called it "the most highhanded outrage ever perpetrated in the Union," worse than the "Whiskey Insurrection," "Shays' Rebellion," or South Carolina's "Nullification," but ended simply by calling "upon the people of Boston, if there are any patriots and lovers of the Union among them," to see that the law was, in the future, "carried into effect." It called on the President to use the army and navy if necessary, but said nothing about breaking up the Union.[17]

The Augusta *Chronicle and Sentinel* reported the affair in Chester County, Pennsylvania, in which a slaveowner was killed by a mob in his attempt to recover a runaway slave, but only suggested that it was a case where "the terrors of the law should be displayed and its majesty vindicated." The Jacksonville (Alabama)

[16] Salisbury *Carolina Watchman,* November 14, 1850.
[17] Mobile *Daily Register,* November 14, 1850.

Republican told of how the slaves of a widow, passing through New York, had been seized and set free. It denounced such action as "robbery" and closed its report with the comment that such deeds would lead to retaliation and a loss of respect for law. The Burns case brought from the New Orleans *Daily Crescent* some bitter words against such papers as the New York *Tribune* and the Washington *Era,* accused them of working to destroy "all harmony, confidence, and good feeling between the North and South," and then ended its editorial by asking how many more such scenes would "be required to raise up a civil war between North and South,—a calamity more to be dreaded than a combination of all the nations of the earth against our existence." The Richmond *Whig* greeted news of the Shadrach rescue with a warning that the violation of Southern rights "will not be suffered to pass or submitted to with impunity," but did not suggest steps to be taken. Its neighbor, the *Enquirer,* supplied this deficiency by recommending the seizure of Boston ships and the levying of a license fee on goods manufactured in any state refusing to suppress abolition societies. There both let the matter rest.[18]

The reaction of these papers, selected at random, was typical of others, and reveals the absence of any deep desire to reopen the sectional strife or to carry out any of the threats made at the time of the acceptance of the Compromise. Most certainly there was no inclination to make good the assertion that *"the continued existence of the United States as one nation depends upon the full and faithful execution of the Fugitive Slave Bill."*

How widely *Uncle Tom's Cabin* circulated in the South is difficult to say. Francis Lieber wrote from Columbia, South Carolina, that *"Uncle Tom's Cabin* sells here rapidly. One book-dealer told me that he cannot supply the demand with sufficient rapidity." The remark of the Milledgeville *Southern Recorder* to the effect that it was tired of "referring to this book and its pernicious influence," and of the Augusta *Chronicle and Sentinel* that "the Southern press, with few exceptions, have rendered Mrs. Stowe a most acceptable

18 Augusta *Chronicle and Sentinel,* September 23, 1852; March 30, 1853; Milledgeville (Ga.) *Southern Recorder,* December 16, 1856; New Orleans *Crescent,* January 5, 1854; Natchez *Mississippi Free Trader,* September 14, 1854; Richmond *Whig,* October 18, 1850; March 4, 1851; Richmond *Enquirer,* February 1, 1850.

service, by their united and zealous efforts to kick her work into consequence and notoriety," would indicate that a goodly number of Georgians had become acquainted with its contents. Even the Macon *Telegraph*'s statement that it refused to "dignify such a thing as 'Uncle Tom's Cabin' with a review" would seem to point in the same direction.[19]

In most cases, however, editors were too incensed by what they had read to hold their pens. They turned on Mrs. Stowe and her book with fury and with little restraint. The New Orleans *Crescent* called her "part quack and part cut-throat," coming as a physician with arsenic in one hand and a pistol in the other, to treat diseases she had "never witnessed." "Without having ever in her life beheld even a mouse," she had suddenly become "a great rat-catcher," modestly insisting "upon burning down our houses in order to rid us of a rat." This paper declared that: "There never before was anything so detestable or so monstrous among women as this. Men, often barbarous and bloody, have sometimes been known to preach like this, but never until now did a female so far forget all the sweet and social instincts of her sex, as to do what Mrs. Stowe has done—endeavor to whet the knife of domestic murder and shake over the innocent head of every matron, maid and babe in the South, the blazing torch of midnight conflagration, the brutal and merciless instruments of death, that are struck to the heart or dash out the brains of the sleeping or the helpless, in the bursting-out of a slave insurrection!" [20]

Parson Brownlow out in Knoxville, Tennessee, was equally violent. Mrs. Stowe was "a coarse, ugly, long-tongued woman," whose "filthy, lying book" had in fact been written by "a hypocritical brother and husband." A bit taken back by his own extreme words, the good parson explained that when a "female so far loses all self-respect as to lend herself to Northern Abolitionists, as a dirty instrument to prowl about through the negro kitchens of the South and hunt up slang with which to satisfy their morbid appetites for slander, she forfeits all claim to respect and the common courtesies

[19] Lieber to Hilliard, February 3, 1853, in Lieber Papers; Milledgeville *Southern Recorder*, December 16, 1856; Augusta *Chronicle and Sentinel*, March 30, 1853; Jacksonville (Ala.) *Republican*, June 15, 1852; Macon *Georgia Telegraph*, March 25, 1853.

[20] New Orleans *Crescent*, January 5, 1854.

of life." With this out of the way, he proceeded to proclaim Mrs. Stowe to be "destitute of all moral sense," reveling in misery, gloating over crime, enjoying slander, "as the Devil does the hypocrisy of these New England saints." Her book was a concoction of "absurdities, falsehoods and inconsistencies," the filthiest volume "ever to emanate from the American press." [21]

The Mobile *Advertiser* accused the author of plagiarism and a morbid copying of Charles Dickens. The *Mississippi Free Trader* saw her book as an expression of that "more crafty, false and base" abolition propaganda which "glides forth in the pleasant paths of literature, and in the garb of meticulous fiction breathes with profound hypocrisy its venomous slanders on the social organization of one half of the American Union." [22] With more of dignity and learning but with no greater approval, the South's one serious literary journal, the *Southern Literary Messenger,* accepted the responsibility for dealing with the work both as a literary effort and as fiction turned to the service of social reform. The task was assigned to George Frederick Holmes. His instructions were as follows: "I would have the review as hot as hellfire, blasting and searing the reputation of the vile wretch in petticoats who could write such a volume." [23]

Holmes too had to make it clear that he violated no Southern codes in dealing harshly with Mrs. Stowe. She might not be "a fishwoman," but she had "placed herself outside the pale of kindly treatment" by intermeddling "with things which concern[ed] her not—to libel and vilify a people . . . , to foment heartburnings and unappeasable hatred between brethren of a common country." But even at that, the reviewer refused to avail himself "of the full benefit of her forfeiture" and concentrated his efforts on her book.

This he found to be "a fiction throughout; a fiction in form; a fiction in its facts; a fiction in its representations and coloring; a fiction in its statements; a fiction in its sentiments, a fiction in its morals, a fiction in its religion; a fiction in its inferences; a fiction equally with regard to the subjects it is designed to expound, and

[21] Knoxville *Whig and Independent Journal,* February 12, November 19, 1853.

[22] Mobile *Advertiser,* quoted in Augusta *Chronicle and Sentinel,* January 9, 1853; Natchez *Mississippi Free Trader,* September 12, 1854.

[23] John R. Thompson to George F. Holmes, August 24, 1852, in George F. Holmes Papers (Manuscript Division, Duke University Library, Durham).

with respect to the manner of their exposition. It is a fiction, not for the sake of more effectually communicating truth; but for the purpose of more effectually disseminating a slander. . . . Fiction is its form and falsehood is its end."

It was, in fact, as this reviewer saw it, "a maze of misinterpretation" sprinkled with bits of truth "prostituted to base uses, and made to minister to the general falsehood." It was useless to attempt to refute a work which reinforced preconceived and malicious prejudices and pictured things, not as they were, but as readers wished them to be. The genius of the work, if it had any, sprang "from intense fanaticism and an earnest purpose"; its central argument gained its strength from the fact that unthinking persons were willing to believe that "any social institution, which can by possibility result in such instances of individual misery, or generate such examples of individual cruelty as are exhibited in this fiction, must be criminal in itself, a violation of all the laws of Nature and of God, and ought to be universally condemned, and consequently immediately abolished."

There was only one way in which to meet such an attack. That was to point out the "graver miseries, worse afflictions, and more horrible crimes familiar to the denizens of our Northern Cities, and incident to the condition of those societies where the much lauded white labor prevails." In this way men could be made to see that to condemn a whole system because of abuses due to "the frailties of humanity, the play of fortuitous circumstances, the native wickedness of particular individuals, and the inability of human wisdom or legislation to repress crime without incidentally ministering to occasional vices," is not only unsound but a danger to all social institutions. When this is recognized, then the vastly superior character of slavery as a labor system can be seen. Its paternal nature will be shown to be vastly superior to the harsh, grasping, unresponsible free system which only breeds millionaires and paupers.[24]

And so *Uncle Tom's Cabin* was dismissed "with the conviction and declaration that every holier purpose of our nature is misguided, every charitable sympathy betrayed, every loftier senti-

[24] George F. Holmes, "Uncle Tom's Cabin," in *Southern Literary Messenger,* XVIII (1852), 721–31. See also *ibid.,* 630–38.

ment polluted, every moral purpose wrenched to wrong, and every patriotic feeling outraged, by its criminal prostitution of the high functions of the imagination to the pernicious intrigues of sectional animosity, and to the petty calumnies of wilful slander."

Lesser lights attempted to answer Mrs. Stowe's book in kind. At least fifteen novels, bearing such titles as *Uncle Robin in His Cabin in Virginia and Tom Without One in Boston, The Lofty and The Lowly*, and *The Master's House*, were published in the years 1852 to 1854. All sought to give a rosy picture of slavery, to show how biased Northerners had been won to its support by seeing it as it was, to reveal the Negro happy under thralldom, or to depict the miseries of the poor in other societies. Not a one of them had any literary merit or made any appeal to universal feelings. They only showed the literary poverty of their section and the powerful impression which Uncle Tom had made, even in the South. The moral charge had, indeed, sunk deep. No converts had been made, but prejudices had been sharpened and the misunderstanding between North and South widened. Uncle Tom had helped the South to state its case a little more clearly to itself. He had added to the self-righteousness of both sides—a dangerous matter under the circumstances.[25]

Northern behavior, irritating as it was, did not, however, heal the breach between Southern factions, nor did it isolate the South from the larger currents of national development. Even while the Compromise struggle was at its height, strong democratic impulses were astir in Southern states, and demands for reforms were to be heard on all sides. Liberals, in backward areas, were insisting on Constitutional changes which would give a more equitable distribution of political power; progressive leaders in nearly every state

[25] [Edwin J. Pringle], *Slavery in the Southern States. By a Carolinian* (2d ed., Cambridge, Mass., 1852), a pamphlet of 53 pages "published at the request of a friend . . . in Boston . . . as an answer to the question, What do you think of 'Uncle Tom's Cabin' at the South"; review of *The Lofty and the Lowly*, in Columbia *Daily South Carolinian*, February 5, 1853; review of *The White Slave of England*, in Augusta *Chronicle and Sentinel*, March 10, 1853; notice of *Uncle Tom's Cabin as it is*, in Jacksonville *Republican*, June 15, 1852. Jeannette Reid Tandy, "Pro-Slavery Propaganda in American Fiction of the Fifties," in *South Atlantic Quarterly*, XXI (1922), 41–50, 170–78, gives a list of ten volumes written in answer to *Uncle Tom's Cabin*. The author has in his possession several volumes which she does not list.

were asking for improvement in agricultural methods, for the revival of Southern commerce, and for the building of factories and railroads. A few would improve Southern schools, check intemperance, put an end to dueling, and lighten conditions for prisoners and the insane. Southern men were to be found in the ranks of the Young Americans, and pride in national greatness was still a Southern right.

Most of the states in the newer South had, in the preceding decades, made their governments, local and state, thoroughly democratic in form if not always in practice. In Alabama, Mississippi, Tennessee, Arkansas, and Texas, "the governor was popularly elected, there was universal manhood suffrage, legislative apportionment in both houses was based on white population, with provisions for periodic reapportionments, and county government was democratic." Georgia, Florida, and Louisiana were not far behind. Only by the counting of slaves as well as whites in apportioning seats in the legislature did they fall behind the leaders.[26]

The demand for democratic reform was, therefore, confined largely to the older Atlantic states. Virginians were particularly disturbed. The constitution of 1830 had left a disproportionate amount of power with the eastern part of the state—a condition that had grown more and more unsatisfactory as the west increased in population and wealth. The legislature had at various times discussed the matter of reapportionment, but disagreement over the suffrage basis had prevented action. Agitation, however, continued, forcing in 1850 the calling of a new constitutional convention.[27]

Here reformers, mostly but not entirely from the west, demanded an equalization of representation, white manhood suffrage, and the popular election of the governor and judges. They wanted biennial sessions of the legislature, an end to the governor's council, and the establishment of a public school system. Eastern conservatives fell back on the old arguments that both persons and property should be represented, and that some freehold or other

[26] Charles S. Sydnor, *The Development of Southern Sectionalism, 1819–1848*, in Wendell H. Stephenson and E. Merton Coulter (eds.), *A History of the South*, V (Baton Rouge, 1948), 283–86.
[27] Fletcher M. Green, *Constitutional Development in the South Atlantic States, 1776–1860* (Chapel Hill, 1930), 254–96; Ambler, *Sectionalism in Virginia*, 251–60.

property or taxation qualification for suffrage was necessary. The rule of mere numbers, they insisted, would result in excessive taxation for railroads and might even endanger the institution of slavery.

After seven months of effort, from January to August, 1851, a new constitution was literally pieced together out of sharply differing interests and opinions. On the whole, it represented a victory for the west and the reformers. "Suffrage was extended. The freehold, tax paying and lease holding qualifications were abolished leaving white male citizenship, age, and residence the only requirements." Cities of over five thousand population were divided into voting wards, and the "legislature was completely reorganized" so that its members would be allotted with some regard to county population. Provision was also made for a complete reapportionment "to take place in 1865 and every ten years thereafter," but the basis of representation was left for future decision. The governorship and most other important offices, including the judiciary, were now to be filled by popular election. The governor's council was abolished along with life tenure for judges and property qualification for officeholding. Taxation was equalized, and some provision was made for funds to be used for primary and free schools. Virginia had, indeed, moved well forward along the democratic road. She had carried out what one of her citizens called "one of the proudest triumphs of popular government which the records of history attest." [28]

North Carolinians also were demanding democratic reforms. The state's constitution required a freehold of fifty acres to vote for members of the senate and permitted the appointment of judges for life by the legislature. The existing system of representation also gave minority control as a result of which forty-four counties, with a majority of 167,067 white people and paying some $1,891 more in taxes, had four fewer senators than the remaining thirty-six counties.

Efforts to remedy these inequalities, which had become tangled with western demands for railroad building, had begun as early as

[28] Fletcher M. Green, "Democracy in the Old South," in *Journal of Southern History*, XII (1946), 3–23; Ambler, *Sectionalism in Virginia*, 261–72; Green, *Constitutional Development in the South Atlantic States*, 287–96.

1840, but it was not until the Democrats took up the freehold requirement in 1848 that the reform effort actually began. Twice bills to give "every freeman" who paid his taxes the right "to vote for members of both branches of the General Assembly" passed the house and the senate but lacked the three-fifths majority necessary to carry an amendment. Three times the Democrats made suffrage their chief issue in the gubernatorial campaign and under Governor David S. Reid, in 1854, succeeded in securing the necessary majority for passage and publication to the people. Opposition now ceased, and in August, 1857, the amendment was ratified by a popular vote of more than three to one.

The moves to limit judicial tenure and to reapportion representation, however, were not successful. With the failure of the latter went western hopes for internal improvements, and this, with stubborn eastern resistance to the taxing of slaves, left the Old North State still acutely conscious of sectional division.[29]

The winds of reform weakened as they blew on southward. In South Carolina, as has been said, the question of domestic reform had become a part of the larger question of the state's relations to the Federal government. A radical group, despairing of leading the state or the South into secession, now advocated a policy of non-participation in the national affairs and, of course, ardently defended the *status quo* in local matters. South Carolina, in the balance of interests and sections and classes which her peculiar system produced, had, they insisted, achieved something quite superior to the rule of majorities. It still drew the best talent in the state into public life and gave this comparatively small spot on the map a disproportionate influence in national affairs. The argument, therefore, that internal conflict over local issues would weaken the state's position in the South and in the nation, held back Orr's moves for popular elections and the equalization of representation. The only constitutional change made in the state during the 1850's was one by which senators were made elective by classes every two years and by which elections were limited to one day only.[30]

The democratic impulse, however, had not been without effect. It

[29] Green, *Constitutional Development in the South Atlantic States*, 265–72.
[30] *Ibid.*, 261–64; White, "National Democrats in South Carolina, 1852 to 1860," *loc. cit.*, 370–78; Schultz, *Nationalism and Sectionalism in South Carolina*, 12–25.

had strengthened Orr's appeal for a new outlook in South Carolina and given him a firmer hold on the western part of the state. Conservatives had been alarmed. Their appeal for moderation in the interest of state harmony had been, to a degree, effective, but it had weakened their position and made South Carolina less inclined toward radical action than she had been for years. Counsels were divided. With the strong hand of Calhoun removed, no arm proved strong enough to bend his bow. Rhett and Hammond could only recommend a negative course. The initiative belonged to Orr and his group.

In Louisiana, in spite of democratic forms, there had been little majority rule. Under the original constitution, which lasted to 1845, the franchise was conferred on all white males who had purchased public land or paid state taxes, and representation was supposedly "equal and uniform" according to the number of registered electors. On the surface, this suggested majority rule. In practice, however, it denied the ballot to two thirds of the adult freemen and permitted the slaveholding planters to dominate the legislature. Early inhabitants complained little of conditions, but the heavy growth of population and the shift of interest strength toward New Orleans in the decades of the 1820's and 1830's brought a sharp demand for reforms. This was met to a surprising degree in the constitutional convention of 1845, in which all property tests for voters and public officials were abolished and seats in the upper house apportioned on the basis of total population (New Orleans being limited to one eighth of the membership) and in the lower house according to the qualified electorate.

These moves were definitely in the direction of democracy. Yet in practice the suffrage reform worked little change because the lesser whites failed to vote. The representation changes, moreover, kept a minority of slaveholders and men of property in complete control of the legislature. A slaveholding minority could check any move that threatened its interests.

Such a situation opened the way for the growing commercial interests of New Orleans, with Whig support, to urge a new convention and new "reforms." In 1852 they had their way and, under the leadership of Judah P. Benjamin, again altered the constitution for the benefit of a minority group.

Limitations on the state's borrowing capacity were wiped out; public subscriptions to internal improvements were authorized; and the General Assembly was empowered to charter specie-paying banks by special or general laws. Then followed the exemption of the dubious Citizens Bank from the safeguards of note registry and specie redemption and the changing of the basis of legislative representation to one of total population, white and Negro. These moves were strictly in the interests of the black parishes and the commercial groups of New Orleans which combined to carry them through. Small wonder that the lesser people believed that the purpose was to secure "banks to steal the money of the people, and . . . railroads to run away with it."

Again, it must be admitted that these moves were hardly democratic. Yet they did stir an aggressive opposition group which gave strength to the Democrats and kept the Louisiana political fight more or less a class conflict. That would make some foreign groups "Lincoln men" in 1860, give Douglas strong support, and produce civil war within the state after secession.[31]

Thus, with the Missouri constitution affording "more efficient guarantees to individual rights" and less opportunity for corruption than any state in the Union, and with Kentucky and Maryland revising their constitutions in 1849 and 1850 to bring the Border States into democratic line, the once-dominant aristocratic planting class had in the main been shorn of its power. The Southern states had become, except in a few minor matters, as democratic as those of the North.[32]

The office seeker now had to solicit the votes of common men as well as those of aristocrats. If the planters were to rule, they must do so with the consent of those who farmed or ran their cattle on open lands. Speeches had to be made, rivals met in debate, wives and children flattered. Many men failed to exercise the franchise even when it was granted, and the larger number of these were unquestionably from the poorer element. Yet the percentage voting

[31] Shugg, *Origins of Class Struggle in Louisiana*, 130–56; James K. Greer, "Louisiana Politics, 1845–1861," in *Louisiana Historical Quarterly* (New Orleans), XII (1929), 381–425, 555–610; XIII (1930), 67–116, 257–303, 444–83, 617–54; Cole, *Whig Party in the South*, 76–78; New Orleans *Bulletin*, August 11, October 6, November 2, 1851.

[32] Green, "Democracy in the Old South," *loc. cit.*, 20.

in the South as compared to population was about the same as that in the New England states.

The rise of men from the lower classes to political prominence in the period is also significant. The best-known cases are those of Joseph E. Brown in Georgia, Andrew Johnson in Tennessee, and Albert Gallatin Brown in Mississippi. These are not, however, isolated cases. A careful study of biographical materials and facts revealed in the manuscript census shows that only some 7.73 per cent of the men who represented Virginia, the Carolinas, Alabama, Mississippi, Louisiana, Georgia, and Tennessee in the House and Senate from 1850 to 1860 were plantation owners or had come from families of plantation owners. Most of them were lawyers, 75 per cent of whom had read law but had not attended law school. Only about one sixth of them had attended college for even a brief period of time, and the great majority of these had gone to their own state universities.[33]

Reform efforts, however, were not confined to politics. The temperance movement found ample reason for existence in the South and equally ample hands to carry it forward. Like the rest of America, and with variations all its own, the South had augmented its joys and weakened its sorrows by a liberal consumption of ardent spirits. The quantity and quality of such support varied with individuals, social groups, and localities, but the universal testimony is that the supply, ranging from imported wines to home-distilled "corn licker," was always more than was reasonably sufficient for the purpose in hand. One writer described the situation in early Alabama as follows: "Public meetings were concluded by scenes of drunkenness and uproar which were revolting. The courts were disturbed by the noise in the streets. Jurors were seen in the box too stupid to perform their duty." Colleges had difficulty with excessive student drinking and more than one prominent public man was notorious for his occasional sprees. The clergy seem to have been considerably less given to excesses than were their fellows to the North, but the situation was, on the whole, one to invite reform in an age much given to reforming.[34]

[33] From study made by Bernard Drell and the author from biographies and manuscript census materials.

[34] J. E. Sanders, *Early Settlers of Alabama* (New Orleans, 1899), 45; Benjamin S.

The great American temperance crusade of the forties and fifties, therefore, knew no sectional lines. Prominent Southern leaders, such as Governor Henry A. Wise of Virginia, Governor Joseph E. Brown of Georgia, Robert Barnwell Rhett, John B. O'Neall, and Robert J. Breckinridge, took up the cause and Southern churches responded with a zeal equal to that fermenting among Northern Protestant sects. Sons of Temperance societies appeared in every corner of the section. Pinning the white ribbon became a major interest in colleges, and in one case, at least, the students petitioned the trustees for ground on which to erect a temperance hall on the campus. Newspapers reported the doings of the Sons of Temperance as a regular part of the news. Local societies were organized into divisional and then into state organizations. Local and traveling speakers appeared at "conventions," and "fairs" and "processions" seem to have been a regular part of society activities.[35]

The *Mississippi Free Trader* described one such fair in Natchez as "one of the most brilliant gatherings this staid old town has witnessed for many a long year, and quite as exciting as the late election [1848] or the California gold fever." P. W. White of Pennsylvania was the speaker at a New Orleans meeting in December, 1849— "a scene imposing and full of interest"—and the anniversary celebration in May following was described as "a grand affair" with much parading, music, and speechmaking. The "Spartan Division" of the Alabama Sons of Temperance went completely Northern: its address was delivered by Miss Frances Cobb. Of the merits of that address, the Jacksonville *Republican* found it difficult to speak "in terms of adequate praise." It was able, however, to declare "the manner of its delivery . . . admirable in every way."[36]

The Sons were equally active in the other Southern states. Tennessee and Kentucky both had strong local and state organizations which not only paraded and sang but which, at times, were able

---

Ewell to William Green, Esq., July 9, 1855 (drinking at William and Mary College), in William Green Papers, Brock Collection (Huntington Library).

[35] E. Merton Coulter, *College Life in the Old South* (New York, 1928), 124–25; Natchez *Mississippi Free Trader*, April 26, 1849.

[36] Natchez *Mississippi Free Trader*, April 25, 1849; New Orleans *Daily Crescent*, December 29, May 23, 1850; Jacksonville *Republican*, May 6, June 27, 1851; Boyd, *Alabama in the Fifties*, 174–77.

to close the local "dram" and "coffee" shops where the "demon rum" held forth. Josiah Flourney, in Georgia, driving from county to county, secured enough signatures to a petition prohibiting the retailing of liquor in the state to produce a bitter struggle in the legislature and ultimately to enable the temperance forces to nominate and run Basil H. Overby for governor in 1855.[37]

The movement was particularly strong in Virginia and North Carolina, where the college students seem to have been unusually active. Quakers and other evangelical groups played an active part in each state but prosperous planters such as General John H. Cocke, who built a temple to the Sons of Temperance on his estate and held office in national temperance societies, were not missing from the ranks.[38]

In Charleston, South Carolina, where Rhett was vice-president of the Young Men's Temperance Society, a temperance hall was dedicated in February, 1850. A local paper spoke of its "chaste design" and its handsome furnishings, and of the "throngs of bright eyes and cheerful faces" which filled the room. Three groups were represented—the Total Abstinence Society, the Order of the Sons of Temperance, and the Rechabites, all "clothed in their respective regalia." [39]

Meanwhile, up in Baltimore, a group of six reformed drunkards were launching their Washingtonian movement, which was to give a new and quite different turn to earlier temperance efforts.

Other reform efforts of the period also found supporters in the South. Dorothea Dix had made an extended tour of the region in 1845–1846. Starting in Kentucky and swinging south to New Orleans and Mobile, she had turned northward to Montgomery and eastward to Augusta and Charleston. She had then returned to New Orleans and made an excursion into Arkansas. At every stop she inspected prisons and hospitals and reported that "Taken as a section, the south showed no great contrast to other sections." In fact, she found "incomparably more to approve than censure" in

---

[37] Memphis *Daily Appeal,* July 14, 1854; Eaton, *History of the Old South,* 496–97; Montgomery, *Cracker Parties,* 135.

[38] Clement Eaton, *Freedom of Thought in the Old South* (Durham, 1940), 323–24.

[39] Charleston *Courier,* February 14, 1850; May 9, 1854; May 29, 1856; Sumter *Black River Watchman,* November 16, 1850.

New Orleans and pronounced the state penitentiary in Georgia "excellently ordered." Hospitals for the insane, on the other hand, were bad. Yet she everywhere found a welcome and the promise of improvements. The next few years bore the fruits of her labors as abundantly here as in the North. In 1848 the legislature of Tennessee appropriated land and money for a hospital large enough to care for 250 patients, and North Carolina authorized taxes for the building of an institution to be known as "Dix Hill." Mississippi, to Miss Dix's surprise, followed in 1850. It was a victory over what had, at first, been "prejudice and a determination not to give a dime." The legislature's appropriation was not only for a hospital "for the mentally ill" but also for the rebuilding and reorganization of the state penitentiary.

Action in Alabama, which seemed possible at this time, was checked by the burning of the state capitol, but plans were not abandoned and her asylum opened on the eve of the Civil War. Texas and South Carolina were also slow to act, but Miss Dix continued her visits even while the slavery controversy neared its climax and, in the end, saw her dreams realized in both states. Since Kentucky and Louisiana had earlier made provision for the separate care of the insane, only Florida and Arkansas were without state asylums in 1861. Only three states, the two Carolinas and Florida, were without state penitentiaries in which some regard was paid to the more humane treatment of prisoners as advocated by Dorothea Dix and her fellow reformers.[40]

Few of the other social reforms that were stirring the North in these years met with wide response in the South. There were a few peace men and a goodly number who were courageous enough to condemn dueling in an individualistic society where the practice still persisted. There were, however, no Brook Farms or Fruitlands or Fourier groups, and woman's rights made no appeal. Both types of effort ran counter to Southern tradition. The early connection of reform leaders with antislavery also played a part, as did the greater

---

[40] Helen E. Marshall, *Dorothea Dix, Forgotten Samaritan* (Chapel Hill, 1937), 111–13. In 1850 there were, in the fourteen Southern states, some 53,794 more illiterate white persons over twenty years of age than in all the rest of the United States; by 1860, there were 61,755 fewer. In 1850 the illiteracy ratio among the native Southern whites was 20.30 per cent.

difficulty of organizing groups and spreading ideas in a rural order. But the sharp reaction against these moves and others that could be designated as "isms" showed that many Southerners were still definitely conscious of national social trends and felt some responsibility for them. Furthermore, the Southern efforts to improve public education were most certainly a part of the larger national effort which Horace Mann and Henry Barnard had launched. They gained strength as the franchise widened and as men from the lower social ranks gained political prominence. But they were slow to become a part of the sectional drive to give the South a social system different from that at the North.

Illiteracy had long been excessively high in the South. The wealthy elements had employed private teachers, established the largest number of academies in the nation, and done fairly well with their own colleges or sent their sons to Northern institutions. Common schools, where they existed, had retained something of the charity idea, and the lower classes had resented them and taken a kind of pride in their lack of "book larnin'." Even where the opportunity existed, they often refused or neglected to send their children to school.[41]

By 1850, however, progressive Southern leaders were thoroughly awakened to the need for free public schools in their section. The next ten years would see a marked improvement. Henry A. Wise's statement that "There should be no distinction between the children of a republic," and Governor Joseph E. Brown's exhortation to "Let the children of the richest and poorest parents in the State, meet in the schoolroom on the terms of perfect equality of right," expressed the democratic spirit behind the move. The support of men as prominent as Yancey in Alabama, Brown in Mississippi, Christopher G. Memminger in South Carolina, and Andrew Johnson in Tennessee showed how firmly the movement had taken hold.

There was, however, much to be done, and the start had to be

[41] Edgar W. Knight, *Public Education in the South* (Boston, 1922), 209–60; Johnson, *Ante-Bellum North Carolina*, 277–82; William F. Perry, "The Genesis of Public Education in Alabama," in *Transactions of the Alabama Historical Society, 1897–1898* (Tuscaloosa), II (1898), 16 ff.; Stephen B. Weeks, "Calvin Henderson Wiley and the Organization of the Common Schools of North Carolina," United States Commissioner of Education, *Report . . . for the year 1896–97* (Washington, 1898), II, 1379–1474.

made from low levels. Progress was bound to be slow. It was, in many states, a case where agitation for improvement constituted most of the gains. That was largely true in Virginia, where under the prodding of an Educational Convention, the legislature increased the educational funds but ignored Governor Wise's recommendation for sound reform. It was equally true in South Carolina, where Henry Sumner made an excellent report on conditions and the remedies required, and two governors attempted without success to secure action. In Georgia it was much the same. There, public meetings advocated the appointment of a state superintendent, adequate funds for schools, and the training of teachers, and Governor Joseph E. Brown urged the legislature to enact such a program. The only result, however, was the appropriation of some $100,000 from the earnings of a state-owned railroad with no plans for its use. Mississippi, meanwhile, paid even less attention to her governor's appeals for education, and a confusion of systems marked her schools to 1860.[42]

The younger states of Texas and Florida did slightly better with plans on paper but made only an inadequate beginning with real school systems before the Civil War. Tallahassee, in Florida, however, did the unusual by laying a town levy and setting up a superior local system. Arkansas also made plans but provided no funds for their realization. The frontier here was too close to permit anything but schools as good or as bad as local conditions dictated.[43]

Progress in the other Southern states was more substantial. North Carolina, with beginnings already soundly made, now rounded out "the best system of public instruction" in the section. In 1853 the legislature created the office of state superintendent and appointed Calvin H. Wiley as its first occupant. For thirteen years he remained in office and "labored for a complete reorganization and improvement" of the schools of the state. He founded the *North Carolina Journal of Education* (1856) and in co-operation with

[42] Knight, *Public Education in the South,* 209–28; Cornelius J. Heatwole, *A History of Education in Virginia* (New York, 1916), 100–22; E. Merton Coulter, *A Short History of Georgia* (Chapel Hill, 1933), 270–71.

[43] Frederick Eby, *The Development of Education in Texas* (New York, 1925), 110–47; Knight, *Public Education in the South.*

Braxton Craven helped to promote a normal college for teacher training. He organized a teachers' convention and spread information widely through writing, lecturing, and personal contacts. Even a civil war could not completely destroy his work.[44]

William Flake Perry did almost as well in Alabama. In 1854 the legislature set up a new educational program. It voted enlarged funds, created the post of state superintendent, provided for teacher examinations, and gave authority to the counties to levy a property tax for schools. Perry, as the first state superintendent, developed a new course of study, began the classification of pupils, and provided better textbooks. In 1856 he established the Alabama Educational Society and the next year, the *Alabama Educational Journal.* Soon school enrollment compared favorably with that of Northwestern states, and a six-month school term was generally accepted.[45]

Tennessee owed its public school system largely to the efforts of Governor Andrew Johnson, under whose administration a general capitation and a property tax were levied for education in 1854. Funds were thus doubled and standards lifted. The state lacked central supervision, but teacher examinations were inaugurated and better schools made possible.[46]

In Kentucky the work of Robert J. Breckinridge as state superintendent was responsible for a two-cent tax on all property for school purposes and a thorough rebuilding of the school system. During his six years in office, which began in 1847, school enrollment increased from 20,000 to over 201,000, and standards were raised to a level comparable to that in schools across the Ohio. With a driving energy he made the most out of his office in spite of political difficulties. The same cannot be said for Louisiana officials of the same period. There the legislature of 1847 had laid a property tax of one mill on the dollar and a capitate tax of one dollar each

[44] Edgar W. Knight, "Calvin Henderson Wiley," in Allen Johnson, Dumas Malone, and Harris E. Starr (eds.), *Dictionary of American Biography* (New York, 1928–1944), XX, 213; Archibald Henderson, *North Carolina: The Old North State and the New* (Chicago, 1941), II, 186–88.

[45] Boyd, *Alabama in the Fifties,* 119–37.

[46] Gerald M. Capers, *The Biography of a River Town; Memphis: Its Heroic Age* (Chapel Hill, 1939), 121–22; F. Garvin Davenport, *Cultural Life in Nashville on the Eve of the Civil War* (Chapel Hill, 1941), 52–55.

on every white male over twenty-one years of age. Alexander Dimity was made superintendent of schools with a salary of $3,000, and plans for a first-class system were drawn up on paper. There most of them remained, and soon politics entered to make the office of superintendent appointive and to cut the salary in half. Some progress, nevertheless, was made, and appropriations for schools between 1847 and 1861 ran well over $3,840,000.[47]

The total for the South does not add up to a great figure. But it was a start. It represented the Southern side of a national movement in which Northern patterns, as a rule, were followed with no indication of sectional embarrassment or envy. The census tells a rather surprising story of achievements. Between 1850 and 1860 public school attendance in the Southern states increased by 413,-013—a gain of 43.2 per cent. The number of schools grew by 9,266, and the number of teachers increased by 10,074. These represented gains of more than 50 per cent in each case. The income of such schools rose from $2,673,910 to $5,269,642—a gain of 97.08 per cent.[48]

The gains, however, had not been uniform; nor did they mean that the South, as a whole, had established a respectable public school system. Only a few states had done that. Most of these, it should be noticed, were Border States. Only the larger cities in other parts of the section had done as well.

Yet the tide had turned, and a remarkable group of state superintendents, well abreast of the national reform movement, had done much with comparatively little. Wiley in North Carolina, Breckinridge in Kentucky, and Perry in Alabama deserve rank among the educational leaders of the nation. The movement in which they played a part was national, not sectional.

[47] Thomas H. Harris, *The Story of Public Education in Louisiana* (New Orleans, 1924), 10–15; E. Merton Coulter, "Robert Jefferson Breckinridge," in *Dictionary of American Biography*, III, 10–11.

[48] Virginia had the largest number of public schools in 1850, and Kentucky the most in 1860. Missouri, however, had the largest absolute gain—2,550 schools. The greatest relative gain was in Texas—249 per cent. How little percentages mean, however, is shown by Florida's gain of 40.58 per cent, which represented an actual increase from 69 schools to only 97. Louisiana led the South both in 1850 and 1860 in income of public schools per pupil, with Mississippi second. The actual cash involved, however, was (1860) only $14.75 and $12.45. The figures dropped to $2.56 in North Carolina and to $2.90 in Tennessee.

Agricultural reform and the attempts to diversify Southern economic life were to a degree, at least, a part of national efforts along these lines. The shift to a sectional purpose, however, was soon so marked that major efforts and accomplishments in this period became a part of the move for Southern economic independence. Yet it must be remembered that the Southern commercial conventions, which talked much of direct trade with Europe, began back in the 1830's; that William Gregg's drive for Southern manufactures opened with praise of New England's accomplishments; and that the moves toward a new agriculture were born of poverty and despair, not hatred of the North.

Nor should it be forgotten that the Young Americans, who regarded Stephen A. Douglas "almost as a demigod" and saw greater things ahead for the youthful republic, included such Southern leaders as Beverly Tucker of Virginia, Senator Yulee of Florida, "Lean Jimmy" Jones of Tennessee, Pierre Soulé of Louisiana, and Robert Toombs and Alexander H. Stephens of Georgia.

It must, therefore, be understood that something besides Southern provincialism and self-consciousness characterized this section in the decade before the Civil War. There were likenesses between North and South as well as differences. The wine of young nationalism was too heady and the temptation to boast too great to permit the Southerner to yield his claims to a share in America's glories. Matthew Fontaine Maury and Elisha Mitchell worked as scientists, not as Southerners. Washington Allston and Joel T. Hart were just artists making their contribution to America's slender output. To charge the Southern politician with an unusual degree of sectionalism is to ignore the attitudes and votes of his Northern and Western colleagues. The nation may have been headed toward civil war, but few Southern men in the early 1850's were conscious of that fact, and fewer were ready to take a hand in bringing it on. The honest conviction that the South had grievances against the antislavery North did not mean that men had ceased to prize a Union in which their rights would be secure. They were not, as Governor Reuben Chapman of Alabama said, insensible to the benefits of such a union, nor to the glories of which it was a monument.

CHAPTER VIII

THE CENTER SHIFTS

THE three years following the Compromise of 1850 amply demonstrated the simple truth that a few immediate concrete issues had been "adjusted" by the democratic process but that nothing permanent had been accomplished. The "finality" idea—if it meant the end of sectional difficulties—was mere wishful thinking. That the solid interests of the day, rushing into a glorious new era of "change and progress," wanted peace and quiet cannot be questioned. There was much to be gotten for each American interest, whether sectional or individual, if only impediments could be removed and government could be free to assist. Yet it was equally clear that fundamental issues which had to do with "right" and "rights" had been only by-passed, not settled. And furthermore, these years had shown that the damage done to the agents and machinery of the democratic process was serious if not fatal.

The old notion that peace had been restored to a troubled nation by another great compromise and that the foolish action of an Illinois Senator was to be the cause of all future troubles calls for much explaining if not revising. Clearsighted men everywhere had treated the Compromise as little more than "a temporary repose." The fugitive-slave section was not being obeyed, and Vermont had already passed her personal-liberty law to make the recovery of runaway slaves impossible. She had set a pattern which nine other Northern states would soon follow. On December 20, 1853, Gerrit Smith had broken the flimsy agreement to avoid the slavery issue in Congress and had bluntly asserted that the Southern claim that slavery was "an exclusively State concern," and that the North had nothing to do with it, was eminently false. "The poor North has much to do with slavery," he said. "It staggers under its load, and smarts under its lash." When charged with "making an Abolition speech," he simply answered: *"I am."* [1]

Said Hendrick B. Wright of Pennsylvania: "I am one of those who believed, that after the great contests the country has so recently passed through, when both the great political parties of the nation seemed to have concluded this warfare, and when the great battle was fought and the victory won—I say, I am one of those who believed that abolitionism was dead and buried; . . . I supposed that it was dead and gone; but like the ghost of Banquo, it is again in this Hall, and before the country." [2]

It was, indeed, in both places, as was also a grim Southern determination to secure equal rights, legal if nothing more, in the territories. Archibald Dixon of Kentucky, Atchison of Missouri, and Phillips of Alabama would soon prove that beyond a doubt.

The political situation had, meanwhile, grown steadily worse. The Whigs as a national party had come dangerously near to the end of their road. The antislavery attitude of its Northern wing had alienated Southerners, and the strife between the Seward faction and Fillmore's followers had wrecked it in the North. It had paid the price—near destruction—in the crushing defeat of 1852. Thousands of party-minded Americans were thus left without an adequate political roof over their heads. The great party that had stood for national harmony and against sectional strife had given way before the poundings of the rising tide of selfish interests.

The Democrats were in better shape only because their party traditions were stronger and because they had won an election against a hapless foe. The incompetent Pierce had been chosen for what he was *not,* rather than for what he *was.* His administration was now rapidly degenerating into a hopeless effort to satisfy conflicting elements and to develop something of party solidarity. In nearly every state faction struggled against faction and threatened the formation of new political combinations for local control. In the South, where little forgiving or forgetting had been done, a state of guerrilla warfare continued with truces only when Northern "aggression" required them. Southern Democrats had already set their price for party loyalty at the high figure of complete re-

[1] *Cong. Globe,* 33 Cong., 1 Sess., Appendix, 50–52.
[2] *Cong. Globe,* 33 Cong., 1 Sess., 89.

spect for "Southern rights," which meant the end of slavery agitation and an equal share in the territories. They had made it possible for opponents to apply the term "Doughface" to Northern party men who supported their claims. They had, in fact, made the "security" of the South depend upon the survival of the Democratic party and its dominance in national affairs.

In the North the New York situation had become a national scandal. The struggle begun in Van Buren's days reached new intensity when President Pierce's appointments favored the Barnburners, and Secretary Marcy openly opposed Daniel S. Dickinson, the conservative Hunker leader. Administration interference with Customhouse appointments completed the transformation of a bitter local struggle into an antiadministration fight and brought a complete split in the New York state democratic convention with two tickets in the field. One group talked of cleansing "the party from the effects of a leprous association." The other called its opponents "traitors" and "seceders." [3]

In Massachusetts the Free-Soil element had widely infiltrated Democratic ranks. After Webster took his stand in support of the Compromise, Free-Soil leaders, such as Charles Sumner and Henry Wilson, openly advocated a coalition with the Democrats and, in 1851, received their reward in the election of Sumner to the Senate.

Opposition to these moves had been led by Caleb Cushing. Early he had rejected the doctrine that it was "the duty of the citizens of Massachusetts to give themselves up to the agitation of the question of slavery abolition in the South," and now, on September 29, 1853, as a member of Pierce's cabinet he bitterly denounced the formation of county coalition tickets as "hostile in the highest degree to the determined policy of the Administration." The President's face was "set . . . like flint" against these "backslidings." [4]

Such outside interference in local affairs turned another critical state situation into one in which the national Democratic organization and its wavering local members were at serious odds. The term

[3] Phillip G. Auchampaugh, *History of the State of New York: Politics and Slavery* (n.p., n.d.), No. 3, pp. 72–77; Roy Nichols, *Franklin Pierce* (Philadelphia, 1931), 450–88.

[4] Quoted in Claude M. Fuess, *Life of Caleb Cushing* (New York, 1923), II, 103-107, 139–40.

"Independent Democrats," which now came into wide use, suggested that first steps were being taken toward new political affiliations.

Party conditions in Ohio were equally chaotic. "The slaveholding democrats are at swords points," wrote Chase, "—and the non-slaveholding democrats not much more amicable." The Compromise measures had "brought a sword and not peace." The Democrats were split into "Old Line" and "Independent" factions with a group of "liberals" in between. Yet the "Independents" were largely Free-Soil men, and Chase called them "Free Democrats" almost as often as "Independents." His and their Democracy was simply one of accommodation, and his thoughts often turned toward a new coalition of Whigs and Democrats and Free-Soilers. The conflict of forces reached a climax early in January, 1854, when the state convention broke into bedlam over an effort to endorse the national platform of 1852. Passions flamed so fiercely that the chairman lost complete control. The effort was dropped and substitute resolutions were passed only when open revolt threatened.[5]

Across the line in Indiana John Bright wielded a despotic hand in Democratic affairs. Recalcitrant editors, and even Governor Joseph A. Wright, were bluntly read out of the party. When the legislature chose John Pettit as Senator, Bright refused to recognize him "as a gentleman or as my friend." The strong Free-Soil element in northern counties and a growing temperance force met with equal contempt. Indiana too had a considerable body of Democratic malcontents who might give substance to the Lafayette *Courier*'s prophecy that a new national party "including the Liberty party, the Free Soil party, the abolitionists, and that portion of the Democrats who sustain the nominees but not the finality resolutions" would soon appear. Douglas' friends, meanwhile, warned him that Bright was an enemy "in spite of pretended friendship." [6]

Douglas' troubles, however, were not confined to Bright. The

[5] Chase to Hamlin, February 25, 1852, in *Diary and Correspondence of Salmon P. Chase*, 240.

[6] Roger Van Bolt, "The Rise of the Republican Party in Indiana" (Ph.D. dissertation, University of Chicago, 1950); Lafayette (Ind.) *Courier*, in Anderson *Indiana True Democrat*, October 14, 1852, quoted in Theodore C. Smith, *The Liberty and Free Soil Parties in the Northwest* (New York, 1897), 262; David L. Yulee to Douglas, January 28, 1853, in Stephen A. Douglas Papers (University of Chicago Library).

northern part of Illinois was, in these years, filling rapidly with men from the Northeast and from abroad. Their political traditions were either non-Democratic or yet unformed. Between 1846 and 1850 the percentage of Democratic votes in twenty-three counties in that area sharply declined. This was unquestionably due in large part to the new arrivals, but there were many old Democrats who were unhappy because of the party's failure to pass liberal land and internal-improvement legislation. Now they were more displeased because of Douglas' failure to control patronage under Pierce. As a correspondent wrote Gustav Koerner, "abolitionism, freesoilism, and other foolish issues have been made in this northern region in our party; & which have so obliterated many of the ancient landmarks, of the party, that any political result in districts which were formerly, and are still Democratic, is now at times uncertain."

To this alarming situation was now added another. In the southern part of the state, Sidney Breese, John McClernand, and William H. Bissell were making trouble and threatening revolt. Some of the difficulty was personal; some grew out of differences on fundamental issues. Thus the Illinois Democracy "in the very wake of a victory which doomed the Whigs to oblivion," found itself, as one writer puts it, "woefully divided." [7]

Conditions in the new state of Iowa were similar to those in Illinois. The Democratic party had dominated elections from the beginning, but land and railroad disappointments had weakened its control, and the heavy inflow of new settlers from the North had increased both Whig and Free-Soil strength. This, combined with a sectional struggle between Democrats around Dubuque and those in the southern part of the state, had made elections close, with the balance threatening to fall into Free-Soil hands. Senators Augustus C. Dodge and George W. Jones, in Washington, found it increasingly difficult to defend administration policies to the satisfaction of their constituents. Party regularity was no virtue in a state that

[7] J. McRoberts to Gustav P. Koerner, December 6, 1851, in "Letters to Gustav Koerner, 1837–1863," *Transactions of the Illinois State Historical Society,* 1907 (Springfield, 1908), 242; John Wright, "The Background and Formation of the Republican Party in Illinois" (Ph.D. dissertation, University of Chicago, 1946), 111.

needed as much Federal aid as did Iowa. A strong political wind could blow it in any direction.[8]

The Democratic family fight in Missouri was more ancient and more bitter. There it centered about the person of Thomas Hart Benton. Slaveholder and stanch party man, Benton had, since the days of Jackson, retained a firm hand on his constituents in spite of his opposition to the Mexican War and to disunion moves of all kinds. His independent attitude reached a climax in his refusal to receive instructions from the Missouri legislature on slavery in the territories, and the fight against him, which Calhoun had fostered, broke out with new fury. Under the leadership of Senator David Atchison, disgruntled Democrats with strong proslavery backing turned on Benton and prevented his re-election to the Senate. It was a costly victory, for as Atchison wrote, "The Whigs, profiting by our divisions, have succeeded in electing six members of Congress, and sixty members of the Legislature." He believed, however, it would pay in the long run, for with Benton "killed" his "heretofore friends . . . will now act with the old Democratic party." How little he understood either Benton or the times was soon clear. Benton was anything but dead, and the struggle in Missouri was only entering a more important phase.[9]

Two things stand out in this all too brief survey of Democratic party conditions: In the first place, in order to hold its Southern strength and to take over any considerable body of former Whigs, the national organization would have to accept a strictly conservative, Constitutional view of slavery's rights and interests; the Pierce administration had already shown that many Democrats were quite willing to do exactly that thing. And secondly, the Northern Democrats were already so badly shattered and divided that fusion movements were the rule and not the exception. Bitter fights within local ranks had caused some men to be read out of the party and had made others choose to be defeated by the Whigs rather than to co-operate with their rivals. The party, furthermore, was not meet-

[8] David Sparks, "The Birth of the Republican Party in Iowa" (Ph.D. dissertation, University of Chicago, 1951).

[9] Atchison to Davis, September 24, 1854, in Jefferson Davis Papers (Manuscript Division, Duke University Library).

ing the needs and demands of a changing era. The Northwest was particularly dissatisfied, and it was becoming increasingly difficult for representatives from that section to harmonize the appeals locally necessary with the national party positions. Many Democrats were as badly off as were the Whigs in having no political roof over their heads. Many were ready to fraternize with Free-Soilers or to bolt the party.

Politicians like Stephen A. Douglas found themselves not only out of step with those who dominated the national organization but in grave danger of losing stride with their own constituents. The Democratic party was simply going to pieces under their feet. Unless it could produce new leadership and a new appeal of some kind which would hold the South and satisfy the Northwest, the Democrats would follow the Whigs into ruin. Whether an appeal could be found which would be concrete enough to meet revolutionary material changes and yet abstract enough to appease aroused moral feelings was very doubtful. The very effort to make it in such a strained and confused atmosphere might only add to the strain and confusion and turn well-marked drifts into precipitant action.

It thus seems clear that the South was going to continue to rule the existing Democratic party and that a new party was bound to come in the North in which the fusion of Whigs and Free-Soilers and dissatisfied Democrats would take place. It was only a question of what act or what event would produce the move. It is entirely possible that even if there had never been a Stephen A. Douglas or a Kansas, something else would have answered. A new social-economic order in the Northeast and the Northwest was in the making. The Democratic party in power and the Whig party in ruin did not serve the purposes of the new age. The Compromise of 1850 had done as well as could have been expected in providing a poorly observed truce of four years' duration. The hour for a change was now at hand. Douglas and Kansas were merely to provide the occasion.

A steady drive for the organization of the territory west of Missouri and Iowa had been on for several years. The normal pressure on the frontier had been augmented by the breaking of the home market in the wheat area of the Old Northwest and by an intense interest in transcontinental railroad building. Restless settlers in western Iowa and Missouri had been looking hopefully across their borders at visions of farms and townsites to be secured and profits to be realized. Railroad promoters had been organizing companies, pressing their representatives in Congress to secure government aid, and stirring the interest of local communities through which railroads would pass as connecting links in the continental span. The representatives of Iowa and Missouri had repeatedly introduced bills in Congress for the organization of the territory, and Douglas, as chairman of the Senate Committee on Territories, had reported such a bill on the last day of the preceding session. Settlers and railroads both required it.[10]

There was, therefore, nothing unusual about the fact that Congressman John G. Miller of Missouri and Senator Dodge of Iowa early in the first session of the Thirty-third Congress introduced bills calling for the organization of the Territory of Nebraska. Nor was it a matter for surprise that on January 4, 1854, Douglas should have reported back from his committee the Dodge bill, which had been referred to it. What was unusual was that Senator Dixon of Kentucky should have told the Senate on January 16 that when this bill came up for consideration he would offer an amendment which would in effect nullify Section 8 of the Missouri Compromise. That portion of the Missouri authorization act which prohibited slavery north of 36° 30', he said, should "not be so construed as to apply to the Territory contemplated by this act, or to any other Territory of the United States; but that the citizens of the several States and Territories . . . [should] be at liberty to take and hold their slaves within any of the Territories of the United States, or to the States to be formed therefrom."

Equally unusual was the fact that on the next day when Douglas announced the date on which he expected the Senate to take up his bill, Senator Sumner gave notice that he would move an amendment to it providing that nothing in it should "be construed

---

[10] P. Orman Ray, *The Repeal of the Missouri Compromise* (Cleveland, 1909), 95–108; Milton, *Eve of Conflict*, 97–114.

to abrogate or in any way contravene" the Missouri Compromise.[11]

Here was an issue raised; here were sides sharply taken. The Missouri Compromise was to be a part of the territorial question. Douglas, whose bill of January 4 had merely said, in the words of the Utah and New Mexican Territorial Acts, that when admitted as a state "the said Territory . . . shall be received into the Union with or without slavery, as their constituents may prescribe at the time of their admission," now had to accept that fact if he had not already done so. If he did not take a position, Dixon and Sumner would see to it that the Senate did. Things were getting out of hand.

In the next few weeks this "Nebraska Bill" evolved into one in which the territory was divided into two parts—Kansas and Nebraska—and the Missouri Compromise was bluntly "repealed" as having been superseded by the new principle of popular sovereignty contained in the 1850 compromise. Who and what were responsible for this remains a mystery. Benton out in Missouri, eager to return to the Senate, had driven Atchison to declare that he would support no bill "to organize a government for the Territory" unless it was without "restrictions upon the subject of slavery." He would vote for no bill that made Nebraska a free-soil territory. He later boasted that he had forced Douglas to his position and should receive credit for the Missouri Compromise section of the act.[12]

Archibald Dixon of Kentucky by his amendment threat and a later conference with Douglas is supposed to have had a strong hand in the matter. The desire to secure Southern support for the quick opening and settling of the territory in the interests of a central railroad to the Pacific is also supposed to have had an influence. It has even been suggested that Douglas saw the chance to revive his weakened party by advocating a return to the good old Demo-

[11] Cong. Globe, 33 Cong., 1 Sess., 87, 115, 175, 186.

[12] Ray, Repeal of the Missouri Compromise, 102–41; Frank H. Hodder, "The Railroad Background of the Kansas-Nebraska Act," in Mississippi Valley Historical Review, XII (1925–1926), 3–22. Professor James C. Malin has recently discovered a Douglas letter of December 17, 1853 (well before his bill was introduced), explaining his program for developing the whole Great Lakes–Mississippi River area, by both water and land transportation. He would check the establishment of permanent Indian reservations and organize the territories as rapidly as possible. He suggested that many railroad lines should be spread westward. As to slavery, he hoped that all would "be willing to sanction and affirm the principles established by the Compromise Measures of 1850."

cratic principle of self-rule, and some charged that it was a cheap trick to win the presidency.[13]

Motives were doubtless quite varied and may not have been clear to the actors themselves. Yet it should be noted that this move did not originate in the South and only indirectly touched that section. Over and over again this fact was noted in the debates which followed, and historians have found no evidence to the contrary. The interesting thing, however, is the constant assumption that somehow the whole business was a Southern move for the benefit of slavery, and that it constituted a base yielding to Southern demands. So insistent was, and still is, this assumption, that the South actually paid the price of it as if it had been a fact in the developments of that day, and in the history of the present. No other single happening so blackened the South's standing with Northern men as this "betrayal of a sacred agreement." It became the proof of the Slave Power's aggression.

Chase and his fellow "Independent Democrats" began it in their "Appeal . . . to the People of the United States." They warned of the "imminent danger . . . [which menaced] the freedom of our institutions or the permanency of our Union." They declared that the passage of the Kansas bill would "open all the unorganized territory of the Union to the ingress of slavery." It was a step towards permanently subjugating "the whole country to the yoke of a slaveholding despotism." It was a yielding to the idea that the Union could "be maintained only by submitting to the demands of slavery." The call was to "rescue . . . the country from the domination of slavery." [14]

Thus begun, the idea of Southern aggression grew steadily to the outbreak of the Civil War. "The *unanimous South* has elected —with its eyes open—to rescind the Missouri Act," wrote Edward Everett Hale to his father. "As every intelligent man knows," said the *Commercial Register* of Sandusky, Ohio, "it is the South alone who . . . is the instigator of all the excitement that may result from this uncalled for and unexpected reagitation of the slavery question." The express purpose of the bill was to give *the South* "a

[13] Mrs. S. B. Dixon, *A True History of the Missouri Compromise and its Repeal* (Cincinnati, 1899), *passim*.

[14] *Cong. Globe*, 33 Cong., 1 Sess., 281–82.

preponderance over the North in the government." "Shall the North lie supinely down and await the welding of chains already forged for its subjection?" it asked. This bill was "the scheme of a weak and imbecile administration; of a corrupt and ambitious demagogue; of grasping, dishonorable Slaveholders." The people must unite "upon a Northern policy" to force "the Slave Power" to "recoil from the deed they [sic] have committed." The *Ohio State Journal* spoke of the bill as "the issue now tendered by the South," and Representative Elihu B. Washburne of Illinois called it the "last attempt of the slave power (aided by its northern allies) to break the old landmarks of freedom." Chase put it more bluntly: "It is *Slavery* that renews the strife. It is Slavery that again wants room. It is Slavery, with its insatiate demands for more slave territory and more slave States."

The New York *Tribune* warned the people of the North that they "must bear in mind that the ground taken by the *South* now is . . . slavery forever and its extension over the whole country." Scornfully it asked: "Men of the North! are you prepared to permit this Southern whipster to rule you longer?" William Cullen Bryant's *Evening Post* simply assumed with Greeley and Benton that this was "the first act in a new Southern drama." Abraham Lincoln would later express the same idea.[15]

Yet the facts were all in the opposite direction. The men who were responsible for the repeal of the Missouri Compromise represented no particular group or section. Two were Democrats; one was a Whig. They came from states which bordered and touched each other on the Mississippi—states which had been settled by upland Southern peoples, many of whom were hostile to slavery, and which had rather unusual reputations for loyalty to the Union and a middle-of-the-road attitude. Not one of them had been represented at the Nashville convention nor would be members of the Confederacy. In none of these states had there been a strong Southern Rights party during the recent Compromise struggle. Threats of

15 E. E. Hale to his father, May 26, 1854 (italics mine), in Edward Everett Hale Papers (New York State Library, Albany); Sandusky (Ohio) *Commercial Register*, February 28, May 25, 27, 1854; Columbus *Ohio State Journal*, May 27, 1854; *Cong. Globe*, 33 Cong., 1 Sess., Appendix, 134 (Salmon P. Chase); New York *Tribune*, July 19, 1855; New York *Evening Post*, quoted in Allan Nevins, *Ordeal of the Union* (New York, 1947), II, 131.

secession were absent. Support of the Compromise was general. Atchison, one of the Democrats, seems to have been occupied in recent years in a fight against Benton and never expressed any interest in Kansas and slavery except that of serving his immediate Missouri constituents. His ambitions seem never to have risen above that of holding his job. Dixon was a Whig who had never been closely associated with the now nearly defunct Southern element. He had not in the past, nor did he now, get its support. If he had either a party or a Southern motive, it was never apparent. His state, like that of Atchison, contained a strong antislavery element. He, like Atchison, certainly had more local reasons for his action than he had Southern ones.

With Douglas it was the same. His problem was one of holding a rapidly dividing constituency together and of looking after the interests of the whole great Northwest. Illinois, his own state, reached from the Lakes to a point southward well below Richmond, Virginia, and its older southern part, where Douglas' strength lay, was, day by day, being overshadowed by the rapid growth of the region about the bustling young city of Chicago. His constituents wanted lands and internal improvements and more foreign immigration—things his national party was not giving. The larger Northwest, of which he was also spokesman, wanted land and water outlets and room to expand westward across lands being reserved for Indians. He was, moreover, far more conscious of the great party upheaval that was occurring than his fellows and of its drifting, leaderless condition. On November 11, 1853, he had written: "Our first duty is to the cause. . . . The party is in a distracted condition and it requires all our wisdom, prudence and energy to consolidate its power and perpetuate its principles." [16]

He was not a proslavery man, nor did he think that there would ever be another slave state added to the Union. Speaking of the "vast territory, stretching from the Mississippi to the Pacific," he had pronounced it "large enough to form at least seventeen new free states." "I think," he continued, "I am safe in assuming that each of these will be free Territories and free States, whether Congress shall prohibit slavery or not." And where would slavery find

[16] Letter to editors of the Springfield *Illinois State Register*, November 11, 1853, reprinted in Ray, *Repeal of the Missouri Compromise*, 185–86.

a region into which to expand? His answer was blunt and positive. "There is none—none at all." Whatever Douglas' motives may have been—to help Atchison, to forward railroad schemes, to check the creation of a permanent Indian barrier across the West, or to provide the sinking Democratic party with a principle and leadership —they did not include benefiting the South by an extension of slavery. And, as we shall see, a unanimous South did not welcome the introduction of his bill or approve of its contents. Few thought it would do what Douglas expected—"impart peace to the country and stability to the Union." [17]

The significance of the Kansas-Nebraska Bill for the South must be looked for in the North. The South had not yet recovered from its last great upset. It was not eager for another. It had not asked for the Douglas move, and its important leaders had played no part in its origin. It would, however, have to bear the brunt of the bitter reactions awakened. It would have to weigh the benefits and the harm to be expected from such a move. The bill, with its repeal feature, had come so unexpectedly that considerable time would have to elapse before men could realize the import of what had happened and make up their minds not only as to the merits of the bill but as to the meaning of the Northern reaction to it. The immediate Southern reaction was, therefore, one of uncertainty and near indifference.

The North, meanwhile, was aflame with anger and indignation. The "inflammable sentences" of the Appeal, in which "Assumptions, arguments, and beliefs were stated in the form of undisputed facts," "fell like sprays of oil" upon a smoldering fire. "The 'Slave Power' was breaking a 'sacred compact' to extend its hellborn tyranny . . . ; the fairest land on earth was being given to the Monster." Month by month the uproar increased and distortions to uphold the assumptions grew apace. Douglas was charged with being a slaveholder. He was planning to move to the South. The Slave Power was about to seize Cuba. Slavery was to be spread over the whole nation. The slave trade would soon be reopened. "The triumph of the measure" would be "the triumph of Slavery and Aristocracy over Liberty and Republicanism." "Never, since

[17] *Cong. Globe,* 30 Cong., 1 Sess., Appendix, 366 ff.

184

Ohio was a State," said one editor, "has there been known so universal and so overwhelming a revulsion of popular sentiment." The same could have been said of nearly every Northern state.[18]

Such a quick and deep reaction to what men wanted to believe regardless of the facts was possible only because the Kansas-Nebraska Act so perfectly lent itself to forces already at work. Thousands of men already believed everything which the Appeal said —believed it of Douglas; believed it of the Democratic administration; believed it of the South and slavery. Furthermore, it provided a reason for doing exactly what thousands of men were about to do anyway. It did not alter the course of events, it merely made it possible for them to happen in a more intense way than they might have been expected to happen sooner or later. Had Chase and Sumner sat themselves down and drawn up a plan ideally suited to their purposes, they could not have done half so well as did Stephen A. Douglas.

This was not a situation in which facts and truth mattered. Neither would have served the purpose. It was one in which the possibilities for inference, interpretation, and distortion counted most heavily. And Stephen A. Douglas and the Kansas-Nebraska Bill offered exactly those possibilities. They made it easy for perfectly honest men to ignore realities and to believe the things they most feared.

Douglas, himself, was no angel. In a time when the temperance crusade was in full swing, he made no effort to hide his occasional excessive use of liquor. He never indulged in the moral platitudes so characteristic of the day or made a public show of religion. He thought that a smooth working of the democratic process required compromise and an observance of Constitutional rights. He was no reformer. He dealt hard blows to his political opponents and took them as well. He talked claptrap when that sufficed but could think clearly and talk straight when necessary. He was a typical Westerner, loyal, boastful, honest, and square-dealing. He was ambitious, shallow and profound by turns, courageous and impetuous. Men loved him or hated and feared him. His qualities were the same in 1854 when he introduced the Kansas-Nebraska Bill and in

[18] Albert J. Beveridge, *Abraham Lincoln, 1809–1858* (Boston, 1928), III, 184, 186–87; Craven, *Coming of the Civil War*, 332–44.

1860 when he courageously, unselfishly, and loyally went through the South in a vain effort to stem the tide against the Union.

He was the type of man whose motives and actions could be easily misrepresented and about whom almost anything could be charged and believed. Men of his day misrepresented him, and historians are still doing it. "Senator Douglas never yet committed an act without a sinister motive," said an Ohio paper in 1854; "a man of dim moral perceptions" whose apprehension of moral considerations was "cloudy and limited," asserts the historian Allan Nevins in 1947.[19]

It was thus not hard for men to believe that Douglas had trampled on "a sacred pledge"; that he had entered into "an atrocious plot" to "open the free territories of the nation to the infamous traffic in men, women and children"; that he intended to bully the people "into tacit complicity in his crimes against God and Man."

It was just as easy to convince them that the Democratic party, in the hands of Southerners and their "doughface" allies, was plotting to bar "the freedom-loving emigrants from Europe" and the "energetic and intelligent laborers from our own land" from "the very heart of the North American continent" so that "the blight of slavery . . . [might] cover the land." Had it not refused to pass the liberal land and internal-improvement legislation so essential to free Western development? Had it not "at the bidding of the slave power" trampled into the dust "the fundamental principles of our Government, our national constitution, the bleeding cause of humanity, the law of God and the public conscience?" Certainly the time had come when "There ought to be something got up where friends of freedom . . . [could] be associated on moral principles, and not be ridden to death by the party hacks, who . . . [were] always the ready tools for the people's oppressors." Ought not all men who believed in freedom hold a convention and "pledge themselves to work together for the overthrow of the slaveholding dynasty"? [20]

19 Sandusky *Commercial Register,* February 22, 1854; Nevins, *Ordeal of the Union,* II, 108–109. Nevins, because of his strong Lincoln bias, sees Douglas as all black in 1854, but all white in 1860. He fails to explain the complete transformation of the man's character in six short years.

20 Madison *Wisconsin Daily State Journal,* March 1, 1854; Milwaukee *Daily Free Democrat,* May 9, 26, 1854.

The moral reasons for a new political deal were reinforced by evidences of economic neglect. "With a treasury overflowing," said the Sandusky *Commercial Register*, "not one dollar can be wrung from it with which to aid and abet Western prosperity and national commerce. Millions can be given for a section of barren territory with which to make another slave mart, because the South demands it, but not one cent for Custom Houses and Harbor Improvements where they are needed." It was easy to pass legislation by which "to fasten the fangs of the monster Slavery upon fair and *free* territory," yet impossible to get anything "for the benefit of Free States and Northern Commerce!" It was up to "the people to say . . . if the word democracy shall be nothing but another name for pro-Slavery and anti-North." [21]

Here were moral and economic reasons enough to complete the work, already so far under way, of taking dissatisfied and mistreated Democrats completely out of the party and into a new union with Free-Soilers and orphaned Whigs. Various names were applied as the force of anti-Nebraska feeling did its work, but in the end the term "Republican," already widely used in Michigan and Wisconsin, became standard. A new party, in the process of forming since Martin Van Buren's rejection in 1844, had at last crystalized—a "Northern party," which Corwin said Chase and his friends had been trying to form for years. Its immediate purpose was to oppose the extension of slavery into the territories, but its ultimate obligations would, of necessity, include the economic and social needs of a section.

The effect which the violent reaction to the Kansas-Nebraska Bill had in producing a fixed stereotype of the South and its institutions in Northern minds is hard to measure. There can be no doubt, however, that it was large. Abolition propaganda and *Uncle Tom's Cabin* had laid a broad foundation. Douglas' bill brought a sense of reality to the most extreme charges that had before been lacking. It forced men to realize that, deep in their hearts, they already believed that "slavery was *wrong* and ought to be restricted"; that somehow it did not jibe with democratic ideals.

Opposition to the bill was conducted on the same high moral plane that the abolitionists had long taken in denouncing slavery

[21] Sandusky *Commercial Register*, April 7, May 31, 1854.

itself. It probably profited from a deep wave of evangelical religious feeling that was sweeping the North, expressing itself in revival meetings and temperance reform. The part which the clergy took in protest and petitions was especially noticeable. A Wisconsin editor charged that in the pulpits of his state "Instead of 'believe in the Lord Jesus Christ and thou shalt be saved,' it was 'beware of the Nebraska Iniquity'! 'No Christian can be a Democrat'!" Seward spoke of the conflict as "an eternal struggle between conservatism and progress, between truth and error, between right and wrong." Chase's speeches were models of righteous indignation. Through conscious and unconscious effort the move against the bill thus took on the air of a great moral crusade against an ignoble foe. Opposition to the extension of slavery became *the slavery issue*. The politician became the outstanding antislavery spokesman.[22]

Sumner set the pattern of vituperation by calling the Kansas-Nebraska Act "a soulless, eyeless monster—horrid, unshapely, and vast," and Benjamin F. Wade spoke of it as a "conspiracy" to spread an institution which had already "sunk" Virginia from first rank in the nation to fifth, "Africanized" her statesmanship, and made her the enemy of progress, the advocate of extended markets for human beings.[23]

William Lloyd Garrison's *Liberator* had long been at work creating a picture of Southerners and their section which abolitionists accepted as the inevitable product of slaveholding. It took for granted brutal, licentious aristocrats in a tumble-down social-economic order. "Their career from the cradle to the grave," wrote Garrison, "is but one of unbridled lust, of filthy amalgamation, of swaggering braggadocio, of haughty domination, of cowardly ruffianism, of boundless dissipation, of matchless insolence, of infinite self-conceit, of unequalled oppression, of more than savage cruelty." They were "monsters, whose arguments . . . [were] the bowie knife and revolver, tar and feathers, the lash, the bludgeon, the halter and the stake." "What is the South," he asked, "but one vast graveyard in which lie buried all noble aspirations, all reverence for human rights, all freedom of speech, all respect for jus-

22 Appleton (Wis.) *Crescent,* May 19, 1856; *Cong. Globe,* 33 Cong., 1 Sess., Appendix, 155.
23 *Cong. Globe,* 33 Cong., 1 Sess., 282, 339.

tice?" Their character was a blending of "the conceit of the peacock with the ferocity of the tiger." Their condition was "the most hopeless of any portion of the human race." [24]

Wendell Phillips spoke of the proud Southern "barons," living in their "massive castles" more like those of the fourteenth century than of the nineteenth. Yet he saw the Old South as a land of desolation and ruin—"the vulture and the wolf returning to the homes once tenanted by women and children; . . . churches with roofs fallen in and proudly emblazoned oak carvings covered with moss"; planters giving up "raising cotton and . . . [taking] to the breeding of men." Even in the Lower South the planter was but an overseer for the North, whose books discounted for him, whose capital sustained him, and whose wharves received the ships freighted with his cotton. The cause of it all—"slavery!" [25]

The Southerner, from whose tobacco-stained lips came "the most villainous oaths . . . possible for the language of Billingsgate to invent," was notoriously lax in matters of sex. There was "probably not a single slaveholder . . . in Virginia" who did "not have sons and daughters in slavery." Six sevenths of all the slaves in that state were reported to have "more or less white blood in their veins." Planters bought and sold their own offspring. *"Gentlemen* of the city, keeping an office, who are unable to own a slave, find no difficulty in hiring one from planters or farmers for purposes of prostitution," quoted the *Liberator* from the New York *Examiner*. "The consequence is," it continued, "that nightly at twilight, there are to be seen, passing from some suburban retreat, colored or black women, to the office of a Colonel in one street, a Doctor in another, a Lawyer in another, and an Editor in another street; and on the following morning until approaching mid-day the streets are streaked with ebony-hued divinities passing from the caresses of *gentlemen* of the first families." [26]

Such pictures of the South had not reached a wide audience, but they created a stereotype for a radical element which now formed an essential part of the new political alliances and which had already been able to thrust forward such leaders as Chase and Sumner and Wade. Only men who accepted this stereotype, at least in

[24] Boston *Liberator*, November 16, 1855; September 12, 19, 1856.
[25] *Ibid.*, January 8, 1847. [26] *Ibid.*, March 28, 1847; January 7, 1853.

part, could have written the "Appeal of the Independent Democrats," and have believed, at least in part, what they were writing.
And now since increasing numbers were ready to believe the Appeal, they were by that very fact made more ready to accept the
stereotype. In the anti-Nebraska press there now began to appear
statements about the South and its people which had a strangely
familiar ring.

The New York *Tribune* was most extreme in its assertions but
Western papers were not far behind. Said the *Tribune:* "Southern
plantations are little less than negro harems and the best recommendation to a slave girl is that she is handsome enough to please
the eye of her master. . . . Of all the Southern presidents hardly
one had failed to leave his mulatto children. . . . The South is a
perfect puddle of amalgamation!" In the South, it insisted, "Lynch
law is inevitable." "We do not expect a community imbedded in
negro slavery . . . to await for the process of law, quick or slow.
. . . We must look for hideous savageism worthy of original Africa
in crime and punishment under such a system." Southerners, it
reported, went around "armed like assassins . . . [and] importa-
tions from the regions of chivalry" to the North often continued
to carry "bowie-knives, sword-canes, and pistols." [27]

Southern college students were described as "impertinent bullies." At Northern institutions they were invariably "the leading
spirits in whatever was bad and corrupting in its influence. They
assumed an air of impertinent superiority which engendered the
bitterest hates in the hearts of the students from Northern States,
and, let but one of such utter a sentence of disparagement of
Slavery . . . [and] a brutal assault was sure to follow. So characteristic of the 'bully' is the Southern student that . . . Northern
institutions where slave holding patronage is bestowed are fast becoming neglected by Free State students." [28]

And, as bad as things were, the worst probably never was known,
"for where liberty is wanting, crime may exist to almost any extent
and be unknown out of the circle of its immediate neighborhood.
. . . In the South the want of publicity, of intercourse, of social
analysis must prevent the great bulk of crimes from ever reaching

27 New York *Tribune*, June 22, 1855; July 11, August 3, 1854.
28 Sandusky *Commercial Register*, March 21, 1856.

the light." Even "the religion of the South without Northern help
. . . would be sheer bankruptcy." [29]

To licentiousness and brutality was, of course, added the charge
of backwardness. "It is most true . . . at the South," said the *Tribune,* "we are not able to discover any productive agency called
genius,—no inventor, savant, artist, or his works. In this department, the Caucasian man there presents one magnificent level, like
the sublime desert . . . , one grand uniform of barrenness, which
rises to sublimity by its extent." "In what iota has she . . . contributed to the inspirations of the century? Nothing. Nothing—
less than nothing. Whenever she could she has laid her hands on
Northern industry and blasted it." Each year renders "her poverty
more transparent and the spread of popular ignorance more de-
plorable." Her people were "maddened ignoramuses . . . without
the capacity required to see the inevitable end which awaits their
insanity," added a Wisconsin editor.[30]

Nor was there hope of betterment in a land "cursed with a system of labor which so . . . [stagnated] her life blood that she . . .
[could] not support good schools even for the children of the
wealthy." And if sent to school at the North, they would be "likely
to learn that there is a better and decenter state of society than that
which renders concubinage not an uncommon evil in the house-
holds of slave plantations." [31]

Nor was it alone a case in which the people were "intellectually
ruined." Norfolk was "commercially a ruin"; Mount Vernon
"domestically another ruin; and Richmond, if not a ruin, might
as well . . . [have been] one as . . . [to have been] sustained by
the trade in human flesh." The fields too were in ruins. "Pride and
folly, and tobacco raising, chewing and spitting" had worn them
out and driven "the chivalry to new lands." And "there were hundreds of thousands of illegitimate mulatto ruins, without the position of manhood and womanhood, liable to be sold by their white
parents or brothers and sisters at any moment, to make up for the
real-estate ruins." [32]

[29] New York *Tribune,* July 15, 1854.
[30] *Ibid.,* January 9, 1855; August 18, 1854; Monroe (Wis.) *Sentinel,* May 2, 1855.
[31] New York *Tribune,* July 3, 1854.
[32] *Ibid.,* October 20, 1854.

And so the tragic work went on of recasting the old abolition stereotypes for wider use. Many Northern men saw what was being done and protested ardently against it. "In the present excited state of the Northern mind," said one editor, "everything defamatory of Southern character and institutions is eagerly seized upon and admitted as truth; and in consequence, our general estimate of Southern life and character is very gross and improper." Yet the whole drift of events was against moderation and clear thinking. Kansas and Preston Brooks and soon even the Supreme Court of the United States seemed bent on giving men additional reasons for "seizing upon" and admitting "as truth" all the things which the abolitionists had charged. Even the writer of the protest quoted above was soon saying that conditions in "decadent New Orleans" were worse than in "the despotic empire of brutalized Austria." [33]

Meanwhile, what of the South? How had Southern men reacted to the Kansas-Nebraska Bill? How had they reacted to the Northern reactions? How had the bill affected the political parties in the South?

The answers to these questions are not as simple and clear-cut as the Northern public supposed them to be. Not everyone approved, and even when they did, their reasons were not always the same. The reactions of Congressmen, who had to take sides at once as debate developed, were one thing; those of the people back home were another; reactions developed under the violent Northern outburst were something else again.

The reaction of Congressmen came first. Dixon, Atchison, and Phillips had played a conspicuous part in the shaping of the Kansas-Nebraska Bill, and they, with Douglas and Jefferson Davis, had influenced President Pierce to accept it as the Democratic administration policy. Their position, as expressed by Dixon, was that the repeal of the Missouri Compromise restrictions on slavery had come from nonslaveholders as an act of "public justice and magnanimity." The "whole country," in his opinion, "believe[d] that *the Missouri compromise act* was a palpable wrong, originally done to the people of the slaveholding States, and that it ought to be repealed" as

[33] Sandusky *Commercial Register*, July 14, 1854; January 22, 1856.

inconsistent with the acts of 1850. He pretended to believe that such a show of fairness, after years of wrong, would put all the states "upon an equal footing" and bring to an end the slavery controversy. His friend Mason of Virginia called the bill "a great healing measure for the purpose of preventing agitation." [34]

Others were not so enthusiastic or so badly informed as to Northern feelings about slavery. George E. Badger of North Carolina thought there had been "no necessity for immediate action in respect to the establishment of these Territories" and Preston Brooks of South Carolina was frank to avow "that it would have been wiser, and in better keeping with the general interests of the country," if territorial organization had been delayed "until the pressing wants of the people . . . had caused them to apply to Congress for relief." William Cullom of Tennessee went further. He called the bill an "ill-advised and dangerous measure; this firebrand, thrust upon our deliberations." The honor of the South, plighted by the act of 1820, was at stake. He begged the country to "rise up as one man and frown down this attempt to advance individual and party objects, under the flimsy pretext of doing justice to the South, when it can only jeopard a nation's peace." The South had not asked for it. "No public meeting of the people, no primary assembly, no convention, no legislative body . . . [had] called for this measure." He had heard no voice from his constituents, and he was certain that no one in the North had "executed a power of attorney to the Senator from Illinois . . . to make this offer, to reopen the fountain of bitter waters, and to renew the dangerous agitation which has heretofore well nigh severed the glorious Union." [35]

Theodore G. Hunt of Louisiana flatly opposed the bill as a violation "of good faith" and "as engendering discord and dissension among the people of the different sections of the country." He denied the truth of the assertion that the repeal of the Missouri Compromise was "a voluntary and spontaneous peace offering from the North to the South." The North was clearly against repeal, and "the South had no interest to move in the matter of slavery in relation to the territory mentioned in the bill." The region would at-

[34] *Cong. Globe,* 33 Cong., 1 Sess., Appendix, 141.
[35] *Ibid.,* 145, 371, 538.

tract few slaves but would soon be filled with free laborers. The effort to keep an equilibrium between slave and free states in Congress was hopeless. Slavery in the United States could not "keep pace with the growth of the white race." [36]

Others expressed like opinions but it was the gnarled old Texan Sam Houston who insisted on having a last word in opposition before the bill came to a vote. "But what would the repeal of this compromise amount to?" he asked. "An abstraction! . . . Will it secure these Territories to the South? No, sir, not at all. . . . We are told by southern, as well as northern gentlemen, those who are for it, and those who are against it, that slavery will never be extended to that territory, that it will never go there; but it is the principle of non-intervention that it is desired to establish."

To Houston, this was an empty abstraction. "It holds a promise to the ear," he said, "but breaks it to the hope. . . . I want no empty promises. They have not been asked for by the South. They are not desired; and so far as I am concerned, they will never be accepted." The only fruits of this bill would be "a tremendous shock" that would "convulse the country from Maine to the Rio Grande." "The South has not asked for it," he repeated. "I, as the most extreme southern Senator upon this floor, do not desire it. If it is a boon that is offered to propitiate the South, I, as a southern man, repudiate it. I reject it. I will have none of it." [37]

The majority, however, were of a different opinion. They may not have asked for it, and they would not have proposed it. They might even regret that it had been offered, because of the agitation and irritation it had cost. "But," as Clayton of Delaware asked, "can a Senator, whose constituents hold slaves, be expected to resist and refuse what the North thus freely offers as a measure due to us? . . . How faith can be violated by us in consenting to their offer, when both parties thus agree to the repeal of a former arrangement of both, it will be difficult for any man to explain." The South must accept it as "an act of justice, long, long delayed." [38]

Over and over again Southern spokesmen asserted that in supporting the bill, they were merely supporting the principle of equality among the states. As frequently, they denied the expectation of any tangible gains to be won. Of more than fifty members

[36] Ibid., 435–39.   [37] Ibid., 339–40.   [38] Ibid., 383.

of the two houses of Congress who spoke on the Kansas-Nebraska Bill, only two expressed confidence that slavery would be established in the territories. Most agreed with Bell of Tennessee, who insisted that Douglas had only offered "a principle, an abstraction —a dangerous temptation to southern Senators—which I fear will prove utterly barren—bearing neither fruit nor flower." He had "enquired with some diligence into the grounds upon which any expectation . . . in the South, that slavery . . . [would] be established in this Territory," was founded, and while a few thought it might, "the greater number, with more reason, concur[red] in the opinion that it never [would]." Robert M. T. Hunter of Virginia confessed that for a moment he permitted the illusion to rest upon his mind that Kansas might become a slave state, but "upon a further examination of the subject" had concluded "that it was utterly hopeless to endeavor to effect any such thing." It was a case, as Houston said, of the South having "to overcome a law of nature more potent than geographical obstacles, before the country . . . [could] be filled by a slave population." He no more doubted that Indiana and Illinois were "non-slaveholding States than that Kansas . . . [would] always be such." Butler of South Carolina, Alfred B. Greenwood of Arkansas, Emerson Etheridge of Tennessee, Stephens of Georgia, John Kerr of North Carolina, Brown of Mississippi, Benton of Missouri, and many others expressed the same conviction. A few, like John R. Franklin of Maryland and John S. Millson of Virginia, even denounced the bill as an aggressive free-soil move. These regions would "forever remain free." To organize was only to invite a flood of free settlers who would never pass the local laws necessary to protect slavery. "I am unwilling to multiply the number of free-soil and non-slaveholding communities," was the way Millson put it.[39]

Yet when the vote was taken only two Southern Senators and nine Representatives voted against the bill. The only conclusion possible is that they had followed "the party line" or had reacted as Southern men against whom they believed a sectional opposition had developed. Later conduct might even suggest that the ardent defense of the "equality principle" had strengthened both the desire and the hope that Kansas might become a slave state!

[39] *Ibid.*, 409, 224, 339, 419, 426.

Opinions regarding the Kansas-Nebraska Act developed slowly among the people and in the press of the South. The debates in Congress received surprisingly little attention, and when they did the comments were usually a pale reflection of some opinion expressed there. The section simply had not recovered from its previous disturbance. As the Richmond *Enquirer* said: "Throughout the South there prevails a repugnance to agitation. We had enough, and too much, excitement during the Compromise Controversy of 1850, and now there exists an indisposition to popular meetings and legislative resolves." [40] Few said anything startling in discussing the repeal of the Missouri Compromise. The Edgefield (South Carolina) *Advertiser* said that as far as it was concerned it would have "to be excused from going into ecstasies over the mere abstract renunciation of gross error." The Winchester *Virginian* saw it as a move *"calculated for no earthly end than the excitement of bitter and prolonged agitation."* [41] The Raleigh *Register* thought it would prove to be only "the rallying cry for another antislavery agitation which . . . [would] throw all that . . . [had] preceded it in the shade." The Parkersburg (Virginia) *Gazette* was of the opinion that this "gift to the South would be another wooden horse from which would issue 'all sorts of plagues to torment the recipients.' " So completely was excitement lacking that J. L. M. Curry was moved to write in July: "It is difficult for us to comprehend, or credit the excitement, that is said to prevail in the North, on account of the Nebraska question. . . . here . . . there is no excitement, no fever on the subject. It is seldom alluded to in private or public and so far as the introduction of slavery is concerned, such a consummation is hardly hoped for." [42]

Newspaper comment throughout the South confirms this judgment. Said the Charleston *Mercury:*

"The spectacle presented by the North and South at the present moment, is well calculated to arrest the attention of thoughtful minds. In the former, we find society convulsed, all the slumbering elements of sectional bitterness roused, and slavery agitation awake

[40] Richmond *Enquirer*, March 2, 1854.

[41] Edgefield (S.C.) *Advertiser*, February 22, March 8, 1854; Winchester *Virginian*, quoted in Richmond *Whig*, January 31, 1854.

[42] Raleigh *Register*, February 1, 1854; Parkersburg (Va.) *Gazette*, quoted in Shanks, *Secession Movement in Virginia*, 50; J. L. M. Curry to C. C. Clay, Jr., July 5, 1854, in Clement C. Clay Papers (Manuscript Division, Duke University Library).

again, after its brief and delusive sleep, strengthened by new accessions, and eager for the onset. Never before have the Northern press approached so near to unanimity in the cause of abolition. Never before were all other issues so far buried, and the sentiment and voice of that whole section so united in war upon the South. . . . Such is the state of things at the North. How is it at the South? All is calm and cosy indifference. The thunders which come rolling from the North, die away before they reach our latitude, or if heard at all, are scarcely heeded. The contrast thus exhibited between the active and fierce energy of the assailant and the quiet apathy of the assailed, is most remarkable. . . . [The North is united in an effort to wipe out what it deems a great outrage, but] if we look now to the South, we will discover great variance on the Nebraska bill. By many, it is regarded with indifference; by some openly opposed; while the mass look upon it as a thing of so little practical good, that it is certainly not worth the labor of an active struggle to maintain it." [43]

The New Orleans *Bee* commented on this same "indifference" and declared that the defeat of the bill would cost the South no sleep. "There neither has been, nor will be any excitement in the South in reference to this measure, the efforts of fire-eaters and demagogues to the contrary notwithstanding," was its blunt assertion. "Something not far from indifference is felt on the subject," it said at another time. "Let the Nebraska bill be rejected tomorrow and the South will sleep quite as sound at night as before. We shall have no revival of the treasonable discussions of 1850!" The *Republican Banner and Nashville Whig* as late as June denied the statement made in a Northern newspaper that the South "warmly favored" the bill and insisted that "the very opposite" was the case. "Its introduction fell coldly upon the Southern public," it said, and "the fierce discussion [in Congress] which followed, awakened no sensation, and its passage or defeat would have produced no widespread excitement. Indeed, we believe that the slaveholders of the South would have preferred its defeat." A questioning of men on the street confirmed this opinion. [44]

Thomas Hart Benton in April called attention to the fact that

[43] Charleston *Tri-Weekly Mercury*, June 21, 1854.
[44] New Orleans *Bee*, May 17, 1854; *ibid.*, quoted in Quincy *Whig*, March 20, 1854; *Republican Banner and Nashville Whig*, June 30, 1854.

although four months had passed since the bill was introduced, "not a petition for it from the class of States for whose benefit the movement . . . [professed] to have been made!—not a word in its favor from the smallest public meeting or private assemblage of any Slave State" had been received. "This," he said, "is the response of the South to this boon tendered to it by northern members under a northern President. It is the response of silence—more emphatic than words." [45]

The Richmond *Enquirer* explained this seeming "want of interest or apathy of feeling" as due to "the dignity and gravity" of Southern character. The absence of "violent explosions of feeling" and "popular demonstrations of excitement" should not be interpreted as meaning an indifference to the "Nebraska controversy." A vital principle was involved, and on behalf of "non-intervention" all the "ardor and energy" of the section would be enlisted. This was no struggle over expedients or measures of a "partial or temporary character." It went deeper. The sole reason for supporting the measure was the vindication of "the equality and sovereignty of the States." The *Enquirer* therefore appealed for Southern unity on grounds of resistance to a Northern effort to humiliate her people by superadding the ordinance of man to the decree of God.[46]

This was getting nearer to solid ground on which a sectional effort could be based. Even though the bill itself was nothing to get excited over, Northern fury was. It called for alertness if not defense. Yet the belief that the bill offered the South little but trouble was widespread, and its provisions were too vague to inspire confidence or produce unity. The debates in Congress had not cleared up a significant question—whether the doctrine that the people of a territory should decide the slavery question for themselves applied during settlement or only when a state government was formed. Most men were intelligent enough to see that if the settlers were to decide in territorial days, the much-talked-of "equality" would exist on paper but not in Kansas. As the Macon *Georgia Telegraph* put it: "What is all this pother about, that we are making over the Nebraska bill? What possible good can any bill assenting to and offering . . . [the idea of squatter sovereignty] do the

[45] *Cong. Globe,* 33 Cong., 1 Sess., Appendix, 561.
[46] Richmond *Enquirer,* March 2, 9, January 7, April 11, 1854.

South, when the Free Soilers have any start of us in the populating of the territory that may be in dispute?" [47]

The *Republican Banner and Nashville Whig* gave the answer in no uncertain terms: "in as much as facilities for the Northern people to emigrate are so much superior to the slave holder, . . . before we could get up in the morning, eat our breakfast, yoke the oxen, and get off the darkies, the Yankees, with the assistance of the squatters, would possess the land and have their quarantines established." The Natchez *Courier* carried the answer a bit further. "Property is very timid"; it said, "it moves not with rapidity; it seldom runs risks, especially where no extraordinary motive induces; and, therefore, long before the first five hundred slave-holders reach those regions, fifty thousand Northern men and foreign emigrants,—all opposed to slavery in the abstract, and utterly unwilling to associate with the system in practice—will have flocked there, formed territorial laws for our exclusion, and set on foot the machinery of State government, which make that exclusion perpetual." [48]

Others denied that squatter sovereignty was the principle established by the bill and insisted that no decision on slavery was possible until the territories were ready for statehood. Few, however, expressed the belief that either Kansas or Nebraska was fitted for slavery. Even the Richmond *Enquirer,* which in early January saw hope for a new slave state, had changed its mind by March, and was saying that "all agree that slavery cannot exist in the territories of Kansas and Nebraska." [49]

The same opinion was widely expressed in the newspapers of the Carolinas and Georgia. Neither the Raleigh *Register* nor the *Standard* thought that slavery had a chance. The Charleston *Mercury* was equally pessimistic. It did not "suppose that slave states would spring up in Nebraska," but it did want "the consolation of seeing a just principle of legislation established." The Columbia *Daily South Carolinian* agreed that "no practical benefits" were to be expected and declared that it would stand by the act only be-

[47] Macon *Georgia Telegraph*, March 7, 1854.

[48] *Republican Banner and Nashville Whig*, March 7, 1854; Natchez *Courier*, June 15, 1854.

[49] Richmond *Enquirer*, January 7, March 9, 1854.

cause it expressed "a sentiment of justice." In Georgia the Augusta *Chronicle and Sentinel* and the Macon *Georgia Telegraph* both saw Douglas' bill as a move to create more free states. It would not give the South "a single inch of slave territory," and its squatter-sovereignty principle would "effectively cripple the progress of slave immigration." It was "a swindle." The South actually gained "nothing . . . except the assertion of the principle, that Congress has no right to determine the institutions of a territory." Neither the *Southern Recorder* nor the Columbus *Enquirer* "entertained any settled opinion as to the probability of slavery being introduced into this region," and one of them called it a gift as subtle and fatal as the poison "which prostrated the fabled strength of Hercules." [50]

Doubts as to any slavery gains were also expressed widely in other states of the Lower South. The Mobile *Daily Advertiser* denounced Douglas for "reopening the slavery excitement" and declared that if he were right in his statement that the people must act before slavery could exist in a territory, then the South had "no interest in his bill." Its neighbor, the *Register,* approved the bill because it did "what no Southern man [had] dared to ask," but it did not express confidence in the measure's ability to spread slavery. The Jacksonville (Alabama) *Republican* was so unimpressed by what the bill offered the South that it dismissed it for news of the Crimean War. The Montgomery *Advertiser* was equally indifferent. It gave little attention to the bill and seemingly accepted the fact that squatter sovereignty was to be applied.[51]

Mississippi and Louisiana papers, on the other hand, had much to say. The Natchez *Courier* insisted that not one person in a thousand "dreamed of the possibility of slavery" in these territories. The bill offered little good and was "fraught with evil." Its defeat would be "a subject of national felicitation." The *Mississippi Free Trader,* while not convinced that squatter sovereignty applied, was

[50] Raleigh *Register,* February 1, 1854; Raleigh *North Carolina Standard,* March 8, 1854; Charleston *Mercury,* January 20, 1854; Columbia *South Carolinian,* October 17, 1854; Augusta *Chronicle and Sentinel,* October 16, 1856; Macon *Georgia Telegraph,* June 6, 1854; Milledgeville *Southern Recorder,* July 15, 1856; Columbus (Ga.) *Enquirer,* June 13, 1854.

[51] Mobile *Daily Advertiser,* February 18, 1854; Mobile *Register,* January 16, 1854; Jacksonville *Republican,* June 6, 1854; Montgomery *Advertiser,* February 1, 7, March 14, 16, 23, July 27, 1854.

certain that if it did slavery was doomed. The whole business was a "fatal delusion." Regardless of Douglas' own personal opinions on the subject, the South must not yield. It was a critical situation.[52]

The New Orleans *Bee* agreed that the situation was critical, but for quite a different reason. The "Nebraska bill" had stirred "the flames of sectional discord" and raised up "wide-spread, tenacious and unyielding" resistance among "the more sober and conservative elements of the northern public." And to what end? "As a measure of practical utility . . . [the bill was] absolutely worthless. Nebraska and Kansas . . . [would] never become slaveholding territories." They were too far north. They would "be filled up almost exclusively by an Eastern population." The bill was "absolutely injurious." The *Crescent* felt much the same way. Nothing valuable had been secured for the South, and new life had been given "to the fanaticism of the North." Nebraska would never become slave territory. In fact, the editor mused, it was a matter for wonderment "that Missouri and Kentucky remained so long and so steadfastly true to the principles of slavery." This "indiscreet, injudicious and uncalled for measure" had brought nothing but antagonism against "the alleged grasping spirit of the South." It summed up the matter in this fashion: "Suppose the North carry its point, what will it take? What Nature has already given it, and legislation can't take away. Nebraska *must* be a Free State.

"Suppose the South prevail: What will it take? The barren privilege of opening to a few slaveholders, a soil where their slaves will be set free as soon as it shall rise into a State.

"What then is gained anywhere? At best, only a general political confusion in a country where there is already a grand surplus; vast turmoil about nothing; an aggravation of abundant ill blood, a most perilous hazarding of the best of all things, the Union."

The New Orleans *Bulletin* was in complete accord with these positions. "Our people are beginning to appreciate the *utter practical worthlessness of the project,*" it said. Southern sentiment was steadily growing against the bill—"a thing not fit to be touched." And like its Whig neighbors, it quarreled with the *Delta* for supporting Douglas and his bill. Approval of Congressional noninter-

[52] Natchez *Courier*, May 11, June 15, 1854; Natchez *Mississippi Free Trader*, March 1, 1854.

vention as a principle could not be condoned even though the *Delta* expected no "practical advantage" to be gained from its application. The line between disputants, it must be noted, was political—Whig against Democrat—but the argument was waged on purely sectional grounds, and the stakes kept to Southern interests.[53]

Even in Tennessee and Arkansas, which were close enough to Kansas to feel the pull of cheap lands, hopes for slavery expansion were not high. The *Union and American* in Nashville, a loyal Democratic sheet, quickly saw the danger in squatter sovereignty and argued long and loud against any suggestion that it was a part of the bill. Its constant harpings on this point suggests fear rather than confidence. It never seemed quite certain of its position. This may have stemmed in part from the fact that its Whig neighbor, the *Republican Banner and Nashville Whig*, steadily insisted that "the principle of squatter sovereignty" had been "incorporated in the bill" and that the so-called "great concession to the South" was "a mockery and humbug." "There will never be another slave state formed out of any territory we now possess or which we may hereafter acquire," was its considered opinion. "Mr. Douglas' bill," it repeated, "goes just far enough to *turn loose all the elements of agitation,* but not far enough to be of the slightest value to the South." The bill was a "free-soil" measure, and both Douglas and Pierce accepted that point of view.[54]

Parson Brownlow, over in Knoxville, denounced the bill on grounds of its worthlessness and its tendency to "arouse the whole anti-slavery feeling of the North." "The infamous Nebraska bill" had rendered powerless the moderate men who had "stood up in the North for the constitutional rights of the South." For its passage the Democratic party deserved destruction. In Memphis, at the other end of the state, the *Daily Appeal* urged the South to be calm but resolute in the face of "the fanatical excitement" the bill had stirred. It praised Douglas for the principle he had advanced but thought the victory was one to be achieved on Northern soil.

[53] New Orleans *Bee*, February 4, March 11, 24, May 17, 29, June 7, 1854; New Orleans *Crescent*, November 14, 1854; New Orleans *Bulletin*, June 7, 1854; New Orleans *Delta*, May 30, 1854.

[54] Nashville *Union and American*, March 7, 11, 18, June 23, 29, July 28, 1854; *Republican Banner and Nashville Whig*, March 9, 18, November 4, 1854.

It made no promise of new slave territory and did not urge migration to Kansas until the summer of 1856. The *Eagle and Enquirer*, on the other hand, was soon denouncing the bill as "unwise and unnecessary." The repeal of the Missouri Compromise not only meant freedom in Kansas but freedom everywhere else. "The North, with its teeming millions, already to migrate at a moment's notice, can always best the South colonizing the territories," it protested. The bill was, therefore, "a measure of freedom, in other words, an antislavery measure." [55]

Arkansas opinion followed the same pattern. Democrats praised the "able, and bold, and patriotic" principle of allowing the settlers to vote slavery in or out of the territories. Few, however, made the bold claim that slavery had thereby been extended. Whigs were dubious. They not only denounced the reopening of agitation but saw no new slave territory either above or below the old Missouri Compromise line. There opinion rested, and local problems seemingly crowded the matter out of Arkansas minds. A strange indifference followed until Kansas "began to bleed." [56]

The question immediately arises as to why the Southern representatives, and, in the end, a large proportion of the people, supported a measure which so many thought injurious or of no practical value to their section. Why did they give such ardent support to the efforts of proslavery men in Kansas? Why were they so bitter when Kansas did not become a slave state?

The answers are not simple, but they seem to turn on the point that Southern reactions in the long run were not to the Kansas-Nebraska Bill and what it offered but rather to the Northern reactions to that bill. The Charleston *Mercury* put its finger on the right spot when it said:

"There is no compact sectional sentiment at the South in favor of the Nebraska and Kansas bill; while at the North there is the most intense hostility to it. What is to be done? Can the South stand listlessly by and see the bill repealed, when this is made the direct is-

[55] Knoxville *Whig and Independent Journal*, November 11, 1854; Memphis *Daily Appeal*, July 1, 15, August 4, September 16, 1854; Memphis *Eagle and Enquirer*, August 3, April 24, 1854.
[56] Granville D. Davis, "Arkansas and the Blood of Kansas," in *Journal of Southern History*, XVI (1950), 431–36.

sue against her, and the bond of union, which once secured, is to be used fiercely for her ruin? If the matter ended with the repeal of the Nebraska bill, it might be permitted. But when, as the adroit plans of the Tribune plainly show, abolitionism intends to stoop to this measure merely because it will unite the North against the South, and secure a triumph which it can press to the worst acts of aggression upon her, how can she remain indifferent to the result? If she prizes the citadel, can she neglect the outposts? There is no alternative for the South. When the North presents a sectional issue, and tenders battle upon it, she must meet it, or abide all the consequences of a victory easily won, by a remorseless and eager foe." [57]

This consciousness of the Northern storm and some realization of its full meaning soon colored every reaction and turned support of the Kansas bill into a sectional matter—a struggle for Southern equal rights against "abolitionism." Governor Thomas Bragg of North Carolina spoke for the whole South when he declared:

"We cannot shut our eyes, and ought not if we could, to the spectacle which has lately been presented in the non-slaveholding States of this Union, and to the efforts which have been made. . . . to array section against section and people against people. . . . The day may come . . . when our Northern brethren will discover that the Southern States intend to be equals in the Union, or independent out of it!" [58]

Antislavery had entered a new and wider phase; a more united North now had to be faced. A more bitter opposition had to be met. The Richmond *Enquirer* confessed that it might have been filled with "astonishment and indignation" by the violent opposition to the bill, if it had not been familiar with "the grasping and ferocious nature of the antislavery fanaticism." No one who understood that would be surprised "that a measure so just in regard to the rights of the South, and so reasonable in its operation and effect, should have provoked such denunciation, however strange in itself." To at least hope that slavery might gain a foothold in Kansas thus became a sectional virtue. Common sense no longer had much to do with it.[59]

[57] Charleston *Mercury,* June 21, 1854.
[58] Quoted in Sitterson, *Secession Movement in North Carolina,* 131.
[59] Richmond *Enquirer,* February 2, 1854.

Democratic party loyalty also aided. It is, however, a question whether the bill gained as much from this as the party gained from its support of the measure. Southern Whigs now began to see new virtue in their once-great rival. Many went over without longer hesitation. Others delayed awhile in a new political party which sought to shift issues and to stress a new national outlook—the Know-Nothings. But the fact that the Democratic administration had given its support to a measure that now symbolized Southern equality, whereas Northern Whigs were almost solidly against it, ended the last hopes of a national Whig revival and added new attractiveness to the Democrats.[60] A small step towards political party unity thus was being taken—an essential step towards Southern nationalism. A long road had yet to be traveled, even to regain the driving forces of 1850, yet the Northern shifts had thrown the South off farther to itself, and Kansas had been given a new meaning in sectional and national affairs.

[60] Speaking for Northern Whigs, Benjamin F. Wade declared: "We certainly cannot have any further political connection with the Whigs of the South." *Cong. Globe,* 33 Cong., 1 Sess., Appendix, 764.

CHAPTER IX

SOWING THE WIND

AFTER the Kansas-Nebraska Bill had done its work, few events in the life of the American nation took a normal course or produced normal reactions. Each side was now convinced that the other was an aggressor. Each believed that things it held dear—dearer perhaps than life itself—were being endangered. Distrust and fear and lack of sound information had, in each section, reduced the purposes of the other to a fixed pattern which became more fixed with every additional brush. Events were thus interpreted in set ways, and reactions ceased to conform to events but took shape from some preconceived notion. Suspicion and distortion became the rule. The trust and understanding so essential to the existence of tolerance and a willingness to reason and compromise were being lost. A complete breakdown of the democratic process could not be far off.

The introduction of a moral issue into politics had, moreover, brought a new type to Congress. These men were not politicians in the usual sense; they were social reformers. Their object was to press the slavery issue, to keep it before the public, and to use the floors of Congress as a wider platform from which to speak. Ordinarily such men as Gerrit Smith, Charles Sumner, Benjamin Wade, and Salmon Chase would not seek office, nor would they appeal favorably to the voters. They were too single-minded and too uncompromising for the usual political game by which the democratic process is made to work. As one of Sumner's friends said of him at the time of his election, "there is nothing of the statesman in him. . . . [He] will say anything, and this stands for courage." "He is essentially a man of emotions and sentiments, and it is very easy for him to believe anything to be true that he wishes to. . . . I do not think he has a truthful mind."[1]

Just now, however, statesmanship and truthfulness were not the important things. As a Maine man wrote: "If a man is 'right on slavery' he possesses all the qualifications that are supposed to be necessary adequately to fulfill the duties of a station that has as much to do with slavery as with the affairs of Jiddah." And Sumner was "right on slavery." As Theodore Parker wrote him: "You once told me that you were in morals, not in politics. Now I hope you will show that you are still in morals, although in politics."[2]

That Sumner, as well as Smith and Wade and Chase, was still "in morals" had been clearly revealed in the Kansas-Nebraska debates. That they were not interested in any practical adjustment was made equally clear. "Sir," cried Sumner, "*nothing can be settled which is not right.*" "I shall be blamed for having treated my subject in the light of so severe a morality," said Smith, after having called the government "a bastard democracy" and religion "a bastard Christianity" for permitting slavery. Chase frankly admitted that he would not vote for his own amendments to Douglas' bill and that they were not offered to help solve the practical problems presented. Well might opponents charge that the object was to embarrass and agitate; well might those who hoped for peace and harmony through the democratic process despair.[3]

Kansas quickly revealed the tragic condition into which the nation had fallen. Here was a wide new region opened at the insistence of Western men to meet the desires of settlers, speculators, railroad promoters, and politicians. It bordered Missouri immediately on the west and, according to all precedents in westward migration, would normally receive the largest number of its early settlers from that state. A majority of the remainder, under normal conditions, would come from the Middle West, north and south of the Ohio River. Due to rather unusual economic pressures at the moment in this area, the flow of population might be expected to be both heavy and rapid. Most of the migrants would, in all proba-

---

[1] Lieber to Hilliard, May 4, 1851; Hilliard to Lieber, December 8, 1854, in Lieber Papers.

[2] New York *Herald*, September 13, 1852; Commager, *Theodore Parker*, 256.

[3] *Cong. Globe*, 33 Cong., 1 Sess., Appendix, 529.

bility, be small men of no great property, but the fact that Missouri, Arkansas, Kentucky, and Tennessee were slave states might, here and there, inspire some slaveholders to take advantage of the opportunity offered by Douglas' squatter-sovereignty doctrine. And if, under such conditions, some conflict of interests, a goodly amount of lawlessness, strife over land claims, drunken sprees, and an occasional murder should occur, they would set no new pattern for life in a raw Western territory. Kansas land surveys had not been completed; Indians were still there; and hunger for choice locations, where towns might spring up or a railroad cross, would of course be intense, and men's hopes in proportion.

It should be noted, furthermore, that western Missouri had long been the point of departure for trappers and traders headed for Santa Fe or the upper Missouri River fur regions. Its people had probably retained more than a normal amount of frontier individualism, self-reliance, pride, and an unwillingness to be pushed around. Their faces were turned westward. Profits in trade with the Indians and the army posts across the border had continued an interest stirred by Spanish gold and the harvest of furs. California and Oregon had kept it going. The mines had given it new life. If these people had a kind of proprietary feeling toward Kansas and her soils, if they should resent any effort artificially stimulated by unfriendly groups to seize it, certainly there would be little unnatural about such attitudes.

Unfortunately, however, slaves were most numerous in the Missouri counties nearest Kansas and along the Missouri River bottom. For several years, masters had been deeply concerned about serious losses from runaways encouraged and aided by abolitionists in Iowa and Illinois. The Quakers and Methodists had been particularly troublesome, and "protective associations" against their efforts had already been formed in several counties. The intense reaction to the Kansas-Nebraska Bill in the free states, therefore, created considerable excitement, but its chief effect, at first, seems to have been only to increase the apprehensions of slaveholders for the security of their human property. Meetings were held in several counties, and new "self-defensive associations" formed. Some speakers told of the expressed purpose of Kansas settlers to destroy

PROMINENT SOUTHERNERS OF THE 1850's. *Top to bottom, left:* Howell Cobb, of Georgia; Jefferson Davis, of Mississippi; James L. Orr, of South Carolina; *center:* Samuel Houston, of Texas; Robert M. T. Hunter, of Virginia; *right:* Andrew Johnson, of Tennessee; James H. Hammond, of South Carolina; Robert Toombs, of Georgia. From *Frank Leslie's Illustrated Newspaper* (New York), IX (April 21, 1860), 327.

"BELLE MEADE," NEAR NASHVILLE, TENNESSEE. Built in 1853, replacing house built in 1830. Historic American Buildings Survey, Library of Congress, photograph by Lester Jones.

SERVANTS' CABIN, NEAR NEW ROADS, LOUISIANA. Typical of former slave quarters throughout the Deep South. Historic American Buildings Survey, Library of Congress, photograph by Richard Koch.

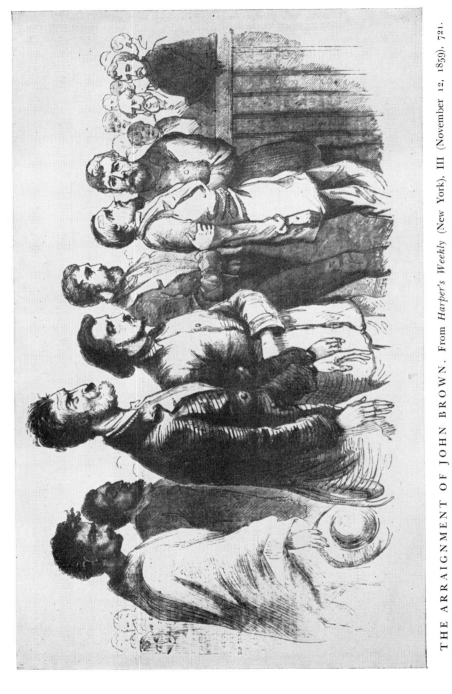

THE ARRAIGNMENT OF JOHN BROWN. From *Harper's Weekly* (New York), III (November 12, 1859), 721.

THE TRIAL OF JOHN BROWN, AT CHARLESTOWN, VIRGINIA, FOR TREASON AND MURDER. From *Harper's Weekly*, III (November 12, 1859), 728.

THE CHARLESTON CONVENTION—INTERIOR OF DOUGLAS' HEADQUARTERS, HIBERNIA HALL, CHARLESTON, SOUTH CAROLINA. From *Frank Leslie's Illustrated Newspaper*, IX (May 5, 1860), 355.

THE DEMOCRATIC CONVENTION AT CHARLESTON,
SOUTH CAROLINA—INTERIOR OF THE HALL OF THE
SOUTH CAROLINA INSTITUTE IN MEETING STREET—
THE CONVENTION IN SESSION. From *Frank Leslie's Illustrated
Newspaper*, IX (May 5, 1860), 359.

slavery *in Missouri*, and one member asked the state legislature to prevent Kansas from becoming an "asylum for abolitionists and freesoilers to harass and destroy our peace and safety." Even Atchison and his friends primarily stressed the need for preparedness against any efforts "to run off your negroes, and depreciate the value of your slaves here." The attitude seems in the early period to have been largely one of local defense. Slavery interests were being alerted. The next step would be aggression.[4]

What happened in Kansas in the next few years, and what men thought happened, played a tragic part in further dividing the already divided North and South and in reducing their differences to an "irrepressible conflict." Out of the Kansas-Nebraska debates there had come a notion, widely accepted in the North, that squatter sovereignty meant a race between free settlers and slaveholders for the possession of Kansas. Victory would belong to the party that was there first with the most. There was also a widespread assumption that the South and slavery had gained "a material advantage" by the passage of the bill. In spite of much denial, Northern men held to this opinion and somehow believed that Southerners were determined to make Kansas a slave state at all cost. Seward had said as much in one of the truly great speeches of the debate. He was confident, however, that unless unfair means were used, "African slave immigration" did not stand a chance against that of the free settlers. "The fountain of slave production" was a frail source compared to the great springs of freemen, native and foreign. So, if the South persisted, his only answer was: "Come on, then, gentlemen of the slave States. Since there is no escaping your challenge, I accept it in behalf of the cause of freedom. We will engage in competition for the virgin soil of Kansas, and God give the victory to the side which is stronger in numbers as it is in right." [5]

That put the issue, as far as the South was concerned, on a new basis that had nothing to do with the fitness or unfitness of Kansas

[4] St. Louis *Daily New Era*, September 23, October 29, 1846; Hannibal *Missouri Courier*, March 2, 1854; St. Louis *Daily Missouri Democrat*, March 4, 1854; Juanita Schoff, "The Proslavery Activities of David R. Atchison" (M.A. thesis, University of Chicago, 1952), 40–89.

[5] *Cong. Globe*, 33 Cong., 1 Sess., Appendix, 768, 771.

for slavery. This was to be a test of sectional strength, a contest of conflicting principles. As Seward put it, there was "suspended on the issue of this contest the political equilibrium between the free and the slave States." And everything hung on that equilibrium because "Slavery and freedom . . . [were] antagonistic elements in this country. . . . They . . . [had] been at war with each other ever since the Government was established, and that war . . . [was] to continue for ever." It would have to end either "in a separation of the antagonistic parties, or in the establishment of superiority by one of the parties." And since entangled economic interests forbade separation, there could be only one outcome. The repeal of the Missouri Compromise had taught the North that anything could be repealed or changed. It had the strength, and Southern aggression in this case might lead the North into drastic retaliatory action that would hasten the inevitable.

Under such circumstances, the mere assertion of the abstract principle of sectional equality in the territories was mockery. If a race was to take place, there must be contestants. If the settlement of Kansas had something to do with the place which the South and her institutions were to hold in American life, then the outcome was not a matter for indifference. Northern attitudes required a new outlook. Some Southerners began to talk of the necessity of making Kansas a slave state.

Meanwhile, theory and talk had given way to action out on the plains of Kansas. There forces, some perfectly normal and some quite the opposite, were writing one of the tragic pages in American history. Taking squatter sovereignty at its face value, the New England Emigrant Aid Company had been incorporated for the purpose of assisting free immigration to Kansas. Already it had started groups westward, and a colony had grown up at Lawrence. Missourians had answered by crossing the border to dominate the elections of a territorial delegate to Congress and of the territorial legislature. Some may have been prospective settlers; most were angry invaders. Neither group, however, had greatly disturbed the normal flow of incoming settlers. Most of these came from the Ohio Valley, and the larger percentage of them were middle-class freemen who could better themselves in a new country. Even the foreign-born soon outnumbered the Missourians. A few slaveholders made the trek, but the percentage was never large, and only two slaves remained to be counted in the Census of 1860.[6]

A considerable amount of lawlessness and confusion existed in Kansas from the beginning. Some of this grew out of land disputes, eagerness for gain and advantage, and personal differences. Much came from the efforts of half-organized bands of Missourians who, having taken a hand in the setting up of government, came over or threatened to come, at intervals, to see that things ran according to their wishes. This was not an entirely unique procedure in westward expansion, and Iowans were doing much the same thing at this very time in Nebraska. But in this case slavery was involved, and the struggle between the sections over slavery expansion was drawing near the breaking point. Yet there is no evidence, other than assumption, that all the Missourians who crossed over into Kansas were slaveholders or that their motive was exclusively that of establishing slavery in the territory. Since some slaves were already there, the enactment of the Missouri slave code along with other Missouri laws does not prove the case. On the other hand, there was much in the Missourians' character and in the circumstances that indicates a more or less spontaneous action to meet what they believed to be an organized effort by a hostile group to put something over on them. Proslavery attitudes under such conditions might mean little or much.[7]

But regardless of what was or was not the purpose or purposes of the Missourians, the free-soil settlers at Lawrence, who had come out to save Kansas from slavery, were thoroughly convinced that all that had been done was a part of a proslavery scheme. Refusing to accept the government as established or to recognize the authority of its acts or its officials, they set up a rival government and asked for its recognition. Individuals or bands of men under such leaders as

---

[6] Craven, *Coming of the Civil War*, 357–67. For sources of Kansas population, see James C. Malin, *John Brown and the Legend of Fifty-Six* (Philadelphia, 1942), 511–15.

[7] Malin, *John Brown and the Legend of Fifty-Six*, 498–511. Malin's comment on the difficulty of getting at the truth in the Kansas story is worthy of quotation: "The history of the Kansas question has been so completely overlaid with propaganda that it is only with great difficulty and at the expense of some tediousness that the historian can reconstruct even an approximate picture of the contemporary scene." *Ibid.*, 31. The writer has relied on Malin's interpretation and materials because the writer is convinced that he affords the only sound treatment of the Kansas story.

John Brown matched violence with violence, and the strife between the supporters of "law and order"—meaning the "proslavery" supporters—and the free-state men at times assumed the proportions of full-scale warfare. "Bleeding Kansas" crowded its way into national consciousness and began to serve causes not its own. Regardless of what was involved in the complex affairs of this western territory, the struggle everywhere—in Kansas itself at times—came to be seen and understood as one between proslavery and free-soil men. Governors who tried to face realities as they found them pleased no one, were denounced by one side or the other and often by both, and in the end gave up, branded as abolitionists or as the tools of slavery.

Yet amid the smoke and confusion of public reaction, sober voices in Kansas constantly qualified both the degree and the character of the struggle. Kansas, to most men east of the Mississippi River, meant what Iowa or any other open region in this depressing period meant—cheap lands and a chance to begin over again. They did not start for Kansas to make it free or slave. They went to make a home. In the fall of 1854 an Independence newspaper declared that anyone who would take the trouble to make a short excursion into the territory would find men from different parts of the country "cozily sheltered in the same cabin," living together in harmony. "They all seek to better their condition in life," it continued, "and to secure, if so be they can, the little lordship of one hundred and sixty acres of mother earth, whereon to propagate no matter what, but opinion least of all." Feelings generated outside, however, could not be escaped. Soon Governor John W. Geary was reporting that "Large parties, both from the North and South, are daily arriving with pre-existing prejudices and hostile feelings, which will greatly increase the difficulty of preserving the peace of the territory." He was right. Soon lawless bands, intent on the service of a cause or interested in plunder or adventure, were roaming about, disturbing the peace and providing the outside world with the kind of news it expected. Yet while this went on, one Lieutenant McIntosh of the regular army could speak of "persons who have no interest in the struggle" but were "quietly living on their claims." A fellow officer threw even more light on the situation by his report that: "There are so many rumors afloat, and so little truth in them, that it is difficult to separate them from falsehood." A third added another angle: "The disorders in the Territory," he said, "have, in fact, changed their character, and consist now of robberies and assassinations, by a set of bandits whom the excitement of the times has attracted hither." His superior officer confirmed this impression. He charged that armed bands belonging to both parties were "taking advantage of the political excitement to commit their own rascally acts." [8]

Thus it seems perfectly clear that no single approach to the Kansas situation gives the whole story. Yet a simple single explanation of affairs was what partisans wanted and received. No other kind would have served their needs. No other would have fitted their expectations or satisfied their honest though twisted beliefs. Southerners had to see Kansas as being unfairly torn from their grasp. Republicans had to see the failure of all administration efforts. Abolitionists had to see the ruthless slaveholder boldly taking every advantage to advance his power. Reporters and politicians gave each what was wanted, and "Kansas 'bled' all over the floors of Congress and over the pages of the country's press." James C. Malin, the only scholar who seems able to deal with Kansas in a thoroughly objective way, shows how the reporters "on the scene" distorted facts and concocted stories to fit the biased needs of the New York *Tribune,* the Chicago *Tribune,* the Boston *Daily Evening Traveller,* and the Cincinnati *Commercial.* The object, he says, was to keep the antislavery issue alive and to show that the responsibility for outrages rested squarely on the shoulders of "Franklin Pierce and the democratic party." On such a fare, the Republican party could grow and prosper.[9]

Opposition papers protested. The St. Louis *Evening News* was moved to write in the spring of 1856: "It is refreshing to turn from the acrimonious wrangles and bitter disputes in Congress, where Kansas affairs are represented as they are *not,* to the peaceful, smiling Territory itself, where we can see things as they are. . . . By our files of western Missouri and Kansas exchanges, we see that the people of the Territory are over head and ears—not in fighting—but in farming." [10]

[8] *Ibid.,* 31–88, especially 78–88, for official materials.   [9] *Ibid.,* 89–116.
[10] St. Louis *Evening News,* April 16, 1856, quoted *ibid.,* 109.

"Proslavery" papers in Kansas charged the "Black Republicans" with a determination "to keep up the excitement in Kansas in order to have some hobby of which to manufacture political capital to carry them through the approaching Presidential election." They complained against the tales of "butchery, massacre and murder" which "lying correspondents and telegraphic reporters" were sending to the press. They charged Republicans, who had defeated every move in Congress to get some settlement of Kansas affairs, with a desire to keep up the cry of "bleeding Kansas" as long as it was politically profitable.

Thus consciously and unconsciously Kansas affairs were twisted to fit a pattern. It could not have been otherwise. What was going on there was something far bigger than the settlement of a new territory. A nation was in the process of dissolution. Kansas was only a symbol—something to be seen and interpreted as proving things men feared or wanted proved. It had become the battleground of ideas, a place where advantages might be gained for parties and factions. The outcome of the struggle there would mean victory of one section and the defeat of another. Right and wrong were involved. Normal conditions were impossible and sound reactions to events equally impossible. Violence was inevitable when so much was at stake. "Bleeding Kansas" as a symbol was more important than "Kansas, the Territory."

Now that Kansas symbolized the conflict between North and South, and between freedom and slavery as themselves the symbols of two sets of values and ways of life, Southerners no longer talked about "the principle of equality." They talked about making Kansas a slave state. The sharp change in Northern feelings as shown by the spring and fall elections of 1854 had thoroughly alarmed those who still counted on Democratic solidarity. Howell Cobb had to admit that the party had "been literally slaughtered in the Northern, Middle and Western States, whilst of the Whig party there is not left even a monumental remembrance." Southern papers took note of the Northern boast that at last there was "a North" which knew its rights and would henceforth defend them. They answered with a plea for a united South. That was the only way to resist "a warfare, unceasing, aggressive, and insulting, waged upon the rights, interests and feelings of the South." It was the only answer to "an arrogant majority, flushed with success," which now threatened to exert its power in the next Congress against the section.[11]

Kansas was a demonstration of this aggression at work. The migration of Missouri men to Kansas, said the Richmond *Enquirer,* was a perfectly normal affair and would have remained so if the New England Emigrant Aid Society had not altered it. It was normal for the Missouri group to have an interest there; it was not normal that the Massachusetts group should. "They did not profess to go there because it was the nearest unoccupied territory, because they preferred it to the other new States and territories, nor to cultivate the lands; but by express bargain with the Boston Emigration Aid Society, to seize upon the territory and exclude slaveholders." [12]

The Charleston *Mercury* viewed the matter in the same light. Abolitionists had gotten up "a kind of fury of emigration to Kansas" for the sole purpose of seizing the territorial government and stamping it with the character of antislavery from the outset. Missourians could not remain "idle spectators of proceedings so hostile to their security." They were "willing that things should . . . [have taken] their natural course, but they . . . [had] no intention of being made the victims of a deliberate Abolition conspiracy." They did not intend that their western border should be settled by people who were sent there "pledged to the one absorbing sentiment of hostility to them." They were not willing to have "an Abolition State got up by subscription in their very sight." And since it was beyond hope "that emigration . . . [would] be allowed to take its natural course, and determine calmly, in the progress of time, what . . . [should] be the institutions of Kansas," the issue had to be met on the North's level. It would "be a struggle of fanaticism and political rancor on one side, and of plain self-defense on the other." [13]

This notion that Missourians and their interests were the pri-

[11] Cobb to James Buchanan, December 5, 1854, in Phillips (ed.), *Correspondence of Toombs, Stephens, and Cobb,* 348; Macon *Georgia Telegraph,* November 7, 1854; Huntsville *Southern Advocate,* January 13, 1855.

[12] Richmond *Enquirer,* December 22, 1855.

[13] Charleston *Mercury,* June 24, 1854.

mary consideration in Kansas seems to have been generally accepted throughout the South during the early period. The Montgomery *Mail* spoke of the absurd belief held in the North that the Kansas bill transferred a "vast territory, consecrated to the genius of freedom, . . . to the cruel Moloch of the slave power," and of the resulting crusade "preached by the St. Bernards of an unholy and impure fanaticism to conquer the new territory." It praised the Missourians for their courage in resisting. "Honor," it declared, "called them imperatively to resent a movement which wore the shape of a deliberate insult to their State. . . . They did not make the issue, it was forced upon them." Self-preservation required prompt action.[14]

The Mobile *Register* likewise justified the Missourians who had only "acted in an emergency that admitted of no delay, on the impregnable principle of self-defense." There may have been some lawlessness, it admitted, but those "who themselves personally disregard the constitution and trample on the laws" have "no right to complain of violence and prate about law." [15]

A new note, however, soon appeared. The Kansas struggle was more than a local affair. The South and her institutions were being attacked in Kansas. Missourians had been fighting the whole section's battle. As the Jacksonville (Alabama) *Republican* put it: "Missourians have nobly defended *our* rights and will continue to defend them, and the South will support its valiant vanguard. . . . The first blow has been struck, and blood has been spilled on the borders of Missouri. The cause of that State is the common cause of all the Southern states." Kansas was only revealing "the burning animosity" which had been engendered against the South and Southern institutions by "long years of incendiarism" at the North. The Kansas "assassins" were the "acknowledged representatives of a large and powerful party in the Northern States . . . the whole spirit of whose political theory . . . [was] hostility to the South." Kansas was but the first step in a program "the final scenes of which they hope[d] to behold realized when, in the language of the traitor Wilson of Massachusetts, 'the Southern mother shall clasp her babe with wilder fondness to her bosom when she hears at her door at midnight the tramp and voice of the black avenger'." The abstrac-

[14] Montgomery *Mail*, May 5, 1855.   [15] Mobile *Register*, May 16, 1855.

tions of the slavery debate had, indeed, become momentously practical in Kansas. "Stripped of all its surroundings of forms," as the
Charleston *Mercury* said, what was happening there was "simply
a war between the North and the South." [16]

As this fact became clear, men stirred from "a long and almost
unaccountable apathy," and talk of concrete action took its place.
"We must meet and repel this assault with the same means" employed by the North, said the *Mercury*. "We must send men to
Kansas, ready to cast in their lot with the proslavery party there
and able to meet Abolitionism on its own issue, and with its own
weapons." "There is more virtue in the gleam of a bayonet or the
whistle of an eager bullet than in all the eloquence of wisdom or
practice of Christian forbearance," echoed the Montgomery *Advertiser and Gazette*. It was of the opinion that thousands of men
would go to Kansas if only the effort were made to enlist them and
facilities offered for their going. Certainly there were tens of thousands who could and would give money if any mode of its application were suggested.[17]

Little that was practical, however, came from such talk. Kansas
was far off and cold. The broad open lands of sunny Texas were
far more inviting. And besides, the migration of slaveholders had
normally been south and west, where cotton lands lured. Only the
upland Southerner, who wanted to leave slavery behind, had gone
north and west.

The movement started out bravely enough. Meetings were held
widely over the Lower South and resolutions were passed with a
will. At Columbus, Georgia, the good citizens resolved that:
"Whereas the action of the non-slaveholding States with regard to
the settlement of Kansas Territory, has thwarted the natural laws
of increase and immigration, and tends to force upon that Territory their peculiar institutions in violation of the spirit and intent
of the Kansas-Nebraska act: it behooves the South and every patriot
who desires to preserve the equality of the Southern States in the
Union to counteract these insidious attempts of Northern Aboli-

---

[16] Jacksonville *Republican*, August 9, 1855; Natchez *Mississippi Free Trader*,
December 7, 1855; Mobile *Register*, November 6, 1855; Charleston *Mercury*, February
22, 1856.

[17] Montgomery *Advertiser and Gazette*, June 14, 1856.

tionists to stifle the free action of the citizens of Kansas in the formation of their social institutions, and thus to convert that magnificent domain into an engine of oppression to the South." The people of Hancock County, Mississippi, a bit more practical, resolved to learn even from their enemies "that unity and combination give strength and success." So they invited their sister counties to join in the "organizing of associations to enable vigorous and patriotic Southern men to immigrate to Kansas, to aid our brethren there, lawfully at the ballot box, and, if necessary, with the cartridge box." They raised over five hundred dollars, at one dollar per member, for the cause.[18]

Other groups, from South Carolina to Arkansas, did equally well at resolving. Since "the battle for the equality of the South in the Union . . . [was] to be settled on the Plains of Kansas," they were ready to "meet rifle with rifle, and knife with knife." Yet most of their efforts ended right there. A few citizens offered to give money to send others to Kansas, but only a handful prepared to go themselves. One E. B. Bell of Edgefield, South Carolina, attempted to raise a body of settlers "to go to Kansas and uphold Southern institutions," and Preston Brooks offered to give $250 whenever one hundred volunteers were ready to leave, but there is no record that he ever had to meet his obligation. The efforts of R. G. Earle of Jacksonville, Alabama, who offered to lead a party of "gentlemen" of substance to Kansas met with equal indifference. Here and there a few individuals, bent on adventure, and willing to take the money offered by some local "Kansas Association," set out for the territory, but the only move from the South of any proportions was the one sponsored by Jefferson Buford of Alabama. Even that one was of little actual significance. Selling his slaves to raise funds, he advertised for three hundred able-bodied men to whom he promised land and support for a year. He originally intended to take women and slaves along, but found the response great enough to enable him to limit the party to men over eighteen years of age. These were to rendezvous at Eufaula, Alabama, Columbus, Georgia, and Montgomery, Alabama, and were to proceed by boat to New Orleans and

[18] Cahawba (Ala.) *Dallas Gazette*, November 2, 1855; Montgomery *Advertiser and Gazette*, January 5, 1856 (reports the Hancock County meeting).

thence, by rail, to Nashville. They were to be organized in companies of fifty, each under its own officers.[19]

When the time of departure arrived, fewer "volunteers" appeared than had been promised. Less than 250 left Montgomery after being blessed by a Methodist minister in a Baptist church, and only 280 men were in the party when it departed from New Orleans. Most of them were poor men who, according to all the evidence available, would have been far more attracted by Buford's promise of forty acres of good Kansas land and support for a year than by any burning desire to make Kansas a slave state.[20]

The effort to meet the North on equal terms in Kansas had been a complete failure. Even the people of Arkansas on the very border of the territory were willing to let the cause in Kansas go by default. The blunt truth of the matter was that Kansas, after all, was only a symbol, and the effort to deal with it as a concrete matter from which nothing concrete was to be expected could produce little action. The Southern people had abandoned it, even though their politicians had not. Voices of protest began to be heard on all sides.

Openly the Charleston *Standard* denounced the effort to colonize Kansas and urged "men of high character and elevated purposes" to discountenance the move. This "raising money, men and arms," it asserted, could only lead to violence and to disunion. Slavery would not be strengthened by extension; it would profit far more by consolidation and improvement. The Charleston *Patriot* and the Winnsboro *Register* joined in the attack. They were frank to admit that the South could not compete with the North in this kind of emigration. Kansas would never be a slave state, and men and money sent there would be permanently lost. This was the point constantly stressed by the *Republican Banner and Nashville Whig*. To race with the North for Kansas was a perfectly futile business. The slaveholders must be beaten. "They cannot 'pack up

[19] Montgomery *Advertiser and Gazette*, January 5, June 14, 1856; Little Rock *True Democrat*, September 3, 1856; Davis, "Arkansas and the Blood of Kansas," *loc. cit.*, 441–43; Charleston *Mercury*, February 4, 1856; Jacksonville *Republican*, March 11, 1856; Charleston *Courier*, June 4, 1856.

[20] Cahawba *Dallas Gazette*, February 8, 1856, for Jefferson Buford's letter of instructions; Montgomery *Journal*, April 7, 1856; Walter L. Fleming, "The Buford Expedition to Kansas," in *American Historical Review*, VI (1900–1901), 38–48.

their all' in a night and be off," it said. And if they could, how many would do it? How many would risk their slave property in Kansas, where security was to be determined by the outcome of a settlement race? [21]

Others simply lost heart because the people did not respond. The *Mississippi Free Trader* lamented the fact that in spite of a clear realization of what "the mercenary fanatics" of the Northern emigrant-aid associations were doing and "the importance of preventing this," the Southern people were doing "nothing, nothing." The South simply would not unite. Not even a majority would unite. Kansas was at the very moment "a theatre of civil war," yet the South slept on in false security. Congressman Henry M. Shaw of North Carolina expressed equal amazement and alarm at "the stolid indifference and the apathy with which the people of the South" were viewing "the fearful struggle . . . going on between the friends of the South & the Rights of the States, . . . and the deadly enemies of both." There was little use in trying to match the North in Kansas when the people felt this way. His colleague William R. Smith of Alabama spoke of the overwhelming advantage which the North possessed for invading Kansas "with homeless foreigners" and of its superior means for travel. "I would not advise the South to continue this fruitless competition," he said. It was a waste of effort.[22]

Most of this criticism of the Southern efforts in Kansas came from Whig and Know-Nothing sources. Their emphasis on national unity and their dislike of agitation made them critical not only of force in Kansas but of the whole sectional controversy. This led papers like the Richmond *Whig* and the Augusta *Chronicle and Sentinel* now to denounce the "Kansas bill" as the cause of all troubles. The *Whig* expressed "sensations much akin to nausea" when forced to allude to the slavery-abolition struggle, and the *Sentinel* wanted an end to the whole strife over slavery. The repeal

21 Charleston *Standard*, quoted in Charleston *Mercury*, February 16, 1856; Boucher, "South Carolina and the South on the Eve of Secession," in Washington University *Studies, Humanistic Series*, VI, No. 2, pp. 100–101; Charleston *Mercury*, March 31, April 9, 1857; *Republican Banner and Nashville Whig*, August 9, 1856.

22 Natchez *Mississippi Free Trader*, September 10, 1856; Sitterson, *Secession Movement in North Carolina*, 138; *Cong. Globe*, 34 Cong., 1 Sess., Appendix, 160 (William R. Smith).

of the Missouri Compromise was a mistake. Colonization of Kansas was impossible. Agitation might aid politicians, but every "right thinking" man in the South knew it was "an evil of the first magnitude." If this were continued, it would array "men of the same language, descent, and Christian faith" against each other in deadly strife. It could only end in civil war. "Let the South declare her determination against all agitators," it urged. Let her representatives in Washington agree to abide by existing legislation, endure no encroachments, and commit none. Then when efforts to raise sectional issues were made they could refuse to waste time on these useless discussions and insist that Congress proceed "to the legitimate business of the country." The Prattville (Alabama) *Statesman* called for "a rope for the neck" of those who had brought the agitation in Kansas. It would have Douglas, "not the black-skinned Douglas, but the black hearted Douglas, be the first to test the strength of it." A speaker at the Know-Nothing state convention in Georgia spoke of the author of the Kansas bill as "Stephen Arnold," a traitor to his country! [23]

Meanwhile in Washington, far removed from the realities of Kansas and shut in by the gloomy walls of House and Senate, men from North and South, angered by Kansas reports and irritated by personal contacts, pretended to be carrying on the nation's business. The Thirty-fourth Congress had assembled early in December, 1855. Political lines were so chaotic that the *Congressional Globe,* which usually classified House members by party, gave up in despair. Kansas and Nebraska had made their own divisions. The attempt to elect a Speaker and organize for work ended in a hopeless deadlock. Day after day and week after week the voting continued with bitter debate over Kansas affairs interspersed. Anti-Nebraska men quickly lined up behind Nathaniel P. Banks of Massachusetts. He was a former Democrat turned Republican, and most of his support, but not all of it, came from that party. The Democrats voted for William A. Richardson of Illinois, and the Know-Nothings, who were not supporting Banks, backed Henry

[23] Richmond *Whig,* quoted in Huntsville *Southern Advocate,* August 8, 1855; Augusta *Chronicle and Sentinel,* October 16, February 26, 1856; Prattville (Ala.) *Statesman,* June 18, 1855; Augusta *Constitutionalist,* July 17, 1856.

M. Fuller of Pennsylvania. Enough votes were always scattered to other candidates to prevent a majority. Not until February 2, when the opposition to Banks had seemingly shifted its support to William Aiken, a Know-Nothing from South Carolina, was it possible to pass a resolution declaring that after three more trials the man who received the largest vote should become speaker. Then the division became strictly sectional, party lines already weak entirely disappeared, and Banks was elected without the aid of a single Southern vote.[24]

Republicans hailed this as a party triumph. It was not exactly that, but it was a *Northern* victory and the Republican party was rapidly becoming the carrier of *Northern* interests. Southerners understood this. Toombs wrote that "The election of Banks has given great hopes to our enemies, and their policy is dangerous in the extreme to us"; Albert Gallatin Brown thought the spirit behind the election "the most vindictive and devilish ever manifested by men living under the same government." "They pursue their objects with a fiendish delight and increasing pertinacity," he said. "It seems to me that the Union of our fathers is hopelessly lost." [25]

President Pierce had not waited for the House to elect its Speaker before submitting his message. He upheld the repeal of the Missouri Compromise and the principle of popular sovereignty but said little about affairs in Kansas. He followed this, however, on January 24, with a special message in which he denounced the emigrant aid societies and upheld the legality of the Kansas legislature as set up by what was being called "the proslavery forces." That was fuel for a fire already burning. The distortions and extravagances of Congressional oratory were now added to the troubles of an already overtroubled nation.

The speeches in House and Senate seldom bore any resemblance to rational discussion of issues. Northerners viewed the New England emigrants as near saints intent only on finding a home in a fair land. They saw the Missourians and other Southerners as fiendish

24 *Cong. Globe,* 34 Cong., 1 Sess., 3–343.

25 Boston *Liberator,* February 8, 1856, headed its editorial, "The North Victorious"; Toombs to Thomas, February 9, 1856, in Phillips (ed.), *Correspondence of Toombs, Stephens, and Cobb,* 361; Ranck, *Albert Gallatin Brown,* 143; Fred H. Harrington, "The First Northern Victory," in *Journal of Southern History,* V (1939), 186–205.

devils bent on inflicting a crime upon this haven. Southerners viewed these same New Englanders as the armed mercenaries of fanaticism, and these same Missourians as honest men defending their property and their vital interests. Northerners charged that Missourians started it all and that their own organizations were but an answer to "blue lodges" already existing and to threats already made. Southerners answered that the New England moves began before the Kansas act had passed and that first settlers were welcomed until their threats against Missouri itself grew too blatant. Few seemed to be interested in what the truth might be. Assertions were as serviceable as facts. Gossip and rumor or wild report obtained from some newspaper served as unquestioned proof.

If such speeches did little to reveal truth, they did much to increase sectional and personal bitterness. From behind the cloak of righteous indignation, Senators and Representatives alike launched violent attacks not only on opponents but on the states they represented. As Representative Augustus E. Maxwell of Florida said, "the watchword of the day . . . [was] 'aggression.' " Senator Henry Wilson of Massachusetts struck out savagely at Atchison and the people of Missouri, while Senator James C. Jones of Tennessee made no effort to conceal his utter contempt for Wilson and Massachusetts. Congressman Mordecai Oliver of Missouri was quick to resent the term "border ruffians" as applied to the citizens of his state, but was equally quick to call New Englanders "intermeddlers." When Representative Henry S. Bennett of Mississippi chided Massachusetts with openly setting at defiance the laws of the nation, William S. Damrell from the Old Bay State sarcastically reminded him of the fact that Massachusetts had *never repudiated her honest debts.*" [26]

There was little of sweetness about such clashes, but they were only mild indications of a temper that would find full expression in the masterful tirade of Charles Sumner and the brutal answer given by Preston S. Brooks.

Sumner was one of those figures who should never have been in politics but whom the abnormal times and issues had put there. He was as extreme, unbalanced, and dangerous as the issues themselves,

[26] *Cong. Globe,* 34 Cong., 1 Sess., Appendix, 496 (Augustus E. Maxwell), 95–102 (Henry Wilson and James C. Jones), 196 (William S. Damrell).

and no picture of him can be drawn which reveals the man so perfectly as his own speech of May 19, 1856. He called it "The Crime Against Kansas." [27]

It was the speech of a learned man in the sense that he could quote from the classics, use fine phrases, and cast his philippic after the pattern of Cicero denouncing Cataline. It was a shockingly shallow performance, abstract and unreal, and lacking in sound grasp of issues. It contained nothing new but only repeated in extreme fashion what others had already said. It was egotistical, generously sprinkled with the personal pronoun, overornate, bombastic, and shot through and through with the arrogance of one speaking for God Himself. It was the speech of an actor, lost in the part he was playing and personally not conscious of any responsibility for what he was saying. It was a dangerous speech because its author could see only one side of a question and assumed there was no other. It was in bad taste because of the cheap personalities indulged in, and unsportsmanlike, because of attack on persons not present.

Yet it had a certain strength because it had that kind of sincerity which belongs to those who do not respect the opinions of others and believe, at the moment, what they are saying because they themselves are saying it. Its "holier than thou" moral tone was not offensive to a people whose emotions were deeply stirred and who sensed a crusade under way. Even its violence and its reliance on rumor in place of fact was acceptable to a people accustomed to Kansas reports. This same overwrought temper caused a speech to be answered and later revenged that might better have been ignored or laughed at.

Cass started to deal with it in the right vein by saying: "I have listened with equal regret and surprise to the speech of the honorable Senator from Massachusetts. Such a speech—the most un-American and unpatriotic that ever grated on the ears of the members of this high body—as I hope never to hear again here or elsewhere."

He should have stopped there, or at least with the next com-

[27] *Ibid.,* 529–44. Charles Sumner's reliance on newspaper reports is interesting. He wrote his friend Theodore Parker that he intended his speech to be "the most thorough philippic ever uttered in a legislative body." Moorfield Storey, *Charles Sumner* (Boston, 1900), 138 ff.

ment, that the speech was open to the "highest censure and disapprobation." But he went on to answer false statements made regarding Michigan. That dignified what he had just denounced.

Douglas also took the sound course when he said that he did "not deem it necessary to say one word" in reply. The temptation to talk, however, was too great and he went on. Even his comment on the ridiculousness of the charge that three fourths of the Senate were guilty of fraud, swindling, crime, and infamy, and his question as to whether Sumner's object was "to provoke some of us to kick him as we would a dog in the street, that he may get sympathy upon the just chastisement," might have served a purpose. But Douglas too went on to defend himself and to weaken the impression which Sumner's speech had made. By the time he had finished, Sumner had been reinstated in a position where some might think he should be punished, not ignored.[28]

Tragically, Preston Brooks, relative of the aged Senator Butler, whom Sumner had unjustifiably attacked, assumed the responsibility for this kind of an answer. He too was the type of man who should never have been in politics. He understood little of the democratic process; he knew as little of tolerance as did Sumner. To him, persons were more important than principles. He was immature enough to think that violence answers violence. A few days later, while the Senator sat writing at his desk after the adjournment of that body, Brooks approached with a small gutta-percha walking stick in his hand.[29] After informing Sumner that he had read his speech and found it a libel on South Carolina and her venerable representative, he struck the Senator some dozen or more times over the head and shoulders with his cane. Sumner, attempting to rise, wrenched his desk from its moorings and, in the confusion, fell to the floor stunned and bleeding. Friends now intervened, and Dr. Cornelius Boyle was called to attend to Sumner's injuries. He found three scalp wounds, only two of which required attention. These were cuts to the skull some two inches long which required two stitches each. When this was completed, Sumner went to his room,

[28] *Cong. Globe,* 34 Cong., 1 Sess., Appendix, 544 (Lewis Cass), 544–46 (Douglas).

[29] The writer has taken the material on Preston S. Brooks's assault from the *Cong. Globe,* 34 Cong., 1 Sess., 1347–67, on the assumption that it gave a balanced official report.

where the doctor visited him an hour later and found the bleeding stopped and the patient "doing very well." Five days later he declared Sumner able to return to his duties—even able to wear his hat.

From that point forward, facts grow dim. Dr. Boyle was dismissed, Sumner taken to the home of Francis Preston Blair, who had recently presided at the convention launching the new Republican party, and other physicians called. They declared Sumner incapacitated "for the time being," and stressed the matter of the shock he had received and the effect of this, due to "the peculiar condition of his nervous system at the time, a condition induced by severe mental exertion, and nervous tension from the loss of sleep for several consecutive nights, also by the peculiar susceptibility of his temperament, which is highly nervous." [30]

It would thus seem that Preston Brooks had been very unfortunate in his selection of the individual whose words he had chosen to answer by blows. He probably intended insult more than the inflicting of severe physical injury, or he would have used a more deadly weapon. Under excitement he was evidently more vigorous than he had intended to be, for all testimony agreed that his blows were delivered with all his strength. That, however, was the least of his offense. His act was rash from any point of view, but it was downright foolhardy at this time to attack any Republican Senator, let alone one to whom the mental and nervous shock would be as great or greater than the physical injury inflicted. Martyrs are always dangerous. In this era when symbols were far more powerful than realities, they were doubly so. "Bleeding Kansas" had wrought unmeasured damage to the nation. "Bleeding Sumner" might do as much.

Again it was not a case in which the facts were important. The question of the seriousness of Sumner's physical injury is one that cannot be answered with complete assurance. Neither can that of Brooks's intentions. Sumner did not return to his seat in the Senate until December, 1859, but he did travel widely and indulge in a strenuous social life. If the testimony of the attending physician before the House committee be accepted, his injury consisted of "nothing but flesh wounds," and he "might have taken a carriage

[30] New York *Tribune,* October 8, 1856.

and driven as far as Baltimore on the next day without any injury."
His "turn for the worse," it should be noted, came with a stream of
sympathetic, but bitter and excited, visitors and the realization of
the intense public interest which the assault had created. Sumner's
conduct in these days, as described by Joshua Giddings in his speech
of July 11, was that of a dramatic actor playing a part. Looking at
the Ohio Representative "with great solemnity of countenance and
deep emotions" he dramatically said: "I sometimes am led to appre-
hend that I may yet be doomed to that heaviest of all afflictions, to
spend my time on earth in a living sepulcher." He was not sham-
ming. "The peculiar susceptibility of his temperament, which is
highly nervous," aggravated by a shock, physical and mental, and
that genuine quality of an actor which merges the man completely
into the part played, were manifesting themselves in the new Sumner, the martyr, the symbol. Where this ended and physical injury
began Sumner did not know, the public did not know, the historian
cannot know.[31]

As to Brooks's intentions, there is equal confusion. Both the
constant charge made by Sumner's friends that a "murderous" assault with a "bludgeon" had been made, and the obvious efforts of
the House committee to show that the weapon used might have
killed, reveal an intention to make the most out of the affair. The
only statement made by Brooks before his act was that he was going to *punish* Sumner for the insults to his state and his relative.
The size of the cane used was well established at the hearings. It
was a hollow gutta-percha stick about one inch in diameter at the
top and five eighths of an inch at the bottom. The rim was about
three sixteenths of an inch in thickness. It broke after four or five
blows. Brooks in his speech of July 14 denied any intention to
murder and spoke of his anticipation of legal punishment for "a
simple assault and battery." He made no effort to strike Sumner
after he fell to the floor. He sent an apology to the Senate for any
infringement of its rights. He paid his fine of $300 in the Wash-
ington court.

This much we know from testimony given under oath at the time.

[31] *Cong. Globe,* 34 Cong., 1 Sess., Appendix, 1119. For valuable aid in understanding
Sumner, the writer is indebted to Dr. Thomas French. See "Alleged Assault upon
Senator Sumner," in *House Reports of Committees,* 34 Cong., 1 Sess., I, No. 182.

Yet there was also the confession of sleepless nights and a decision not to use a cowhide whip. There was also, beyond doubt, the realization of the chances being taken in striking any person over the head with any kind of a walking stick. The existence of blind anger and the striking of savage blows that were heard throughout the Senate chamber were attested to by a dozen witnesses. That he intended to render Sumner unconscious, however, is an inference that finds no justification whatsoever in anything said or done.

These are the only facts available. They are important only as contrast to the fiction which quickly took their place and to which the great majority of Americans reacted.[32]

Excitement and bitterness in Congress reached new levels with the Brooks-Sumner affair. Kansas had been far off and somewhat abstract to most members. Here was something concrete right at hand which satisfied every preconceived notion and served every purpose. A demonstration of free-soil and of "border ruffian" tactics had appeared in Congress.

A startling difference in approach to the assault by Southerners and Northerners was apparent at once. Most Southerners viewed it as a strictly personal affair between one individual who had used insulting language and another individual who rightly resented such flagrant irresponsibility. Sumner deserved to be checked and the use of physical retaliation in the form of a caning was pardonable even though subject to legal penalties. The official status of the individuals and the attention which the Senate and the House should pay to the matter were Constitutional questions, questions of jurisdiction. Some openly approved of Brooks's act and thought the fact that the Senate was not in session at the moment divested it of any official significance. Others did not approve of the use of physical force or of the time and place of the assault. All seemed to hold Sumner in complete contempt and to consider his words scurrilous and offensive. His was the kind of irritating performance that was becoming all too common among Northern antislavery politicians.[33]

[32] *Cong. Globe*, 34 Cong., 1 Sess., Appendix, 632, 831–33. See Brooks to J. H. Brooks, May 23, 1856, quoted in Boucher, "South Carolina and the South on the Eve of Secession," in Washington University *Studies, Humanistic Series*, VI, No. 2, p. 115.

[33] These are general impressions gained from a survey of opinion over the whole

Northerners, on the other hand, ignored the personal angle. Sumner had spoken for freedom. He "was not the mere representative of a State, or party, or section. He labored for the elevation of our Government and of mankind . . . and the blow which struck him to the earth, throbbed in the temples of twenty-five millions of people." He had said nothing against slavery and slaveholders that was not "called for"; perhaps he had not said enough. He had not "uttered a sentence or a paragraph not strictly authorized by the rules" of the Senate. The attack was thus upon freedom of speech. "The crime . . . [was] against the most vital principles of the Constitution, against the Government itself, against the sovereignty of Massachusetts, against the people of the United States, against Christianity and civilization." It could be justified only "by a code of morals unknown to the more enlightened civilization of the free states. . . . It [had] resulted from the manners, customs, and habits of our slaveholding population." Among them it was customary to see personal security violated and "God's image . . . daily assailed, disfigured and mutilated." In the South, when one man spoke disrespectfully of another, revenge was sought in violence. Slavery was back of it all. Sumner's "hatred of slavery was the *head and front of his offending*." [34]

From such a point of view, Brooks represented "the slave power." His action revealed its methods. His cane became the symbol of its intention to check free speech, to use force because it could not meet argument, to "bully" the North into submission. Brooks had intended murder. Sumner was near death.

The press in both sections reflected these attitudes and usually went a step further. Facts became less and less important and were bent to fit stereotypes already set up. Reactions, in turn, produced their own reactions as the gulf between the sections widened. In the North, even Kansas was forgotten for the moment. "The brutal assault . . . has aroused a deeper feeling in the public heart of the North than any other event of the past ten years," said the New York *Times*. The rights of all people, regardless of party, had been assailed. The liberties of the republic were in peril. The blow

South. The remarks of John H. Savage of Tennessee were typical of the attitude toward Sumner's speech: "for vulgarity, malice, falsehood, slander, and literary thieving, it has no parallel in any age or any nation." *Cong. Globe,* 34 Cong., 1 Sess., Appendix, 913.

[34] *Ibid.,* 1118–20, 873.

struck at Sumner put an end to freedom of speech in a place where "without freedom of speech, there . . . [could] be no freedom of any kind."

The attack, moreover, was regarded as "ferocious and deadly." It had been carried out with "a loaded bludgeon." Sumner had been felled to the earth "and when down," beaten "as if he were a rebellious slave." The very fact that "Brooks continued to assail with furious violence his fallen and bleeding victim long after he had become insensible," and until he was "forcibly interrupted by a third person," proved that he "intended to commit a murder." The "murderous weapon" used and "the whole circumstances of the case," moreover, proved "on the part of the assailant a murderous intention." Yes, if "two gentlemen from New York" had not come to the rescue, "Brooks, having broken his cane, might have ended with drawing a bowie-knife and stabbing his insensible victim to the heart." [35]

Sumner, of course, in such reporting, was badly wounded. The New York *Herald* told of the "consultation of physicians" the day following the assault, and a week later stated that as "yet no one was admitted to see him." Wendell Phillips cried to a Boston audience: "Sir, he *must* not die . . . he shall yet come forth from that sick-chamber, and every gallant heart in the Commonwealth be ready to kiss his very footsteps." The inference was clear: Sumner's life hung by a thread.[36]

Most serious, however, was the studied effort to picture Brooks as a typical Southerner and his act as an expression of a settled Southern policy. The Springfield (Massachusetts) *Republican* saw the assault as "akin to the war upon the people of Kansas." The two things together showed "how lordly and impudent Slavery . . . [had] become." The New York *Tribune* declared that through this "outrage" the South had lost the support of those who once defended her. They could not respect a people who had no "better arguments than fists, canes, knives and revolvers" and who were "determined to stifle freedom of speech by personal violence and

[35] Anderson, "Slavery Issue as a Factor in Massachusetts Politics"; New York *Times*, May 26, June 3, 1856; Springfield (Mass.) *Republican*, May 24, 1856; New York *Tribune*, May 24, 27, 1856.
[36] *Works of Charles Sumner*, IV, 312.

assault." If Southerners were so "tyrannical, imperious and over-bearing" that the criticism of a Southern state or a Southern politician meant punishment and chastisement by any self-elected avenger, then republicans and freemen could no longer defend them from the "epithets which they proved themselves to deserve." In fact, said the *Tribune*, Brooks's act had reduced the issue to the question "whether there is to be any more liberty of speech north of Mason and Dixon's line, even in the ten mile square of the District of Columbia. South of that, liberty has long since departed; but whether the common ground where the national representatives meet is to be turned into a slave plantation where Northern members act under the lash, the bowie-knife, and the pistol, is a question to be settled."

The *Tribune* was sure that unless the Northern people were "the poltroons they are taken for by the hostile slavebreeders and slave-drivers of the South," they would soon be heard from. But if not, then they deserved to have their "noses flattened" and their "skins blackened," and to be set to work "under taskmasters." They would be in a land where "the scepter of the self-appointed oligarchy . . . [was] a gutta-percha cane, backed by pistols and a bowie-knife under the flap of the coat, and its patron saint . . . Bully Brooks." [37]

More moderate papers did their best to counteract distortion and abuse. The Washington *Evening Star* denounced those who exaggerated Sumner's wounds and denied the statement that Brooks had struck Sumner "after he was prostrated." It described Sumner's speech as "little more than a tissue of personal accusations and assault" and declared that his charges were made without the slightest effort to sustain their truth except by citing paragraphs from unreliable newspapers. It did not justify Brooks, but it did insist that Sumner's attack on Butler was "far better suited to some low doggery in a region . . . wherein Billingsgate is uttered with impunity" and that his abuse of Douglas would "have graced the foulest mouthed fishwoman in all London." The Cincinnati *Enquirer*, while "regretting and condemning . . . the mode and measure of redress" that had been adopted by Brooks, still felt that those who provoked such attacks and those who applauded "the assailant of

[37] Springfield *Republican*, May 24, 1856; New York *Tribune*, May 26, October 11, 1856; Boston *Transcript*, May 26, 1856; Boston *Liberator*, May 20, 1856.

age and station" were not without blame. It noted the fact that no editor could indulge in such liberties with another person's character without getting his poor skull treated "with wooden substances." Even the Boston *Courier* was inclined to wonder if the citizens of other states would have listened dispassionately to such "insulting and provoking charges" if launched against their commonwealths. It confessed that it would have despised a son of Massachusetts who would have done so.[38]

That the South universally approved of Brooks's action was taken for granted by the majority of Northerners. Yet that was not the case. All shades of opinion were present. One thing, however, was clear. Few persons reacted to the assault on its own merits separated from its sectional implications. There was naturally no sympathy for Sumner and little criticism of Brooks personally. Approval of the assault was general in South Carolina, where state pride was high and where Senator Butler was loved and respected. Brooks had "truthfully carried out the will of the State." He had administered legitimate punishment for "an uncalled for outrage." If there was any criticism, it was for the use of a cane instead of a cowhide. Some thought he ought to be made governor. At least every voter in his district should "turn out to a man" and send him back to Congress with an overwhelming vote. The influential Charleston *Mercury* was disposed at first "to condemn the act in the most unmeasured terms" as a violation of the right of speech guaranteed by the Constitution and as a "reply by blows to argument or to invective itself." It soon, however, came to the conclusion that Brooks had "simply done his duty." Neither Massachusetts nor Sumner had any respect for law and, therefore, could not claim the protection of the law. Where "the code of honor . . . [was] not respected" by men who indulged in the violent abuse of others, there was "only one appeal and that . . . [was] to caning." Seemingly the *Mercury*'s attitude was heavily influenced by Northern opinion and its final reaction was one of rejoicing that the affair had aligned the sections more solidly against each other.[39]

[38] Washington *Evening Star*, June 2, 1856; Cincinnati *Enquirer*, May 27, 31, 1856; Boston *Courier*, quoted in Nashville *Union and American*, June 4, 1856.

[39] Jackson (Miss.) *Southron*, May 28, 1856; Athens (Ga.) *Southern Watchman*, June 4, 18, 1856; Columbia *Daily South Carolinian*, July 23, 1856; Charleston *Mercury*, June 13, 21, 1856.

The Charleston *Courier* was silent at first on the assault, reporting it as news, without comment. It was, however, soon caught in the enthusiasm which greeted Brooks's return home and did its part "to do honor to a man who [had] stood forth so nobly in defense of the fame of South Carolina and the honor of South Carolinians." Its reports of the banquets and gifts bestowed wherever Brooks appeared and its approval of his appeal to sectional feelings were as enthusiastic as those of the *Mercury*. Only one faint note of discord was heard. A writer in the Charleston *Evening News* rose up boldly to say that Brooks was "wrong, wrong, wrong,—wrong in chastising Sumner, wrong in method, wrong in place." "What has Mr. Butler, or Mr. Brooks, or South Carolina, gained by the thrashing of that man?" he asked. "Just nothing," was his answer.[40]

Outside of South Carolina, opinion was less unanimous. There was approval and there was disapproval on various grounds. Many Virginians commended the purpose back of the attack but condemned the method. The Richmond *Enquirer* said it was a case of "shameful submission to insult" or "the finding of some adequate redress." Since a gentleman could not answer abolitionists in the language of "the brothel," there wasn't much to do but to inflict personal chastisement. A Georgia editor thought that "Sumner got no more than his deserts" but regretted that the place in which "just punishment" had been administered had turned a "simply personal matter" into a public affair. An Alabama paper carried it a bit further. It justified Brooks "in the cause and manner of his rebuke to Mr. Sumner," but could not "acquit him of censure for the *place* and *time* chosen to inflict it." Yet the editor found it hard to censure a man who was establishing, in Congress, the principle "that a private wrong has a remedy in a personal responsibility to the injured party." [41]

The condemnation of "time and place" was widespread. The Nashville *Daily Union and American* reported that it was found in nearly all the Southern papers received. It added, however, that most exchanges thought the provocation merited punishment. As for itself, it could only say that "When the voice of abolitionism

---

[40] Charleston *Courier*, August 29, 1856; Charleston *Evening News*, June 10, 1856.
[41] Shanks, *Secession Movement in Virginia*, 51; Richmond *Enquirer*, June 4, 1856; Augusta *Constitutionalist*, July 25, 1856; Huntsville *Southern Advocate*, June 4, 1856.

ceases to war upon our Constitutional rights, and its echoes no longer vibrate in the halls of Congress, then and not until then, can they claim those halls as a place of refuge, when they fly from the spirit of insulted honor and slandered manhood they have invoked."

Time and place also worried the Columbus (Georgia) *Enquirer,* the Raymond (Mississippi) *Hinds County Gazette,* and the Memphis *Appeal.* The Senatorial chamber was no place to settle personal matters. Canes were not as bad as "Sharp's Rifles" but it would have been better for some old lady about Washington to have spanked Mr. Sumner. The Nashville *Union and American* had a better suggestion. Sumner should have been kicked from one end of Pennsylvania Avenue to the other. Perhaps it would have been most appropriate to have had a Negro do the job.[42]

Nor was condemnation of Brooks and his assault lacking. A Nashville editor called it "a gross outrage" that could not be justified. The lack of sympathy for Sumner "should not prevent Southern men of all parties from raising their voices in strong and earnest rebuke and condemnation of the desecration, by such brutality, of the Halls of the National Legislature." The effects abroad of such an affair would be deeply injurious to the national character. South Carolina's reception and gifts to Brooks would, moreover, "bring ridicule and disgrace" upon the South.[43]

The Macon *Georgia Telegraph* confessed "a deep mortification and chagrin over this occurrence." It excited unfeigned sorrow and mortification. That any Southern man should have done such a thing—not in a moment of frenzied passion, but long after the shafts had hit, festered, and rankled—was a matter for deep regret. It would be worth a thousand speeches and arguments to abolitionism. It would give "a stronger impetus to Black Republicanism than anything else which could be imagined of a hundred times its importance." Truly, "an unwise friend is more terrible than a score of enemies." [44]

[42] Nashville *Daily Union and American,* June 1, 3, 1856; Richmond *Dispatch,* June 3, 1856; Columbus *Enquirer,* May 29, 1856; Raymond (Miss.) *Hinds County Gazette,* June 4, 1856; Memphis *Appeal,* May 31, 1856; Nashville *Union and American,* May 28, 1856.

[43] *Republican Banner and Nashville Whig,* May 27, 1856.

[44] Macon *Georgia Telegraph,* May 27, 1856.

The Mobile *Advertiser* was even more outspoken. Brooks's rash act admitted of no justification. It had given Sumner's speech, which otherwise would scarcely have reached the public ear, thousands of readers and had "done more harm to the South . . . and the country, than the combined skill, talent, diligence and malignity of the whole abolition crew could have effected in a twelvemonth." Sound-thinking, unprejudiced men everywhere would know that Sumner's speech was abominable, despite all the whitewashing resolutions Massachusetts might pass, and that Brooks's assault was rash, unwise, and utterly indefensible, no matter how many gold-headed canes Columbia, Charleston, and other towns might give him. Yet the damage to the country at home and its standing abroad was irreparable. Its neighbor, the Mobile *Daily Register,* was equally blunt about the damage. Writing under the maxim "It is an ill wind that blows nobody good," its editor noted that Sumner had been well whipped, Brooks well abused, but that the free-soil press and the newsboys everywhere in the North were feasting on the affair "with all the gusto of hungry vultures gathered around a carcass fragrant with attractive odors. To these dealers in garbage Mr. Brooks . . . [was] a benefactor. And if it . . . [were] a good thing to lay the foundations for a dissolution of the Union in a sentiment of extreme malevolence on the part of the North against the South, then must Brooks and Sumner both be regarded as patriots of a very high order." Never before had such a vile defamation of the South, its men, and its institutions been known. Onto slavery had been heaped the charge of being parent to "every species of ruffianism, brutality and blackguardism." The object was to inspire the whole North "with a fierce and bitter enmity towards the South." Papers once friendly had now joined in "these raving denunciations and unscrupulous slanders." The South was being forced into Northern consciousness as a land of brutal bullies whose whole aim was to silence their opponents with revolvers, clubs, and bowie knives. The South must begin to live unto herself.[45]

New Orleans newspapers were just as harsh on Brooks and as apprehensive of the results. The *Bee* bemoaned the fact that Sumner had "been whipped into notoriety, if not into eminence." He

[45] Mobile *Advertiser,* May 29, June 1, 1856; Mobile *Register,* June 5, 15, July 26, 1856.

was now the symbol of the whole North, whereas his assailant was represented as the ideal of an undivided Southern sentiment. Their affair was pictured as Puritanism in strife with the brutal and barbarous slaveholding states. The result was a redoubling of abolitionist zeal, a new flaring up of the smoldering abolition fires. These things, if nothing else, should have admonished Mr. Brooks of the wisdom of restraining his zeal. The *Picayune* saw nothing but folly in Brooks's action. It was to be "deeply deplored" and "severely reprehended." It would help Sumner's "bad cause" more than half a dozen of his "frantic speeches." Reasoning and patriotic men would not be moved by his oratory, but sympathizers would be found for him and his words by an attack on his Senatorial privileges, his freedom of speech, and the use of force against him where reply was as free as attack. "Mr. Brooks, in suffering his temper to overmaster his judgement," only "lifted Mr. Sumner into a high place with his followers, and armed him with new capacity for mischief. The assault was, therefore, not only wrong in principle, but exceedingly impolitic." [46]

This was strong language but it was moderate compared to that of the Louisville *Journal,* which defended Sumner and urged the expulsion of Brooks from Congress. It bitterly attacked South Carolina for its attitude towards him and insisted that her soil grew the worst men in the nation. It would have agreed with Gazaway B. Lamar that Brooks's act "was unjustifiable, unmanly, illtimed, illadvised . . . and totally indefensible as to time, place and manner." [47]

Kansas and Brooks had indeed brought a profound change in Northern thinking. The impression was now widespread that an aggressive "Slave Power," willing to resort to brute force in order to have its way, was definitely on the march. The young Republican party had made the most of the situation. From small local beginnings, it had blossomed out into national organization and now stood forth as a serious contender in the approaching Presidential election. A deeper moral feeling of indignation against slavery as

[46] New Orleans *Bee,* June 3, 1856; New Orleans *Picayune,* May 27, 1856.

[47] Louisville *Journal,* quoted in Nashville *Union and American,* June 1, 1856; Gazaway B. Lamar to Cobb, May 31, 1856, in Phillips (ed.), *Correspondence of Toombs, Stephens, and Cobb,* 365–66.

236

the author of all national ills had been kindled. Plain men throughout the section had set themselves in the name of democracy and Christianity to resist further aggression. The North itself had taken the offensive.

In the South, far less excitement existed. Men were not less indignant nor less determined. They too were on the defensive against aggression. Northern ferment alarmed them. The speeches of Northern men in Congress and the editorials in Northern newspapers revealed a new and threatening attitude toward the South and her institutions. These were more extreme, more distorted, more inclined to challenge, than in earlier days. They were much more unfair. The South had not schemed and plotted to seize Kansas. It had acted there only in defense of rights restored by the repeal of the Missouri Compromise as an act of delayed justice—a move to restore equality among the states. What they saw in Kansas was, therefore, Northern refusal to permit squatter sovereignty to work fairly.

As to Brooks, he was just a Southern man acting in defense of honor and against personal abuse. He might deserve the sympathy of self-respecting men, but he did not head a Southern drive against freedom of speech or any other sacred thing. His act did not herald the dawn of an era of bullying. In fact, it meant nothing as far as the South as a section was concerned. Yet everywhere Southern men met the unfair assertion of sectional aggression. They found themselves maligned, charged with Brooks's guilt. They heard themselves, their ways, and their morals held up to scorn. They had but one choice. It did no good to explain or to protest. They might just as well accept the facts and prepare for defense.

Such attitudes led extremists to urge secession. Rhett and Yancey and Ruffin and their kind were ready to act. They were, however, still well in advance of public opinion. The vast majority still held their faith in the democratic process. They still believed that through political bargaining a satisfactory balance of interests might be achieved. A Presidential election was at hand. Southern votes were in demand. A price could be set. If enough of political unity could be achieved at home to influence the national parties, they might be kept "safe" on slavery. The best sectional defense might be found in the national political party.

Local political unity, however, would be difficult to achieve. Although recent events had built a powerful Republican party out of divergent elements in the North, and had forced the Northern Democrats into an "alarming" amount of agreement on social and economic issues, they had not brought any large degree of political unity to the South. The Southern Democrats had profited, to some extent, from the heavy drift of Northern Whigs into Republican ranks, but the opposition at home was still strong, and the question as to what extent the Know-Nothings, now making their appearance, were to take the place of the old Whigs was not settled. It would not be known until after the coming election how much Kansas and Brooks and Northern critics had done to make old political rivals love each other.

The rise of the Know-Nothing or American party in the South had not been due to any great reaction either to foreigners or to Catholics in their midst. These were too few and too well integrated into Southern life to produce serious hostile reactions. A sounder reason lay in the reluctance of old Whigs to join the Democrats and in a repugnance to the growing sectional strife. Old rivalries were as powerful as new issues in the movement and local conditions were always an important factor. The demands that native-born Americans should rule America and that the Union should be maintained and preserved, appealed to those who had been Whigs even though they felt little inclination to resist the "aggressive policy and corrupting tendencies of the Roman Catholic Church." Here, at least, was a place to go when the old party failed.

The secret character of the Americans in early days made transition from old associations to new ones easy. It also added a favorable element of surprise when unannounced candidates received a heavy vote or were unexpectedly swept into office. It proved, however, to be a most vulnerable spot in the organization. Opponents pointed out the danger in political secrecy and the un-American character of such underground movements. This, with the offense to loyal foreign-born citizens, weakened the appeal of the Know-Nothings as a permanent party and ruined its chances of becoming the much-needed new national organization with which to combat the Republicans.

The political situation in the South, however, gave the party an opening. Local differences were still stronger than sectional fears. Just when first steps to operate were taken in various corners of the South is not always clear, but by 1853 and 1854 Know-Nothing influence was being felt in local elections throughout the section. Maryland and Louisiana, with strong Catholic populations, were the first Southern states in which an American council was formed. The need for a new party, however, was wider than religious prejudices, and organization followed rapidly in the other states. A gradual affiliation with the national organization and the adoption of the national ritual soon brought the movement to maturity and practical political effort. Old Whigs and disgruntled Democrats had found a new, if only temporary, political home.[48]

Surprising successes in local elections in the first days kindled high hopes and precipitated bitter struggles between Americans and Democrats. In the Baltimore municipal election of 1854, the new party gained control of the city council and, in New Orleans, under the name of "Independents," after much rioting and bloodshed, won all the municipal offices except those of mayor and three recordships. Local successes in Montgomery, Louisville, Richmond, and Nashville indicated a rapid spread of the movement and gave needed encouragement toward co-operation with the national organization. The so-called Philadelphia platform of June 5, 1855, was, as a result, widely endorsed throughout the South and secrecy and ritual generally abandoned. Other moves to widen party appeal also appeared. In some places the cause of temperance was espoused and corruption attacked, and everywhere the effort was made to clear the organization of the charge that it was nothing but the old Whig party under a new name. State conventions now became the rule. Open campaigns were conducted. Platforms were presented to the voters. In other words, the Americans were now ready to contest with the Democrats for local and national control.[49]

State elections in 1855 and 1856 seemed to promise much. In the Border States particularly, the party showed new strength. Four

[48] Benjamin Tuska, *Know-Nothingism in Baltimore, 1854–1860* (New York, [1930?]), pamphlet.
[49] W. Darrell Overdyke, *The Know-Nothing Party in the South* (Baton Rouge, 1950), 73–90.

of the six Congressmen elected in Maryland and a large majority of the legislature were Americans. In Kentucky the party completely swept the field, electing the governor, the lieutenant governor, the attorney general, six Congressmen, and a majority of the state legislators. They made substantial gains in Tennessee, losing the governorship but electing five of the ten Congressmen and gaining an equality in the legislature. Henry A. Wise checked advances in Virginia with a spectacular campaign, but the Americans did manage to elect one Congressman and sixty-two members of the state legislature. A three-way split in Missouri aided the party, and its more than forty thousand votes for governor was only 5 per cent less than that of the victorious Democrats.

In the other Southern states, outside of Louisiana, where the party retained its early strength, the Americans created considerable alarm but did not really threaten. The showing both in North Carolina and Georgia was respectable. That in Mississippi and Florida, only fair. Arkansas, Texas, and Alabama, in spite of such names as Sam Houston, Jeremiah Clemens, Henry Hilliard, and Albert Pike on American rolls, remained firmly Democratic.

All in all, the party had done exceedingly well in its short life, and hopes were high. The basic weaknesses of the party were only beginning to be recognized. The national organization was yet to face the slavery issue. Withdrawals from the party were as yet unimportant.[50]

The Presidential campaign of 1856 thus found the South divided much along old lines. Know-Nothings had replaced the Whigs to an uncertain degree, and the Democrats had unquestionably profited to an equally uncertain degree from the part which their party had played in national affairs. Since there was little in the South to create active hostility either to foreigners or to Catholics, the campaign there returned largely to earlier patterns. The Americans took up the old Whig role of promoting national harmony. The Democrats continued to proclaim themselves the defenders of Southern rights against Northern aggression.

[50] *Ibid.*, 9–126; Sitterson, *Secession Movement in North Carolina*, 131–32; Percy L. Rainwater, *Mississippi, Storm Center of Secession, 1856–1861* (Baton Rouge, 1938), 32–33; Dorman, *Party Politics in Alabama*, 101–24.

Americans cried down the slavery issue, condemned Democratic policies that had brought on strife in Kansas, and insisted that squatter sovereignty as a policy was of no benefit to the South. Kenneth Rayner from North Carolina worked hard to commit the national council to a statement that the question of slavery did not come within the purview of party objects, and to persuade it to abide by its first position that Congress ought not to legislate upon slavery in the territories. He failed, but the substitution of meaningless resolutions did not greatly weaken Southern support of Fillmore; it only gave added reason for charges against the Democrats. The Atlanta *Intelligencer* wanted to know who alone was responsible for the war that raged in Kansas. Who had brought the republic "to the verge of the precipice—the trembling verge now shaking beneath . . . [the nation's] feet"? Who had armed one section of the Union against the other? Who was responsible for the blood that stained the soil of the "debatable land"? The answer was clear: *"The Democratic party!"* The blame rested squarely upon those who had repealed the Missouri Compromise. They had brought the Republican party into being. They had pushed the nation to the border of disruption. The Augusta *Chronicle and Sentinel* went a step further. It asserted that abolitionism itself had been dying out and men had been breathing freer "because they no longer apprehended impending ruin to the government." Then "in utter contempt of pledges, . . . [and] in most shameful violation of plighted faith," Democratic demagogues had "sprung the mind" and plunged the country into turmoil and agitation ten times greater than it had known before. The *Sentinel* could find no language harsh enough for those who thus selfishly turned the country topsy-turvy and staked "the existence of the Union upon the result of their games for political power." It begged the conservative men of both sections to "arise and sternly demand that agitation of the slavery question . . . cease."[51]

The same cry came from American editors throughout the section with added words against the squatter-sovereignty doctrine.

[51] Richmond *Whig,* quoted and approved in Huntsville *Southern Advocate,* August 8, 1856; Overdyke, *Know-Nothing Party in the South,* 129–32; Atlanta *Intelligencer,* quoted in Rome *Courier,* September 6, 1856; Augusta *Chronicle and Sentinel,* October 16, 1856.

Diligently they pointed to the fact that Southern Democrats held one opinion and Northern Democrats another as to the time when the people of a territory might act on slavery. They made much of the part which the foreign immigrant was playing in winning Kansas for freedom. Always they deplored the growing sectional strife and held abolitionists and disunionists equally guilty of its production. "May Heaven, in the munificence of mercy," cried the New Orleans *Crescent,* "take pity on these misguided men! They know not what they do!" [52]

Southern Democrats fought the Americans at first on the basis of secrecy and Whig antecedents. As the campaign advanced, however, and a steady stream of prominent Know-Nothings abandoned their party and came to Buchanan's support, they centered their attention primarily on the national situation. Their real enemy was the Republican party. "Know-nothingism in the Northern States," they charged, was "an abolition movement in its origin, purpose, organization, tendency and effect." It was one with the Republicans. The whole North was united in "that deep-seated and deadly hostility to the South which long years of incendiarism . . . [had] engendered." Southern Americans, deluded "by the false though specious pretenses of a counterfeit patriotism," should reflect upon their position and "view the present juncture of affairs in the light of reason." There was "but one party to be relied on in the emergency." That party had "never proved faithless. . . . For Southerners to linger longer in the embraces of Know Nothingism . . . [was] giving aid and comfort to . . . [the South's] most deadly enemies." [53]

This plea for Southern unity grew stronger as it became increasingly apparent that the Americans had reached their crest in the local elections of 1855. The realization that Fillmore had little chance for election stressed the importance of centering strength where it would yield largest sectional returns. The election, after all, was not just a contest between parties; it was a struggle between sections over issues fundamental to Southern interests and values.

[52] *Republican Banner and Nashville Whig,* May 22, 29, 31, September 24, 25, 1856; New Orleans *Crescent,* October 8, 1856; Augusta *Chronicle and Sentinel,* August 1, 22, 30, October 8, 1856.

[53] Richmond *Enquirer,* January 25, 1855; Natchez *Mississippi Free Trader,* December 7, 1855.

Slavery "has become a great, live, earnest, practical question," said
the Nashville *Patriot*. "It is wrestling . . . for its very life." The
"Black Republican party" had declared war—an "internecine war
—war to the knife and to the hilt." For the first time in our history
a sectional contest for the presidency had been precipitated by the
organization of a powerful party in the North based on an "avowed
and unrelenting hostility to the domestic institutions and the equal
constitutional rights of the Southern States." Its hope of success lay
in securing the united vote of the North. Its defeat depended on a
united Southern vote.[54]

As the campaign neared its close, thoughtful men began to consider the consequences of political defeat. What would be the meaning of a Republican victory? What should the South do if John C.
Frémont was elected? These were serious questions. Already a New
Orleans editor had declared that the election would show whether
the Northern people preferred "niggers . . . [and] a false,
wretched, miserable and resultless philanthropy, to their own race
and color and the Union and all its countless blessings." The vote
would be on the slavery platform, and if the vote were averse, then,
said the editor, the parties to the present compact had "better commence making arrangements for a dissolution of co-partnership."
There would be no use "in attempting to continue the business."
If the North as the senior partner of the concern insisted that he
had a right, whenever it suited his will and pleasure, "to insult,
oppress and grind to the very earth" the South, as the junior
partner, then all the latter could do would be to seek release "from
the degrading thraldom." Much was made of the purely sectional
character of the Republican party. Its "very organization evinced
a hostility to the Southern States." Its campaign methods had aimed
at creating a strictly sectional feeling. Its speakers had "poured forth
a foul stream of vituperation upon the Southern people," and had
"left no means, however wicked, untried to excite irreconcilable
hatred of them in the minds of the people of the North." [55]

Frémont's election, to extremists, therefore, meant complete ruin

[54] Nashville *Patriot*, quoted in Huntsville *Southern Advocate*, August 30, 1856;
Mobile *Register*, April 9, 1856; New Orleans *Daily Crescent*, October 7, 1856; New
Orleans *Daily Picayune*, October 7, 1856.
[55] New Orleans *Daily Crescent*, June 19, 1855; New Orleans *Daily Picayune*, No
vember 2, 1856.

to the South. Should that "miserable faction" succeed, the Missouri Compromise would be restored, Kansas would become a free state, the Fugitive Slave Law would be repealed, insurrection and servile war would be kindled in the South, the amalgamation of the races would be enforced, and the torch would be put to Southern homes and the knife to Southern throats. To the people of the South the question was simply one as to "whether they would tamely couch at the feet of their despoilers, or like their ancient forefathers, openly defy their enemies, and assert their independence."

Faced with such a situation, there could be but one answer. "If Frémont should be elected President, the Union of these States . . . would not, and should not long survive." Honor and interest alike, said a Mississippi editor, demanded "that the South should forthwith withdraw from all connection with the North and establish an independent Confederacy." He thought the people were ripe for such a move; that they would do it in peace and quiet if possible, but "in war and blood" if necessary. Governor Wise of Virginia was of the same opinion and declared that he could "arm and equip 50,000 men the next morning, ready for revolution." He would wait for no overt act. To tell him "that Virginia and her fourteen sister slave States" should submit "to the election of a black Republican" when such an election "would be an open, overt proclamation of public war," was to tell him they were "already subjugated and degraded." Frantically he invited the governors of the Carolinas to meet him in conference. Even the failure to achieve little more than a social gathering did not check his belief that a revolution was at hand.[56]

Moderates would not go so far. They would, at least, wait for some overt act to justify extreme action. The mere fact of Frémont's election "in a Constitutional and lawful manner" afforded no grounds for radical measures. It was well to prepare, but not to act. Delay, however, should be conditional. The always moderate Augusta *Chronicle and Sentinel* expressed it this way:

"We have for years been convinced that the Union between

[56] Columbia *Daily South Carolinian*, September 13, October 3, 1856; Port Gibson (Miss.) *Southern Reveille*, October 30, 1856; Raleigh *North Carolina Standard*, April 2, September 24, 1856; Judge P. T. Scruggs to John B. Sale, October 4, 1856, quoted in Rainwater, *Mississippi, Storm Center of Secession*, 38; Augusta *Daily Constitutionalist*, September 20, 1856.

North and South must one day cease, unless an utter revolution in men's sentiments and conduct can be brought about. In one respect we agree with the . . . [extremists] and admit that disunion *must* come sooner or later, but we place the event upon quite a different contingency. They place it upon the election of Fremont—*we* on the continuance of slavery agitation. . . . This continual and irritating agitation of the slavery question must cease, or the Union cannot exist." [57]

Few there were, however, who expected the agitation to cease. The "virus of Abolition fanaticism . . . [was] too deep seated in the political system" and the rewards of agitation too great. The election of Buchanan, said another conservative, would hold the country together four years longer. It would not stop the forces now supporting Frémont. The South should, therefore, support the Democratic candidate and use the time thus gained in preparation for the final break.

The results of the election were both encouraging and alarming to the South. Buchanan's election meant four more years under a friendly administration. But Buchanan's vote had been only 1,838,169 against 1,341,264 for Frémont. The Republican gains were phenomenal. The party had definitely established itself as the future power in the North. The American party, on the other hand, had carried only one state—Maryland. It had polled only 473,465 votes in the South as against 601,587 for Buchanan. It had made substantial gains over the Whig vote of 1852, but it showed neither national nor local promise for the future. As an effort to carry forward the old tradition of sectional harmony, it had made little progress. Southerners might well conclude that their only hope for maintaining their place in national life and in protecting their peculiar interests lay in the Democratic party. That seemed to be the opinion of the newer leadership which events were pushing forward—a leadership that had as little interest in making the democratic process work as did Chase and Wade and Sumner.

[57] Augusta *Chronicle and Sentinel,* October 9, 1856; Augusta *Daily Constitutionalist,* September 20, 1856.

CHAPTER X

THE HARVEST

THE election of 1856 taught the Southern people much. They were not facing a temporary political excitement. They were meeting a moral crusade bent on putting an end to slavery extension, if not to slavery itself, and one that was determined to break Southern political influence at Washington. A struggle for power, because power determined policies, was now well under way. "The freesoil war against the South is to be continued unto the bitter end," said the New Orleans *Crescent*. It would be even more "malignant, remorseless and vindictive" than before. The enemy, for they were countrymen only in name, were already preparing for 1860. Bleeding Kansas was being invoked again. Falsehoods about the South and her people were being retold. Reports that the slave trade would be reopened and Cuba seized were being circulated as facts even though not a half-dozen reputable papers in the South advocated such measures. No, the South would not be "let alone," although "to be let alone" was all she asked.[1]

The strength shown by the Republicans in the late election gave them every inducement to continue their exertions, to organize their forces for renewed effort. And Kansas was there waiting to serve their purposes. Already it had produced an almost "unanimous decision" for Frémont in the nonslaveholding states. The old assertion that the abolition party, notwithstanding its noisy obtrusions, was only a faction "without respectability and destitute

[1] New Orleans *Crescent*, November 17, 1856; *De Bow's Review* (New Orleans), XXIII (1857), 462–74, for an interesting description of the change that had come over the North.

of power," could no longer pass current. Conservatives were every-where falling before those whose slogan was "war against slavery, constitution or no constitution." Was it the rabble which passed personal-liberty laws? Was it a handful of fanatics who had sup-ported Frémont? No! The South could no longer look to the con-servatives of the North to protect her rights. She must be united for self-protection. Slaveholders and "free white citizens" without slaves must join hands against "the would-be aristocracy of Boston and New Haven" which was seeking to "debase the white working men to the level of negroes, to deaden their aspirations, accustom them to the coarsest social distinctions, founded on mere wealth, and teach them to bear like negroes the scoffs and taunts of their superiors, whilst they fulfil[led] the most menial and servile of-fices." No middle ground was left—not because the South was un-willing to yield much for the sake of peace, but because the anti-slavery sentiment would never stop short "of the total overthrow of Southern social and political institutions." The South was being assailed. She must defend herself.[2]

It was this feeling which now gave added strength to the moves for Southern economic and social independence. The realization of heavy Southern dependence on others and the effort to remedy the situation had begun back in the preceding decade. The crisis of 1850 had been followed by much talk and some action. Republican growth and Kansas now added to each.

In 1849 the Sumter *Banner* had urged the necessity of "bringing up the rising generation to MECHANICAL BUSINESS." It was the only way to be free from "Northern foes." "In what part of the South," it asked, "can be found Engineers, Carpenters, painters, engine builders, masons or architects but what are Northerners?" With shame it confessed that Southerners cultivated with Northern implements, although they could easily manufacture them. They secured most of their comforts and conveniences such as plate, car-riages, saddles, furniture, books, and carpets from Northern sources. It was time for the South to drop the foolish argument "that the mechanic is no gentleman—that it is degrading." One look at his-tory, at the halls of Congress, yes, at Southern ancestors, would

[2] New Orleans *Bee*, November 8, 1856; Richmond *Enquirer*, September 12, 1856; Charleston *Mercury*, December 25, 1856.

prove that "the mechanic arts . . . [were] the arm of civilization." [3]

In 1850 James D. B. De Bow, convinced that the Southern cup of forbearance was filled to overflowing, had offered a complete program with which to meet Northern aggression. He would have the South build her own ships and conduct her own trade with foreign powers; manufacture at home every bale of cotton; diversify her industry, and build roads and railroads; cease the annual migrations to Northern watering places; educate all children at home and encourage a native literature. He would "light up the torches . . . [of industry] on every hill-top, by the side of every stream, from the shores of the Delaware to the furthest extremes of the Rio Grande—from the Ohio to the capes of Florida." [4]

Reports of cotton mills being set up in North Carolina and Georgia; of a planter buying shoes for his slaves in Petersburg instead of Boston; of flour mills and an iron foundry being established in Knoxville; of the remarkable progress being made in cotton manufactories by William Gregg at Graniteville and Edwin Holt at Alamance, and in the iron industry by Joseph R. Anderson at the Tredegar works in Richmond—all indicated some progress in practice from much preaching. Yet these represented only beginnings. Economic independence was still a long way off. [5]

The new sectional bitterness after 1854, therefore, only produced more complaints against dependence and more urging of improvement efforts. Said the New Orleans *Daily Crescent:*

"We import from Massachusetts, Ohio, New York, and Connecticut all our machinery, our domestic utensils, our cloths, our fashions, and a great deal of our provisions. Our steamboats are built at Cincinnati, and our steamships at New York; our mills and machinery come from Boston; our cottons, our linens, our ploughs, our hats, our printing paper, the very pavement on which we ride and walk are brought from the same places. . . .

[3] Sumter *Banner,* April 18, 1849; *De Bow's Review,* X (1851), 106–108.

[4] *De Bow's Review,* IX (1850), 120–24.

[5] Augusta *Chronicle and Sentinel,* January 21, 1851; Petersburg (Va.) *Intelligencer,* quoted in Huntsville *Southern Advocate,* August 22, 1855; Knoxville *Whig and Independent Journal,* September 17, 1853; New Orleans *Daily Crescent,* November 6, 1855; Broadus Mitchell, *William Gregg, Factory Master of the Old South* (Chapel Hill, 1928), 15–48; Thomas P. Martin (ed.), "The Advent of William Gregg and the Graniteville Company," in *Journal of Southern History,* XI (1945), 389–423.

"This state of affairs cannot continue forever. The *vis inertiae* that has been so long and justly charged against Southern character must give way to a new impulse and we must manufacture as well as produce." [6]

This was the same old complaint and the same old remedy. Even the growing protest against teaching Negro slaves the various trades and thereby robbing white artisans of their opportunities was not exactly new. It had been common in the 1840's. Although most Southerners thought the Negro's place was in the fields, many masters had long felt justified in turning capable Negroes into carpenters, masons, cobblers, and weavers. A few both advocated and practiced the use of slaves as factory workers. The experiments tried in different places, they said, were highly successful and promised much for the future. At the Tredegar Iron Works in Richmond, for instance, Anderson both owned and hired slaves, taught them all the skills, and when his white mechanics struck, used slaves almost exclusively. The tobacco factories of Virginia and North Carolina had used slave labor from the beginning. There was no reason, said its advocates, why such efforts might not be extended.[7]

What *was* new in this period came from the pen of a North Carolina nonslaveholder who had wandered widely in the West and North and even more widely in his thinking. His name was Hinton Rowan Helper, and his book was entitled, *The Impending Crisis of the South: How to Meet It*. The work began with the familiar dirge in which Southern backwardness was held up in contrast to Northern progress. Southern dependence was stressed in telling fashion:

"In one way or another we are more or less subservient to the North every day of our lives. In infancy we are swaddled in Northern muslin; in childhood we are humored with Northern gewgaws; in youth we are instructed out of Northern books; at the age of maturity we sow our 'wild oats' on Northern soil; in middle-life we

6 New Orleans *Daily Crescent*, July 20, 1855.

7 Wetumpka (Ala.) *Southern Dial, and African Monitor*, May 20, 1858; Natchez *Mississippi Free Trader*, May 12, 1849; New Orleans *Daily Picayune*, November 12, 1858; Kathleen Bruce, "Slave Labor in the Virginian Iron Industry," in *William and Mary College Quarterly* (Williamsburg), Ser. II, Vol. VI (1926), 289–302; VII (1927), 21–31; Kathleen Bruce, *Virginia Iron Manufacture in the Slave Era* (New York, 1931), 231–58.

exhaust our wealth . . . in giving aid and succor to every department of Northern power; in the decline of life we remedy our eyesight with Northern spectacles, and support our infirmities with Northern canes; in old age we are drugged with Northern physic; and, finally, when we die, our inanimate bodies, shrouded in Northern cambric, are stretched upon the bier, borne to the grave in a Northern carriage, entombed with a Northern spade, and memorized with a Northern slab!" [8]

With this out of the way, Helper piled up statistics and then attempted to give the reasons and the remedy. The cause, he thought, was apparent to anyone who could read. It was Negro slavery. The remedy was as simple—abolition of slavery. The cost? Nothing! Increased value of lands alone would more than compensate. Increased yields and greater diversity of crops would be clear profit. "Slavery," he wrote, "lies at the root of all the shame, poverty, ignorance, tyranny and imbecility of the South; slavery must be thoroughly eradicated; let this be done, and a glorious future will await us." [9]

For the slaveholders, Helper had only contempt. They were fewer in number, he thought, than the census reported. They were indolent, overbearing, "so depraved, that there . . . [was] scarcely a spark of honor or magnanimity to be found amongst them." It would be sheer folly to expect voluntary justice from them. Action must come from the nonslaveholders. They must shake themselves loose from this oligarchy, assert their liberties and their power, "strike for the freedom of the South" through the ballot box. They must organize for independent political action, wrest the franchise from the slaveholder, cease to patronize him, tax his slaves, reject his newspapers, and put him and his slavery "on the road to ultimate extinction." The battle was for justice and for the prosperity of the masses.

Helper's statistics were selected and sorted for his purposes. Other writings and later conduct cast considerable doubt on his sincerity.

[8] Hinton R. Helper, *The Impending Crisis of the South: How to Meet It* (New York, 1857), 23. See also speech of Albert Pike at meeting of the Southern Commercial Convention in New Orleans, in Herbert Wender, *Southern Commercial Conventions, 1837–1859*, Johns Hopkins University *Studies in Historical and Political Science*, Ser. XLVIII, No. 4 (Baltimore, 1930), 149–51.

[9] Helper, *Impending Crisis of the South*, 153.

Ascribing to slavery all the ills of the South and to free labor all of the virtues of the North was farfetched and erroneous. The fact remains, however, that he had struck a heavy blow in a vulnerable spot at a crucial time. The economics of slavery needed probing. The class appeal, on social, economic, and political grounds, was the most dangerous one that could be made in a stratified society. The quick negative response south of Mason and Dixon's line proved that the blow had landed. The wide use of the book soon to be made in the North revealed a keen understanding of the importance of the weapon that had been placed in antislavery hands.[10]

Helper's analysis and remedy were too extreme to produce any practical efforts at reform in the South. Few of the forgotten men for whom it was written had a chance to read it. Slaveholders denounced it as "incendiary, insurrectionary, and hostile to the peace and domestic tranquility of the country." They called its author a "poor traitor to his native sod and native skies," a "scoundrel beneath the level of contempt and infamy," "one of the most miserable renegades and mendacious miscreants the world has ever seen." When Senator Henry Wilson of Massachusetts quoted the book in a bitter attack on the South, Senator Asa Biggs of North Carolina charged that Helper had left his native state after being detected in theft; that he was "a dishonest, degraded and disgraced man . . . an apostate son, ruined in fortune and character . . . catering to a diseased appetite at the North to obtain a miserable living by slander upon the land of his birth." [11]

That seemed to satisfy Southern feelings until the spring of 1859, when a group of prominent Northern men began collecting a fund for the printing of one hundred thousand copies of a compendium of the *Crisis* as a Republican campaign document. This move, endorsed by sixty-eight Republicans in Congress, produced intense excitement and brought acrimonious debate when the House attempted to elect a Speaker. Coming as it did about the same time as the John Brown raid, it added fuel to an already dangerous conflagration. Under the new excitement, the sale of Helper's book at the North mounted by leaps and bounds, and men caught with it in

[10] Hugh T. Lefler, "Hinton Rowan Helper, Advocate of a 'White America,'" in James D. Eggleston (ed.), *Southern Sketches* (Charlottesville), No. I (1935), 42 pp.
[11] Quotations are from *ibid.*, 21.

their possession at the South were dealt with as public enemies. Editors refuted its assertions; citizens in some places publicly burned all available copies; the authorities of Guilford County, North Carolina, arrested the Reverend Daniel Worth for circulating the book and later forced him to flee the state. The more industrious attempted to reveal in pamphlet or book the distortion in Helper's statistics and the fallacies in his conclusions.[12]

If Southerners were unwilling to accept Helper's advice on how to improve their economic situation, they were quite eager to listen to those who suggested less drastic steps. They were not interested in a social revolution, but they did want economic betterment.

The idea of building a Southern mercantile class by the encouragement of direct trade with Europe had been advanced at different times. The Northern merchant who came and went with the seasons provided another glaring example of Southern weakness. The dependence on New York for the financing of planting and marketing crops was equally galling. The practice of receiving payment for cotton in drafts on New York banks or sterling bills to be sold there proved particularly humiliating when the panic of 1857 rendered exchange almost worthless. The absurdity of a great exporting city like New Orleans being "stranded because of a money panic in Wall Street," of cotton selling on the New York market for ten cents a pound while in London it brought eighteen or nineteen, was enough to stir sectional resentment. It was time to seek permanent emancipation from a system which was "wringing millions of hard earned dollars from Southern pockets." Direct trade with Europe through local merchants with their own ships was clearly the remedy. Norfolk, Charleston, and New Orleans must become ports through which the trade not only of the South but of the Northwest as well would find its way to the outside world. Coastal cities must be linked with both Europe and the interior.[13]

So, along with the interest in direct European trade, went a de-

12 William Polk, "The Hated Helper," in *South Atlantic Quarterly,* XXX (1931), 181 ff.; David R. Barbee, "Hinton Rowan Helper," in *Tyler's Quarterly Historical and Genealogical Magazine* (Richmond), XV (1933–1934), 144 ff.

13 Robert R. Russel, *Economic Aspects of Southern Sectionalism, 1840–1861,* in University of Illinois *Studies in the Social Sciences,* XI, Nos. 1–2 (Urbana, 1924), 103; Richmond *Enquirer,* December 17, 1855.

mand for the expansion of the Southern railway system. "Extend the iron rails and send the steam horse into all sections of the country," urged the Mobile *Daily Advertiser*. By increasing internal trade, it continued, the South would add to its population, hurry the development of its resources, turn its capital to better use, and, in the end, enjoy "a good measure of the independence so much declaimed about." State aid must be given, public interest aroused, sectional patriotism stirred; the Northwest must be tied to the South, and Europe and South America made friends.[14]

In the field of agriculture, improvements for sectional strength had already made sound headway. Southern patriots such as Edmund Ruffin, James H. Hammond, J. D. B. De Bow, and Charles W. Howard, and the editors of a half-dozen excellent agricultural papers, had by preaching and practice wrought a veritable revolution in this important field. Farmers and planters, however, still needed prodding to "raise their own corn, their own cattle, [and] their own pork." "Let the farmer . . . make his own bread, his meat, raise a few colts and hay to feed them," urged De Bow. "Let him increase the quantity of corn and forage until he can spare a little; . . . let him remember the old saying, 'a master's footsteps are manure to his land'." It was by such efforts, added Ruffin, that the South could be strengthened "against the plundering and oppression of tariffs to protect Northern interests, compromises (so-called) to swell Northern power, pensions and bounty laws for the same purpose." It was to Southern deficiencies in foodstuffs, flocks, and herds as much as in manufactured goods, charged the New Orleans *Daily Crescent*, "that most of the outrages perpetrated upon us by the fanatics of the North . . . [were] to be attributed." "Were we practically independent," it continued, "we could afford to laugh to scorn their ravings and their threats." [15]

Under sectional excitement the moves for intellectual and social independence also took on a new importance. Why should the South

---

[14] Mobile *Daily Advertiser*, January 17, 1855.

[15] Craven, *Coming of the Civil War*, 272–302; Avery Craven, *Edmund Ruffin, Southerner; A Study in Secession* (New York, 1932), 49–95; Craven, *Soil Exhaustion . . . of Virginia and Maryland*, 122–61; New Orleans *Daily Crescent*, July 20, 1855; November 12, 1856; *De Bow's Review*, XIV (1853), 34–46; Edmund Ruffin, *An Address on the Opposite Results of Exhausting and Fertilizing Systems of Agriculture* (Charleston, 1853).

send its sons and daughters North to school and college? Why turn them over for education to those who, while rifling their pockets, slandered their parents and country? Northern schools were "hotbeds of abolitionism, under the control of implacable enemies of the South and of her patriarchical institutions." In them children were educated "from Southern orthodoxy and gentility into that Yankee selfishness and sordidness" so much denounced. In the Northern colleges young men were being "constantly exposed to the danger of imbibing doctrines subversive to all old institutions, and of all established tenets respecting religion, law, morality, property, and government." Editors and lecturers, "unchecked by a healthy public opinion," were discussing everything as though nothing were settled, nothing sacred. Was it safe, at an age when boys naturally hated restraint, when their minds were most susceptible to impression, to crowd them into Dartmouth, Harvard, Yale, Amherst, Hamilton, and Brown, where they would be encouraged to "give free reins to inclinations, appetite and passion"? These were hotbeds of political heresy and higher law—of hatred for the South. Even if Southern institutions were inferior, and they were not, it would be better that Southern "sons remained in honest ignorance and at the plough-handle, than that their plastic minds be imbued with doctrines subversive to their country's peace and honor, and at war with the very fundamental principles upon which the whole superstructure of the society they . . . [found] at home . . . [was] based." [16]

With such statements went a demand for the improvement of Southern schools, the employment only of Southern teachers, and the use of Southern textbooks. Teacher training and a greater respect for the teaching profession were preached if not always practiced. A Virginia paper, evidently indulging in a bit of wishful thinking, declared that "The first young men of the state in point of talent, education and respectability" had now turned their attention to teaching. It was the employment of none but native sons that had wrought the change.

[16] Huntsville *Southern Advocate*, September 18, 1856; Richmond *Enquirer*, September 1, December 29, 1855; Memphis *Daily Avalanche*, August 6, 1859; *De Bow's Review*, X (1851), 362–63.

There was, however, much yet to be done. Bitterly did Parson Brownlow denounce the Memphis school trustees for importing "a gang of low-flung nutmeg dealers" from Connecticut to teach their children. Teachers should be "native here and to the manor born," said a Mississippi writer. "Let us establish schools for the education of teachers here at home," he urged, "and employ them at salaries sufficient to make their avocation respectable and desirable." He would banish and burn instantly every textbook which "by implication" inculcated anything contrary to Southern opinion.[17]

This demand for orthodox Southern textbooks was widespread. The realization that the section was dependent on the North for such books was exceedingly embarrassing, and the assumption that they contained insidious propaganda was freely made without investigation. Even when they contained no direct attacks on Southern ways, most of them, it was asserted, implied Southern inferiority. One reformer told of a text which said that the "slaveholder ought not to be despised since slavery . . . [was] not his own, but the sin of his fathers," and which expressed pity for his condition with the hope that this great misfortune would "soon be removed from his midst." One singled out one of Peter Parley's books which admitted that Southern slaves were well treated and were given enough to eat, drink, and wear but concluded by saying that, in spite of this, slavery was not conducive to the happiness of either the whites or the Negroes. Another went the whole way and insisted that any books coming out of a region so rife with religious, political, and social heresies must be dangerous.

It was, however, "the bitter poison of Abolition prejudices and opinions" which was being "diffused into the minds of Southern children" before they were able to think for themselves, of which most complained. This was "the serpent coiled among flowers and striking the tender hand of childhood, stretching innocently forth to gather the flowers that sheltered it." This was the thing which demanded immediate attention and called for the preparation of texts "at the South by Southern men . . . with an especial eye to

[17] Ambler, *Sectionalism in Virginia,* 281; Natchez *Mississippi Free Trader,* November 6, 1857.

[Southern] institutions." Children must be taught that slavery was a good, a blessing to both master and slave.[18]

The need for a distinctly Southern literature was just as pressing. Thralldom of any kind was humiliating, but "dependence for knowledge"—knowledge of good and evil—was simply disastrous. Southern people were obliged to read Northern books because there were none better to be had. Some were, therefore, "more familiar with such abominable works as Mrs. Stowe's 'Uncle Tom's Cabin,' and the abolition sermons of Theodore Parker, than with the constitutionalism which [had] made the nation great." Calhoun and Duff Green had tried to encourage printing houses in the South, but the people "preferred the trashy stuff of Boston, Cincinnati and New York, to the pure, healthful, home-made productions of Southern pens." They subscribed for the antislavery *Saturday Evening Post,* for "Harper's semi-English and Putnam's Free Soil Magazines," and neglected their own *Southern Literary Messenger* and the *Southern Quarterly Review.* Southern men owed it to themselves, said the Richmond *Enquirer,* "to turn away from Northern publishers" and to support "home literature." "Intellectual vassalage" must end. Works of "pre-eminent merit" from the North, such as those by a William H. Prescott or a George Ticknor, could be tolerated, but the indiscriminate preference for anything Northern over anything written by a Southerner was degrading and corrupting. Even the use of Northern type and paper was a useless aiding of foes. These were now available at home. The South could write and publish its own books on its own paper if its people wanted independence badly enough.[19]

Another step towards independence which Southern patriots now thought should be taken was that of "summering at home." A kind of "ridiculous snobbery" had long been carrying Southerners to

[18] Augusta *Constitutionalist,* December 18, 1856; Mobile *Daily Register,* August 26, 1856.

[19] Wetumpka *Southern Dial, and African Monitor,* December 1, 1858; Natchez *Mississippi Free Trader,* July 31, 1857; Huntsville *Southern Advocate,* September 5, 1855; Montgomery *Mail,* May 9, 1855; Memphis *Appeal,* January 16, 1859; Jay B. Hubbell, "Literary Nationalism in the Old South," in David K. Jackson (ed.), *American Studies in Honor of William Kenneth Boyd* (Durham, 1940), 175–220; Eugene Current-García, "Southern Literary Criticism and the Sectional Dilemma," in *Journal of Southern History,* XV (1949), 325–41.

Newport, Saratoga, Niagara, or other "crowded pleasure-places" at the North. It was "fashionable folly and nothing more." It was foolish in the first place because there were plenty of healthy and pleasant places in the South—yes, fashionable places, where Southerners could enjoy far more genteel companionship without "troubling the agitators and fanatics of the North." Why travel "long leagues" to enrich those who immediately turned around and denounced you? And in the second place Southerners ought to spend their time and money in places where they and their institutions were respected—where their money was made and their attention required by business. Then Southern watering places would be built up, Southern trade would flourish in the summer months instead of languishing as at present, and Northerners would have more respect for the common sense of Southerners as a whole.[20]

Northern aggression also gave new incentive to defend slavery. That, of course, required no capital or planning. It was more in line with Southern abilities. In fact, the proslavery argument was now rounded out to its final and most extreme statement. While other moves lagged a bit, and sometimes came to little, the defenders of slavery were able to create a whole new "sociology for the South." This is significant because it came in answer to those opposing slavery extension, not primarily to those condemning slavery *per se*. It shows how completely nonextension had become the new antislavery movement and how much greater was the actual threat of injury in such a drive. Nonextension carried a denial of an equal right to share in the territories. It threatened Southern influence in government. It gave strength to the refusal to enforce the Fugitive Slave Law. It labeled slavery a blight that must not touch virgin soil, a barrier across the path of progress. Earlier attacks had stressed the abstract; here were things concrete. A sharper, more comprehensive defense was required.

The old arguments from history and the Bible were, of course, repeated, but the emphasis was no longer on the abstract. The purpose now was to prove the soundness and naturalness of slavery and the superiority of society under it. There was "something wrong and rotten in Free Society," and, as one writer put it, "the great

---

[20] Montgomery *Mail*, March 29, 1855; New Orleans *Daily Crescent*, June 27, 1855; New Orleans *Daily Picayune*, May 18, 1856.

question now to be resolved by experiment, statistics and ratiocination . . . [was] not whether black slavery be excusable, but whether slavery in some form be not natural and necessary." The scenes of want and destitution exhibited under liberty and *laissez faire* in Europe and in our own industrial Northeast were causing thoughtful men on both continents to turn toward slavery as a remedy. The "sufferings of the laboring millions" under freedom had warned "the wise and the good of the necessity of change." [21]

If thinkers such as Carlyle and Newman found hope for a better society in a return to *white* slavery, how could anyone question the justice and soundness of Southern *Negro* slavery? Here was an "inferior race" rescued from the horrors of African life, from "a vast continent of sin, misery and superstition," and brought into contact with Christianity and civilization. "Why the Supreme Being saw fit to create or to produce such a race" no one could answer. But that the Negro was particularly fitted to be a slave was apparent to all. Thomas R. R. Cobb went into details: "His black color peculiarly fits him for the endurance of the heat of long-continued summers. The arched leg and receding heel seem to indicate a natural preparation for strength and endurance. The absence of nervous irritability gives to him a complete exemption from those inflammatory diseases so destructive in hot and damp atmospheres, and hence the remarkable fact, that the ravages of that scourge of the tropics, the yellow fever, never reach the negro race. In other portions of the body, especially the formation of the pelvis, naturalists have discovered a well-defined deterioration in the negro which, a late learned observer, Vrolik, of Amsterdam, has declared, shows 'a degradation in type, and an approach towards the lower form of animals.' So the arched dome of the head and the perpendicularity of the vertebral column are said, by an observant writer, to be characteristic, and to fit the negro peculiarly for the bearing of burdens upon the head." [22]

Yet even with such splendid equipment the Negro, Southerners

[21] Richmond *Enquirer*, January 29, 1855.

[22] Rev. Josiah Priest, *Bible Defense of Slavery; and origin, fortunes, and history of the negro race* (Glasgow, Ky., 1852), 99; Samuel B. Howe, *Slavery not Sinful* (New Brunswick, N.J., 1856), 80; Thomas R. R. Cobb, *An Inquiry into the Law of Negro Slavery in the United States of America* (Philadelphia, Savannah, 1858), I, 23–24; *Southern Dial* (Wetumpka, Ala.), I, No. 1 (1857), 31–35.

insisted, was helpless without the guidance and control supplied by slavery. He would not work without someone to make him do so. Indolence benumbed his "feeble intellect . . . and inflame[d] his vile passions" and drove him "into the extremes of savage barbarism." Without slavery he would sink into poverty and want, into vice and plunder, into disease and death.

Slavery thus made him into a useful member of society and rewarded him with a bit of civilization and Christianity. There were twice as many Negro church members in the South as had been won to Christ by all "other missionary efforts" combined. In fact, it appeared that an "All-wise Providence" had permitted slavery to exist in order to spread the light of the gospel. Seemingly God had forced the Negro upon the Southern cavalier, who would have preferred the white indentured servant, so that the African might, by association, make the most rapid progress out of his "original degradation." [23]

Dr. Josiah C. Nott, a Mobile physician and later professor of anatomy at the University of Louisiana, gave the argument quite a different turn. From his medical practice among slaves he was convinced that the Negro constituted a different species from the whites. He did not believe that the two had sprung from a single pair of progenitors. He insisted that "the Mosaic account [of creation] sheds no satisfactory light on this question" and that the clergy after two thousand years of discussion had only proven that they knew nothing about it. He, therefore, concluded that there had been many creations, not just one. Some animals on the present earth were different from those before the Flood, and must have been created since Noah gathered the few in his locality into the Ark. New lands, rising out of the sea, were known to produce their own peculiar type of vegetation. The wide variety of human types in different parts of the world seemed to indicate that it was the same with mankind.

Physical forces, he argued, could not change one species into an-

23 William G. Brownlow and Rev. A. Pryne, *Ought American Slavery to be Perpetuated?* (Philadelphia, 1858), 253; N. L. Rice, *Ten Letters on the Subject of Slavery Addressed to the Delegates from the Georgetown Association to the Last General Assembly of the Presbyterian Church* (St. Louis, 1855), *passim;* Thornton Stringfellow, *Scriptural and Statistical Views in Favor of Slavery* (Richmond, 1856), 68; *Duties of Masters to Servants: Three Prize Essays* (Charleston, 1851), 7–46.

other regardless of the changes they might make within a single species. They could not make a white man out of a Negro, nor a Negro out of a white man. The two races had existed for thousands of years without basic changes in physical characteristics, and nowhere could a relationship be shown between them. The Negro was clearly a separate and inferior creation. Nature had from the beginning destined him for servitude.

Thus the good doctor, who was recommending mesmerism as a form of treatment for certain ill-defined nervous disorders and suggesting that yellow fever was spread by insects (he even mentioned the mosquito), would turn to science for justification of the South's peculiar institution. He was laying the foundations for an "Aryan" superiority doctrine.

Such bold thinking shocked the Southern clergy. Was not the Bible, when correctly interpreted, sufficient defense for slavery? Could a society which prized stability above all else tolerate such unorthodox thinking? Men would have to choose between science and Moses and St. Paul. It would take more than the learning and logic of Josiah Nott to force the South to give up the Bible.[24]

The clergy, however, had a contribution all their own. Slavery, like sin, they proclaimed had come because of Adam's fall. In the imperfect state of human society, it pleased God to allow this evil to exist as a check on greater evils. It was not God's purpose in "the present dispensation of religion that 'all ill should be banished from this sublunary state and the earth be converted into a paradise.' " Nor was it the business of the church to be waging "war upon every form of human ill, whether social, civil, political or moral, and to patronize every expedient which a romantic benevolence may suggest as likely to contribute to human comfort and to mitigate the inconsequences of life." "The church had 'no commission to construct society afresh, to adjust its elements in different proportions, to rearrange the distribution of its classes, or to change the forms of its political constitutions.' " It "had no authority to interfere with slavery as a political institution." Its duty was simply

24 Josiah C. Nott, *Two Lectures on the Natural History of the Caucasian and Negro Races* (Mobile, 1844), pamphlet in Huntington Library; Josiah C. Nott and George R. Gliddon, *Types of Mankind: or, Ethnological Researches* (Philadelphia, 1854), *passim.* For reviews see Richmond *Enquirer,* April 29, July 6, 1854.

that of softening the personal relationships in slavery—in stressing the mutual obligations of servants and masters.[25]

Slavery thus viewed was a responsibility not to be taken lightly. "I thank God," said Frederick Ross, "he has given this great work to that type of the noble family of Japheth best qualified to do it,— the Cavalier stock,—the gentleman and lady of England and France, born to command, and softened and refined under our Southern sky." Masters had duties to servants—duties to the Negroes as their property and duties to them as social beings. Slavery as practiced in the American South had little relationship to the imaginary picture presented by Northern fanatics. It was a paternal relationship. Some even objected to the word "slavery." [26]

Such a system, defenders said, produced a superior social-economic order. Disorder and isms so abundant in the North did not exist in the South. Religion and politics were not mixed; spirit rappings were not heard; bloomerism had never taken hold; Millerites and Mormons were not to be found. New England was a natural breeder of anarchy. Her people had a "peculiar taste for insubordination to the laws and for schemes of mischief which seem[ed] inherent to the dollars proclivities of Yankeedom." The South, on the other hand, had none of these "poisonous weeds and fungi" and "no persecution for conscience sake." Slavery prevented labor troubles, kept the lower class orderly, and gave justice instead of charity to the infirm and aged.[27]

George Fitzhugh of Virginia climaxed the new proslavery argument with his two volumes, *Sociology for the South* and *Cannibals All!* The first of these denounced "free trade and universal liberty" as expressions of the selfish exploitation of the many by the few, of a war of wits against the guileless, and the cultivation and praise of "avarice, caution, circumspection and hard dealing." Slavery, on the other hand, stressed the responsibility of the strong for the weak, the adjustment of a labor system to the Negro's capacities, and a

[25] William S. Jenkins, *Pro-Slavery Thought in the Old South* (Chapel Hill, 1935), 207–18.

[26] F. A. Ross, *Position of the Southern Church in Relation to Slavery, as illustrated in a Letter of Dr. F. A. Ross to Rev. Albert Barnes with an introduction by a Constitutional Presbyterian* (New York, 1857), 68.

[27] Macon *Georgia Telegraph*, July 25, 1854; Milledgeville *Southern Recorder*, July 24, 1860.

more just distribution of the necessities of life among workers. Free society had failed and was everywhere drifting toward socialism. Slavery gave all the benefits of socialism without any of its evils. Free labor was everywhere harassed by want and worry; the slave was ever "cheerful, happy and contented, free from jealousy, malignity, and envy, and at peace with all around him." The one was "a system of antagonism and war; the other, of peace and fraternity." [28]

The second volume had as its chief aim to show "that *Labor makes values, and Wit exploitates and accumulates them.*" Its subtitle was *Slaves Without Masters;* its general conclusion "that the unrestricted exploitation of so-called free society, is more oppressive to the laborer than domestic slavery."

Back of Fitzhugh's thinking lay the idea that labor alone creates wealth and that an equal amount of one kind of labor should be given for another kind. The "profits" made from free labor were, therefore, "the amount of the products of such labor, which the employer, by means of the command which capital or skill" gave him, took away, exacted or "exploitated" from the free laborer, and those of slave labor, the proportion which the master was able to appropriate. Thus all those who were successful in living without producing what they accumulated were consuming their fellow men. And in a free society "the respectable way of living" was to make other people work for you and to pay them as little as possible. The workers thus became slaves without the benefits of care in sickness and old age and a plenty of food and shelter. They were slaves without masters—slaves without the benefits of slavery.

In a slave society, on the other hand, the master was forced to accept responsibility for the welfare of his workers. Children, the aged, and the infirm worked not at all, yet received all the comforts and necessaries of life. Those who toiled had reasonable hours, certain subsistence, and complete freedom from worry. In a way both the master and the land were their property. Free labor had "not a thousandth part of the rights and liberties of negro slaves."

As civilization advanced, said Fitzhugh, capital would accumulate

---

[28] George Fitzhugh, *Sociology for the South; or, The Failure of Free Society* (Richmond, 1854), *passim;* Harvey Wish, *George Fitzhugh, Propagandist of the Old South* (Baton Rouge, 1943), 82–93.

in fewer hands, land would become the property of a small proportion of the population, and the chances for individual employment
and certain subsistence would decline. Then slavery alone would
solve the problem of capital and labor. Only in slavery, which identified their interests, could they live in harmonious and friendly relations. Conditions in England showed that society was nearing the
stage of strife and civil exploitation, and the arguments of socialists,
Utopians, and other reformers asking for change only proved the
complete failure of free society. Only the great open West prevented
American society from showing equal confusion and decay. Thus
slavery, with its happy workers, well treated in every way and having security without responsibility, was not only a more just system
but the one to which the world would ultimately come.[29]

Fitzhugh, of course, had ignored the discontent that existed in
his own society—the threat of slave insurrections, which, at the
very time he wrote, was reaching a new high. He had, however,
bluntly questioned the soundness of trends in Northern life and
the justice of social-economic relationships in a financial-industrial
order under which the living of the many was passing into the hands
of the few and great fortunes were being accumulated as poverty
deepened, and in which ferment and disorder characterized the
process of adjustment from an old age into a new. Seward confidently called it "Progress." Lincoln was beginning to talk of it
as the evidence of soundness under democracy. Yet there was also
much of unrest and uncertainty. Depressions recurred; regions supplying raw materials and markets were being reduced to a grum-
bling colonial status; some men even talked of "wage slavery." The
possibilities for "the good life" in urban centers had not been entirely realized. Nor did the machine necessarily recognize the dignity
and divinity of the individual or give him the opportunity for self-
expression. And most serious in its social consequences, the greater
interdependence of mankind in the age that was dawning did not
proportionately increase the feeling of responsibility in the strong
for the dependent.[30]

[29] George Fitzhugh, *Cannibals All! or, Slaves Without Masters* (Richmond, 1857),
passim; Wish, *George Fitzhugh,* 160–93.
[30] Harvey Wish, "The Slave Insurrection Panic of 1856," in *Journal of Southern
History,* V (1939), 206–22.

Fitzhugh had lifted the slavery struggle to new levels. He had turned the argument around. He had assumed the soundness and justice of slavery and was asking, with many others, whether finance-industrialism and majority rule offer in themselves any protection for the weak or a fair distribution to those who toiled. That was a disturbing question to raise just as the Northeast was confidently entering this modern world, financing and marketing Southern crops, manufacturing or importing her goods, and making an effort to convince the farmers of the West that they too would soon share in the profits and benefits of finance and industry. In the face of existing conditions, it was not exactly comforting to have a man ask whether freedom always gave equality.

It should thus be noted that Fitzhugh's proslavery thinking was turning toward the creation of a possible science of society in which slavery was rationalized into an eternal principle. He and his friends George Frederick Holmes in Virginia and Henry Hughes in Mississippi were, in their praise of slavery as a corrective of the social-economic ills of the day, lifting the argument well above emotional levels and, like Josiah Nott, giving it a wider and more universal connotation. Hughes even repudiated the word slavery, because it implied that the bondsman labored for the master's benefit alone, whereas his work was beneficial to himself and to the state as well. He insisted that "the societary organization of the United States" might better be known as "Warranteeism." It was, he said, an "organization whose essentials every society just to itself, must incorporate." He was, of course, speaking only of the South. Northern society belonged in the failure category.[31]

Nor were the Southern efforts to end dependence and to escape from a colonial status, which now began in earnest, any more pleasing to the North than the implications in the new proslavery argument. They were in fact a bit more disturbing. Although not completely successful in all lines and a complete failure in some, real progress soon began to be made in others, and prospects were bright enough to worry Northern competitors. The move for direct trade with Europe was one that came to little. Colonel Dudley Mann, in

[31] H. G. Duncan and W. L. Duncan, "The Development of Sociology in the Old South," in *American Journal of Sociology* (Chicago), XXXIX (1933–1934), 651–56.

Virginia, projected a line of steamers from the Chesapeake to England, secured a charter from the legislature, and opened books for the subscription of stock. The public response was encouraging, but action was delayed and interest soon dwindled. The outbreak of the Civil War put an end even to talk. Other projects aimed at lines from Norfolk to France, and one from New Orleans to Liverpool. Neither got beyond the planning stage. A few coastwise sailing-packet lines were all that came out of the elaborate proposals of individuals and conventions.[32]

The efforts to diversify Southern life and develop manufactures made better headway. How much recent propaganda helped we cannot say. Conditions were favorable and improvement had already begun. Yet the gains made from 1850 to 1860 were substantial enough to suggest the beginnings of a new era. The value of Southern manufactures increased by 96.5 per cent. In the cotton mill industry the gain was 43 per cent, and in the production of bar, sheet, and railroad iron, 63 per cent. Woolen manufactures more than doubled, while clothing, shoes, paper, cotton gins, carriages, and wagons all showed remarkable gains. Virginia and North Carolina factories, by June, 1860, were producing 61 per cent of all the plug, smoking, and snuff tobacco manufactured in the United States. The value of flour and meal ground was nearly thirty-eight million dollars and of lumber, sawed and planed, more than nineteen and a half millions. Richmond boasted the largest grain mills in the world, and one of her mills had a capacity of a thousand barrels of flour a day. North Carolina furnished 60 per cent of the nation's turpentine, and the lumber industry as a whole employed some sixteen thousand persons.[33]

Virginia led the section, but Georgia was not far behind. The Richmond *Enquirer* in September, 1859, noted the fact that a ship clearing for Charleston carried carwheels and spikes from the Tredegar Iron Works, and 1,300 kegs of nails from the Old Dominion Nail Factory for the use of the Memphis and Charleston Railway. A second ship, for New Orleans, carried from Rhom's Eagle Foundry "Thirteen stationary engines for cotton and sugar plantations, the last of 70 sent in the past few weeks." On the same ship, destined for the Mobile markets, were 14 engines from the Shockoe

[32] Russel, *Economic Aspects of Southern Sectionalism*, 120–21. [33] *Ibid.*, 228–30.

Machine Shops and parcels of brogans from the shoe factory of Alex. Hill & Company. Cotton factories and tobacco factories in Richmond, Petersburg, Danville, and Lynchburg added to Virginia's prosperity and hopes and gave her, year by year, a stronger Border State outlook.[34]

Georgia, meanwhile, was moving forward rapidly in industry, especially in the manufacture of cotton goods. By 1860 her 33 mills were capitalized at $2,126,103 and employed 2,813 hands. Their product was valued at $2,371,207, or a gain of over 69 per cent for the decade. Macon boasted not only of cotton mills but of foundries and machine shops. A rolling mill and nail factory had been set up near Cartersville; Baldwin County had a pottery works; Augusta insisted that the harness and saddles turned out by the establishment of Hatch and Begbie were far superior to anything coming from the North. In all, Georgia had in 1860 an income of almost $17,000,000 from her manufacturing plants and well deserved the title "Massachusetts of the South." [35]

Although financially hampered by the panic of 1857, Gregg's factory at Graniteville, South Carolina, had continued to prosper. Profits in the early fifties ranged from 8 to 18 per cent, and substantial improvements and expansion had been possible. His village, by 1859, had grown to some nine hundred people and the capital to $400,000. On the eve of civil war Gregg was planning large additions to his plant which would have included dyeing, bleaching, and the making of Canton flannel.[36]

Daniel Pratt at his Prattville, Alabama, factory had also prospered. From small beginnings in 1833 he had developed the most successful cotton gin factory in the South, had added saw and planing mills, a flour mill, a gristmill, and what was probably the leading cotton factory of the state. Like Gregg, he made a fortune for himself, and as did the firm of Barnett and Marks at Tallassee and Major David Scott at Scottsville, he set a model for industry in Alabama which, if civil war had not intervened, might have begun the great developments of a generation later.[37]

34 Richmond *Enquirer*, September 29, 1859.

35 Coulter, *Short History of Georgia*, 265–66; Avery Craven, "Georgia and the South," in *Georgia Historical Quarterly*, XXIII (1939), 219–35.

36 Mitchell, *William Gregg, Factory Master of the Old South*, 91–131.

37 Albert B. Moore, *History of Alabama and Her People* (Chicago, 1927), I, 409–12.

Edwin Holt, in North Carolina, kept pace with these other leaders and his famous "Alamance plaids," introduced in the 1850's, pioneered the making of colored cotton cloth in the South. By 1861 he was working twelve hundred spindles and ninety-six looms. He too built homes for his workers, sold them supplies from a company store, and was as painstaking with their religious life as were the proprietors at Lowell.[38]

These developments and others in the iron and hemp industries did not amount to the arrival of the Industrial Revolution at the South, but they did mark a change both in the efforts and in the attitudes of some Southern men and women. In a way they revealed the link with national trends as well as the effort toward the future and showed possibilities rather than comparative accomplishments. Whether the South had begun a permanent shift toward a greater diversity of its economic life is a matter for speculation. Most certainly, if it had, the Civil War ultimately ended its efforts and left developments to new forces in later days.

Railroad building in the South always labored under serious handicaps. Population in a rural world was scattered and light. The movement of crops to market was a seasonal business and one not heavily dependent on the railroad. Southern rivers were plentiful and, in high water, navigable far into the interior. They were ideal for carrying the bulky but comparatively light Southern staples which kept well and could easily await floodtime. Capital, moreover, was tied up in land and labor, and managerial ability was attracted and held to planting by custom and sectional values.

Yet Southern men did understand the importance of the railroad and did share in the national impulse to build. Earlier efforts had resulted in local lines in most of the states east of the Mississippi and in numerous projects to link the coast with the interior. Shortage of funds and rivalries between cities and companies hindered progress, but by the 1850's enough had been accomplished to justify further planning and the rounding out of systems. In this era the South Carolina Canal and Railroad Company, which had long run its trains from Charleston to Hamburg, was able to cross into Augusta and link up with the Georgia Railroad to Atlanta. There the Georgia Central from Savannah connected, and the Western and

[38] Eaton, *History of the Old South*, 427–28.

Atlantic soon made possible connections at Chattanooga with lines running north and west to Nashville and Memphis. With the completion of the Southwestern Road from Richmond to Knoxville and the East Tennessee and Georgia Road to Dalton on the Western and Atlantic, the Atlantic Coast at Norfolk, Charleston, and Savannah was linked with the Mississippi at Memphis. The little junction point, at various times called White Hall, Terminus, and Marthasville, now became the thriving city of Atlanta, important enough one day to bring William T. Sherman in its direction.[39]

The second set of developments of sectional import had to do with the efforts of Mobile and New Orleans to reach northward toward the Ohio. Both cities, as cotton export centers, felt the threat of Memphis and her eastern connections, and the eastward pull of trade by rail from the upper Northwest. The Mobile and Ohio, chartered in 1848, crept slowly northward through eastern Mississippi with county, state, and Federal aid, to connect with the Illinois Central at Cairo in 1859. Much of its track, however, was at that time not ready for actual use, and a bridge across the Ohio was still lacking. Not until 1861 was the road in full operation. The New Orleans project moved even slower. Its charter was granted in 1850, but construction was slow and finances always short. With difficulty it made its way northward through Jackson, Mississippi, and across the border into Tennessee. A branch line into Memphis and connections to Columbus, Kentucky, were the final achievements before the outbreak of war.[40]

There was also much local railroad building in these years, especially in the seaboard states. Governor Wise of Virginia boasted of the lines that were being pushed out from Richmond, Norfolk, and Alexandria. All the principal cities of Georgia were connected by rail and, through Savannah and Charleston, with the seacoast. North Carolina had at last completed a line from Goldsboro west and south across the state to Raleigh and Charlotte. Louisville, Kentucky, and Nashville, Tennessee, were joined in 1859, and the

[39] Ulrich B. Phillips, *A History of Transportation in the Eastern Cotton Belt to 1860* (New York, 1908), 132–331.

[40] Robert S. Cotterill, "Southern Railroads and Western Trade, 1840–1850," in *Mississippi Valley Historical Review*, III (1916–1917), 427–41; Robert S. Cotterill, *The Old South* (Glendale, 1936), 180–85, 215–27; Thomas D. Clark, *The Beginning of the L & N; . . . 1836–1860* (Louisville, 1933), *passim*.

foundations of one of the South's important railroads thus were laid. With the steamboats on her rivers and with railroad lines from the Mississippi to the sea, and from the Ohio to the gulf, the South by 1860 was, as rural worlds go, quite adequately supplied with transportation facilities.

The agricultural achievements at the South in the two decades before the Civil War deserve far more recognition than they have been accorded. Long addicted to single cash crops, which were produced by shallow cultivation under the heaviest rainfall in the nation, the South had known the worst of soil depletion and ruined lands. Under the teachings of such reformers as John Taylor of Caroline and Edmund Ruffin, the old tobacco regions had, by 1850, made remarkable progress toward recovery. By the use of marl, better plowing, and crop rotation, lands had been restored and destruction, to a degree, ended. Now with the wider use of guano, lime, bone, and superphosphates, and with greater supplies of manure, the section was ready to reap the benefits of earlier experiments. Crops were diversified and specialized for new markets. Clover and other legumes became a part of crop rotations. Subsoil and contour plowing were combined with underground drainage to check erosion. The number of slaves was reduced, and those that were retained were carefully selected and trained. Better machinery was invented and put to use. Maryland opened an agricultural college, and Virginia schools set up professorships to teach the science of agriculture. Stock was increased and improved breeds introduced. Reliance for profits was placed on many items instead of on one. Truck gardening flourished in several centers along the coast— great quantities of peas, potatoes, tomatoes, cabbages, strawberries, and watermelons went by night boats in the season to Baltimore, Philadelphia, New York, and even to Boston. The dairy flourished near the cities; and farmers, large and small, were selling their wheat, their tobacco, hogs, cattle, and other surplus items at prices which enabled them to farm well and to improve their lands.[41]

In the Cotton Belt of the Southeast, nearly equal progress was being made. Reformers such as James H. Hammond, Thomas J. and David W. Dickson, Charles W. Howard, Richard S. Hard-

[41] Craven, *Soil Exhaustion . . . of Virginia and Maryland*, 152–61; Craven, *Edmund Ruffin*, 49–95.

wick, and Richard Peters led the way. Hammond brought Edmund Ruffin to South Carolina to search for marl beds and to preach improved methods. At Red Cliff and Silver Bluff he developed model plantations given to diversified crops, and practiced farming at its scientific best. The Dickson brothers brought improved methods to cotton and corn in the fields of Georgia, made skilled farmers out of slaves, developed new strains of cotton and new implements for the cultivation of corn. Hardwick made his contribution in hillside ditching and soil conservation. He was the pioneer of horizontal plowing in the Lower South. Howard bitterly criticized the use of costly slave labor on less valuable lands and searched far and wide for grasses that would fit into sensible crop rotations. The wider use of alfalfa was largely due to his efforts. Peters gave his efforts to improving Southern cattle. He stocked his own farm with Durhams and Ayrshires and later brought in Brahman cattle to cross with other breeds in the attempt to produce a hardier type and one better fitted to Southern conditions. He imported Merino sheep and crossed them with native stocks, and his last venture was a profitable experiment with Angora goats.[42]

Others gave their attention to the improvement of Southern horticulture. Robert Nelson, at his nursery in Macon, Georgia, produced better varieties of early peaches and, with others, helped to put this famous Georgia industry on a commercial basis. A small shipment to New York in 1853 sold at fifty cents each. By 1861 the annual sales from a young orchard near Columbus had reached $7,500. By the end of the decade peaches in carload lots were going from Georgia to New York. Markets had also been found in California and as far away as New Zealand. Apples and grapes also came in for improvement, and both were soon on a commercial basis. Early vegetables and strawberries from the Lower South were also reaching Northern markets before 1860. A new day for a new kind

[42] James C. Bonner, "Genesis of Agricultural Reform in the Cotton Belt," in *Journal of Southern History*, IX (1943), 475–500; Avery Craven, "The Agricultural Reformers of the Ante-Bellum South," in *American Historical Review*, XXXIII (1927–1928), 302–14; Weymouth T. Jordan, "Noah B. Cloud's Activities on Behalf of Southern Agriculture," in *Agricultural History*, XXV (1951), 53–58; James C. Bonner, "The Plantation Overseer and Southern Nationalism As Revealed in the Career of Garland D. Harmon," *ibid.*, XIX (1945), 1–11; James C. Bonner, "The Angora Goat: A Footnote in Southern Agricultural History," *ibid.*, XXI (1947), 42–46.

of agriculture was most certainly in the making when war interrupted. It had brought here, as in the tobacco world, new profits from diversified efforts and had here, as in Virginia, forced new attitudes toward the management of slaves. Numbers were being reduced to profitable levels, and the management of slaves was being adjusted to the needs for more skill and greater co-operation between master and servant.[43]

The moves for social and intellectual independence also brought some results. Northern papers were soon commenting on the absence of Southern men and women from Saratoga and Newport, but Southern complaints against summer migrations were still frequent enough to suggest no great interruption. Developments in education, on the other hand, were quite marked. By 1860 responsibility for public education was generally accepted, and higher education had moved forward faster than in any other part of the nation. Academies of varying quality still retained their popularity, and most of the state universities enjoyed a new prosperity. The University of Virginia could boast of students from every Southern state, and her enrollment of 606 surpassed that of Harvard or Yale. The University of North Carolina grew rapidly in numbers and distinction, and modest revivals were experienced at Alabama and Mississippi. In 1860 the cornerstone of the new University of the South was laid at Sewanee—a conscious move towards Southern educational independence. Meanwhile, a few students left Northern colleges to continue their studies in Southern institutions. One group of medical students in Philadelphia seceded as a body and set up a school of their own in Richmond. Yet the rolls at Harvard, Yale, and Princeton still contained the names of a goodly number of Southern boys, and complaints against that fact were still to be heard. Much talk had not convinced all Southerners that a superior education could be had at home.[44]

The quality of higher education in the South, nevertheless, was

[43] James C. Bonner, "Advancing Trends in Southern Agriculture, 1840–1860," in *Agricultural History*, XXII (1948), 248–59; Charleston *Mercury*, January 13, 1860.

[44] New York *Evening Mirror*, quoted in Jacksonville *Republican*, October 23, 1855; New Orleans *Daily Crescent*, June 27, 1855; New Orleans *Daily Picayune*, May 18, 1856; Montgomery *Mail*, March 29, 1855. There were 65 Southerners at Harvard in the 1860–1861 session. Some 257 Harvard graduates served in the Confederate Army. In 1860 the South had one for every 162 inhabitants in college; the North had one

definitely improving. The greatest handicap lay in the bitter rivalry between religious sects, which resulted in more denominational colleges than could be supported adequately and in a distrust and jealousy of the state universities. Age and sectional consciousness, however, were having their effect. Standards were being lifted. The University of Virginia stood well to the front in quality as well as in numbers. In 1860 it had a faculty of twenty, of whom thirteen were in the Literary and Scientific School, five in the Medical School, and two in the Law School. Of the eight "Professors" in the Literary and Scientific School, six have been deemed worthy of inclusion in the *Dictionary of American Biography*. Both of the "Professors" in the Law School are so honored. Few institutions in the United States, early or late, have boasted a more distinguished faculty than that which contained Basil L. Gildersleeve in Greek, M. Schele de Vere in Modern Languages, Albert Bledsoe in Mathematics, Francis H. Smith in Natural Philosophy, George F. Holmes in History and General Literature, and John B. Minor and James P. Holcombe in Law. In this group also, until 1853, was William B. Rogers, the noted scientist who was later to found the Massachusetts Institute of Technology.

Virginia's library, started by Thomas Jefferson, now had thirty thousand volumes, and her Board of Visitors in 1857 had appropriated $2,000 for new apparatus for natural philosophy, $700 for chemical apparatus, and $1,500 for specimens for comparative anatomy. While Greek and Latin still held the lead in the course of study, it is interesting to notice that for the 220 students in Latin, there were 180 in Chemistry, 211 in Mathematics, 127 in Natural Philosophy, and 113 in History and Literature.[45]

Other Southern universities could hardly match Virginia, yet with David L. Swain as president, the student body at the University of North Carolina grew from 165 in 1845 to nearly 500 in 1860. Its faculty contained in the 1850's such eminent scholars as Elisha Mitchell in Chemistry, Mineralogy, and Geology, J. De Bernière Hooper in Latin and French, Manuel Fetter in Greek, and William H. Battle in Law. Here too sciences received new emphasis, and

---

for every 317. Edward Ingle, *Southern Sidelights: A Picture of Social and Economic Life in the South a Generation before the War* (New York, 1896), 143.

45 *Catalogue of the University of Virginia, 1859–1860* (Richmond, 1860), 4–7, 22–37.

constitutional and international law found a place in the course of study. Perhaps because of strong competition from denominational colleges, President Swain also included the study of the Bible. Under his direction Chapel Hill began to take on something of the charm that still marks its ways.

Elsewhere less was accomplished. The University of Georgia was torn with strife and lost such outstanding men as John and Joseph LeConte, Charles S. Venable, and Charles F. McCay to the University of South Carolina, which still retained something of its earlier glories with James H. Thornwell as president and Francis Lieber on its faculty. At Alabama, in spite of strong competition from denominational schools, the University attracted such high-grade scholars as Frederick A. P. Barnard, Michael Tuomey, and John W. Mallet. Barnard, who filled the chair of Chemistry and Natural History, left Alabama in 1854 for the University of Mississippi, where in 1856 he became its president and then its chancellor. His later career as president of Columbia University in New York City would suggest that the Southern universities of this period were not without talented instruction. The distinguished scientific work of such men as Mitchell, Tuomey, LeConte, and Mallet at these schools, and that of Francis S. Holmes at the College of Charleston, would indicate both the time and the encouragement for research.[46]

Denominational colleges also played their part in supplying the South with higher education. Methodists, Baptists, and Presbyterians were particularly active in founding if not always adequately supporting colleges. Many stressed the training of preachers, but the protection of their young people from the "immorality and unorthodox thinking" supposedly characteristic of the universities was also a purpose. Some secured and held scholarly teachers; others

---

[46] Henderson, *North Carolina: The Old North State and the New*, II, 131–38; Coulter, *College Life in the Old South*, 247–63; Benjamin M. Palmer, *The Life and Letters of James Henley Thornwell* (Richmond, 1875), 325–96; Charles F. Thwing, "Frederick Augustus Porter Barnard," in *Dictionary of American Biography*, I, 619–21; W. W. Kemp, "John LeConte," *ibid.*, XI, 88–89; George P. Merrill, "Joseph LeConte," *ibid.*, 90–91; Edgar W. Knight, "Charles Francis McCay," *ibid.*, 577–78; Charles W. Dabney, "Charles Scott Venable," *ibid.*, XIX, 245–46; Thomas C. Johnson, Jr., *Scientific Interests in the Old South* (New York, 1936), 27–28, 187–88; James H. Easterby, *A History of the College of Charleston . . .* (Charleston, 1935), 124.

placed piety above learning. Enrollments varied greatly and resources even more. A few of the larger, well-established schools might at their peak have around two hundred or more students; the smaller ones, just enough to keep their doors open. Standards were seldom high, yet the service rendered to church and state by such schools as Randolph-Macon, Hampden-Sydney, Davidson, Emory, Wofford, Howard, and Transylvania seems to have been out of all proportion to their resources.[47]

The production of Southern textbooks lagged. A few books bearing a distinctly Southern flavor were produced in different fields, but none was of sufficient quality to sweep the section. In 1858 the history classes at the Citadel in Charleston, South Carolina, were still being taught that the manners and morals of the upper Southern group were distinguished by "luxurious and expansive hospitality" but were "too generally addicted to the vices of card-playing, gambling and intemperance." Peter Parley's much despised texts were still in wide use. Southern boys still learned that the states were divided into towns and counties; they heard much of the onions and broomcorn raised in Connecticut, but little about Louisiana and her sugar, and read that slaves were "worse treated in the American States than in any part of the world."

Publishing in the South remained backward in spite of complaints and encouragement. A few concerns in different cities published a few books but seemingly did not greatly restrict the Southern business of such Northern publishers as Ticknor and Fields, J. B. Lippincott, and G. P. Putnam. One writer has asserted that, in 1856, the Southern states manufactured only $750,000 worth of books out of the nation's total of $16,000,000. Hinton Helper declared in his much-quoted volume that out of more than 300 publishers in the United States, less than 30 were in the South, and of these, half were in the city of Baltimore. These figures, however, like others in his book, must have been slightly juggled, for in O. A. Roorbach's *Bibliotheca Americana* for 1852, out of some 550 publishers of books listed, approximately 100 were in the South. The output, at any rate, was never large, and the fact that the sales of Ticknor and Fields, located at Boston in the heart of the abolition

[47] Albea Godbold, *The Church College of the Old South* (Durham, 1944), 3-45.

belt, reached a high-water mark in the years 1859 and 1860 seems
to indicate that propaganda had not improved matters to any great
extent.[48] As George W. Bagby wrote in 1861:

"Southern patriotism never was proof against Northern newspapers and picture magazines. If the angel Gabriel had gone into
the very heart of the South, if he had even taken his seat on the
top of the office of the *Charleston Mercury* and there proclaimed
the immediate approach of the Day of Judgment, that would not
have hindered the hottest secessionist from buying the *New York
Herald* and subscribing for *Harper's Magazine.*" [49]

The exact amount of Southern publishing done in the years immediately before the outbreak of war is hard to determine. J. W.
Randolph and West and Johnston in Richmond, Evans and Cogs-
well in Charleston, and S. H. Goetzel and Company in Mobile were
probably the outstanding firms in the section. Strother and Mariam
in Raleigh, and Burke, Boykin and Company in Macon were lesser
concerns of importance. All did local printing, and their output
of books consisted largely of second-rate volumes by local writers.
Randolph seems to have done better than the others; but books
by Southern writers did not sell in the North, and Southern writers
of ability usually preferred a Northern publisher because of better
distribution facilities. The Southern publisher was, therefore, always at a disadvantage in the quality of the material he was offered
and in the market in which he had to sell it. For these reasons the
best product of the Southern press was always the newspaper. Its
editor, more than any other person, spoke to and for the people of
the section. Only the clergyman rivaled him in influence. Through
the columns of their papers, such men as William Olds, John Forsyth, Richard Yeadon, George W. Kendall, William W. Holden,
the Rhett brothers, and a dozen others equally gifted helped to
shape Southern opinion and to give direction to Southern action.
Through them the South became articulate.

In the periodical field, some progress was made and some South-

[48] Warren S. Tryon, "The Publications of Ticknor and Fields in the South, 1840–
1865," in *Journal of Southern History*, XIV (1948), 305–30.
[49] Quoted in Hubbell, "Literary Nationalism in the Old South," in Jackson (ed.),
American Studies in Honor of William Kenneth Boyd, 217–18.

ern weaknesses startlingly revealed. Southern agricultural papers, such as the *Southern Planter,* the *Southern Cultivator,* and the *Soil of the South,* seem to have prospered in this period, but the *Southern Literary Messenger* could complain in 1855 that *Harper's Magazine* had five times as many subscribers south of the Potomac, and the *Southern Quarterly Review* would have to suspend publication in 1857 for lack of support. *Russell's Magazine,* founded in Charleston in that same year, fared no better. In 1860 it too "struck upon breakers and sank." Perhaps it was, as one writer has suggested, that the contributors to these magazines were too much in earnest and believed that it was their mission on earth to elevate even though it cost the last subscriber. *De Bow's Review,* with its more general coverage, did manage to survive but had, at all times, good reason to complain of Southern neglect. In the end, however, it had to become a voice of radical Southern opinion.

Perhaps it was the vigor of the newspaper and the preoccupation with immediate political problems which caused the call for a distinctly Southern literature to go largely unheeded. Perhaps the trouble lay deeper, in certain fixed notions of what constituted literature and a failure to appreciate the rich literary materials that lay all about. It may have been that a mere demand for a certain type of output to meet an emergency is not the way to secure a native literature. Whatever the cause, the results were meager. Southern literature did not blossom on demand. William Gilmore Simms was still active and in the ten years before 1860 added to his already long list of books such titles as *Katharine Walton, The Sword and the Distaff, The Forayers, Eutaw,* and *The Cassique of Kiawah.* Just how much more sectional these volumes were than his earlier ones is a question. That he, himself, had become more conscious of the South's plight and more active in her defense is quite apparent. But he had from the first made use of Southern materials. Most certainly his larger patterns had not changed.

The little group that gathered around him in Charleston, moreover, followed an older romantic tradition. To it belong the young poets Henry Timrod and Paul Hamilton Hayne. Both had begun to write, but neither as yet went much below the surface. As one critic has said of Timrod: "[He showed] all the rootlessness of one who had learned the technique, had mastered the art of poetic reference and communication, but had never really had anything to say." That had to come with war and its aftermath.[50]

The really worth-while literary contribution of the period came from quite outside the orthodox group and also found its first expression, as a rule, in the newspaper, not in the literary magazine. It was the work of a group of Southern humorists who caught and exaggerated the homely vices, virtues, crudities, and foibles of the plain people at work and play. There was a boisterous, ridiculous quality about the tales they told of life in out-of-the-way corners. The humor was broad and sometimes brash, but there was realism there and freshness which appealed to the storytelling rural peoples. It had begun back with Augustus Baldwin Longstreet's *Georgia Scenes,* and continued in William Tappan Thompson's *Major Jones's Courtship* and Johnson Jones Hooper's *Adventures of Simon Suggs.* It now found expression in Joseph G. Baldwin's *The Flush Times of Alabama and Mississippi* and in the early writings of George Washington Harris and Richard Malcolm Johnston. The last two were only beginning their work, but they had already tapped the rich veins that would one day yield *Sut Lovingood's Yarns* and *Georgia Sketches.*[51]

The South was thus richer in literary ability than it knew or than the North suspected, but little of its production had come from the sectional call for intellectual independence. Professor Jay B. Hubbell is probably right when he says that the gain was largely in the new respect for the writer which now came with the realization of the need for a sectional literature as a defense against slurs and attack. The politicians and the public now began to realize that the spoken word was not enough.

There had been much talk in these years of unrest and apprehension to the effect that North and South now constituted two peoples, and about the tendency of political parties to divide at the sectional line. More and more was heard the statement that separation was inevitable, that the South would ultimately be forced to secede or yield her way of life. Such statements usually met a quick reply—an affirmation of loyalty to the Union and a reminder of

[50] Edd Winfield Parks, *Segments of Southern Thought* (Athens, 1938), 83–95.
[51] *Ibid.,* 215–34.

its value. Yet the feeling was there, and the Southern commercial conventions, which year after year had passed resolutions in favor of direct trade with Europe and of building factories and forwarding railroads, steadily drifted into radical hands. Southern rights took up more time. Hostility towards the North was more often expressed. Politicians were more in evidence. Some charged that the Savannah meeting in 1856 was a conclave of "brazen faced disunionists," treasonable in its purposes and hostile to the national government. The next year's meeting at Knoxville was even more section-conscious, and from that time forward it was clearly understood that the politicians had taken control. The commercial conventions had become little more than meetings to forward Southern nationalism.[52]

The election of James Buchanan and the inclusion of Southern leaders in his Cabinet, however, tended to calm the atmosphere and to crowd the radical spokesmen temporarily aside. Where there was open strife, it was between the party factions in the states from which Cabinet appointments had been made. Old Southern Rights Democrats in Georgia were angered at Cobb's selection, and the Hunter group in Virginia were displeased by the choice of Floyd. But even these factions acquiesced when Buchanan proved too stubborn, and the inclusion of two more Southerners, Jacob Thompson of Mississippi and Aaron V. Brown of Tennessee, produced a general feeling of confidence.

The South, moreover, was prosperous. Cotton prices were high; the new industrial plants were paying dividends; diversified agriculture, with widening markets, was yielding greater returns to the farmers in the Border and Eastern Seaboard states than they had known for a generation. The larger political situation was comparatively quiet. The Know-Nothings, like the Whigs before them, had split on the slavery issue, and in spite of some efforts to continue as a major party, it steadily melted away. The Democrats were thus left to dominate. Their old feuds had left wounds that had not entirely healed, but they could afford a degree of division against competition that often could call itself nothing but the "Opposition Party." The political turmoil which the young and vigorous Repub-

[52] Wender, *Southern Commercial Conventions*, 170.

licans were producing in the North was entirely lacking. Only the threat of Northern aggression troubled a people whose way of life was undergoing no spectacular social-economic changes.

The Kansas question, however, was still unsettled. And Kansas had become the symbol of "right" and "rights" and "the balance of power in government." Most Southerners now realized that the North had won the race for numerical supremacy. They also understood that Kansas would ultimately become a free state. The exact meaning of squatter sovereignty, however, had not been determined, and whether the people could decide for or against slavery in territorial days or must wait until statehood was a matter still hotly debated. Southern Democrats were almost unanimous in their insistence that the equality promised by the Kansas-Nebraska Act prevented any interference with the entrance or existence of slavery until a state constitution was framed. That, somehow, would satisfy Southern pride, and might even give slight hope that, through some legal loophole, Kansas might temporarily be won. At least the equality fiction would be upheld.

The majority of Northerners, on the other hand, were of the opposite opinion. They were, at least, certain that, with numerical supremacy and the Declaration of Independence on their side, Kansas *ought* to be free at all times. Perhaps there was also some loophole by which this could be achieved regardless of squatter-sovereignty interpretations. At any rate, the problem thus presented to the new administration was to hold a badly divided party together and to stop the valuable uses to which the Republicans were putting Kansas.

With this in mind, the President-elect, who had vacillated between the two conflicting points of view, now turned to the Supreme Court. From a friend on the Court, he learned that a decision would soon be delivered in the case of Dred Scott, a Missouri Negro who was suing for his freedom on grounds of having lived on free territory. The case had first been taken up in conference, and a majority had decided to dispose of it by a refusal to assume jurisdiction. This would have left Scott in slavery, as the Missouri courts, from which appeal had come, had ruled. Then two minority judges had determined to file a dissenting opinion justifying the Republican contention that Congress had full power to deal with slavery in the territories—a move which had led Judge James M. Wayne to insist that the majority also discuss Congressional powers.

After considerable disagreement on grounds for opinions and some pressure on the part of Buchanan, the majority now took the fatal step. Although not voting as a unit on all points, they held that Scott, as a Negro, did not have a citizen's right to maintain a suit in a Federal court; that Congress had no right to exclude slavery from any territory; and that, as a result, the Missouri Compromise was, and had been all along, unconstitutional. This was the decision which Buchanan, in his inaugural, had prophesied would end the slavery conflict.[53]

The furor which greeted this decision in the North was not matched by rejoicing in the South. Bitter denunciation of the court was not balanced by words of praise. In fact, the famous Dred Scott decision received scant attention in the South. The reasons are obvious. In the first place, there was nothing new or worthy of notice to Southerners in the assertion that a Negro was not a citizen with the right to maintain suit in court. Southerners had long taken that for granted. Nor was there anything new to Southerners in the pronouncement on the Missouri Compromise. They had maintained for years that it was unconstitutional and had taken its repeal in the Kansas-Nebraska Act as a move towards delayed justice. True, agreement by the Supreme Court even on commonplaces was gratifying, but what had been gained? As the Augusta *Constitutionalist* said, it would "not take away the occupation of demagogues, nor cure the madness of the antislavery fanatics of the North." These two classes would "continue to agitate the subject of slavery and only grow more lawless and insane, as the weight of popular and legal condemnation accumulate[d] upon them." They would simply turn against the Court. They would plead the "higher law" against any decision.[54]

Kansas, however, was another matter. To what happened there the South could not be indifferent. The new administration was

[53] Roy F. Nichols, *The Disruption of American Democracy* (New York, 1948), 63–66, 71–73; Frank H. Hodder, "Some Phases of the Dred Scott Case," in *Mississippi Valley Historical Review*, XVI (1929–1930), 3–22.

[54] Sitterson, *Secession Movement in North Carolina*, 140; Schultz, *Nationalism and Sectionalism in South Carolina*, 135; Augusta *Constitutionalist*, March 18, 1857.

expected to see that Southern interests in the territory were protected. Yet just what that now meant was not clear. From a theoretical point of view, all that the South could ask was that slaveholders, along with free men, might go to Kansas, and that a majority there would be permitted to decide for freedom or for slavery. The whole situation, however, had become hopelessly confused. If the time of deciding had been agreed upon by all, much difficulty might have been avoided, but not all of it. There was too much distrust abroad. Because of irregularities, distortions, and the importance now attached to the outcome, no unfavorable decision could possibly be accepted as a fair and impartial one. Many Southerners had come to feel that unless Kansas became a slave state justice had not been done. The whole business, including the Kansas-Nebraska Act itself, was a cheat and a fraud. The North was determined to have the advantage at all cost. The South was being done out of its rights. Its people had become sensitive and suspicious. Their self-respect was at stake. Their equality in the Union was at issue. They began talking anew of sending settlers to Kansas. A few began to say that here was the final sectional issue.[55]

Some, on the other hand, saw nothing to be gained by further effort. "The battle between North and South," said one, "has been fought, and the North is the victor. . . . A dissolution of this Union, at no distant day, is inevitable." Another wrote: "Two distinct and rival systems of society and civilization are bound together in this confederacy, the Northern and the Southern. For ours, we ask no particular privileges; we have stood on the defensive; we have made no war upon others, and only ask a fair opportunity of extending, by our own exertions, the institutions we have loved and valued at home. But the people of the North deny us this right, and insist that their civilization shall engross all the territories that the vast power of the Union can conquer or purchase, while ours shall never pass its present boundaries." [56]

Such a situation could not long continue. The "progress of sectionalism had been more rapid during the past year" than at any time since the foundation of the government. The final break could

[55] Augusta *Constitutionalist*, September 7, 1856.

[56] S. C. Elson to Hammond, April 7, 1856, in Hammond Papers (Division of Manuscripts, Library of Congress); Natchez *Mississippi Free Trader*, August 18, 1857.

not be far off. "Either the Abolition North, or the States Right South," wrote a Virginia editor, "must be morally and politically crushed, in the approaching conflict. The cry will be 'no quarter.' When the curtain falls over the campaign of 1860, it will hide only the victor and the dead." [57]

[57] Charleston *Mercury,* October 25, 1858; Norfolk (Va.) *Statesman,* quoted in Natchez *Mississippi Free Trader,* July 14, 1857.

CHAPTER XI

KANSAS, DOUGLAS, AND JOHN BROWN

AS PRESIDENT BUCHANAN developed his program, the object was undoubtedly more the ending of the Kansas troubles and the checking of Republicans than one of pleasing the South. He needed a new Democratic state. Governor Geary, who had done exceedingly well, must be replaced by a man of greater prestige. The Kansas question must be gotten out of politics. With this in mind, he somehow persuaded Robert J. Walker, his old colleague in Polk's Cabinet, to undertake the job. Walker was reluctant to leave a promising business career but was won over by the assurance "that the actual bona fide residents of the territory of Kansas, by a fair and regular vote, unaffected by fraud or violence . . . [would] be permitted, in adopting their state constitution, to decide for themselves what . . . [would] be their social institutions." When he left Washington, he clearly believed that the administration would insist on a popular referendum on any constitution adopted. He may even have dreamed of some day returning in triumph as the Senator from the new state.[1]

Yet before Walker arrived in Kansas, Frederick P. Stanton, who had gone on ahead to act as secretary of the territory, had discovered that plans concocted in Washington had little relationship to the realities in Kansas. The combination of speculation, frontier lawlessness, and local ambitions made the smooth working out of a Democratic machine and a peaceful settlement of internal conflicts almost impossible. Surveyor General John Calhoun, his chief clerk, L. A. Maclean, and the recent district attorney, Andrew J. Isacks, had already made up their minds to control the setting up of government. They did not welcome interference. They had already made

---

[1] Nichols, *Disruption of American Democracy*, 94–98.

life miserable for Stanton before Walker arrived to deliver his well-worked-over inaugural address.

That address, undoubtedly shaped in part by the immediate surroundings, marked the end of the radical Southerner's confidence in Walker and, to a degree, in Buchanan. Walker first stressed the fact that unless the constitution framed was submitted to the people, it would, in all probability, be rejected by Congress. He then spoke of the glorious future possible in Kansas and of the needlessness of a quarrel over slavery. He was certain that climate, not politics, would determine the outcome. Kansas was unsuitable for slavery. The South would have to look to the Indian territory, westward and south, for her slave state.[2]

"We are betrayed," wrote Thomas W. Thomas. "Our victory is turned to ashes on our lips." Walker had traveled to Kansas through the North, "gathering up a free-soil suite," speaking from the same platform with the abolitionist Charles Robinson, "and attempting to mask his vile hypocrisy with the flimsy twaddle of a slave state in the Indian country south of Kansas." He was a traitor, and his master in the White House seemingly knew his opinions before he left Washington.[3]

The New Orleans *Crescent* was equally violent:

"So far as Kansas is concerned, the South has been irredeemably sold by the present administration—by an administration that went into power on her votes—which votes were cast for Mr. Buchanan on the faith of solemn pledges that the rights of the South should be vindicated and respected in case of his election. The word of promise has been kept to the ear, only to be violently wrenched in pieces to the hope." [4]

Old Whigs and Americans now saw back of the whole Kansas business what one of them called the "cloven foot of National Democracy," which had aimed at a free Kansas from the beginning. The "betrayed and insulted South" would soon discover that the Kansas-Nebraska Bill was introduced "to prevent the further extension of slavery." Northerners understood how squatter sover-

---

[2] *Ibid.,* 103–16; John Calhoun to Douglas, April 2, 1857, in Douglas Papers.

[3] Thomas to Stephens, June 15, 1857, in Phillips (ed.), *Correspondence of Toombs, Stephens, and Cobb,* 400–401.

[4] New Orleans *Crescent,* July 17, 1857.

eignty would work. They had from the first intended that aliens as well as natives should have a vote there. The South had been "duped." Well might Buchanan and Douglas laugh at the foolish Southern wing of their party.[5]

Howell Cobb attempted to defend the administration and declared that the President had not wished "Walker or any other official . . . to use his position to affect the decision of the slavery question, one way or the other." He was, he declared, "indifferent to that decision, so it was fairly and honestly made by the people of Kansas, and this was the position of every member of the cabinet." He denied that there was any purpose to influence the results by forcing the submission of the Constitution to the people. Yet he had to admit, as Toombs said, that Walker had raised "the devil all over the South." It might mean the ruination of Buchanan and his administration as well.[6]

Many in the South were thus prepared to view Walker's every move with suspicion. His efforts to persuade the free-soil residents to take part in the election of the territorial legislature was seen in some quarters as the first steps toward giving them control. When he threw out fraudulent votes from Oxford and McGee precincts, most of which were Democratic, more were convinced of his determination to thwart Southern interests. He was interfering and refusing to allow the people themselves to run their own affairs. The inference, of course, was that squatter sovereignty gave them the right to corruption if they wanted it.

The climax in Walker's conduct, however, was reached in his refusal to accept the work of the proslavery constitutional convention and its notorious Lecompton Constitution, which protected slave property already in Kansas by declaring that "the right of the owner of a slave . . . is . . . as inviolable as the right of the owner of any property whatever." Nor would he accept the convention's proposal to force the people to vote either for the new constitution with slavery or for the constitution without slavery as a fulfillment of the submission promises made to him in Washington or his

[5] Mobile *Daily Advertiser*, December 6, 1857; Augusta *Chronicle and Sentinel*, July 7, 1857.
[6] Cobb to Stephens, June 18, 1857, in Phillips (ed.), *Correspondence of Toombs, Stephens, and Cobb*, 402–403; Toombs to W. W. Burwell, July 11, 1857, *ibid.*, 403.

promises made to the people in Kansas. That, according to the radical Southern view, was the last straw. Walker was trying to get a certain kind of constitution. He was going to give final decision on the constitution to men who had refused to vote for members of the convention. That was rank favoritism. If free-soilers had refused to participate in the formation of the constitution, it was their own fault. This was a legal document, and the convention had the right to submit it for ratification or not to do so. Kansas should be accepted as a slave state! [7]

Hostile Southern opinion unquestionably had its effects on Buchanan. Thompson and Cobb in his Cabinet had felt the pressure from their home states, and Thompson, through a subordinate sent to Kansas on "official business," may have influenced the final decision on submission. At any rate, Buchanan now turned against Walker and committed his administration to the Lecompton Constitution. That brought the revolt of Stephen A. Douglas, who would soon be campaigning for re-election in Illinois, and whose political life hung on a fair application of squatter sovereignty in Kansas. Southern radicals now had a new villain against whom to vent their anger and their disappointment. Democratic party politics, as well as Southern rights, were involved. The situation was getting back where principles and abstractions could be talked about, and difficult, concrete action, such as sending settlers to Kansas, could be forgotten. Southerners were more at home with the abstractions.

The importance of this shift can hardly be overestimated. Kansas had always been an artificial issue. In spite of talk, there were at all times grave doubts in the minds of thinking men as to any benefits for the South to be gained there. They had said in the beginning that nature had forbidden slavery, and they had quickly learned that if it had not, Northern emigration had. They had in reality

[7] Stephens to the voters of the Eighth Congressional District of Georgia, August 14, 1857, *ibid.*, 410–11; Toombs to Burwell, July 11, 1857, *ibid.*, 403–404; Hammond to Perry, December 31, 1857, in Perry Papers; Perry to Hammond, March 7, 1858, in Hammond Papers (Division of Manuscripts, Library of Congress); William P. Miles to Hammond, November 10, 1858, *ibid.;* Augusta *Chronicle and Sentinel,* July 7, August 5, 7, 1857; Macon *Georgia Telegraph,* May 12, 1857; New Orleans *Daily Crescent,* July 17, 1857; Columbia *Daily South Carolinian,* July 21, 1857; Lawrence Keitt to Miles, June 15, 1857, in William Porcher Miles Papers (University of North Carolina Library).

been contending only for a principle, for self-respect and pride. Yet results depended on action—the taking of important specific steps which slaveholders were not prepared to take. They had, now and then, tried to fool themselves with the idea that maybe Kansas might be made a slave state. They really knew better all the time. Even a temporary triumph would be overturned as soon as Kansas could speak for herself. The steady decline in the number of slaves carried there and kept there was clear evidence of Southern failure regardless of equal rights. Atchison told friends in South Carolina in June, 1857, not to raise any more money and to give up the effort to send emigrants. It was a hopeless business.[8]

Some Southerners had all along warned against building up false hope in regard to Kansas. The Montgomery *Advertiser and Gazette* was astonished at the number of persons in its own community who thought the Kansas-Nebraska Act was designed to make Kansas a slave state. Anyone who could read, it insisted, should have known that this act neither established nor prohibited slavery. It only left the people free to act as they chose. Southerners were wrong in saying that squatter sovereignty was a trick to cheat them. It had only given an opportunity which the South had not seized. Edmund Ruffin was even more realistic. He admitted that the Lecompton Constitution was the work of a minority and that if Kansas was made a slave state under it, the result would be only "an apparent gain and victory to the South, but in a bad cause, and the slavery feature . . . [would] be certainly struck out of the constitution within a year after Kansas . . . [was] a state." James L. Orr, who visited Kansas during the Walker regime, insisted that the governor had *made* no public opinion in Kansas but had only "conformed to *what was public opinion*" when he got there. Orr's Carolina supporters, therefore, "reluctantly yielded to the opinion that Kansas never . . . [could] be a Slave State," but that "it was well at least to make it a sound Democratic State, with a strong leaven of Southern sympathy in its population." Some even concluded that, after all, there was nothing to alarm the public mind in submitting a constitution to the people for ratification.[9]

[8] Charleston *Courier*, August 27, 1857.

[9] Montgomery *Advertiser and Gazette*, August 8, 1857; Edmund Ruffin Diary (Division of Manuscripts, Library of Congress), January 5, 1858; Edgefield *Advertiser*, quoted in Schultz, *Nationalism and Sectionalism in South Carolina*, 141.

Andrew G. Magrath came near the truth when he questioned the genuineness of Southern fervor for Kansas because of the great doubt widely entertained regarding "the adoption of that territory for slave labor." It was, he insisted, "only when Southerners were forced to view the question as one involving the denial of their right in the territory," that they became determined. Just what tangible good the South could gain from the Lecompton Constitution must have puzzled him as it puzzled most thinking Southerners.[10]

The transfer of the struggle for Southern rights from the plains of Kansas to the halls of Congress, from action to debate, from physical to political strife marked a new stage in sectional affairs. It sealed the fate of the Democratic party. It brought the nation a step closer to civil war. Nevertheless, the immediate effect of Buchanan's decision to support the Lecompton Constitution was to ease the Southern mind to a degree. It brought the administration into line with radical Southern opinion. It upheld the fiction of sectional equality. It enabled loyal Democrats to boast that their party was still true to its pledges.

Extremists, nevertheless, continued to threaten. Governor Joseph E. Brown declared that if Congress rejected Kansas it was his "imperative duty to call a convention which . . . [would] determine the *status* of Georgia with reference to the Union." In Mississippi, where both the Democratic state convention and the legislature had condemned Walker for "gratuitously throwing the might of his judgment and official position against the ultimate success of the proslavery party," talk of secession was again widespread. Many believed that "an early dissolution of the Union was inevitable." Some thought it highly desirable. As Albert Gallatin Brown said, "we mean neither to be defrauded of our rights in the name of the Union nor to surrender them for the shadow when the substance has been wrested from us." [11]

In Alabama Governor John A. Winston, disgusted with the Kan-

10 Andrew G. Magrath to Miles, February 18, 1858, in Miles Papers.

11 Joseph E. Brown to Stephens, February 9, 1858, in Phillips (ed.), *Correspondence of Toombs, Stephens, and Cobb*, 431; Rainwater, *Mississippi, Storm Center of Secession*, 47–55; Natchez *Mississippi Free Trader*, January 15, 1858.

sas situation, bluntly declared that the Union was not the paramount good either to his state or to his section, and the senate asked his successor to call an election for delegates to a state convention which might determine the steps necessary for the protection of Alabama's rights and honor. Yancey was more than ever convinced that the Democratic party could not be relied on for the protection of Southern rights. Safety demanded the formation of a strictly sectional political organization. With Rhett and Ruffin he now bent his efforts toward the awakening of Southern consciousness.[12]

Yet in spite of extreme expressions, the general drift was in the other direction. Interest in Kansas had begun to wane. The Whig-American press was quick to denounce the talk of secession and to insist that "the really sensible portion of the people" were "not so lost to all consciousness of their prosperous, influential and happy condition, as to wish to sever the ties which . . . [bound] together a nation whose very name . . . [was] symbolic of grandeur and power." The editor of the Richmond *Dispatch* complained of being "tired of the very word Kansas." He was "fatigued with Lecompton." The whole business had become a bore. If this nation had to go to pieces, he hoped it would be over something more tangible than Kansas. Parson Brownlow wanted to "sink Kansas from the face of God's green earth after a third day's notice." His Whig and American friends did not care a cent for Kansas or for its Lecompton fraud. C. W. Dudley in South Carolina was so disgusted with the disunion talk in his state that he was "strongly tempted to sell out & move to some other state that promise[d] some security in its past history, from the injudicial agitations of . . . [his] own."[13]

Soon, too, the Democrats began to divide and weaken. Some would let Kansas go; others just forgot about Kansas and turned their attention to Stephen A. Douglas. A conservative wave started across the South, a wave which was to last until John Brown struck at Harpers Ferry. In Virginia, Wise and Hunter split on Kansas.

[12] Dorman, *Party Politics in Alabama,* 143; William L. Yancey to James S. Slaughter, June 15, 1858, advising the formation of committees of public safety to "free the Southern heart" and "instruct the Southern mind" so as to "precipitate the cotton states into a revolution," in the Montgomery *Confederation,* May 26, 1860.
[13] Okolona (Miss.) *Prairie News,* April 22, 1858; Richmond *Dispatch,* quoted in Augusta *Chronicle and Sentinel,* March 27, 1858; Knoxville *Whig,* May 8, 1858; C. W. Dudley to Perry, September 25, 1856, in Perry Papers.

Since natural conditions would ultimately make a free state, Wise favored a submission of the whole constitution to the people. Hunter, on the other hand, believed that the loss of Kansas would end all hopes of extending slavery and of achieving equality in the nation. The *South,* recently established by Roger A. Pryor, backed Hunter's stand, but the *Enquirer* insisted that the Kansas question had "given trouble enough to the country." It hoped Congress would accept the Lecompton Constitution, admit Kansas, and then let Kansas put an end to slavery as she might please. Peace and quiet were the things wanted. "The dissolution of the Union would be more than a pastime." It was a calamity to be postponed as long as possible.[14]

Even Pryor's *South* accepted the Kansas rejection of Lecompton as satisfactory, with the remark that slavery in the territories was a matter of little immediate interest. By March, 1858, the *Enquirer,* while admitting that there were secessionists in the South, rejoiced that they were "few and feeble." Fortunately "for the Confederacy, for the American people, for the cause of constitutional liberty and the institution of slavery," the "true sense of the South" was for preserving of the Union "by endorsing the Constitution strictly and rigidly." It was disgusted with those who brooded "over the imaginary evils" which the South sustained under the Federal Union and who "lost sight of the blessings of liberty and self government." Virginia had no interest, under King Cotton, in becoming again the colony of "Old England" in order to be disconnected from "New England." She would even hesitate to join a Southern confederacy if the slave trade were to be reopened.

A group of former Whigs, meanwhile, under the lead of Alexander H. H. Stuart and John M. Botts, set about attempting to organize "the conservative Union sentiments of the country" into an effective instrument with which to oppose the Democrats. Before long some Whigs were even ready to support a Republican for office in preference to a Democratic secessionist. So marked was the Virginia reaction that Ruffin was convinced that there were "scarcely a dozen men in Virginia . . . who [would] now even

---

[14] Woodville *Republican,* quoted in Augusta *Chronicle and Sentinel,* September 5, 1857; Shanks, *Secession Movement in Virginia,* 55–56; Richmond *Enquirer,* January 7, March 1, 1858.

speak openly, much less act, in defense of the South to the extent that was avowed generally a year or two ago." [15]

What was true of Virginia was also true of North Carolina and to a large degree of South Carolina and Georgia. Jonathan Worth spoke for the majority of North Carolinians when he declared that there was "Not a particle of the excitement" prevailing in Congress "among any class of our people." They were for any course in relation to the Lecompton Constitution that would put an end to agitation. They knew that slavery could not long exist in Kansas. The South was fighting for a shadow. From South Carolina a writer declared that he had never "known such a perfect calm in the public mind regarding the relations of the State with the General Government and Federal politics." He felt that South Carolina was "fast becoming (if not already so) one of the most conservative Democratic States in the Union."

Perhaps this was, in part, due to the earnest desire of Senator James H. Hammond to keep South Carolina "in the rank with the South" and "not beyond the reach of any portion." He would have the *Mercury* "avoid faction language & extremeism" and "attempt to conciliate the South—the whole South." He would "at least . . . try the Union after the Free States . . . [had] the ascendency" for he believed they had sense enough "to drop all this abolitionism." He would "in short contemplate an honorable & influential position *in* the Union," and yet show that the South was not "unable or afraid to 'let it slide.' " "Senator Hammond has given the death blow to disunion & Revolution," wrote Benjamin F. Perry in his journal. "Orr & Keitt go with him. They are as conservative now as I am." [16]

The people of Georgia were equally calm in spite of their governor's radical talk. As one citizen wrote Alexander H. Stephens: "There does not seem to be much excitement, and I think nine-tenths of the intelligent portion of the people are, like myself,

[15] Richmond *Enquirer*, March 2, June 18, 1858; Richmond *Whig*, September 30, 1859; Ruffin Diary, May 16, 1858.

[16] Sitterson, *Secession Movement in North Carolina*, 142–43; Jonathan Worth to John A. Gilmer, March 9, 1858, in J. G. de Roulhac Hamilton (ed.), *The Correspondence of Jonathan Worth* (Raleigh, 1909), I, 55; Edgefield (S.C.) *Confederation*, September 24, 1858; William Gilmore Simms to Miles, November 23, March 22, 1858, in Miles Papers; Benjamin F. Perry Journal, August 29, 1858, in Perry Papers.

anxious to get rid of this Kansas matter in almost any way, as it seems nothing can be made of it, either beneficially to the South or to our party. . . . Considering that Kansas is *really* a free state, and there being no possible chance of it being a slave State, even say that it is admitted under Lecompton, . . . I dont think *much fire* can be *raised up* in Georgia upon this subject." [17]

He was right. Through Cobb's efforts the harsh attacks on Walker, and indirectly on the administration, were effectively checked. The price, however, was heavy. Governor Brown was "forced down the middle" against his natural inclinations, and the already serious breach between Cobb and the "regular" Democrats was thereby widened. Henceforth Brown would set his own course without reference to the national party's needs and wishes. Domestic interests would crowd national problems aside. Both Cobb and the nation would one day pay heavily for the calm that now ensued.

Opinion in the Border States followed about the same general pattern. The Whig-Americans sharply opposed the administration's efforts to get rid of the Kansas problem through the Lecompton Constitution and decried all slavery agitation as destructive of national harmony. Many welcomed the Louisiana move to revive the Whig party on a national basis, but soon accepted the role of "opposition" in the hope of gathering in more disgruntled Democrats. Kentuckians generally endorsed Senator John J. Crittenden's scathing attack on the Lecompton Constitution as the product of chicanery and fraud, and welcomed the support of the powerful Louisville *Democrat* as an indication of Democratic disintegration.

In Tennessee, Nashville papers went out of their way to explain that the Republican party was not abolitionist and to encourage Southern moderation. They insisted that the noisy minority in Republican ranks was being pushed aside and that there was "so much conservatism in the North" that a radical like William H. Seward "could not receive a larger vote than was given to Birney in 1844." They urged the Southern people, in turn, to reject fire-eater leadership and the Southern press to stop quoting radical Northern statements to the neglect of more "representative opinion." They were

17 P. B. Sweatt to Stephens, April 6, 1858, in Alexander H. Stephens Papers (Division of Manuscripts, Library of Congress).

certain that "the masses of the Northern people" respected the "rights of the South" and loved "the Union *as it was.*" [18]

Democrats, here as elsewhere, more and more saw the Kansas issue in terms of the administration's fight with Douglas. They gave more attention to their own internal affairs than to either Kansas directly or to the "opposition." They did, however, meet Whig assertions regarding the conservative character of Republicans by pointing to the extreme statements of such leaders as Seward and Chase. They charged that these men, in periods of excitement, established a control that could not be broken even in periods of calm. After all, said the Nashville *Union and American,* there were "demagogues" in the Republican ranks, and until the conservatives put them aside there could be no peace.[19]

Nor were conservative trends and internal dissensions entirely absent from the Gulf States. A New Orleans paper rebuked "the old and hitherto leading states of the South" for their "selfish and narrow-minded policy" in opposing the acquisition of Cuba and the laying of tariff duties beneficial to the sugar industry. It suspected that "incompatibilities of temper and tendency, discrepancies of opinion and diversity of interests" between Southern states had to be eliminated before union and co-operation in the section itself were possible. It thought that South Carolina was trying to cut the garments for the other states according to her pattern. She would "frame the policies for the South for the benefit of those who could not compete with Louisiana, Texas, &c." Another editor condemned the efforts to secure Kansas as "squabbling over worthless . . . Territorial abstractions." Kansas, he said, "was gone and with her every chance likely to flow from our territorial possessions as a nation." Not another slave state would "ever be admitted into the Confederacy." The true Southern policy then was to secure what it now had and not to waste its "strength upon abstractions having neither practical worth nor value." So since the section stood "no chance whatever in the Territories" it should ignore them and devote its efforts elsewhere. The wise move in the interests

[18] Washington *National Intelligencer,* June 23, 1857; *Cong. Globe,* 35 Cong., 1 Sess., 1153–59; Augusta *Chronicle and Sentinel,* April 1, 1858; Nashville *Patriot,* September 16, 1859; *Republican Banner and Nashville Whig,* quoted in Nashville *Union and American,* October 18, 1859; *ibid.,* November 4, February 7, November 30, 1858.

[19] Nashville *Union and American,* October 18, 1859.

of slavery was to make it secure in the Border States from Maryland to Missouri. It was time to praise Southern stability under slavery as opposed to the strife and turmoil of the North under free labor. Conservative men of the North too might listen to such an appeal instead of to the "irrepressible conflict" talk of Seward, which certainly did not represent the true opinions of the North.[20]

Alabama and Mississippi also felt the reaction. Yancey had not ceased his efforts to inflame the Southern mind and just now was pushing Edmund Ruffin's League of United Southerners with all his accustomed zeal. Opposition, however, had developed. Critics accused him of attempting to divide, not to unite, Southern sentiment. He was going too fast. The people were "not going to be precipitated into a revolution for past aggressions." Nor should outsiders judge the temper of Alabama by "the over-zealous indiscretions of a few hot-headed very erratic and unstable, though honest politicians." The "great masses of the people of Alabama" were not of that kind. Some might have been driven to believe the two great sections of the Union were divided beyond reconciliation, but more were convinced that this government, "if rightly administered . . . as its founders intended" was "the noblest government ever devised by the wit of man." Such citizens would tell the world "that the day had not yet come" when this Union could be dissolved "upon the frivolous matter of the rejection of the Lecompton Constitution." In fact, said the Cahawba (Ala.) *Dallas Gazette,* most of the wrongs of which the South had been complaining were imaginary. The section had not as yet suffered any very serious injury. Why become so upset over anticipated mischief? The truth was that if the people would look around them and realize that they still enjoyed their lands and their Negroes, that heaven had "smiled propitiously upon and blessed them—that a generous soil had yielded a heavy harvest in return for their labor," they would have little enthusiasm for girding on their armor against "anticipated evils, or in favor of a string of abstractions so contradictory and impractical that it would puzzle the shrewdest metaphysician of the age to expound them." The Southern agitator was the section's worst enemy.[21]

20 New Orleans *Daily Delta,* March 16, 1859; August 28, 1858; New Orleans *Daily Crescent,* December 1, July 20, 1859; New Orleans *Picayune,* November 7, 1858.
21 Auburn (Ala.) *Gazette,* August 19, 1858; Montgomery *Confederation,* July 31,

The bitter feud between Jefferson Davis and Albert Gallatin Brown, which represented something of a class struggle as well as a personal one, intensified attitudes in Mississippi in these fateful years. Brown became increasingly radical; Davis was surprisingly conservative. Their loyal followers reflected their opinions. In Congress Brown supported the Lecompton Constitution as a peace measure and came home to deliver a fiery speech in defense of his position and to denounce Douglas and his stand on Kansas. He was through with all compromises for saving the Union. He "would make a refusal to acquire territory because it was to be slave territory, a cause for disunion." Davis, on the other hand, clung to the hope that sectional differences could be settled. He went North by ship when Congress adjourned, making while at sea a speech in which he spoke of disunionists as "mosquitoes around the ox," annoying but never killing. He accepted an honorary degree at Bowdoin College along with antislavery William P. Fessenden and at Portland, Maine, delivered an address, definitely moderate in tone, in which he admitted that the people of a territory, by refusing to pass "laws and police regulations" necessary to give security to slave property, could practically debar its existence.[22]

The radical Southern press and that friendly to Brown were rather hard on Davis for his conciliatory attitude and his expressed belief in Northern good will, but he had his defenders. He, rather than Brown, shaped the Mississippi Democratic policy, begun that year, of loyalty to the national organization in an effort to control its course. It was based on Davis' firm conviction that the differences between the views of the "temperate, true men" of both sections were less than he had formerly supposed.[23]

On Douglas' break with the administration over the Lecompton Constitution, Southern opinion was again divided. Many angrily

---

1858; Mobile *Advertiser and Gazette*, August 17, 1859; Tuscaloosa (Ala.) *Monitor*, April 15, 1858; May 28, 1859; Cahawba *Dallas Gazette*, May 13, 1859.

[22] Ranck, *Albert Gallatin Brown*, 160–64; Dunbar Rowland (ed.), *Jefferson Davis, Constitutionalist, His Letters, Papers and Speeches* (Jackson, Miss., 1923), III, 271–73, 299, 339–46 (Davis' statement repeated to Mississippi legislature on November 16, 1858); Charleston *Mercury*, August 10, 1858.

[23] Montgomery *Advertiser and Gazette*, November 25, 1858; Charleston *Mercury*, October 16, 1858; Raymond *Hinds County Gazette*, September 23, October 26, 1858; Rainwater, *Mississippi, Storm Center of Secession*, 63; Rowland (ed.), *Jefferson Davis, Constitutionalist*, III, 498.

denounced him as a traitor. He was nothing but a selfish politician. His speeches in the Senate on the Kansas question, said the Charleston *Mercury*, were "the clap-trap of a demagogue. . . . He should . . . [be] held up to the country in his true light, as a self-seeking renegade, truckling to the antislavery sentiment of his people." He could now be considered "the great leader of the Black Republicans." The *Southern Reveille* thought his defection "so gross, so shameful a betrayal of the confidence and trust of his friends, that though he should wash in the waters of Jordan, we should still doubt him." He was more to be feared than a thousand Lincolns. He had put an impassable gulf between himself and the Southern people.[24]

Over and over again they classed him as a "Black Republican." Some professed to see no difference between Douglas and Seward. As a matter of fact, Douglas' doctrines were far more dangerous, because they were "much more easily reduced to practical adoption." Some hoped for his defeat in Illinois. If it were just a question of Douglas or a Black Republican, argued the Nashville *Union and American*, it might be possible to prefer Douglas to Lincoln. But in this case there was a principle at stake, and it might be "better to be defeated for a principle than to yield to Douglas." At best it was a choice of evils. The unfortunate Illinois Democrats were being asked to choose between surrender to "anti-Lecomptonism" and defeat. Might it not be "better for the friends of truth and the advocates of sound principles to submit for a while to the triumph of their worst enemies, than to compromise with error and play second to malcontents and rebels in their own party?" Anyway, Abraham Lincoln wasn't so bad. He was "a sound, safe and conservative man" even though he was a Republican. He had at least forced Douglas to reveal his hand.

For those who still clung to Douglas because he seemed to be the only Democrat with any chance of being elected President in 1860, the Columbus (Georgia) *Sun* had a word. "If we are to have a Republican President," it said, "let us have an out and out, 'dyed in the wool' one, that we may know where to meet him and prepare

---

24 Charleston *Mercury*, December 12, 25, 1857; April 12, 1858; Port Gibson *Southern Reveille*, December 29, 1858; Mobile *Register*, December 13, 1858; Mobile *Advertiser and Gazette*, October 23, 1858.

to fend off the blow where we know it will fall, rather than one who, while he holds out the hand of pretended friendship, stabs us in the heart with a dagger which he has concealed beneath the cloak of hypocrisy." [25]

These attitudes toward Douglas, however, were only part of the story. Some frankly defended his stand and wished him well in his campaign for re-election to the Senate. They could see nothing new or alarming in his position and they could not withhold their admiration for his gallant fight against great odds. "Whatever may be our opinion of Judge Douglas as a man and as a politician," said one editor, "his present position and his bold and manly bearing, command our unqalified admiration. . . . He is now giving evidence of abilities that entitle him to rank among the greatest men of the nation. . . . If he should succeed against such odds [as he faces in Illinois], he must be rebaptized. The cognomen of 'Little Giant' would no longer be appropriate—he should be called 'Coeur de Lion' of America." Another asked why he should be victimized because of imputed squatter sovereignty when there was nothing practical in the doctrine anyhow. Did not Orr, Stephens, Jefferson Davis, Andrew Johnson, George W. Jones, and many others hold exactly the same opinions? Douglas' alleged treason, said a third, consisted in "simply refusing to 'back down' from the position he had always occupied when it suited the convenience of Mr. Buchanan and the Democratic party." The real traitors were those who, once his friends, now unfairly turned against him. "Whilst he is standing in the open field, stripped to the girth, his noble bosom bared to the thick-flying, death-dealing bullets of our foes," complained the *Georgia Telegraph*, "cowardly assassins are sticking stilettoes into his back." Some even "prayed for his defeat" by a "dyed-in-the-wool Abolitionist, a no-more-slave-states, and death-to-slavery candidate." Some charged that he had "gone over to Black Republicanism." How absurd! Just because he now differed with the administration did not mean that he had forsaken the Democrats or the rights of the South. Douglas "would be as

---

[25] Augusta *Chronicle and Sentinel*, October 31, 1858; Milledgeville *Southern Recorder*, September 13, 1859; Nashville *Union and American*, July 11, 1858; Louisville *Journal*, quoted *ibid.*, September 1, 1858; Columbus *Daily Sun*, quoted in Augusta *Chronicle and Sentinel*, October 6, 1858.

much out of place in the foul atmosphere of free-soilism as a bird in a coal pit." [26]

Men who felt this way about Douglas hoped, of course, that he would triumph in Illinois. Even if he had been somewhat irregular in recent months, he had "never indulged in any of those denunciations of the South and her 'peculiar institution' that . . . [were] so characteristic of the black-hearted Abolitionist that oppose[d] him." He had, after all, defended the Dred Scott decision and stood up for Southern rights in the common territories. Even his opposition to the Lecompton Constitution was not based on opposition to slavery but on the fact that it was not submitted to the vote of the people. For these reasons, the preference and sympathy of intelligent Southerners ought to be decidedly with him. As the Monticello (Mississippi) *Journal* said: "We cannot afford to throw him overboard unless he is guilty of some greater offense than he has yet committed. We may need his services in the next great battle which we will have to fight with our abolition enemies with Seward at their head." [27]

So it was a duty to side with Douglas, "not against the Administration but against the Black Republicans." No matter "what the sins of Douglas against the Administration," he had not "sinned a tenth part as much as Lincoln,"—Lincoln, who was "a malignantly, indecent and abominable Abolitionist of the meanest, dirtiest, and most virulent type." That was the reason, said the New Orleans *Crescent*, "that ninety per cent of the Southern Democracy want[ed] him to defeat Lincoln." [28]

[26] The Douglas Papers contain many friendly letters from the South. The following were selected at random: Logan McKnight, New Orleans, December 25, 1857; K. B. Sewall, Mobile, December 31, 1857; John L. Payton, Staunton, Va., February 23, 1858; Joshua Madden, Bellforte, Ala., March 3, 1858; Thomas Lloyd, Jacksonville, Ala., March 10, 1858; Thomas C. Teasdale, Mobile, March 15, 1858; Fred L. Roberts, Edenton, N.C., May 8, 1858; Thomas P. Atkinson, Danville, Va., July 19, 1858; Thomas W. Honan, Donaldsonville, La., August 17, 1858; George W. Lamar, Augusta, August 21, 1858; James Gardner, Augusta, October 12, 1858; W. H. Ryan, Demopolis, Ala., November 2, 1858; L. C. Leland, Panola, Miss., November 6, 1858; *Republican Banner and Nashville Whig*, August 1, 1858; Huntsville *Southern Advocate*, December 30, 1858; Athens *Watchman*, October 21, 1858; Macon *Georgia Telegraph*, December 15, 1857; August 16, 1858; Natchez *Mississippi Free Trader*, September 20, October 25, 1858.

[27] Montgomery *Confederation*, August 3, 1856; Monticello (Miss.) *Journal*, quoted in Natchez *Mississippi Free Trader*, March 12, 1859.

[28] New Orleans *Daily Delta*, August 20, 1858; New Orleans *Crescent*, September

Some supported Douglas not because they approved of the course he had taken but because they feared the effects of defeat on party unity. "The Democratic party has a battle before them in 1860, that will be to them destiny," said the *Georgia Telegraph*. "Let the faithful bury divisions, or it will be to them a Waterloo." "Douglas will not fall alone," warned the New Orleans *Bee*, "but like Sampson of old, will pull down his enemies with him." The Richmond *Enquirer* also was alarmed at the "intestine feuds and sectional quarrels" in Democratic ranks. The campaign in Illinois was being marked by "violent denunciation and opprobrious epithets" applied by Democratic factions to each other. The "virulence of the press" suggested "the violent antipathies of . . . antagonistic parties rather than the friendly and accordant sympathies of papers in the fellowship of the same party. . . . And thus," it said, "we fear, will be wasted away the main strength of the Northern Democracy upon a question involving no vital principle of party," but upon which the passions and prejudices of partisans have been violently arrayed. "This was political folly." "Judge Douglas should not be ostracized by any portion of the Democracy." He had long fought manfully for the party and its principles, and, "right or wrong upon the Lecompton question," he should have the united support of Democracy in Illinois. "This administration," it continued, "cannot afford to see Douglas defeated. . . . The defeat of Douglas would indicate the impotency and imbecility of senseless rage, rather than a calm considerate punishment for a grave political offense." The *Enquirer* closed its editorial with an appeal to Illinois Democrats to cease their quarreling in the interests of party success and the safety of the Union.[29]

Martin J. Crawford took a slightly different approach. "The truth is," he wrote to Alexander H. Stephens, "that Douglas has no more idea of going off from Democracy than I have, and as we shall have to defend him in our next race in '60 I see no use of making testimony against ourselves." He saw that Douglas had taken a position on Kansas from which he could not retreat without losing face in Illinois. Only officeholders there were with Buchanan, and

---

21, October 2, 1858; Richmond *Enquirer*, June 15, 1858. The *Crescent* said that the Austin *Gazette* and the Paulding (Miss.) *Clarion* were Douglas papers.

[29] Richmond *Enquirer*, June 19, 1858; Macon *Georgia Telegraph*, September 15, 1858; New Orleans *Bee*, August 13, 1858.

the South had already "made all out of Kansas that was in it." So why now take attitudes toward Douglas from which it would be difficult to "back track"? [30]

The New Orleans *Crescent* carried the idea a little further. Douglas, as a shrewd politician, knew full well that if Kansas were admitted as a slave state, "there would be no Democratic party at the North worth speaking of, and that the freesoil element in that portion of the confederacy would unquestionably elect the next President of the United States." The handwriting was already on the wall. Douglas had seen that he must either "modify the political complexion of the Democratic party, so as to adapt it to the increasing intensity of the anti-slavery sentiment of the North," or give up all hope of it "regaining its ascendency in any Northern State." The inevitable consequence of his triumph would, therefore, be either that the Democratic party "as the great conservator of the constitutional rights of the South" would be essentially demoralized, or that the party would be "completely broken up and denationalized." With the Northwestern Democracy behind him, Douglas would be "in a position to offer the Democratic party the alternative of a probable success in the next Presidential election, if they . . . [would] accept the modified platform he . . . [had] prepared for them, and him as their candidate, or of certain defeat and permanent destruction as a party if they . . . [did] not." [31]

If the Democratic party chose to accept Douglas' terms, and thus forfeited its character as the protector and friend of the South, the Mobile *Register* was certain that Southern men would unanimously repudiate it. They had made their last concessions to anti-slavery sentiment in the interest of party harmony. They were ready to stand alone in a sectional party for their constitutional rights or to seek safety outside the Union. That was the other side of the picture.

Most of those who for one reason or other defended Douglas remained favorable even after he had expanded and clarified his posi-

[30] Martin J. Crawford to Stephens, September 8, 1858, in Stephens Papers (Division of Manuscripts, Library of Congress).

[31] New Orleans *Crescent*, December 15, 1858; Mobile *Register*, quoted in Montgomery *Advertiser and Gazette*, November 12, 1858.

KANSAS, DOUGLAS, AND JOHN BROWN

tion before the people of Illinois. They thought, at times, that he was "composed in about equal parts of the elements of first-rate buncombe, provincial politician, and a tolerably enlarged, liberal and comprehensive statesman," but insisted that he was still the defender of vital Southern interests. His first Chicago speech disappointed those who hoped that he had made peace with the administration before he left Washington; his Freeport speech embittered others. To have abandoned the only construction of squatter sovereignty which could give the South any security of its rights was more than some spokesmen could bear. They confessed the error of their earlier approval and became indifferent to the outcome of the Illinois election. Douglas had at last openly admitted "in all its hideous proportions" the true meaning of his doctrine. He had fallen before "the power of the spoils." The majority, however, professed to see nothing new or dangerous in anything Douglas was saying. The Richmond *Enquirer* scorned "the ludicrous attempt to construe Judge Douglas' speech at Freeport into a squatter sovereignty, anti–Dred Scott pronunciamento. The Illinois statesman," it declared, "never did better service to the constitutional rights of the South than will be effected by following up the frank and manly suggestion of that speech." Douglas had simply shown that the present Federal legislation was inadequate to protect slavery in the territories. He was only describing a situation as it existed. Congressman Orr and Jefferson Davis had said the same thing. Any thinking man should realize that without friendly local legislation and local police regulations, slavery could not exist in any locality. That was just plain common sense. The Norfolk *Argus,* the Washington *States,* the Augusta *Constitutionalist,* the New Orleans *Delta,* said the *Enquirer,* all agreed that this was the case, and all remained loyal to Douglas.[32]

The *Enquirer* was right. Orr had said that in every slaveholding community of the Union there were local regulations which alone made slavery possible, and without which it could not exist. If the

---

[32] New Orleans *Daily Delta,* July 20, 1858; Augusta *Constitutionalist,* July 23, 1858; Nashville *Union and American,* October 3, 24, 1858; Augusta *Chronicle and Sentinel,* September 22, 1858; Richmond *Enquirer,* September 10, 30, October 12, 21, 1858. See also Augusta *Constitutionalist,* September 24, November 13, 20, 25, 1858; New Orleans *Delta,* September 10, 11, 22, October 6, 16, 27, 1858.

people of a territory refused to enact such regulations, there was no remedy. They could thus exclude slavery as effectively as though the power to do so were "vested in the Territorial legislature." Davis had been as explicit. At Bangor, Maine, he had pointed out the necessity for laws and police regulations to protect slave property and had insisted that slavery could not be forced upon any community, state or territorial, where the people refused to act. "Though the right would remain," he concluded, "the owner [of slaves] would be practically debarred, by the circumstances of the case, from taking slave property into a Territory where the sense of the inhabitants was opposed to its introduction." [33]

Thus, as the New Orleans *Delta* editorialized, what Senator Douglas said at Freeport was "not the expression of a new principle, or any principle at all, as a rule of action, either in Congress or the Territories." It was simply "the statement of a legal proposition" which could not be controverted and which had long ago been "enunciated by leading Southern men, as the basis of their demand for affirmative legislation, on the part of Congress, for the protection of slaveholders in the Territories." Douglas was on solid ground. He had said nothing inconsistent with the principles of the Dred Scott decision.[34]

A year later, however, when Douglas ended all confusion as to his views by an article published in *Harper's Magazine,* his early defenders began to draw back. Even the Richmond *Enquirer* was "obliged to separate from him." When Douglas asserted that the residents of a territory, through the action of their legislature, could "rightfully and legally, exclude the introduction of slave property . . . or abrogate the right to hold slaves already introduced," he was propounding doctrine more dangerous to the South than that of Seward himself. This article was an "incendiary document" calculated to produce anarchy and bloodshed in the territories. Douglas had launched the last and "most dangerous phase which anti-slavery agitation" had assumed.[35]

Some suggested proscribing *Harper's Magazine* for publishing

[33] Richmond *Enquirer,* September 30, 1858; Rowland (ed.), *Jefferson Davis, Constitutionalist,* III, 299.

[34] New Orleans *Daily Delta,* September 11, 1858.

[35] Richmond *Enquirer,* August 30, 1859.

the article, but the Nashville *Patriot* objected. It thought a great service had been rendered the South. The people now knew exactly what Douglas was advocating. Whereas before he had had "numerous defenders" in the section, they were now few, "very few." Whereas earlier he had been "sailing before a strong wind with fine prospects of reaching the haven of the Charleston nomination,—his battered hulk now . . . [floated] in a windless, currentless sea."

The New Orleans *Delta* was equally disillusioned. This was the weakest document Douglas had ever produced. The doctrines it offered were nothing but "short-cuts to all the ends of Black Republicanism." If his program was carried into effect, the South would be "deprived of all her rights in the Territories," and the "common property" of all the states would be surrendered to the "absolute control of the anti-slavery majority." Only those who thought in purely political terms could continue to tolerate Douglas.[36]

The political chaos which had helped to produce what seemed, at least, to be a period of calm was everywhere apparent in the state elections of 1859. The national Congress of the preceding winter had yielded little but futile partisan conflict over Cuba, tariffs, homesteads, and internal improvements. The administration had "punished" Douglas by removing him from the chairmanship of the Committee on Territories, and government appropriations had been withheld even from the Post Office through equally petty maneuvering. It seemed to be an excellent time for conservative union groups, based on old Whig and American foundations, to stage something of a comeback.

Since Southern local elections were soon to take place in Louisiana, Georgia, North Carolina, Tennessee, and Kentucky—all states once dominated by the Whigs—and in Virginia, Alabama, and Mississippi, in each of which the Democrats were sharply divided, the opportunity seemed to be at hand. Whig leaders of other days, North and South, began to correspond and to dream of a great Union party which might come to power in 1860.

In Virginia, Kentucky, and Tennessee such groups held state

[36] Nashville *Patriot*, October 31, 1859; New Orleans *Daily Delta*, September 15, 1859.

conventions and plotted a campaign, aimed against both Democratic corruption and the rising tide of sectionalism. They labored under heavy disadvantages, but the reluctance of Democratic factions to endorse Buchanan's administration and the bitter rivalry between Democratic leaders gave encouragement. At least they could lay foundations for 1860.

The outcome, in the main, was encouraging. In Virginia, the moderate Democrat, John Letcher, won the governorship over the fire-eater, William L. Goggin, largely because of nonpartisan support from the western part of the state. In Tennessee the opposition gained four Congressmen; in Kentucky, three; and in North Carolina, two. In Alabama the opposition did not organize but threw its vote to the moderate, Andrew B. Moore, who won easily over an opponent advocating the opening of the slave trade and a more vigorous defense of Southern rights. Results in Georgia, Louisiana, and Mississippi were less encouraging, but in Texas the Unionist, Sam Houston, running as an independent, defeated the radical, H. R. Runnels. In all, with the exception of Mississippi, the trends were toward the conservative. Most moderates were satisfied. They had again mustered their forces. They were ready for a better effort on a national scale in 1860.

From another angle, however, the cause of national harmony was less promising. Beyond question Kansas had done great damage to Democratic unity and had only mildly aided the conservative opposition. It had also widened the rift between North and South to an alarming degree. The South had suffered no concrete losses, for slavery was in no great need for expansion, and few slaveholders would normally have gone to Kansas at this time. The whole difficulty lay in the fact that rights were involved and that the equality of the South in national affairs was being still further threatened. Kansas, as has been said, had become a symbol, and what happened there meant a loss or a gain of power for one section or the other. That was why the South had struggled for what so many knew was "a mere shadow." That was why, when a definite outcome had been reached, Kansas so quickly lost its force, and a calm ensued. During the later part of 1858 and the spring and summer of 1859, the South was comparatively quiet and the tide seemed to be turning. Even the rabid Charleston *Mercury* took friendly notice of the fact that the New England Society of that city had, on December 22, celebrated its fortieth anniversary. It spoke of the handsome dinner served at the Mills House and of the toasts "responded to with great spirit and happy effect." It chose to print, among others, the following:

> *New England.*
> *What though they boast of fairer lands,*
> *Give me New England's hallowed soil;*
> *The fearless hearts, the swarthy hands,*
> *Stamped with the heraldry of toil.*
>
> .   .   .   .
>
> *I love her for each noble deed,*
> *Wrought by the iron wills of yore;*
> *The Pilgrim hands that sowed the seed*
> *Of freedom on her sterile shore.*

> *The Common School System: it stands, an imperishable monument to its founders. Its influence, like silent and genial rain upon the early seed, will produce through all time a glorious harvest.*[37]

Then on October 16 all was suddenly changed. That night an old man, half mad, who knew nought of peace or calm save in strife, accepted the responsibility for a nation's failure to get on with its problems. If reason and tolerance had ever been a part of John Brown's makeup, experiences in Kansas had thoroughly eliminated them. His hands were already bloody, and bitter hatred and thirst for vengeance in his twisted mind took on the pattern of a great mission to be performed. Northern friends, such as Gerrit Smith, Samuel G. Howe, George L. Stearns, Thomas Wentworth Higginson, and Theodore Parker, gave financial aid, and a few, at least, knew something of his plans. Thus encouraged, he rented a farm on the Maryland side of the Potomac above Harpers Ferry and made ready for a bold stroke at the institution of slavery. During the late summer he gathered his forces and supplies, 21 kindred souls and 198 Sharps rifles and 950 pikes. His purpose was to seize

[37] Charleston *Mercury*, December 23, 1858; Cole, *Whig Party in the South*, 309–43.

the arsenal at the Ferry, stir and arm the slaves on neighboring plantations, and thus launch a movement that would somehow serve the larger cause of freedom.

The effort ended in pathetic failure. The arsenal was seized, a few planters brought in as hostages, and a few innocent lives taken in the first hours of surprise. But the slaves did not rise in rebellion nor the countryside cringe in terror as expected. The militia and regular troops that quickly appeared did not behave as those Brown had faced in Kansas. Most of his men were quickly killed or captured, and he himself, cruelly wounded, was soon a prisoner. The fiasco was over. Childish in conception and hopelessly inadequate in execution, it amounted to little more, in action, than a local disturbance. Its meaning, however, was tragically national. News of the raid spread like wildfire throughout the nation. Men talked of little else. Somehow people understood that something epoch-making had occurred.[38]

Stripped of all sentimental associations, the John Brown raid was nothing more or less than the efforts of a band of irresponsible armed outlaws. In open violation of all law and order, they had seized public property, kidnapped individuals, and committed murder. They had, moreover, attempted to incite a slave insurrection and, according to the laws of Virginia, had committed treason against the state. For this, John Brown was given a remarkably fair trial in the county court and, on November 2, sentenced to be hanged a month later. When the sentence had been executed, the whole affair was officially at an end. The man, John Brown, was dead. John Brown, the symbol of fanaticism on the one hand and of courage and idealism on the other, was, however, much alive.

Southern reaction to the John Brown raid was quick and violent. It moved on an accumulation of distrust and fear that had been forming for a generation. Harpers Ferry fitted on to a whole chain of acts and attitudes that had been mounting toward just such a

[38] Oswald G. Villard, *John Brown; A Biography Fifty Years After* (Boston, 1910), *passim;* Robert Penn Warren, *John Brown; The Making of a Martyr* (New York, 1929), 311–81; Malin, *John Brown and the Legend of Fifty-Six, passim; Senate Reports,* 36 Cong., 1 Sess., No. 278.

climax. Even if the leader of this attempt on the South was insane, his was only an extreme manifestation of a milder brand of insanity revealed by every abolitionist. Certainly not all of his twenty-one men were mentally ill save in the same sense that Higginson, Parker, John Greenleaf Whittier, and others were afflicted. They and the friends behind them knew what they were doing. The crusade was on. The time for action was at hand. Southerners could not miss the point or fail to see its sectional significance. To apply the "higher law" was no worse than to preach it. The incitement of a slave insurrection was only the fanatic's expression of a widespread feeling towards slavery. The only question was: "What next?" [39]

Immediate reactions, however, varied with time and place. Intense excitement prevailed for weeks around Harpers Ferry and throughout Virginia. "The public mind of the State" rolled and tossed "as the storm-whipped billows of an angry sea." During the days before Brown's execution, rumors of rescue efforts and of new raids were rife. Every stranger was viewed with suspicion and everything Northern freely denounced. Governor Wise did not help matters by sending troops into the region and by showing a willingness to make political capital out of the affair. The fire-eating Edmund Ruffin did his part by rushing to the scene and appropriating the captured pikes to distribute with suitable labels to the Southern governors. [40]

Many people, however, simply refused to believe the facts as first reported or that anyone was insane enough to make such an attempt. Even when the truth became known, they were inclined to drop the matter when Brown had paid the penalty. Not until the connection of prominent Northerners with the affair was revealed and not until Northern opinion favorable to Brown appeared did they sullenly accept the sectional implications. Then a wave of indignation, hatred, and fear swept across the whole South to give it a unity it had not known before. Men who had refused to recognize the existence of an "irrepressible conflict" now accepted it as a matter of course. Talk of secession became general. The demand

[39] Nashville *Gazette*, November 4, 1859; Raleigh *North Carolina Standard*, October 29, 1859.

[40] Richmond *Enquirer*, November 20, 21, 22, 1859; Shanks, *Secession Movement in Virginia*, 86; Craven, *Edmund Ruffin*, 178–80.

for drastic action in dealing with Brown was nearly universal. The reason was not a realization of the dangers in slaveholding which some Northerners thought Brown's raid had inspired but rather a conviction, reluctantly reached by many, that Southern life and interests could no longer be preserved within the Union. As one editor put it:

"Before the Harper's Ferry emeute disunion had about died out in Virginia, but that event, coupled with the expression of Northern sentiment in support of that emeute and the course of the Northern Press, have shaken and disrupted all regard for the Union and there are but few men who do not look to a certain and a not distant day when dissolution must ensue." [41]

Brown himself was, in all probability, "a poor, wretched monomaniac." His raid had been put down without great difficulty. It had even served a purpose in demonstrating to North and South alike the loyalty and contentment of the slave. No, the importance of the event could not be measured by its immediate magnitude. Brown had intended to start a movement that would have turned "our fair Republic" into "another Saint Domingo." If he had succeeded "our soil would have reeked with human gore." No one who had read of his merciless butchery of helpless, unarmed men in Kansas could doubt that he was a "fiend incarnate." Yet Northern men, even conservative men, were speaking of him as a martyr and a hero. What did it mean? What did it reveal? If Brown had robbed a bank in Virginia and had killed men, no one would have said a word against his execution. But here, because his effort was at "robbery of slave property," he was a hero and his action "just that of a 'misguided man.'" Northern papers were ridiculing Virginia and the whole South for being so excited over "an insignificant riot." They were suggesting that Brown be pardoned or sent to an asylum for the good effect it would have on Northern opinion. A few had gone the whole way to speak of Brown's martyrdom, to accept his motives and forget his deeds, to ask men to withhold their judgments until history had selected its heroes.[42]

[41] Charleston *Mercury*, October 19, 1859; Richmond *Dispatch,* October 17, 1859; Richmond *Enquirer,* December 2, November 25, 1859. For Northern approval of Brown, see James Redpath, *Echoes of Harper's Ferry* (Boston, 1860), *passim*.
[42] Natchez *Mississippi Free Trader,* December 6, 1859; Columbus *Enquirer,* De-

Only one conclusion could be reached. Brown and his deeds were the legitimate offspring of the forces that had created the Republican party, had encouraged the fugitive slaves, and had denied to the South its equal, constitutional rights in the Union. Brown's guilt was even less than that of Seward with his "higher law." The one had preached an "irrepressible conflict"; the other had begun it. As the resolutions of the Tennessee legislature said, the Harpers Ferry outbreak was "the natural fruit of this treasonable 'irrepressible conflict' doctrine put forth by the great head of the Black Republican party and echoed by his subordinates." The guilt was a section's guilt. It began with Brown and ran back to those who had given material and moral support; to the Republicans who had opposed slavery's expansion; to a whole people who had tolerated the attacks on slavery. This was "but the beginning of the end. The Abolitionists, through their great leaders . . . [had] declared that the war between the North and the South must go on until slavery . . . [had] been driven from the land." The "Harper's Ferry tragedy" was like a great meteor disclosing in its lurid flash the width and depth of that abyss which divided "two nations, apparently one." [43]

The lesson to be gained was the necessity of Southern unity. The South must look after its own interests. The white nonslaveholder had as much at stake as did the master of a hundred slaves. All were threatened. The triumph of the Republican party in 1860 would seal the fate of slavery and with it the Southern way of life. Connection with the North was a standing invitation to insurrection. Said Governor William H. Gist of South Carolina, "if the South does not now unite for her defense, we will deserve the execration of posterity." [44]

The calm of the past few months now gave way to tenseness and despair. Secession might be a lesser evil than submission to the avowed hostility and aggressions of the North. At least some steps should be taken immediately in preparation for the worst that

cember 6, 1859; Richmond *Enquirer,* November 14, 11, 1859; Craven, *Coming of the Civil War,* 408–409.

[43] Charleston *Mercury,* December 16, 1859; Memphis *Avalanche,* October 26, 1859; Mobile *Register,* October 25, 1859.

[44] Henry D. Capers, *The Life and Times of C. G. Memminger* (Richmond, 1893), 239.

might occur. "Vigilance committees" and "committees of correspondence" were set up in many places. Strangers were watched with suspicion and sometimes threatened by force. The British consul in Charleston wrote: "I do not exaggerate in designating the present state of affairs in the Southern country as a reign of terror. Persons are torn away from their residences and pursuits; sometimes 'tarred and feathered'; 'ridden upon rails,' or cruelly whipped; letters are opened at the Post Offices; discussion upon slavery is entirely prohibited under penalty of expulsion, with or without violence from the country. The Northern merchants and 'Travellers' are leaving in great numbers." [45]

Under the intense excitement, state legislatures made appropriations for the organization and equipment of their militia "for active and efficient service." Armories were put in order. Guns were purchased, and military companies were soon drilling in businesslike fashion all over the South. Local factions forgot their differences, and South Carolina and Mississippi hopefully sent out agents to urge again the holding of a Southern convention to secure unity "in measures of defense."

In his message to the legislature of South Carolina, Governor Gist declared that "the intention of the North" had been "clearly evinced by the action of the few," and the legislature responded by sending Christopher G. Memminger as "Commissioner" to the state of Virginia to express sympathy and to urge a meeting of all the slaveholding states. The Mississippi legislature had, in the meantime, declared that the election of a Republican President would be sufficient reason for a council of the Southern states, had accepted South Carolina's proposal for such a meeting, and, in turn, had dispatched Peter B. Starke off to Virginia.[46]

These commissioners found Virginia more calm than had been expected and public opinion not yet prepared for action. Virginians feared the move was "a mere excuse for disunion." They listened to Memminger's impassioned plea but took no action. The Mis-

---

[45] Quoted in Laura A. White, "The South in the 1850's as Seen by British Consuls," *Journal of Southern History,* I (1935), 44.

[46] Capers, *Life and Times of C. G. Memminger,* 244–82; Ollinger Crenshaw, "Christopher G. Memminger's Mission to Virginia, 1860," in *Journal of Southern History,* VIII (1942), 334–49; Dwight L. Dumond, *The Secession Movement, 1860–1861* (New York, 1931), 28–31.

sissippi commissioner fared no better, and the total result of all efforts was a Virginia resolution to the effect that direct legislation by the several states would be more effective just now than action by a convention. Sadly Memminger wrote his friend, William Porcher Miles: "I am very sorry to be brought to the conclusion that Virginia is not prepared to do anything—and that the possible apprehension of Disunion will cause the Legislature to decline our conference." [47] Miles's reply was prophetic: "I am deeply pained and mortified to hear that Virginia is so utterly apathetic. . . . We *further South,* must act and 'drag her along.' "

Yet all agreed that the confusion in Virginia politics, which made each faction fearful of taking a mistaken step, had much to do with the refusal to co-operate with the other Southern states. A joint committee of her two houses had already accepted the fact of Northern hostility to the lives and institutions of the South and had recommended that the militia be placed in readiness for service, commercial independence be achieved, and co-operation with other states in such a program be encouraged. John C. Rutherford bluntly told the House of Delegates that the Union was in danger. Northerners had "honored, with high office, admirers of Brown and endorsers of Helper." The bonds of party and religion had been severed. The "active and fanatical hostility" to slavery now threatened to cut the few remaining ties. [48]

Something tragically important had taken place in Southern attitudes. A plain North Carolina citizen put it this way:

"I have always been a fervid Union man but I confess the endorsement of the Harpers Ferry outrage and Helper's infernal doctrine has shaken my fidelity and . . . I am willing to take the chances of every probable evil that may arise from disunion, sooner than submit any longer to Northern insolence and Northern outrage." [49]

[47] Memminger to Miles, June 30, 1860, in Miles Papers; Memminger's report to Governor William H. Gist, February 13, 1860, in Capers, *Life and Times of C. G. Memminger,* 280–81; Miles to Memminger, February 3, 1860, in Christopher G. Memminger Papers (University of North Carolina Library).

[48] Quoted in Shanks, *Secession Movement in Virginia,* 97–101.

[49] William A. Walsh to L. O'B. Branch, December 8, 1859, in L. O'B. Branch Papers (University of North Carolina Library).

CHAPTER XII

THE CAMPAIGN OF 1860

I
T WAS unfortunate that the Presidential election of 1860 had to follow so closely on the heels of the John Brown raid. Political campaigns in the United States are not conducive to calm, rational discussion and understanding. They tend to exaggeration. They create the impression that a crisis has been reached and that something vital is at stake. Emotions are aroused even though nothing but commonplaces and personalities are involved. Men talk of defeat as though it implied disaster.

As a matter of fact, however, the fears expressed have seldom been genuine enough to prevent the acceptance of defeat in good temper. Morals or the fundamental structure of the political or social system have seldom been involved. Campaign oratory has been good-humoredly discounted, and the right of the majority to rule has not been questioned.

This was not to be the case in 1860. The John Brown raid had cleared the air and forced many Northerners to admit that, while they abhorred violence, they found themselves approving both of Brown's motives and of his purposes. The day was coming to an end when they could accept slavery as both legal and immoral. They were, in fact, determined to put it on the road to ultimate extinction. Seward, with his "higher law" and his "irrepressible conflict," was not much ahead of Northern public opinion.

Southerners had understood all this even before the average Northerner had done so. They knew, however, what most Northerners did not seem to comprehend: that slavery represented an economic investment, the loss of which would bankrupt the section, and that the "peculiar institution" was so entwined with Southern life that its abrupt ending would shatter the fundamental struc-

ture of their social system. A race question would be created. A
labor problem would be thrust upon them. The burden of lifting
a whole race from forced dependence and ignorance to responsible
citizenship would be placed upon their shoulders. To meet these
problems the political structure would have to be completely re-
made and the agencies for the care of the poor, the aged, the halt,
and the blind be greatly extended. In fact, they would be faced with
revolution.

This would have been bad enough had it been brought forward
as a great national reform movement to be gradually worked out
through legal action and without economic loss. To face it as a moral
crusade whose agents need not respect life nor law nor property
was intolerable. If Republicans had spawned John Brown and if
they somehow excused his actions or saw his raid as an insignificant
affair, Republican success could only mean Southern ruin.

The campaign of 1860 would, therefore, regardless of what else
might be involved, turn on the issue of the security of slavery in or
out of the Union: its equal treatment with any other kind of property. It would be largely a contest, in the South, between those who
thought that the end had come and that a Republican victory
would prove it, and those who were willing to give the Union further trial. John Brown had done this to politics.

This situation was one, of course, toward which the nation had
been drifting for a decade. The basic issues that had to do not only
with lands, tariffs, internal improvements, and financial policies
but also with the larger matter of national character in the modern
world were being covered over and symbolized by the slavery issue with all its own powerful moral and democratic implications.
The power struggle, the question of the nature of our form of
government, the rights of minorities, and the relation of government to business—these great issues were now so tangled with the
slavery issue that only the merits or lack of them in slavery itself
seemed to influence men's thinking. On this issue alone the fate
of the Union now hung. On this alone, the abilities of the democratic process, now largely a matter of national party solidarity,
would be tested—tested in an atmosphere strained and vitiated by
John Brown's violence.

The party situation itself was bad enough. The Whig party was

313

no longer a national organization, but few of its Southern members had been able to settle themselves comfortably into any other group. The Know-Nothings had caught up many of them for a brief period, but that party also had broken to pieces on the same rocks that had wrecked the Whigs. A slow drift into Democratic ranks seemed to be the only course open. Yet Whig tradition had been definitely national. Its great appeal had been to sectional harmony. Only necessity, therefore, could force "unreconstructed Whigs" into a party that stressed sectional rights and indulged in talk of secession. Many still hoped for the creation of a "constitutional, law-abiding party embracing both the North and the South." A few even dreamed of a revival of the old party itself. Their waverings were enough to encourage some Republicans to believe that votes might be secured in the South. In fact, Virginia and other Border State Whigs had been seriously considering a union with conservative Republicans, and overtures were being made back and forth between their leaders and prominent Republicans in New York.[1]

The Democratic party, itself, had been slowly disintegrating ever since the election of James K. Polk. The old Jacksonian element at the North, with strong Locofoco leanings, had made the first break. Failure to look after Northwestern interests, in terms of land and internal improvements, next took its toll. Then had come difficulties over Texas and Oregon and the more serious disputes over slavery in the territories. Northern and Southern extremists alike had deserted in droves, and those who remained to keep the party still in power were divided into quarreling factions. The Whigs owed their victory in 1848 largely to the irregularity of Southern Democrats, and the Democrats won the next two Presidential elections more because of the weakness of their opponents than because of their own unity. Kansas and Douglas had provided the proverbial last straw. Bitter and unforgiving factions rendered the condition of the party desperate. It was in no condition to meet sturdy opposition.

[1] Columbus *Daily Enquirer*, October 25, 1859; New York *Tribune*, July 25, 1859; Shanks, *Secession Movement in Virginia*, 101–102. The Wyndham Robertson Papers are filled with such material.

Yet it now faced a young and rising Republican party that had lost much of its earlier idealism, had developed a well-rounded economic program, and had learned much of practical politics from such masters as Seward, Weed, Simon Cameron, and Lincoln. It was strictly a sectional party, but its appeal had broadened to attract all classes in the North. It was unquestionably the party in step with "progress," the carrier of the social-economic values essential to the emergency of financial-industrial capitalism. It was, nevertheless, still the party that had been born to oppose the expansion of slavery, and it still held in its ranks a strong antislavery element. Seward by his "higher law" and "irrepressible conflict" doctrines may have been prophesying the inevitable triumph of free labor and of urban industrial society, but to the South he was merely threatening the destruction of slavery, the inauguration of a race war, and the reduction of the South and her ways to a perpetual colonial status.

The immediate difficulty lay in the fact that Stephen A. Douglas, by his recent conduct, had won the loyal support of Northern Democrats and lost that of a majority of his Southern supporters. The administration forces hated him even more than did his Southern foes, and both were determined to prevent his nomination at the coming convention in Charleston. Yet all thinking persons knew that no other Democrat had the slightest chance of becoming President. It was either Douglas or defeat. He alone could cope with Republican strength in the Northwest. He alone could make anything like a national appeal.[2]

There were those, however, who for revenge or because of fears and a growing feeling of desperation were willing to take a chance. It might be better to run the risk of destroying the Democratic party than to surrender Southern equality by accepting the Douglas interpretation of squatter sovereignty. Rights were more valuable than the Union. Northern attitudes had now been clearly revealed. There would be no compromise. Since the break would have to come sooner or later, why delay?

The tragedy of it all lay in the fact that to the political party Americans had delegated the inauguration and carrying out of na-

[2] Montgomery *Confederation*, March 24, 1860.

tional policies. A sectional party meant sectional legislation. A disruption of parties meant the breakdown of the whole democratic process.

During the winter and spring, 1859–1860, there was much discussion in the South as to whether Douglas could be accepted as the Democratic nominee, and as to what the South should do in case he was successful. The majority of the politicians, as has been said, were unquestionably against Douglas. His doctrines, declared Governor Wise, were "the most direct road to the ends of B. Republicanism." The *Mississippian* called him the "most profligate of all political reprobates; the most unbearable of all political bores; a 'turbulent demagogue;' a miserable thimblerigger with remarkable capacity to betray." It would be treason for any Southerner to support him at Charleston. With his eloquence, his ambition, and his depravity, he was "the most dangerous man in the limits of the Confederacy." Already some talked of Southern delegates seceding from the convention if he was nominated.[3]

Not all Democrats, however, were so extreme in their opinions. A few backed Douglas, because they thought him "a practical statesman" who had been denounced by extremists North and South for keeping to the middle of the road. They found "as much to praise as to condemn in his course." Others, such as Robert Toombs and Alexander H. Stephens, in Georgia, understood the necessity of holding the Douglas support even though they disliked the man himself. Unless he did something worse than he had yet done, they would support him "most cordially" if nominated. Many honestly believed that opposition to Douglas was confined to a few extrem-

[3] Nashville *Patriot*, October 7, 1859; Henry J. Wise to F. Woods, July 6, 1859, in Brock Collection; Rainwater, *Mississippi, Storm Center of Secession*, 111; Augusta *Chronicle and Sentinel*, April 6, 1860; Charleston *News*, quoted in Augusta *Chronicle and Sentinel*, August 20, 1859; Albert Gallatin Brown to Douglas, September 10, 1859, in Douglas Papers, threatening to bolt the convention if equal protection to slavery in territories were not guaranteed. The Augusta *Chronicle and Sentinel*, August 21, 1859, said of Douglas: "He possesses the eloquence of a Demosthenes, the ambition of a Caesar and the general character of a Cataline. His political creed is as changeable as the popular will; delighting in public applause, he has never had the courage or the honesty to maintain his opinions against public opposition. . . . In short, he is a most accomplished demagogue as well as an unprincipled political traitor."

ists and would soon be checked by the sober masses. In the months before the convention friends from every state in the South wrote to assure him of their loyalty and to report favorable reactions in their localities. When it became apparent that delegations hostile to his nomination were being chosen, they laid the blame to corrupt leadership and insisted that the majority of the people were still with him. Many of his correspondents boasted of being plain citizens without great political influence, but John Forsyth of the Mobile *Register,* James Gardner and Henry Cleveland of the Augusta *Constitutionalist,* J. J. Seibels of the Montgomery *Confederation,* and John Maginnis of the New Orleans *True Delta* were editors to be reckoned with in any campaign. They were powerful enough to ruin the chances of any possible Southern candidate and to keep the decision on Douglas in doubt to the very end.[4]

The Congress which met in December, 1859, provided further evidence that the democratic process had ceased to work. Men came armed. Debate gave way to harangues and personalities. Disorder and confusion interfered with business and physical clashes between members were common occurrences. Senator Hammond told of reluctantly purchasing and loading a revolver because "the oldest and most conservative" members were doing so. "I keep a pistol now in my drawer in the Senate," he wrote, "as a matter of *duty* to my section & to reinforce it in either House." A member of the House, reporting a near fight between Owen Lovejoy of Illinois and Pryor of Virginia, wrote that he said not a word "but quietly cocked my Revolver in my pocket and took my position in the midst of the mob . . . [resolved] to sell my blood out at the highest possible price." [5]

The election of a Speaker in the House again produced strife and, in the end, a complete deadlock. Through December and January

[4] Huntsville *Southern Advocate,* February 8, 1860; Natchez *Mississippi Free Trader,* March 12, 1859; Toombs to Stephens, January 11, 1860, in Phillips (ed.), *Correspondence of Toombs, Stephens, and Cobb,* 455–56. There are more than 225 letters from the South in the Douglas Papers for the period January, 1859, to May, 1860.

[5] Hammond to Lieber, April 19, 1860, in Lieber Papers; Crawford to Stephens, April 8, 1860, in Stephens Papers (Division of Manuscripts, Library of Congress); D. H. Hamilton to Miles, December 9, 1859, in Miles Papers, urging him to "carry arms."

the struggle went on. Democratic factions refused to co-operate; Whig-Americans, encouraged by their recent successes, went their independent way; Republicans, weakened a bit, could not secure the votes necessary to elect John Sherman, who had gained the bitter hatred of the opposition by support of the effort to print a compendium of Helper's *Impending Crisis*. The situation seemed hopeless, and threats of making this the occasion for an open break were to be heard on all sides. Governor Gist of South Carolina was ready to back such a move with armed troops, assuring his friends that if they decided "upon consultation . . . to make the issue of force in Washington" they should write or telegraph him and he would "have a regiment in or near Washington in the shortest possible time." Not until a deal had been made behind the scenes for the election of minor officers was William Pennington, a New Jersey Whig, named Speaker. When news of this event reached the public, the Richmond *Enquirer* appeared in mourning strips with the statement that it was "appropriate that our venerated sheet should record the disastrous deed in tokens of deepest mourning." [6]

Two months' time had been wasted. Sectional and party rifts had been widened. It was, however, just as well, for the remainder of the session was to contribute little save the storing up of bitterness for the Charleston convention. Republicans spent most of their time in a more or less successful search for corruption in the Democratic administration. Democratic factions fought each other with Stephen A. Douglas' fortunes the stakes. Homesteads, tariffs, and internal improvements were pressed enough to show what might have been the normal course of interest if slavery had not interfered. But men were in no mood for looking after "the business of the nation." Instead they threatened and talked of things sectional.[7]

Alfred Iverson of Georgia warned that a Republican victory in 1860 would result in the breakup of the Union. The South was prepared to defend its rights even at such a cost. Brown of Mississippi, who in the preceding session had bluntly rejected Douglas' doctrine that the people of a territory could by unfriendly action get rid of slavery, now went a step further. On January 18 he intro-

[6] Governor Gist to Miles, December 20, 1859, in Miles Papers; Richmond *Enquirer*, February 2, 1860.

[7] Nichols, *Disruption of American Democracy*, 270–87.

318

duced two resolutions to the effect that it was the duty both of the territorial legislatures and of Congress to protect all types of property in the territories. His colleague, Jefferson Davis, in good Calhoun fashion, followed with a more elaborate set of resolutions on "the Relations of States." As later somewhat revised, the fourth of these read:

"That neither Congress nor a Territorial Legislature, whether by direct legislation or legislation of an indirect and unfriendly character, possesses power to annul or impair the constitutional right of any citizen of the United States to take his slave property into the common Territories, and there hold and enjoy the same while the territorial condition remains."

The fifth resolution stated that if it was demonstrated that the judiciary and executive authorities did not have the means to give such protection and if the territorial government failed to do so, it would be the duty of Congress to act. Not until the people of a territory had rightfully formed a constitution to be admitted as a state into the Union had they any right to decide whether slavery should exist or not.[8]

Here was advice for the platform committee at Charleston—advice which ran directly counter to Douglas' position and to the terms on which he had said he would accept the nomination. It represented, moreover, a complete reversal of the old standard Southern position on the subject.

While Congress blundered away its time, Democrats, North and South, had been selecting their delegates to the national convention now called to meet on April 23. It had proved anything but a harmonious task. It was, however, soon clear that Douglas would have a fairly solid block of support in the North, where New England and the Northwest, in spite of bitter administration opposition, had given him majority delegations. He seemed also to have an even chance of gaining California's votes. The Middle States were less certain. New Jersey had chosen a divided delegation and Pennsylvania a compromise one of which Douglas men constituted one

8 *Cong. Globe*, 36 Cong., 2 Sess., 12, 494; Ranck, *Albert Gallatin Brown*, 166–67; Rowland (ed.), *Jefferson Davis, Constitutionalist*, IV, 203–204; Douglas to J. B. Dorr, June 22, 1859, in Washington *Daily National Intelligencer*, June 24, 1859.

third and unfriendly traders the remainder. New York, of course, was as usual badly divided. Some thirty-five votes were apparently pledged to Douglas, but a contesting delegation had already been chosen under Fernando Wood's leadership in New York City, and everyone knew that most New York politicians were an unstable lot when temptation appeared.[9]

At the South the situation was far more serious. The Alabama legislature, meeting just after the John Brown raid, had provided funds for the organizing and equipping of a volunteer corps of some eight thousand men. It had also arranged for the military training of two young men from each county who were then obligated to drill the local militia. This, however, was little more than had been done under excitement in other Southern states. The really dangerous steps came with the passage of resolutions calling attention to the possibility of antislavery seizure "of the government itself" in the approaching election, and requiring the governor, in case of a Republican victory in 1860, to call for the election of delegates to a convention "to consider, determine, and to do whatever . . . the rights, interests, and honor of the State of Alabama require to be done for their protection." The Democratic state convention followed this up at its meeting in January, 1860, with a resolution which its delegates were instructed to offer as a plank in the national platform:

"Resolved that it is the duty of the General Government, by all proper legislation, to secure an entry into those territories to all the citizens of the United States, together with their property of every description, and that the same shall remain protected by the United States while the Territories are under its authority."

If these resolves or their equivalent were not accepted, the delegates were "positively instructed" to withdraw from the national convention. Yancey had had his way. Forsyth and Seibels had not been able to seat their delegates or to control the chairmanship. The people may have been on their side and willing to stop with the "Cincinnati Platform" of 1856. The politicians most certainly were not.[10]

9 Milton, *Eve of Conflict,* 372–73.

10 Alabama *Acts,* 1859–1860, pp. 258–97; *Proceedings of the Democratic State Convention* [of Alabama] *held in the City of Montgomery, commencing Wednesday,*

No other Southern state imposed such obligations on its delegates, but it was well understood that there were many individuals who would support such measures. The Davis resolutions in Congress were generally accepted as Mississippi's ultimatum and as meaning that her delegates as a body would follow Alabama's lead. Elsewhere unanimous action was in doubt. Dependence would have to be placed on circumstances and individuals.[11]

In Virginia the struggle between Hunter and Wise, both of whom wanted the nomination, shaped events. Hunter's ability to control the delegation turned the Wise support to Douglas, and the convention simply reaffirmed the Cincinnati Platform on slavery. The North Carolina delegation was predominantly conservative. Most of its members would also be content with reaffirming the action of 1856, and would not ask for further protection of slavery in the territories. They might even support Douglas as the only man capable of holding the Northern states.

The situation in South Carolina was complicated. In spite of a noticeable reaction against extremes in the past few years, there had always been a radical sectional element to be considered. It now refused to take part in the choosing of delegates to the convention but expected to control their actions. This resulted in the election of a majority of "genuine supporters of the national Democracy" with Orr in complete charge. "The only concession made to the strongly sectional opinions of a few of the delegates was a resolution stating that a territorial government could not directly or by unfriendly legislation exclude slavery." Delegates were not bound to support any particular candidate or to withdraw if demands were not met. The next move was up to the radicals.[12]

Cobb's ambitions for the Presidential nomination produced considerable confusion in Georgia. He was in desperate need of a vote of confidence both for himself and for the administration of which

---

January 11, 1860 (Montgomery, 1860); J. I. Horn to Douglas, March 11, 1860, in Douglas Papers.

[11] See denunciation of Alabama's course, in New Orleans *Bee*, January 18, 1860; Albert Gallatin Brown to Douglas, September 10, 1859, in Douglas Papers; Rainwater, *Mississippi, Storm Center of Secession,* 117–18.

[12] Shanks, *Secession Movement in Virginia,* 104; Sitterson, *Secession Movement in North Carolina,* 162–64; Rhett to Miles, March 28, April 11, 1860, in Miles Papers; Schultz, *Nationalism and Sectionalism in South Carolina,* 212–13.

he was a part. Public opinion, however, was badly divided, and trends were conservative. An irregular convention called early by his friends resolved to send delegates to Charleston and instructed them to support the party nominee if the platform protected Southern rights. It also agreed to present Cobb's name to the convention. The Democratic executive committee, however, called a second convention, at which strong anti-Cobb sentiment developed. After bitter strife a delegation of twice the usual size, composed of both factions, was chosen and instructed to vote as a unit. Cobb was thus repudiated, and Georgia's political confusion was passed on to Charleston.[13]

The delegations from the other Southern states were largely the product of local, personal rivalries and, while often pledged to support a favorite son, might be counted on to run with the tide at Charleston. Tennessee was offering Andrew Johnson on a slavery platform that "neither conflicted with Douglas' views nor compromised his friends." Kentucky, with Missouri in agreement, would present James Guthrie on a similar platform. Both delegations, however, contained men who would prefer Douglas. Texas, after a conservative swing back to Houston before the John Brown raid, was again in radical hands, while Louisiana was divided between the followers of Soulé, who backed Douglas, and the supporters of Slidell, who in the name of the administration would fight him at every step. Florida adopted resolutions condemning the Douglas doctrine regarding slavery in the territories but expressed no preference for candidates. The radical element in the Democratic party, however, was definitely in control and Governor Madison S. Perry had recommended withdrawal from the Union in case of Republican success. Her militia was already drilling. In Arkansas the anti-Douglas forces had triumphed. The state convention reaffirmed the Cincinnati Platform, denied the power either of Congress or of the territorial legislature to impair the rights of "any citizen to take his slave property" into the common territories, and declared that this right should be recognized before voting on candidates should begin. If this was refused, the delegates should withdraw.[14]

13 Montgomery, *Cracker Parties*, 237–38.
14 George M. Pascal informed Douglas, April 17, 1860, in Douglas Papers, that

The temper and spirit shown in the election of delegates forecast accurately the character of the coming convention. They had revealed the bold determination on the part of a radical group to force a sectional showdown on issues—a willingness to rule or ruin. They had made it perfectly clear that the South was not of one mind, even that a majority had not had its way—and that, in times of stress and uncertainty, a small but determined group of politicians might dominate the confused majority. What was even more alarming was the willingness to stake everything on an abstraction in the name of *rights* and to ignore the cold facts and the tragic consequences that might be involved. Fears and apprehensions, hatred and vengeance, and a reckless willingness to gamble with heavy stakes had characterized men's actions. Reason and common sense had played little part. The conventions had demonstrated the fact that sometimes the opportunity to make speeches, to press issues that might better be left alone, and to demand the recognition of abstract values could do as much harm to the democratic process as the neglect of civic obligations: that even frequent campaigns and elections could sometimes be a disadvantage.

As the day of the convention drew near, rumors floated about to the effect that the place of meeting would be changed and that Douglas had asked that his name be withdrawn. Either, if true, might have helped the situation. Unfortunately they were only rumors. The convention would meet in Charleston, and Douglas would remain in the running.

A place worse than Charleston, South Carolina, in which to hold the convention could not have been selected. She was unique even among Southern cities. Colorful and quaint in "her dim old faded ways," she had given to all that she had touched and all that had touched her a peculiarly native twist. She had churches "that might have come from the England of Christopher Wren," but somehow they were not English. "Along the reaches of East Bay and the harbor end of Queen Street" there were "rows of close-set old

---

the Texas delegation was pledged to withdraw from the convention if necessary to secure his defeat. See also J. W. Singleton to Douglas, January 7, 1860, *ibid.*; Dodd, "Secession Movement in Florida," *loc. cit.*, 45–47; Lewis, "From Nationalism to Disunion," 328–29.

houses that might have come from some French seaport, but . . . [bore] the precise markings of no one in particular." They, like all the rest, were just Charlestonian. She had done the same to her people whether they came from England, France, the West Indies, or New England. They too had become thoroughly native, and provincial enough to be proud of the fact. They spoke a brogue all their own, thought and acted with an independence that was often irritating to those outside. Proud and sensitive, they had ever been quick to resent interference or hostile criticism, always jealous of their honor. Under their leadership, the state of South Carolina had nullified the tariff, had been first to pronounce slavery "a positive good," and had stood always at the front with the threat of secession if Southern rights were not respected. So extreme had been her protests against "being pushed around" and rendered inferior that in the present crisis she had not dared to take the lead for fear of doing damage to the cause. The worthy citizens of Charleston were not, however, expecting or expected to stand quietly aside while the visiting politicians played their game. Even a national Democratic convention in town for only a few days might expect to feel the mighty impress of old Charleston. John C. Calhoun was asleep in St. Philip's churchyard, but Robert Barnwell Rhett still walked her streets.[15]

Regardless of all her virtues, Charleston was not large in size, nor did she possess the facilities for housing and feeding a great convention. The Mills House and the Charleston House were adequate for ordinary crowds that might come at race week or to local political gatherings, but even with five and six delegates assigned to a room they could not hope to care for the crowds, official and unofficial, that now began to arrive by train and boat. Some would find accommodations in the lesser lodginghouses and in private homes. Many delegates, however, were forced to sleep, dormitory fashion, in public halls fitted temporarily with cots or on ships at the wharf. Lack of proper rest would take its toll in nerves and tempers.

Nor was the food sufficient. Charlestonians generally ate at home. Many planters from the outside maintained town houses and sup-

---

[15] Bayard Wooten and Samuel G. Stoney, *Charleston, Azaleas and Old Bricks* (Boston, 1937), 1–3.

plied them from their country gardens. A generous hospitality took care of friends and relatives. The strain on public eating places was, therefore, never heavy, so that now, in spite of the excessive charge of $5.00 per day for board and lodging generally demanded, tables were scantily supplied, and hungry visitors and delegates were the rule. Only Southerners who found friendly doors always open to them escaped the pangs of hunger.[16]

Other conditions were also unsatisfactory. The weather for a time was unseasonably hot. Then it rained and turned cold. Few delegates were prepared for either extreme. Institute Hall, where the convention met, was not large enough, and the noise from the cobbled streets outside poured through the open windows to augment that of overcrowded gallery and floor. Visitors who had come for a gay time, and Charleston men and women who viewed it all as a kind of personal affair, made the galleries, with their cheers and hisses, a part of the convention. Few could hear what was going on unless some unusual speaker had the floor.[17]

As funds gave out and visitors began to leave, the people of Charleston dominated the galleries, waved and shouted to their friends on the floor, and created an atmosphere favorable to bombast and radical action. Northerners became conscious of that subtle ability which Charlestonians possessed of making others conscious of the fact that they were outsiders.

Amid such surroundings, one of the fateful events in American history was to take place.

The delegates who now began converging on Charleston may be roughly divided into four groups. There were the Douglas men, who constituted a majority of the delegates, but many of whom

[16] Charleston *Courier*, April 19, 20, 23, 24, 25, 1860; Charleston *Mercury*, April 21, 23, 25, 1860; Murat Halstead, *A History of the National Political Conventions of the Current Campaign* (Columbus, Ohio, 1860), 1–18. On talk of changing the place of meeting, see George W. Sanders to Douglas, March 26, 1860; John R. Jeffries to Douglas, March 26, 1860, in Douglas Papers. Jeffries wrote: "I regret exceedingly that the place of meeting of the National convention has not been changed to Baltimore as the very unfavorable reports about accommodations at Charleston will deter many of your friends (outsiders) from meeting with us at the latter place." See also William H. Trescot to Miles, February 22, 1860, in Miles Papers.

[17] One of Yancey's first efforts was to have the streets near the convention hall covered with straw.

came from states that would go Republican in the coming election; they were well organized and determined. Then there were those who did not like Douglas and talked of R. M. T. Hunter of Virginia, James Guthrie of Kentucky, or Jefferson Davis of Mississippi, but who would probably support the man and the platform adopted by the convention. Next were the traders, seeking advantage where it might be found and perfectly willing to add their part to the confusion as the best way to their ends. Lastly were those who came determined to defeat Douglas at all cost—administration men and radical Southerners.[18]

The real contest was clearly over Douglas, whose possible nomination radical Southern leaders had skillfully turned into an acceptance of Southern inequality. Out of this could be forged the weapon for which Rhett and Yancey had been searching. In January, Rhett had written: "So long as the Democratic party, as a 'National' organization, exists in power at the South, and so long as our public men trim their sails with an eye to either its power or enmity, just so long need we hope for no southern action for our disenthralment and security. The South must dissever itself from the rotten Northern element. After the Charleston Convention we must have a Southern-Rights Democratic party organized on principles and with States-Rights candidates upon whom to rally." He went on to admit that there was no hope of state rights men controlling the convention and stressed the importance of securing the secession of the Alabama and Mississippi delegations from that body as the first step in dissolving the Union in case of a Republican victory. It was useless, he thought, "to talk about checking the North or dissolving the Union with unanimity and without division at the South." It was simply a case of "men having both nerve and self-sacrificing patriotism" taking the lead and "controlling and compelling their inferior contemporaries." [19]

[18] I. I. Jones to Douglas, April 20, 1860; E. D. Beach to Douglas, April 12, 1860; S. W. Johnson to Douglas, April 12, 1860; P. A. Hoyne to Douglas, April 12, 1860, in Douglas Papers; New York *Herald,* April 22, 1860.

[19] In October, 1859, the Charleston *Mercury* had published a six-point program for the South which the South Carolina legislature should issue as "a declaration of the rights of the South," and which must be affirmed by the convention if the Southern members were to remain in the body. White, *Robert Barnwell Rhett,* 157; Rhett to Miles, January 17, 1860, in Miles Papers; John W. Du Bose, *The Life and Times of William Lowndes Yancey* (New York, 1942), I, 362.

Yancey had declared his "aims and objects" were "to cast before the people of the South as great a mass of wrongs committed on them, injuries and insults" that had been done, as possible, and thus to "produce spirit enough . . . to call forth a Lexington, to fight a Bunker's hill, to drive the foe from the city" of Southern rights. He would "fire the Southern heart" so that "at the proper moment, by one organized, concerted action" he could "precipitate the cotton States into a revolution." [20]

Much of this was, of course, just Southern bombast, but Yancey was in the convention at the head of the Alabama delegation with its threatening resolutions, and Rhett was busy outside directing opinion and pressure. They were thus in a position to make the most for the larger cause out of the Douglas issue. Soon after arriving at Charleston the delegations from Georgia, Florida, Louisiana, Texas, Arkansas, and Mississippi met and agreed to stand with Alabama on her platform as the best means of checking the "Little Giant." They were willing to work with the administration forces under Senators Slidell, Bright, and James A. Bayard to force the adoption of a platform embodying the Alabama demands before the nomination of a candidate was made.

The convention was formally opened on Monday morning, April 23. Strife marked its proceedings from the beginning. Thomas B. Flournoy of Arkansas, a Douglas man, was made temporary chairman, and committees were appointed without much difficulty. The choice of Caleb Cushing as permanent chairman, through administration pressure on Oregon and California delegates, was, however, a clear defeat for the Douglas forces, who now countered with a clever move in the committee on organization. At its first meeting this committee agreed to resubmit the rules of 1856. At a second meeting, however, of which the members from Missouri, Louisiana, and Texas were not notified, the following new rule was added: "That in any State which has not provided or directed by its state convention how its vote may be given, the convention will recognize the right of each delegate to cast his individual vote." Since there were numerous Douglas men in unfriendly noninstructed delegations, this freed them to vote as they pleased.[21]

[20] Du Bose, *Life and Times of William Lowndes Yancey*, I, 376.
[21] Halstead, *National Political Conventions*, 18–30; Du Bose, *Life and Times of*

Against this procedure Southern members protested bitterly but more than righted the balance next day when they forced through their plan for making the platform before choosing the nominee. Just why the Douglas delegates agreed to this is not clear. Perhaps they thought they could dictate the platform and were willing to be rid of those who were pledged to withdraw if the Alabama resolves were not included. They could then command the two thirds necessary to nominate their candidate. This seemed more certain when they were able to seat the friendly New York Regency delegation and exclude the hostile Fernando Wood group.

Internal strife reached its climax on Friday when the platform committee reported its inability to reach an agreement and submitted three proposals. The majority report was that drawn by the fifteen Southerners and their California and Oregon colleagues. It denied the right of any territorial legislature to abolish slavery, to prohibit its introduction, or to destroy or impair its rights; and declared it the duty of the Federal government to protect the rights of persons and property on the high seas, in the territories, or wherever else its constitutional authority extended. It was, in substance, what Alabama had demanded as the condition on which its delegates would remain in the convention. It was what Stephen A. Douglas had said he would not accept as his platform.

The second, or minority proposal, was the Cincinnati Platform with the added statement that questions regarding the rights of property in states and territories, arising under the Constitution, were judicial in character and that the Democratic party was pledged to abide by and faithfully carry out such determination of these questions as the Supreme Court had made or might make.

The third proposal was that of Benjamin F. Butler, which simply reaffirmed the Cincinnati Platform.[22]

William Lowndes Yancey, II, 453–54; Murray McConnel to Douglas, April 22, 1860, in Douglas Papers.

[22] Austin L. Venable, "The Conflict Between the Douglas and Yancey Forces in the Charleston Convention," in *Journal of Southern History,* VIII (1942), 226–41; Milton, *Eve of Conflict,* 433–35; Nichols, *Disruption of American Democracy,* 298–300, gives essential paragraphs of each proposal; Halstead, *National Political Conventions,* 30–37; H. B. Payne to Douglas, March 17, 1860, in Douglas Papers, gives the program of "the conspirators" as then developing.

In presenting the majority proposal, Waightstill W. Avery of North Carolina spoke of the distrust with which the people of the South viewed the Northern wing of the party and the necessity of restoring confidence among those whose material interests alone were involved and who would cast the majority of Democratic votes. He denied that their proposals dealt with an abstraction and argued that Mexico, Cuba, and Central America might some day be United States possessions in which slavery would require protection. It was not a great speech, but it left no doubts as to Southern demands.

Henry B. Payne of Ohio presented and spoke for the minority proposals. His plea was for party harmony on the principle of squatter sovereignty and the equally sound doctrine of nonintervention by Congress. He made it perfectly clear that if the majority proposal were made the platform, not one electoral vote could be expected from the North. "I do not believe we can elect a single member of Congress in the whole Northwest, outside of Lower Egypt, on the doctrine of intervention," were his words.[23]

Complete disagreement was thus revealed and the stage set for the flow of oratory which everyone knew had long been preparing. After an intermission and a few preliminary speeches, Yancey asked for the floor. It was the moment for which the galleries and the radical South had been waiting. Amid rounds of applause and a shower of flowers, he reached the platform and, when order was restored, began to speak in his usual restrained but confident manner. Brushing aside any attempt at compromise, he insisted that Southern men were there to save their Constitutional rights. A squatter-sovereignty platform would mean their ruin. Rather the party go down to utter defeat than to yield on principle. The cause of the present difficulty was clear. Northern Democrats had held slavery to be an evil when they should have proclaimed it a positive good. If they had taken that ground, they would have triumphed. Because they had not done so, Southern property was now invaded; their institutions were at stake; their peace had been destroyed. If Northern men were now enabled to consummate their designs, Southern honor and lives would rest upon "a great heaving volcano of passion and crime." Northern rights and institutions and laws

[23] Halstead, *National Political Conventions,* 38–51.

had not been invaded and assailed. Their peace and property were not at stake. Was the South "asking any too much" when it asked the Northern delegates to yield in this matter as brothers, to quiet Southern doubts? [24]

It was late when Yancey finished, and George E. Pugh of Ohio began his reply with the blunt words: "I thank God we have had one true and honest man from the South to speak to us, who hides behind no equivocal expressions!" Sarcastically, he pointed to the inconsistency of demands for intervention from Southern men who had once denounced it. Must the Democratic party become the tool of three hundred thousand slaveholders? Must Northern men avow slavery to be right and its extension desirable? "Gentlemen of the South," he cried, "you mistake us—you mistake us! We will not do it." [25]

The crisis had been reached. The efforts of the Douglas forces to secure a vote threw the convention into an uproar. The chairman's calls for order went unheeded while the delegates surged "about like the waves of the sea," shouting and pushing. Sheer exhaustion brought adjournment near midnight.

When the convention reassembled on Saturday, men realized that the party of Jefferson and Jackson was on the verge of disruption. Compromises were suggested, and the proposed platforms were turned back to the committee for reconsideration. This produced revisions and concessions in each proposal, but they still remained separate and unsatisfactory to opponents. Filibuster and angry debate only widened the gap and forced a vote on the platforms as they stood. Both sides showed startling indifference to consequences.

On Monday, April 30, the voting began. The Douglas supporters had evidently used the Sabbath to good advantage and carried the motion to substitute the minority for the majority report by a vote of 165 to 138. Then, because some thought the risk too great, they agreed to drop the resolution referring squatter sovereignty to the Supreme Court but pushed through the planks reaffirming the Cincinnati statement on slavery, pledging protection to naturalized citizens, denouncing the personal-liberty laws, and favoring support

[24] Du Bose, *Life and Times of William Lowndes Yancey*, II, 457–58.
[25] *Ibid.*, 458–60; Charleston *Mercury*, April 28, 29, 1860.

to a Pacific railroad and the acquisition of Cuba. On these planks Southern delegates generally refused to vote.

At this point, if the Alabama instructions had been strictly followed, withdrawal from the convention should have begun. That it did not may have been due to the influence of the administration leaders. They were of the opinion that the only way to defeat Douglas was to remain in the convention, and they had made good use of the Sunday interlude to impress this point of view upon the more conservative Southerners. The Virginia delegates, anxious to nominate Hunter, had given their support. Richard Taylor of Louisiana had labored to bring the Alabama group into conference, and there is some evidence that even Yancey agreed to postpone action. Only the stubborn opposition of John A. Winston is supposed to have kept the delegation in line. But whatever the reason, the Southern delegates now hesitated while Charles E. Stuart of Michigan took the floor. Whether he lost his temper because of the hostile atmosphere, or whether his speech was part of a planned program to drive enough Southern delegations out to make Douglas' nomination possible, we do not know. At any rate, he became sarcastic and offensive. When he had finished, all hope of co-operation or compromise was ended.[26]

With an angry protest against the denial of Southern rights, Leroy P. Walker led the Alabama delegates from the hall followed by Mississippi, Louisiana, South Carolina, Florida, and Texas. Setting themselves up in a neighboring hall as a Constitutional Democratic convention, they were soon joined by one delegate from Virginia, two each from Georgia and Delaware, three from Missouri, and four from Arkansas. The New York delegation under Fernando Wood, which had been rejected by the regular convention, expected to be admitted but were refused as not having been a part of the original convention. Organized with Senator James A. Bayard of Delaware as chairman, they adopted the majority platform and impatiently awaited overtures, which never came, from Institute Hall.[27]

[26] Richard Taylor, *Destruction and Reconstruction: Personal Experiences of the Late War* (New York, 1879), 12; Du Bose, *Life and Times of William Lowndes Yancey*, II, 466–67.

[27] Halstead, *National Political Conventions*, 61–68, 72–73; Nichols, *Disruption of American Democracy*, 304–305, 306–309. It is quite clear that the South Carolina dele-

Some members of the seceding delegations had gone out under protest. Two thirds of the Georgia group and a majority of the Arkansas delegates did not withdraw until the second day. Two members from South Carolina, two from Arkansas, and eight from Georgia remained in the convention. These, together with the Border State and New York delegations, now brought forward a new compromise proposition on the slavery issue and one requiring a two-thirds vote of the full convention for the Presidential nomination. The first of these, soon known as the "Tennessee resolution," was not acted upon, but the second, to the dismay of the Douglas supporters, was passed. Trial votes soon showed that no group would yield and that no candidate could be chosen. They, therefore, adjourned to meet on June 18 in Baltimore.

The seceders' convention received this unexpected news in awkward silence. Its delegations had gained nothing and they would now have to return home and plan for a permanent break or fight to retain their old seats. Since Douglas had failed of nomination, some hoped for a reunited convention at Baltimore with a Southern candidate and a revised platform. Some wished to issue an address to the nation explaining their position and actions. Others would have none of it. Friction developed over charges of attempting to destroy the Union and the only action possible was adjournment to meet on June 11 in Richmond.

Between conventions, public opinion changed little. Southern-rights groups approved the conduct of their delegates, while the opposition remained critical. In Montgomery, for instance, the *Weekly Advertiser* spoke of the delegates "walking firmly [out of the convention] in the path of duty and honor . . . bearing with them the respect and admiration of a nation," while its neighbor, the *Confederation*, warned Yancey that the people would soon "demonstrate to him in terms more convincing than his own fiery and glittering eloquence, that he is most egregiously mistaken in supposing them willing to follow him to the natural, logical and inevitable consequence of his present course, viz: a dissolution of the Union for any present existing cause, or for anything proposed

gation had not intended to withdraw, but did so under local pressure. See Rhett to Miles, April 11, May 12, 1860, in Miles Papers; Perry to Franklin Garland, in Charleston *Courier*, May 19, 1860.

to be done or left undone, by the *Democracy of the North*." [28]

It is interesting to notice, however, that the *Advertiser* bluntly denied that this was "a disunion movement." It was only a movement "to uphold the Constitution." It was not even a move to form "a Southern sectional organization." The Democratic state convention took a like position, and Yancey's hope of making the break complete and final could not be realized even in Alabama. Only South Carolina and Florida were willing to go that far. [29]

Most states returned their original delegations to the Baltimore convention with replacements from dissatisfied areas, but also accredited them to Richmond. Only in Alabama, Louisiana, and Georgia did the Douglas forces revolt and send contesting delegations. Whether men who had seceded at Charleston would be admitted at Baltimore was, of course, a question. But hopes for peace and the nomination of a Southern man were general. A reluctance to see the Democracy broken up was everywhere apparent. [30]

What happened at Baltimore and Richmond was only the culmination of the disruption begun at Charleston. The Douglas delegates came to Baltimore determined to view *secession* at Charleston as *resignation* from the convention. The credentials of such persons should, therefore, be referred to a committee and their readmission based on a willingness to abide by the action of the convention. Southerners, supported by many Northerners, insisted that the state conventions alone had the power to appoint or dismiss delegates. Withdrawal at Charleston had not vacated seats. Returning delegates should be accepted without question.

This again produced a majority and a minority report with "steam-roller tactics" employed to carry the Douglas contention. It was, therefore, clear that wherever contesting delegates or delegations had appeared, Douglas men would be favored. Harmony was out of the question. Bitter and disgusted, twenty-five of the Virginia

[28] The Columbus *Cornerstone* called the withdrawal "silly" and the New Orleans *Bee* agreed, May 8, 1860; Montgomery *Weekly Advertiser*, May 16, 1860; Montgomery *Confederation*, May 19, 1860.

[29] Mongomery *Advertiser*, May 16, 1860; Dorman, *Party Politics in Alabama*, 157–58.

[30] It should be noted that a local meeting in northern Arkansas did send three delegates. Memphis *Weekly Appeal*, May 15, 1860; Macon *Georgia Telegraph*, May 12, 1860; Huntsville *Southern Advocate*, June 13, 1860.

delegates, sixteen from North Carolina, and nineteen from Tennessee walked out of the convention. California, Oregon, and half of Maryland followed, and next day most of the delegates from Kentucky, Missouri, and Arkansas joined them. With only thirteen full delegations left, the convention went ahead to nominate Douglas, with Herschel V. Johnson of Georgia as his running mate.

The seceders, meanwhile, joined by the Florida delegation, which had been in the city but not in the convention, assembled in the Maryland Institute Hall, adopted the Charleston majority platform, and nominated John C. Breckinridge and Joseph Lane as its candidates. The Richmond convention, which had awaited the outcome at Baltimore, now reconvened and endorsed these candidates. The Democratic party was hopelessly divided.[31]

Men of the South were not blind to the seriousness of what was taking place, nor was there universal approval. Said the Memphis *Appeal:*

"It has been the just pride of the Democratic party that it was *National,* organized and having its members in every State, County, township, civil district and neighborhood in the whole country, —indeed it is believed that there is not a precinct in the whole Union in which Democratic votes are not polled.

"The odium of the Black-Republican party has been that it is *Sectional* without organization of members in one-half of the States of the Union." [32] Would the "plain, calm and good men" of the South now hazard their prosperity by permitting a group of "restless and reckless or misguided men" to destroy the *national* party and to build a Southern party as *sectional* as the Republican party itself? The *Appeal* was certain that the real Democrats would not do so, for they knew that the only reason Yancey and his kind had remained in the Democratic party was "to precipitate the Cotton States into a Revolution."

The *Southern Advocate* objected bitterly to the Yancey group "prating of Southern Rights as if they were the whole South," talk-

---

[31] In the case of Alabama and Louisiana the old delegations were to be rejected. In Arkansas and Georgia the new members were to be admitted along with the old and the vote divided between the two. Since there were no contesting delegations from Texas, Mississippi, and Delaware, these delegations were to be admitted.

[32] Memphis *Appeal,* May 19, 1860.

ing "of Southern interests as if they owned all the negroes in the South," shouting about "Southern honor as if they were the only people in the South!" It would have the nation know that there were "planters, farmers, working and business men" in the South who could "not be dictated to nor led by the nose." They could think for themselves, and they did not think as did Yancey. Governor Letcher of Virginia felt the same way and declared that "such marplots as Yancey" were "not Democrats in feeling or principle." For the same reason the Montgomery *Confederation* insisted that the withdrawal of the partisans of Rhett and Yancey from the Democratic party was "the removal of a millstone from around its neck." It was a matter "for profound congratulations." [33]

Organized resistance, however, came not only from Democrats who remained loyal but also from old Whig and American men who now launched a new organization called the Constitutional Union party. While Alexander H. Stephens, John Forsyth, and Pierre Soulé labored for Douglas in their respective states, John J. Crittenden, John M. Botts, John Bell, and other old Whigs had now picked up where they left off when the John Brown raid interrupted and had joined with Northern friends of other days in an effort to restore national harmony. The movement had its main strength in the Border States of Virginia, Kentucky, and Tennessee. There the Whigs had once been strong and the breakup of the party had been slow. It was actually reorganized in Virginia in 1858–1859 and made a strong showing in the state elections. The "Opposition" party both in Kentucky and Tennessee had meanwhile held its own with the Democrats. As one man wrote of Kentucky, "the great, sound, conservative, central heart of the Commonwealth" is "for the Union the Constitution—the whole flag, every stripe & every star in its place." The American party had used the cry "The Constitution and the Union," and Virginians in 1858 had sometimes spoken of their movement as "Constitutional Union." Wherever the Whigs had once been strong the new party found the seedbed prepared.[34]

[33] Huntsville *Southern Advocate*, June 13, 1860; Governor John Letcher to George W. Jones, April 29, 1860, in Brock Collection; Montgomery *Confederation*, June 15, 1860.

[34] Shanks, *Secession Movement in Virginia*, 118; Thomas W. Riley to Crittenden, February 8, 1860, in John J. Crittenden Papers; Wyndham Robertson Papers (Uni-

Two other factors contributed to the growth of the party in the South. In the first place, the Border States had more and more come to occupy a unique position in the section itself. Their economic life was more diversified than that of the Cotton Kingdom. Their agriculture was increasingly like that of the North, and in cities such as Baltimore, Richmond, Louisville, Nashville, and Memphis industry and commerce had made rapid strides. As their economic life changed, Northern markets had become more important to them, and even slavery had altered its character to a degree. It was more widely and, in some ways, more thinly spread. It was more paternal and yet to a larger degree dependent on the sale of surplus workers to the Lower South. More slaves were employed at tasks requiring skill and intelligence. More slaves were being hired out by their owners. Some men in the Cotton South were opposed to including these border peoples in a Southern Confederacy because they expected them soon to become "unsound" on the slavery question.

The Memphis *Morning Bulletin* summed up the situation for Tennessee and Kentucky in the following fashion: "Tennessee and Kentucky must from their position be Union States. They can have nothing to hope for out of the Union. South Carolina, North Carolina, Georgia, Alabama, Florida, Louisiana and Texas, have their sea-coasts and harbors, and each one of them might become a State, make treaties and have commerce with other nations. Not so with the States of the West. Union with them is a principle of life; disunion is a principle of death. Louisiana must not be permitted to close the mouth of the Mississippi to them. . . . The Sea, the sea, we will never be cut off from the sea. We want no frowning bastions to confront us on our way to Europe. We want no intermeddling of petty officials, we want to pass through no custom houses but those of the national government." [35]

The second factor in the rise of the Constitutional Union party was the fundamentally conservative, Union-loving attitude of the majority of the Southern people. Douglas owed his Southern support to the existence of such an attitude, but there were many

versity of Chicago Library) contain interesting correspondence between a Virginia Whig and prominent Northern leaders. See Craven, *Edmund Ruffin*, 221–24.

[35] Memphis *Morning Bulletin,* January 28, 1860.

who distrusted him and were ready for a new party based on the old Whig principle of national harmony. They were weary of the continued agitation of the slavery question and the use which the "ranting politicians" had made of it. For years there had been no respite. Talk of disunion had now become frank and open. Seward had declared the conflict "irrepressible" and Southerners "had added to the fury" by senseless agitation for the reopening of the slave trade and a Congressional slave code for the territories. It was time to call a halt. "Sectionalism has had its day," said the Baltimore *American,* "the profound spirit of a nation at peace with itself . . . [wants] only to be left undisturbed in the tranquil pursuit of its material progress and its domestic duty." [36]

Virginia had shown where she stood by her refusal to go into a Southern conference at South Carolina's invitation. Tennessee, said a Nashville editor, had "not forgotten the motto of her illustrious son,—'the Federal Union it shall be preserved.'" "The South is not ready to dissolve the Union," commented the Augusta *Chronicle and Sentinel,* "nor . . . prepared to declare for dissolution" on any existing issue. "Let the hot-heads take warning," it concluded; "let them learn that, however loud the press and the politician may clamor for a reorganization of the government, the people will not heed them." [37]

On ground thus prepared, concrete efforts towards the organization of a party for the campaign of 1860 developed rather spontaneously in different corners of the Border States. Alexander H. H. Stuart, Wyndham Robertson, and other Virginians were early in correspondence with Washington Hunt in New York in regard to such a move, and an "Opposition" meeting in Nashville, Tennessee, on February 12, 1859, adopted resolutions nominating John Bell "as a suitable candidate for the presidency." In Kentucky, meantime, the "Opposition" had adopted the name "National Union Party" with Crittenden as its recognized leader and a determination to "struggle to the last for the Union as it was." [38]

[36] *Republican Banner and Nashville Whig,* January 1, 1860; Baltimore *American,* January 5, 1860.

[37] Baltimore *American,* January 13, 1860; Augusta *Chronicle and Sentinel,* March 14, 1860.

[38] Parks, *John Bell of Tennessee,* 389; Lexington *Kentucky Statesman,* March 20, 1860.

Events now moved rapidly. Union meetings, sponsored by such stanch old Whigs as Henry C. Carey in Philadelphia and Parson Brownlow in East Tennessee, brought old friends together and generated new enthusiasm for "the Constitution and the Union." On January 6, 1860, the *Republican Banner and Nashville Whig* raised the standard of John Bell for President, and a few days later opposition members in the Tennessee legislature called a state convention for February 22. On the same day that the convention met, a group of thirty old Whig and American leaders issued an appeal "To the People of the United States" declaring that neither the Democrats nor the Republicans could safely be entrusted with the management of public affairs and that a new national party must be organized. The appeal was signed by such prominent men as Washington Hunt, John P. Kennedy, William A. Graham, John J. Crittenden, William C. Rives, Francis Granger, and Parson Brownlow. It urged conservatives everywhere to send delegates to a national convention to be held in Baltimore on the ninth of May.[39]

Only twenty-four states answered the call, but from the South only Louisiana was missing. Since Crittenden, who had done more for the movement than any other, refused to be a candidate, the convention was forced to look elsewhere. Sam Houston of Texas, Edward Everett of Massachusetts, John McLean of Ohio, Graham of North Carolina, and Rives of Virginia all received substantial support, but John Bell of Tennessee took the lead on the first ballot and was easily nominated on the second. Everett was then unanimously named as his running mate. The platform followed the old Whig tradition of evasion and "recognize[d] no principle other than the Constitution of the country, the union of the States, and the enforcement of the laws." It went on, however, to pledge the party to protect and defend "the rights of the people and of the States reëstablished, and the government again placed in that condition of justice, fraternity, and equality which . . . has solemnly bound every citizen . . . to maintain a more perfect union, establish justice, insure domestic tranquillity, . . . and secure the blessings of liberty to ourselves and our posterity." [40]

[39] *Republican Banner and Nashville Whig,* January 8, 1860.
[40] Parks, *John Bell of Tennessee,* 339–60; Stanwood, *History of the Presidency,* 288–90.

With the nomination of Lincoln by the Republicans at Chicago, the stage was set for the campaign on which the fate of the nation rested. At the South it would be little more than an exhibition of confusion and folly. The Breckinridge Democrats had taken their stand on the issue of Congressional protection of slavery in the territories. Events had already proved that they had not the slightest chance of securing acceptance of their doctrine, and it was equally clear that they would have gained nothing concrete if they had. Yet they had made it the symbol of Southern rights and equality. As one writer said: "It is merely a war of opinions and words, —a discussion upon abstract principle from which no advantage can be gained by either side, and the worst results must inevitably ensue for both." For it they had rejected Douglas, whose friendship for the South had been repeatedly demonstrated, wrecked the only political party that had served Southern interests, and made the election of a hated "Black Republican" almost a certainty. Few among them honestly believed that Breckinridge could be elected either by popular vote or by throwing the election into the House. Seemingly their only hope was to secure a united South which could force concessions or, if this failed, to secede. Their weapons must be fear and pride.[41]

On the surface, this staking all on *principle* appears to be an extreme, perhaps foolish, effort in defense of slavery against supposed Northern aggression. The constant harping on Kansas and John Brown's raid as the first thrusts in a wide abolition advance and the systematic spreading of wild rumors of abolition-inspired Negro insurrections fit into such a pattern. The reports of troubles in Texas, of towns burned down, of families poisoned, and of women and children murdered produced a state of near hysteria in many parts of the South throughout the election year. What the Republicans in power might do to slavery was thus thrust forward as the burning question of the day. "We think it may be assumed as an admitted fact that the Northern people have determined to subjugate the South," said the Oxford (Mississippi) *Mercury*, "and that too, at no very distant period." Lincoln and

41 Nashville *Republican Banner,* March 29, 1860; John Cichrone to Douglas, April 12, 1860, in Douglas Papers, enclosing letter from Anthony Dugro: "There is hardly a chance for any other Democrat to be elected to the Presidency but Stephen A. Douglas. Some may say that such a state of affairs . . . is to be deplored, but such *is* the *state*."

Seward had both bluntly declared their intention to destroy slavery. The *Mercury* was convinced that the Puritans of New England would deluge the land in blood and that their "hungry hordes already had their gaze fixed on the fertile and smiling fields of the South." Such a people were never satisfied "unless engaged in a strife with their neighbors." They had left England in the beginning because they had not the privilege "of burning witches, cropping Quaker ears, and burning Catholics." They had now determined to conquer and pillage the South.[42]

Yet back of what appeared on the surface, and what was hidden in the blind emotionalism of the immediate, lay the brutal fact that the emerging modern world had reduced the South to a permanent minority in a colonial status and had condemned its labor system as both unjust and inefficient. Douglas had not created the forces that made Kansas free. Squatter sovereignty had not done it. That was only an abstract doctrine never applied. The Industrial Revolution was the real culprit. Douglas had simply recognized inevitable trends and had adjusted his course to them. But because Southern men resented what "progress" had done to them, they saw in Douglas the symbol of it all and hated him accordingly. By rejecting him they were attempting to repudiate the great forces of change that threatened their civilization. It did not make sense, but the frustrated, apprehensive body of Southern Democrats, not knowing what to think or do, could only follow the aggressive few who pretended to know the remedy. They had walked out of the Charleston convention under the impression that they were upholding a principle.

A small number of leaders may have planned the destruction of the Union from the first, but the majority probably aimed at nothing more than forcing concessions. Having made the break, however, and having met the equally determined Douglas forces,

<hr>

[42] Ollinger Crenshaw, *The Slave States in the Presidential Election of 1860* (Baltimore, 1945), 89–111; Rome *Courier*, August 28, 1860, noticed posters placed in the post office warning people against insurrections. The Nashville *Republican Banner*, September 8, 1860, reported a speech by L. Q. C. Lamar in which he excited his audience by tales of abolition threats to the extent that their hair stood out "like quills upon the fretful porcupine," and they saw the Northern "Goths and Vandals" descending upon them. See also Oxford (Miss.) *Mercury*, quoted in Natchez *Mississippi Free Trader*, June 13, 1860.

they had to save their faces by going ahead. Now in the campaign they must stress past injustices and anticipated dangers. Since a united South alone could possibly influence Northern policy and since failure would suggest secession, they had to face the hard fact that even a majority of the Southern people were against them.[43]

Neither the Douglas men nor the Bell supporters would tolerate a deliberate effort to break up the Union. Some would even accept the election of Lincoln or, at least, wait for some overt act before considering extreme action. A few among them were willing to support the effort to secure Congressional protection for slavery in the territories, but most saw it only as a useless abstraction, offensive to all groups at the North. And, probably of equal importance, traditional dislike of Democrats and memories of bitter struggles back in Whig days made unity now an impossibility.

Since Douglas had an even chance of winning Missouri and since the Bell forces were strong in every Border State, it was clear from the start that unless the Breckinridge Democrats clarified their position they stood little chance of achieving the solid front so essential to their plans. They therefore quickly repudiated their radical wing and made strenuous efforts to refute the charge of attempting to break up the Union. In his only campaign speech Breckinridge flatly denied that he was a disunionist or that he was connected with an organization whose aim was disunion. One of his ardent supporters, Humphrey Marshall, when asked if he proposed secession if Lincoln were elected, answered: "Emphatically no! It is a remedy for no evil under heaven. It would be political suicide." In conservative states like North Carolina, Virginia, and Kentucky, the Breckinridge press and speakers went out of their way to stress their loyalty. Because a few extremists supported the ticket, they contended, this was no reason for fixing the charge of disunion on the candidate or party. Yancey himself on one occasion, at least, spoke humorously of this charge as if to deny it, and Jefferson Davis refused throughout the campaign to say what he would do if Lincoln were elected. Yet the extreme

[43] Charleston *Mercury*, May 3, 1860: "We suppose there was not a man, in or out of the Charleston Convention, who did not anticipate the proposal of a new compromise on the rights of the States in the Territories, as a necessary consequence of the withdrawal of the Cotton States from the Convention."

pronouncements of Rhett, Laurence M. Keitt, Clement C. Clay, Richard T. Archer, and other fire-eaters kept the idea of "a plot" for secession alive and provided abundant campaign material for both the Douglas and the Bell forces.[44]

Democratic denial of secession guilt was accompanied by harsh denunciation of both opposing parties for failure to support the Southern cause. By dividing the South, it was charged, they were encouraging the Republicans and weakening resistance to injustice. They were in truth submissionists. They were responsible for the infiltration of the fanatical abolitionists who were now inciting the Negroes to violence. They might just as well be campaigning for Lincoln because Douglas and Lincoln were equally hostile to the South, and Bell was little better. "Now what difference is it to the people," asked the Montgomery *Daily Mail*, "whether Lincoln or Douglas shall be elected? The same ends are sought by each, and we do not see any reason to choose between them." "Mr. Douglas personifies, perhaps better than Seward himself, the 'irrepressible conflict,' " said the New Orleans *Courier*. "Wherever he shows himself, wherever he speaks, Mr. Douglas makes an irrepressible conflict, for everywhere does he assail common rights to the injury of the South." "John Bell," added a Mississippi orator, "was a political 'Judas Iscariot.' " [45]

The Douglas and Bell supporters generally showed a friendly spirit toward each other. Near the end, in a few places, they united their forces. Their common plea was for national unity, and their one great charge against the Breckinridge party was its direct and indirect drive towards secession. Both opposition parties made this their central appeal. The Nashville *Republican Banner* expressed their opinion when it said that "Southern prosperity can be attained in the Union much more surely than under any other auspices—especially under the auspices of fire-eaters and wild abstractionists." The interests of North and South were one, it insisted,

[44] Crenshaw, *Slave States in the Presidential Election of 1860*, p. 160; Richmond *Examiner*, August 14, 1860; Sitterson, *Secession Movement in North Carolina*, 171; Shanks, *Secession Movement in Virginia*, 112.

[45] Montgomery *Daily Mail*, July 6, 1860; New Orleans *Courier*, quoted in Nashville *Republican Banner*, August 1, 1860; Crenshaw, *Slave States in the Presidential Election of 1860*, p. 266.

and prosperity could be attained only by pursuing those interests together "in the bonds of closest union." [46]

The Constitutional Union forces, however, had a distinct advantage over the Douglas group. The broad sweeping character of their platform made it possible for them to adjust their appeal to the peculiar and differing local interests and attitudes. Where the Democrats were forced to accept and defend the generally unpopular squatter-sovereignty doctrine, some Whigs in Maryland could follow Henry Winter Davis in a near affiliation with the Republicans; and some in Kentucky could play with the idea of backing Edward Bates on a conservative national program, while their fellows in Mississippi and Alabama could agree with the Breckinridge Democrats on almost everything but disunion. They could appeal to the Border State consciousness of being in a dangerously exposed position in case of war or as the outer rim of a Southern confederacy. They could, at the same time, permit the Cotton State Whigs to threaten secession in case of Lincoln's election. They made enough headway to permit Bell through most of July to think that he had some chance of being elected. [47]

On the other hand, it was early clear that while Douglas could muster considerable strength in the Border States, he could do little in the Lower South. His Alabama and Louisiana friends remained loyal and active, but they could not stem the emotional tide. Sensing the danger and realizing the importance of the South's decision, Douglas determined on a bold stroke. He would tour the South and do what no candidate for the presidency had ever done—deliver a series of campaign speeches. Twice he crossed the border. His first trip took him into Virginia, North Carolina, and Maryland; his second, into Missouri, Tennessee, Georgia, and Alabama. Here, of course, he defended his record and his program, but the greater purpose seems to have been service to the cause of union—he would "crush out utterly and forever the disunion party."

The high light of his first tour was the speech at Norfolk, Virginia, where he faced a none too friendly audience from the steps

[46] Nashville *Republican Banner*, August 5, 1860.
[47] Parks, *John Bell of Tennessee*, 361–88.

of the City Hall. Bluntly he told them that he wanted the vote of no man unless he desired the Union maintained and preserved intact by the faithful execution of every act, every line and letter of the Constitution. He then frankly answered two loaded questions propounded by Breckinridge supporters: 1. "On Lincoln's election will the South be justified in seceding?" 2. "If the South secede before an overt act of Lincoln, will you advise or vindicate resistance by force?" To the first, he replied that no Constitutional election justified secession; and to the second he asserted that it was the President's duty to enforce the laws, and that he, Douglas, pledged his assistance. That took courage, but there was no flinching, no evasion. He only asked that Breckinridge answer the same questions! [48]

Southern extremists were furious, but Douglas held his ground and a few days later at Raleigh, North Carolina, was even more emphatic. He would hang every man higher than Haman who would resist by force the execution of any provision of the Constitution. He made it clear, as he had done elsewhere, that his Northwest, dependent on the Mississippi River, must insist on the preservation of the Union. He would say later at Baltimore that he was ready to bury Southern disunionism and Northern abolitionism in the same grave.[49]

Douglas' second trip southward took him into the heart of the Cotton Kingdom and of the Breckinridge support. He was weary and worn from much speaking, and audiences were hostile when once he passed Memphis. His purpose was now clear. He told a St. Louis crowd that he was not there to ask for their votes; he was there to make an appeal "on behalf of the Union and the peace of the country." The radical press called his tour "impudent," "disgraceful," and "indefensible," and Douglas was convinced, at one point, that an effort had been made to wreck his train. Yet as he crossed Tennessee and Georgia there were few disturbances among the thousands who came to hear him speak. Alexander H. Stephens stood by his side in Georgia, and John Forsyth welcomed him in Alabama, where he ended his travels and awaited election returns. He had made a gallant and unselfish effort for national unity. He

[48] Richmond *Enquirer*, September 1, 1860; Milton, *Eve of Conflict*, 492–93.
[49] Charleston *Mercury*, September 3, 1860; Milton, *Eve of Conflict*, 493–94.

had proved his courage and his devotion to what he honestly believed were the deeper interests of the South. His failure was now, as it had been in the past, due to the fact that he stood in the middle of the road. These days belonged to extremists.[50]

Douglas had come too late. Fear and treachery had already done their work. The Freeport speech, which, as the *Southern Advocate* said, "at the time, gave no offense to Southern men," had now become "the whole stock in trade" of the Breckinridge campaign. It was "quoted and abused" and "distorted." Yet it had been used with damaging effect. Douglas' very presence in the South at this moment was evidence of the hopelessness of his cause. Already the mysterious Knights of the Golden Circle had been organized, and bodies of "Minute Men" were being formed in different localities "for the purpose of preventing Lincoln's inauguration in case of his election." A blue cockade was their insignia. "While the professional Union-shriekers . . . are ceaselessly crying out 'this glorious Union,'" boasted the Nashville *Union and American,* "the great masses of the people, regardless of former party affiliations, are settling down in the conviction that now is the time to settle forever the vexed question that has permeated every department of life, and now menaces a sudden and violent disruption of our Government." "Let then Tennessee arm herself," it continued. "Let her militia be put in training, her volunteer companies clean their muskets and brush up their tactics, and let new ones be formed." [51]

Class and race appeal had also made their appearance. When the wealthy Dr. Stephen Duncan in Mississippi remarked on the absurdity of "any cotton or sugar planter allowing the thought of disunion to enter his mind," the Natchez *Free Trader* was quick to remind him that "brains, not money; principles, not accidental position" ruled the South, and that the men who made four thousand bales of cotton and owned five hundred Negroes did not have as much influence as the "humblest mechanic" with "correct principles." Its neighbor, the Vicksburg *Whig,* maintained that the men who did not "own the toe-nail of a negro" and would sell one

[50] Milton, *Eve of Conflict,* 497–500.

[51] Huntsville *Southern Advocate,* September 12, 1860; W. T. Tillman to Hammond, October 9, 1860, in Hammond Papers (Division of Manuscripts, Library of Congress); Nashville *Union and American,* October 20, 1860. For pledge of the "Minute Men," see Selma *Alabama State Sentinel,* November 28, 1860.

if they had him, were the ones with the greatest interest in preserving Southern rights. For, as Senator Albert Gallatin Brown argued, the nonslaveholder received all the benefits of a slave society without bearing its burdens. The small farmer and the mechanic had the value of their lands and of their labor increased by the high living standards of the planter class.[52]

They had, moreover, all the advantages of a white skin in a Negro-slave society. If the Negro were free, the nonslaveholder would face a tragic fate. The Negro would insist that he be treated as an equal; that he go to the white man's table, share the white man's bed, and that his son be permitted to marry the white man's daughter and his daughter the white man's son! That, of course, would produce a race war from which the rich man would flee. The poor white man would be left alone to wage the bloody battle.

A distorted picture of Lincoln and his program accompanied such an appeal. Seward had been "thrust aside in the nominating Convention," asserted the Charleston *Mercury,* "because he was disposed to temporize with the South, and lacked the necessary nerve to carry through the measures of Southern subjugation." Lincoln, on the other hand, "possessed the decision of character and the earnestness required" to put down Southern resistance to oppression. He was "the *beau ideal* of a relentless, dogged, free-soil border-ruffian, . . . a vulgar mobocrat and a Southern hater in political opinions." The Richmond *Enquirer* saw him as "an illiterate partisan . . . possessed only of his inveterate hatred of slavery and his openly avowed predilections of negro equality." He surpassed Seward only "in the bitterness of his prejudices and in the insanity of his fanaticism." His election would mean "negro equality," "Northern domination," and "continued aggression." [53]

The efforts of Douglas and Bell men to counteract such appeals to fear and pride had met with little success in the Lower South. It was, therefore, perfectly clear in the closing weeks of the campaign that the Southern vote would be badly split and that unless some fusion of tickets could be achieved Lincoln would become

[52] Natchez *Mississippi Free Trader,* September 25, 1860; Vicksburg *Whig,* October 24, 1860; Jackson *Mississippian,* October 10, 1860.

[53] Charleston *Mercury,* October 15, 1860; Richmond *Enquirer,* May 21, 1860; Nashville *Union and American,* October 24, 1860: Walhalla (S.C.) *Keowee Courier,* August 18, 1860.

President. Fusion, however, presented serious problems. The contest in the South had been a bitter one, waged almost exclusively among Breckinridge, Bell, and Douglas. There had been a few Lincoln supporters in the Border States, but the Republican party had been largely ignored for the enemy near at hand. While Douglas and Bell men had stood together against the Breckinridge forces, they had not united, and the possibility of one or the other candidate withdrawing was slight. Neither had shown any inclination whatsoever to fuse with his common opponent. All had come to realize that division meant defeat, but no one was inclined to yield.[54]

The heavy Republican drift in October elections at the North, however, brought a sharp realization of impending disaster. "Cannot all the Southern people, Bell men, Breckinridge men, and Douglas men, band together to resist the Abolition foe?" asked the Montgomery *Advertiser*. "Let us drop all dissensions," it pleaded, "and form a UNION OF THE SOUTH FOR THE SAKE OF THE SOUTH." The Milledgeville *Southern Recorder,* the Nashville *Union and American,* the Augusta *Chronicle and Sentinel,* and other conservative papers offered the same advice. Jefferson Davis urged the withdrawal of all candidates opposed to Lincoln and agreement on one fusion leader. Bell and Breckinridge were said to have agreed, but Douglas refused on grounds that he would take more Northern votes from Lincoln than would any other. Cobb and Thompson in Buchanan's Cabinet labored for fusion in New York and watched a fusion torchlight parade there with kindled hopes but with little confidence. They knew that some men at the South had made up their minds that it would be either Breckinridge or Lincoln.[55]

Election day thus found the South still divided and uncertain as to what its course might be. Only South Carolina had taken any positive steps. Her governor had, on October 5, written to all the other Southern governors, except Houston of Texas, saying that he was calling a convention and wished for a full and free inter-

[54] Nashville *Republican Banner,* August 30, 1860.

[55] Percy Scott Flippin, *Herschel V. Johnson of Georgia, State Rights Unionist* (Richmond, 1931), 137–39; Montgomery *Advertiser,* October 17, 1860; Milledgeville *Southern Recorder,* October 23, 1860; Nashville *Union and American,* October 12, 1860; Augusta *Chronicle and Sentinel,* July 13, 1860; Nichols, *Disruption of American Democracy,* 336.

change of opinion. Then on October 12 he had issued a call for a special session of the legislature for November 5 to choose electors and to take action "if deemed advisable for the safety and protection of the State." A few days later, a group of prominent Carolina officials, including all but two of her Congressional delegation, met at Senator Hammond's home and agreed that secession should be the program if Lincoln were elected. South Carolina was following Laurence Keitt's suggestion. "This state," he said, ". . . will have to lead. . . . If we wait for Ala. we will wait eternally. There's not the slightest confidence in her leading off. She has no man strong enough to lead. Yancey . . . lacks the elements—Davis in Miss. is far more promising. But we must rely on ourselves in moving off." [56]

The election returns confirmed the direct forecast. Lincoln polled 1,866,452 votes, Douglas 1,376,957, Breckinridge, 849,781, and Bell, 588,879. Lincoln had been legally elected without fraud or manipulation. Even if his opponents had fused on one ticket, he still would have won. He would be a minority President, but no one could question his Constitutional right to the office. Douglas, although in second place, had carried but one slave state—Missouri; Bell had been victorious only in Virginia, Kentucky, and Tennessee; the remaining slave states as a bloc had gone to Breckinridge. His vote, like that of Lincoln in the North, had been heavily sectional. He had, it is true, gained far more votes in the North than Lincoln had won in the South, yet he had not been able to secure a majority in his own section. Union sentiment, though divided, was still strong. What to do next was still an open question.

[56] Keitt to Miles, October 3, 1860, in Miles Papers.

CHAPTER XIII

SECESSION

W HAT the South should do in case of Lincoln's election had been discussed at intervals throughout the campaign. Opinion had varied. Few Southerners could contemplate Republican victory without dismay, and many thought that some kind of "resistance" should be offered. Opinion on the form that this should take, however, was generally vague and confused. Most seemed to think that it was not a matter for separate state action. The South as a whole, or at least the Cotton States, should confer and act in unison. Beyond that, there was little agreement.[1]

A few, unquestionably, were bold for immediate secession. The Rhett group in South Carolina "were looking to an immediate convention to carry the state out of the Union while the resentment over the election was still at its height." Congressman Porcher Miles was "sick and disgusted" with bluster, threats, manifestoes, and resolutions, and hoped that the state would act swiftly with a minimum of talk if Lincoln were elected. Keitt and William W. Boyce were both on record for immediate secession. Even James L. Orr, by August, was saying that "no Black Republican President . . . [should] ever execute any law within our borders unless at the point of the bayonet and over the dead bodies of . . . [our] slain sons." A Tennessee speaker announced, "amid great applause," that he would never submit to become a "white slave of the Northern abolitionists" and that the Cotton States should be allowed to

[1] New Orleans *Bee*, September 3, 1860; *Republican Banner and Nashville Whig*, April 17, 1860; Augusta *Chronicle and Sentinel*, June 10, 1860; Walhalla *Keowee Courier*, August 18, 1860; New Orleans *Crescent*, December 10, 1860; Augusta *Constitutionalist*, December 10, 1860; Baton Rouge *Gazette and Comet*, November 24, 1860.

349

prescribe a remedy. A Florida meeting resolved that the citizens of that state were no longer safe in the Union and that the banner of secession should be raised. In Alabama and Texas some campaign speakers openly advocated secession if the Republicans were victorious, while in Georgia an Atlanta newspaper declared: "Let the consequences be what they may—whether the Potomac is crimsoned in human gore, and Pennsylvania Avenue is paved ten fathoms in depth with mangled bodies or whether the last vestige of liberty is swept from the face of the American Continent, the South will never submit to such humiliation and degradation as the inauguration of Abraham Lincoln." [2]

The majority, however, were less rash. Though increasingly conscious of the fact that Lincoln's election was inevitable, they somehow refused to face the "cold facts" as the secessionists presented them. An Augusta editor complained that they were "eating and drinking and making merry, marrying and giving in marriage, while beneath their feet [was] the rumbling volcano"; that they laughed and sang while the Union was rocking "in the throes of an earthquake." Reckless of the danger ahead, the South was moving along in its accustomed ways. Why could men not see that they stood face to face with revolution and a new reign of terror? Lincoln's election would force the issue of "Union or Disunion!" [3]

There were those, however, who were not indifferent to the drift of events and who had no thought of secession. They were convinced that there was "no evil existing—no evil threatened even in the excited imagination of those mad disunionists—for which the remedies secured to us by the Federal Union and its Constitutional guarantees . . . [were] not fully adequate, and vastly to be preferred, under all circumstances, to any remedy of secession or revolution." True, Lincoln's election would be "a calamity" but it would not offer an excuse "for hasty and precipitate action on

[2] White, *Robert Barnwell Rhett*, 173; Miles to Hammond, August 5, 1860, in Hammond Papers (Division of Manuscripts, Library of Congress); Orr, quoted in Charles E. Cauthen, "Secession and Civil War in South Carolina" (Ph.D. dissertation, University of North Carolina, 1937), 49; Nashville *Republican Banner*, September 11, 1860; William W. Davis, *Civil War and Reconstruction in Florida* (New York, 1913), 42; Houston (Texas) *Tri-Weekly Telegraph*, October 4, 1860; Dorman, *Party Politics in Alabama*, 162; Dumond, *Secession Movement*, 104; New Orleans *True Delta*, November 10, 17, 1860; New Orleans *Daily Picayune*, December 4, 5, 1860.

[3] Augusta *Chronicle and Sentinel*, October 2, 1860.

the part of the South." What harm could he do? He would have only a veto power and could do nothing to injure the South until the Senate and the Supreme Court were radically changed. Furthermore, if he disregarded "his official oath by a violation of the well-defined principles of the Constitution, his power to do mischief would be taken from him,—not by violence or civil war, with all the domestic horrors attending it,—but by the legal process of impeachment and removal from office." Circumscribed as he would be, he might even "go out of office quite a favorite of the Southern people." At least they should give him a trial.[4]

The *Southern Recorder* had a different reason for not fearing Lincoln. "We attach no more importance to Black Republican resolutions," it said, "than we do to Democratic ones. Resolutions are the veriest clap-trap to catch votes; and we have shown time and again that the 'protection' resolution of Mr. Breckinridge's party was a political move without the least particle of honesty in it. . . . The Black Republican party is no more honest in our opinion than the Breckinridge party, and we attach, as we have said, about as much importance to their resolutions." Anyway, love of country should be greater than hatred for present wrongs. The eyes of monarchical Europe were upon the United States eager to see whether a Republican government could stand the test. True statesmanship demanded at least one more honest effort, in the name of Democracy and Republicanism, to bring the sections to an understanding. It was "a strange, sad sight," said the Augusta *Chronicle and Sentinel,* "to see a great, free, prosperous, happy people" about to give up their experiment in democratic government. How could they justify this, asked a Virginian, "to the rest of Christendom, to posterity, or even to . . . [their] own sober second thought." [5]

Some denied "the Constitutional right of peaceful secession." It was "the most senseless thing ever discussed by wise men," said one

[4] Nashville *Republican Banner,* November 7, 1860; New Orleans *Bee,* October 18, 1860; Memphis *Appeal,* October 24, 1860; Tuscumbia *North Alabamian,* August 3, 1860; Perry, in the Walhalla *Keowee Courier,* September 1, 1860.

[5] Milledgeville *Southern Recorder,* October 30, 1860; Augusta *Chronicle and Sentinel,* September 19, 1860; D. H. Mahan to J. E. Davidson, November 1, 1860, in James D. Davidson Papers (McCormick Collection, State Historical Society of Wisconsin, Madison).

editor. Even if a state or every person in it held that such a state
had a right to secede, yet if the other states happened to think there
had been no violation of the organic law "except by the attempt
at secession, and choose to attempt coercion," then the seceding
party would come face to face with revolution and the final test
of *all right, might!* "The right of secession," he continued, "is not
worth a fig, so long as others choose to test that right by force. No
argument can determine this question save the sword." The effort
would, therefore, result either in "treason" if the move failed or
in "a glorious revolution" if it succeeded. Secession could only produce "a test of strength." It was an "arrogant humbug." Revolution was the word, and not secession, said Judge Sharkey of Mississippi. There was but one way to get out of the Union and that was
by wading through blood. He did not "intend to become a traitor
to the best government under the sun, because a few disaffected
politicians were determined to become so." [6]

Strange as it may seem, after all that had been said, the election
of Abraham Lincoln produced something of a shock at the South.
Some had hoped against their better judgment and were not quite
emotionally prepared for the reality. Others had evidently drifted
along or had been pushed into positions. They were now the victims of their uncertainty or indifference. Many had been reacting
to an accumulation of evils rather than to immediate ills and were,
therefore, somewhat confused as to their real feelings about the
specific matter of political defeat. Reactions, as a result, varied from
impulsive demands for immediate secession, born of anger or despair, to complete willingness to abide peaceably by the outcome.
Most opinion, however, lay between the two extremes. The aim
was primarily peace.[7]

A Tennessee editor was honest enough to confess that the cry
of disunion had been raised so often that few had taken it seriously
during the campaign. Evidently the "Northern sectionalists" had
believed it to be "all talk," or they would not have tried their mad

[6] Augusta *Chronicle and Sentinel,* September 18, October 9, 19, 1860; Memphis
Appeal, November 17, 1860; Natchez *Courier,* October 25, 1860.

[7] Stephens to J. Henly Smith, November 8, 1860, in Phillips (ed.), *Correspondence
of Toombs, Stephens, and Cobb,* 502–503; Shanks, *Secession Movement in Virginia,*
120–24.

experiment of sectional political dominance, while most intelligent Southerners had assumed that it was "an idle menace, made to sway Northern sentiment." Now that it turned out that the Cotton States were in earnest, it behoved "all patriots to review their opinions calmly and dispassionately,"—opinions formed under the erroneous impression that men of "the extreme South" were prepared for unlimited submission to Lincoln's election. The situation had evidently become so serious that Tennessee, together with Virginia, Kentucky, and North Carolina, should assume "the glorious and Christian mission of peace-makers." [8]

Middle-of-the-road men generally agreed that the important thing was to remain cool and to avoid any rash and ill-advised moves—"to act as becomes citizens of a great and sovereign State, neither singing hosannas to the Union or unnecessarily rushing into hasty and precipitate movements." Free and intelligent discussion, in which men were "as willing to receive the truth as to impart it," would probably do more good just now than action of any kind. Said the Virginia *Whig:* "Let there be no passion, no excitement, no wildness on the part of any of us, either in view of what is already passed, or in view of the possibilities of the future." Rather let men "patiently and dignifiedly await the development of events," and remain "calm, deliberate and enlightened." [9]

A Georgia editor called attention to the fact that much Republican strength had little to do with opposition to the South but came from "an undying hatred" of the Democratic party. Southerners were inclined to forget "the proscriptiveness, the tyranny, the corruption of the Democratic party, made more especially manifest and loathsome by James Buchanan and his administration." Wyndham Robertson, in like vein, complained: "The possession of the power of the Federal Government by the Democratic party . . . furnished the pretext . . . to confound the whole slaveholding interest as absolutely identical with Democracy, and thus to turn and direct opposition, for whatever cause, to the policy and acts of the Democratic party, into opposition to the slaveholding interests." The inference, of course, was that the Republicans were less

[8] Nashville *Union and American*, November 11, 1860.
[9] Montgomery *Confederation*, November 23, 1860; Augusta *Chronicle and Sentinel*, November 8, 11, 16, 1860; Richmond *Whig*, November 16, 1860.

hostile to the South and her institutions than campaign talk had indicated. The South might have less to fear than had been supposed.[10]

Uncertain reactions such as these were the rule just after the election when, as one correspondent reported, "Every man feels that something terrible is impending." The situation was probably best expressed by an Alabama editor who wrote: "It is useless to disguise the fact that we are face to face with the most alarming and critical exigency that has ever befallen the Republic. The people of Alabama and of the South *must act*. As to *how to act*, we confess we are not now prepared to say." Under such circumstances the soundest advice came in a single word from the New Orleans *Bee:* "WAIT." [11]

Positive attitudes, however, were not long in developing. Union men, especially in the Border States, were soon declaring that "the mere triumph of the Black Republicans at the ballot box . . . [was] no sufficient cause for a dissolution of the Union." Lincoln should be given a trial. The South had no right to judge him "by anything but his acts" and these could only be known after his inauguration. Until he had committed some "overt act" there was not the shadow of an excuse for extreme action. The Constitution with its guarantees was still there and instead of "having been exhausted, . . . [had] not yet been fairly tried." The government might not be as perfect as could be desired; it might not protect in person and property as fully as might be wished; but where was the guarantee of a better in its place? [12]

After all, Lincoln's election was simply "one of those results of our system of free government," and it was every man's duty to acquiesce both when its workings suited his personal and sectional preferences and when they did not. If this was not done all government would soon sink into a struggle between contending factions

[10] Augusta *Chronicle and Sentinel*, November 8, 1860; Wyndham Robertson, *Speech on the State of the Country* (n.p., n.d.), pamphlet. The Thomasville (Ga.) *Enquirer*, November 16, 1860, suggested that the nine Northern states that had passed laws to counteract the Fugitive Slave Act should be declared out of the Union and their Presidential vote be rejected.

[11] New York *Herald*, November 9, 1860; Montgomery *Confederation*, November 23, 1860; New Orleans *Bee*, November 8, 1860.

[12] Raleigh *North Carolina Standard*, November 27, 1860; New Orleans *Bee*, November 9, December 4, 1860; New Orleans *Picayune*, November 15, 1860.

and end in anarchy and constantly recurring revolution. Thus the South in giving Lincoln a fair trial would "but discharge her duty to the founders of the Republic and exhibit to the world the dignity of a brave and gallant people, who, while asking nothing but what is right, are calmly self-reliant in their ability to repel whatever of wrong may be attempted." The sectional quarrel in the final analysis was between extremists "over issues that . . . [had] no real substance in them." Not a single man of sense believed that the territories could ever become the home of a slave population, and the people of Virginia, Kentucky, and Tennessee, at least, were not going to have "their domains made into a common battlefield, stained with fraternal blood" because of the "cultivated metaphysical temperament" of South Carolina.[13]

This unwillingness to be "dragged" into secession by radical states was widely expressed. "South Carolina and Alabama may be very dear," said a Virginian, "but we recoil from entire ruin on their account. Slavery may be a strong bond of union between tobacco and cotton, but we do not feel altogether ready to sink the tobacco for the welfare of the cotton." He believed the present relations of the various states were the best that could be devised, and he did not wish his state to gravitate either toward New York or toward Alabama. "We shall not be dragged," was his emphatic conclusion, "and if the attempt is persisted in, let South Carolina, and let Alabama go their way and we will go ours." He was not going to be caught by what a Tennessee editor called "the old South Carolina trick" of relying on excitement to drag the rest of the South into revolution.[14]

Conservatives also talked of the economic losses involved in a break with the North, of the heavy cost of setting up a new confederation. Already some areas were threatening secession from such a government if formed. One writer noted that "the passions of the hour . . . [would] soon pass away, and self-interest . . . [would] dictate political action." Then the northern tier of slave states would find its interests diverse from the others; slavery would lose its hold; and the line of the Ohio River would be replaced by

[13] Memphis *Morning Bulletin*, November 8, 10, 13, 1860.
[14] Charlottesville (Va.) *Review*, quoted in Richmond *Enquirer*, November 22, 1860; Nashville *Republican Banner*, November 13, 1860.

an imaginary line farther south. Then would come another split, another secession. Only a despotism could prevent it.[15]

Very few conservatives were, on the other hand, ready for complete submission. Most were thoroughly conscious of the fact that Lincoln's election was "a sectional triumph over the Constitutional rights of the South," and that a union of the slaveholding states for some decisive action was demanded. They were not, however, ready for secession until "all honorable, wise and prudent means" had been exhausted and until all "peaceful and forceful resistance" within the Union had proved unavailing. They would "tolerate" Lincoln until he "should violate the Constitution and interfere with the Constitutional rights of the South." Then they would stand shoulder to shoulder with their brethren without the slightest hesitation.[16]

Their constant plea was for co-operation. They feared the effects of hasty action by some excited state. They were not in complete agreement on what to do, but most of them wanted a convention of delegates from all the Southern states to discuss the crisis and to agree on some common plan for action. Some were for the convention preparing an ultimatum to be sent to the governor of each Northern state; some would have the convention call a national convention to secure "an authoritative guarantee from the Northern States of the Union, that every cause that had made . . . [living under Lincoln's] dominion objectionable and odious . . . [should] be removed." Some merely wanted unity for the sake of strength in secession and the stronger pressure it would give upon the North and world opinion.[17]

The conservatives were at all times handicapped by the negative character of their argument. They could be called "timid men and frightened old women": "submissionists" willing to yield the honor

[15] Montgomery *Confederation*, October 4, 1860; W. S. Pettigrew to his brother, November 2, 1860, in Pettigrew Papers; Natchez *Mississippi Free Trader*, November 13, 1860; Natchez *Courier*, November 24, 1860.
[16] Milledgeville *Southern Recorder*, November 16, 27, December 4, 1860; Nashville *Republican Banner*, October 23, 1860.
[17] Savannah *Republican*, November 14, 1860. Governor Beriah Magoffin of Kentucky, on December 9, 1860, urged all the Southern governors to meet in conference. The governors of Mississippi and Alabama sent commissioners to other states for conferences and some state conventions did the same. This provided a degree of co-operation but left each state free to act for itself.

of their section. Not so the radicals. Emotion was on their side. They could still make use of fear and pride; uncertainty and confusion were equally valuable. They were ready for immediate secession.[18]

Many had reluctantly reached the conclusion that the situation was hopeless and that "the North prefer[red] *Sectionalism* to *Nationalism*—an antislavery platform to the Constitution of the country." As Benjamin H. Hill, always "a Union man and a conservative," had earlier said: "We do not fear Mr. Lincoln, but we do fear the fanaticism he represents, the sectionalism that will triumph in his election, and the *passions* which his success will engender. . . . We do not like the current that is bearing us on, but we are beginning to feel that we will go with it because we must." John Forsyth felt the same way. He had labored manfully for Douglas only to see both North and South cast a sectional vote. The election of any President was a matter of temporary importance; but once the fact was clearly established, as it had been in this election, that "henceforth and forever the North and the South would be arrayed as hostile sections in a contest which could end only by the subjection of one or the other, and in which the weaker would rapidly become still weaker and the stronger gain strength," then it was clear beyond a doubt "that the Union between these two sections . . . [had] practically ceased to exist, and that its mere forms . . . [were] but as chains binding together deadly enemies sharing a common doom." Henceforth conservative effort must be directed less toward preserving the Union than toward warding off the shock attendant upon its dissolution—"to build up a new house while the old one . . . [was] being pulled down" or "to so pull down the house as not to be buried in its ruins." He was convinced, as was James M. Mason in Virginia, that "we have no choice but to accept the 'irrepressible conflict.' " [19]

Some demanded secession because they feared the invasion of Southern rights and safety. They talked of the Wide-Awakes, a half million strong, "bent on conquering the South." They charged Lincoln with open hostility to slavery and described his program

<hr/>

[18] Columbus (Ga.) *Times*, November 8, 1860.

[19] Milledgeville *Southern Recorder*, November 6, 1860; John Forsyth, quoted in Montgomery *Confederation*, November 23, 1860.

for the "peaceful" but "ultimate extinction" of the institution. They repeated the charge of a "conspiracy with the slaves, extending from Virginia to Texas," of "the alarm among all classes . . . for the safety of their lives and homes," and of the necessity for a constant guard against the "midnight assassination, conflagration, and servile war." They complained much of the personal-liberty laws and the open defiance of the Fugitive Slave Act. Yet in spite of such talk, it was quite apparent that the intense excitement and the demand for quick action was not due to immediate danger, to the loss of runaway slaves, or even to Lincoln's election.

"Mr. Lincoln is little more than a cipher in the present account," said the Richmond *Enquirer*. "The significant fact which menaces the South, is not that Abe Lincoln is elected President, but that the Northern people, by a sectional vote have elected a President for the avowed purpose of aggression on Southern rights. . . . This is *a declaration of war. This is an act of war*." [20]

The language was strong but hardly convincing. It lacked something. The New Orleans *Daily Crescent* supplied another element. The Northern people, in electing Lincoln, had "perpetrated a *deliberate, cold-blooded insult and outrage* upon the people of the slave-holding States." The campaign had been waged on a platform of "inextinguishable hatred" which if carried out would leave "no right or property or franchise or interest of the South worth maintaining." A writer in the Augusta *Constitutionalist* carried the idea a little further. He wanted to show that Lincoln's election was "more *an insult than an injury*." He argued that, as far as any "material interest" was concerned, *"the danger . . .* [was] *remote and contingent*." The matter of equality in the territories was "a mere abstraction" of little importance. The claim that it was a Constitutional right was of recent origin in complete contradiction of earlier opinion. Northern personal-liberty laws were obnoxious, but the Border States, which lost most of the slaves because of them, were bitterly opposed to secession. No, Southern grievances from the election of Lincoln were "not *tangible ones*" nor those from "immediate wrong." That election was only an evidence on which Southerners could "ground an apprehension of future wrong." The

[20] Montgomery *Daily Mail*, November 19, December 8, 1860; Richmond *Enquirer*, November 19, 1860.

"true reason of hostility and the necessary ground for separation" was *"incompatibility."* [21]

The very vagueness of the term was significant. It evidently referred in part to the denial of Southern "equality in the Union." Equality or independence, Lincoln had said at another time, were what *all* the people wanted. Yet the writer was sure that "something besides Equality" was needed. All the wrongs of the past did not justify secession, and the fact that they would have been overlooked or winked at had any other candidate than Lincoln been elected was proof of that fact. What the South demanded, besides its just and equal rights, was "absolute and perfect *peace* on this matter of slavery." The North must stop the eternal warfare on the institution.

In other words, the Republican party was growing strong enough to have its way and to set the pattern for American life in the days ahead. Either it must yield something in its values or the South would be forced to choose between independence and reconstruction. An increasing number of Southern men were reaching the conclusion that now or never there must "be a permanent adjustment and settlement of the matters of differences between the Black Republicans of the North and the people of the South." There was also a growing realization that what they were asking could not be granted. The whole situation had too much of the quality of the inevitable about it. That was the reason why "the abstract disquisition of the right of secession" scarcely entered into the attitude of radicals. "The people, in fact, do not pause to inquire whether secession is a rightful or revolutionary resort," wrote one man. "They are acting under a sense of long continued aggression and insupportable injustice inflicted by the North, and of which the election of Abraham Lincoln is less the culminating point than the proof of a settled and deliberate policy, and of the existence of the power requisite to carry it into effect." [22]

While others talked, South Carolina was beginning to act. There secession sentiment was strong, and the question had become one

[21] New Orleans *Crescent,* November 9, 1860; Augusta *Constitutionalist,* December 11, 1860.

[22] Nashville *Union and American,* November 25, 1860; New Orleans *Bee,* December 4, 1860.

largely of separate state action or of action only in co-operation with other states. The sheer force of events had largely destroyed the movement under Orr which had hoped and believed that Southern interests could be protected with the Union through participation with the Democratic party. In spite of damage done by John Brown, this group had held control up to the meeting of the Charleston convention. Its disintegration from that point on provides an interesting study of the way in which public opinion is formed and operates. The South Carolina delegation chosen to represent it at Charleston had been largely conservative and, according to Rhett, had not the slightest notion of seceding when it arrived. Under the excitement and local pride generated by the convention, however, all but two delegates followed Alabama's lead. Benjamin F. Perry's speech in defense of his action in refusing to secede was met with open disapproval, and the extremists were able to replace all the old delegation by a more radical one to be sent to Richmond. Nothing of a violent nature had happened that will explain this complete reversal and upsetting of the Orr-led movement of the past five or six years. Nor is there any surface explanation for the steady drift toward the near unanimity of sentiment for breaking up the Union which now prevailed. One by one, conservatives had fallen into line and turned the issue strictly into one of the method to be employed. Fear of public disapproval for nonconformity seemed to be more prevalent than fear of Lincoln's administration.[23]

Senators James H. Hammond and James Chesnut, Jr., in Washington, away from local influences, were slow to commit themselves. Hammond especially was conservative and wished assurance that Georgia and the Gulf States would support secession before he was willing to give it a trial. Orr too was objecting unless Alabama, Mississippi, and Georgia would co-operate—a rather safe position—and John E. Ashmore and other prominent leaders were outspoken enough in opposition to separate state action as to cause Rhett and the *Mercury* suddenly to become quiet on the issue. Even the effort

[23] Charles E. Cauthen, "South Carolina's Decision to Lead the Secession Movement," in *North Carolina Historical Review* (Raleigh), XVIII (1941), 360–72; Boucher, "South Carolina and the South on the Eve of Secession," in Washington University *Studies, Humanistic Series,* VI, No. 2, *passim;* Schultz, *Nationalism and Sectionalism in South Carolina,* 223–30; J. J. Pettigrew to W. S. Pettigrew, October 24, 1860, in Pettigrew Papers.

to force candidates for the legislature in the October election to declare their position had failed. Yet it was now becoming perfectly clear that no other state was willing to take the lead, and new assurance that the action of one state would induce others to follow was being given by the commissioners of Alabama and Mississippi. Even the word from Georgia's governor was encouraging. Perhaps, in spite of past experiences, South Carolina might again be justified in taking the lead.[24]

Since the legislature still retained the archaic right to choose the state's Presidential electors, it had stood by after its preliminary session to await the election returns. It now prepared to face the problem of passing a convention bill. Radicals pressed for an early date; conservatives would delay for the purpose of securing the assured co-operation of other states. Then again for reasons for which there is no surface explanation, men who until now had been counted conservative took the radical step. Senator Chesnut declared for immediate separate action; Congressman Milledge L. Bonham took a like stand; and Federal Judge Andrew G. Magrath and District Attorney James Conner announced their resignations. Three days later Senator Hammond, who had thought "Magrath and all those fellows were great asses for resigning," did the same thing. He confessed, however, that "It is an epidemic and very foolish." Magrath's remarks to the Charleston crowd which serenaded him are equally revealing. He spoke of the wrongs heaped upon the South until forbearance was a crime, of the "revolution" now begun, of the hope for a united South but the willingness of South Carolina to meet the issue alone.[25]

The emotions generating in Charleston, where the *Mercury* offices were displaying the state flag and a group of too-optimistic Georgians were helping the natives to celebrate the connection of Savannah and Charleston by rail, quickly passed to Columbia and the legislature. Whereas it had seemed for a time that the conven-

[24] James Chesnut to Hammond, October 17, October 27, 1860, in Hammond Papers (Division of Manuscripts, Library of Congress); Augusta *Constitutionalist*, August 7, 1860, for Orr's letter.

[25] Charleston *Mercury*, November 3, 7, 8, 1860; Chesnut to Hammond, November 15, 1860; Hammond to M. C. M. Hammond, November 12, 1860, in Hammond Papers (Division of Manuscripts, Library of Congress); report of "Serenade to Judge Magrath" and of his speech, in Charleston *Mercury*, November 8, 1860.

tion could be held back until January, opposition to quick action now completely collapsed, and the date for the election of delegates was set for December 6 and the meeting of the convention for December 17.[26]

In spite of reported conservative reactions in Charleston and parts of the interior, the secessionists everywhere elected their delegates and dominated the convention. An opposition leader as outstanding as Perry in the conservative back country could muster only 225 votes as against 1,300 given to his opponents. There was, therefore, no reason for delay when the convention assembled in the Baptist Church in Columbia or why James L. Orr, the only one-time conservative whose name appeared on the tally for president, should receive more than a handful of votes. Consequently, on its first day of meeting, the convention, by a vote of 159 to 0, adopted a secession resolution and appointed a committee to draw up an ordinance.[27]

A "fortunate" smallpox "epidemic" in Columbia then gave an excuse for transferring the meetings to the far more appropriate Charleston, where the final dramatic steps of taking South Carolina out of the Union would be completed. When the delegates had reconvened in Institute Hall, after a noisy welcome with bands and military companies at the station, they soon discovered the difficulty of doing business with Charleston taking part from the gallery. Next day they moved to the smaller St. Andrew's Hall, where, on December 20, the ordinance of secession was presented and adopted. That evening, again in Institute Hall, with no effort to restrain the crowd, the ceremony of signing was completed.

In their declaration of the immediate causes which induced and justified secession, they talked much of Revolutionary days, but stressed only three matters: the personal-liberty laws passed in the

[26] "The most exciting incident was the unfurling of the State Flag of South Carolina from the upper window of the *Mercury* office, which was greeted with vociferous cheers, proclaiming in trumpet tones, that 'the colors were to be nailed to the mast.' " Charleston *Mercury*, November 8, 1860. See also *ibid.*, November 13, 14, 15, 21 ("The time is rapidly approaching when the people of South Carolina must determine for themselves the place they will occupy in history"); White, *Robert Barnwell Rhett*, 181–84; Walhalla *Keowee Courier*, December 1, 1860.

[27] Kibler, *Benjamin F. Perry*, 343–45; *Journal of the Convention of the People of South Carolina, Held in 1860, 1861 and 1862, together with the Ordinances, Reports, Resolutions, Etc.* (Columbia, 1862), 7–9.

North, the agitation against slaveholding, and the election of a sectional President. For these reasons South Carolina declared her intention to resume "her position among the nations of the world." [28]

South Carolina had not acted without some encouragement from her neighbors. The commissioners from both Mississippi and Alabama, as well as Governor Madison S. Perry of Florida and Howell Cobb of Georgia, had come to witness the secession proceedings, and the Alabama representative had spoken at one of the sessions with considerable assurance as to the course his state would take. It was generally assumed that South Carolina was merely "leading off," that there was now "no hope for the Union." At least that was what Governor Francis W. Pickens said to Caleb Cushing, whom President Buchanan had sent in the vain hope of delaying, if not preventing, South Carolina's action. [29]

Already on November 14 Governor John J. Pettus of Mississippi had issued a call convening the legislature into extraordinary session some twelve days later. The purpose was to consider "the propriety and necessity of providing surer and better safeguards for the lives, liberties, and property of her citizens" than had been found or was to be hoped for, in "Black Republican oaths." He also assembled the state's delegation in Congress to secure advice on the nature of the message he would deliver to the legislature. The issue was again between co-operation and separate state action, and the delegates, with the single exception of Jefferson Davis, advised the latter. [30]

Thus supported, the governor informed the legislature of the grave dangers which threatened and of the remedy to be found in "the reserved rights of the states to withdraw from injury and oppression." The legislature responded by providing for the election of delegates to a state convention to meet at Jackson on January 7, 1861. It also asked the governor to appoint commissioners to visit the other slaveholding states, to inform them of Mississippi's action, and to urge co-operation for "common defense and safety."

The contest over the election of delegates to the convention re-

[28] Charleston *Mercury,* December 21, 1860; *Declaration of the Immediate Causes which Induce and Justify the Secession of South Carolina from the Federal Union; and the Ordinance of Secession* (Charleston, 1860), 3–4.
[29] Fuess, *Life of Caleb Cushing,* II, 273–74.
[30] Rainwater, *Mississippi, Storm Center of Secession,* 168.

vealed the confused and divided state of opinion. Opposition to secession sentiment, although embracing a wide variety of opinion, was somehow ultimately satisfied with a demand for co-operation with the other slave states. A meeting to organize such opinion held at Vicksburg on November 29 was not largely attended but did attract a group of highly respected and capable men. The resolutions adopted declared that there were yet sufficient remedies for all ills within the Union and that until these had been tried and had failed there was no excuse for secession. Even then it should be carried out only by the co-operation of all the slaveholding states.[31]

Throughout the campaign conservatives denounced secession as a surrender of Southern rights, a cowardly fleeing from the enemy, and an abandonment of sound Constitutional positions. Republicans had combined and conspired to get control of the government. They should be resisted, not left unopposed to enjoy the spoils. Furthermore, the move for secession among the Cotton States was an abandonment of the Border States and the courting of a civil war that would fall most heavily upon them. Certainly no drastic steps should be taken until all the slave states should agree. It was scarcely necessary for the radicals to meet such arguments. They had only to assert the futility of further efforts on the part of a humiliated South against an arrogant North flushed with victory. They could answer that the Border States, because they were slave states, would soon be forced to join their fellows in resistance and that a show of force and resistance was the only language Republicans could understand. Civil war would not result, and the hopes for reuniting the nation on a sound basis would be strengthened by a solid South that had possessed the courage to act in defense of its rights. It was the old appeal to pride and fear, and where men were confused, apprehensive, and uncertain, it was effective. Only 60 per cent of those who had voted in the Presidential election six weeks before took the trouble to go to the polls. The separate state secessionists would dominate the convention, but the vote had been close enough to leave considerable doubt as to the true attitude of the people of Mississippi.

When the convention met on January 7 South Carolina was al-

---

[31] Vicksburg *Whig*, November 10, 15, 30, 1860; Natchez *Courier*, November 17, 19, 20, 24, 1860.

ready out of the Union. The effect was all that the radicals had hoped. Secession was taken for granted. An ordinance for that purpose had already been prepared. Feeble efforts to oppose or delay were quickly brushed aside. Even the move to submit the ordinance to the people for ratification was defeated 70 to 29, and the final vote on adoption, on January 9, stood 85 to 15. Mississippi too had "crossed the Rubicon." [32]

Affairs in Alabama had moved as rapidly. There the legislature had earlier provided for the calling of a state convention if the Republicans won the presidency. Governor Moore, however, was uncertain as to just when Lincoln should be considered elected. Was it on November 6, or later on December 5 when the electors cast their ballots? He was open to advice on the matter, he said, and as a result received much—most of it conflicting. At length, under pressure, he selected December 24 as the day for the election of delegates and January 7 as the day for the meeting of the convention. That immediately launched one of the bitterest campaigns in the history of the state. [33]

The contest was seemingly between extremists of the Yancey type, who advocated immediate secession by separate state action, and the co-operationists, who wanted to advise with all the other slave states in a Southern convention. Yet the co-operationists ranged in opinion from those who would secede as soon as others agreed, to out-and-out Unionists, who would act neither because of past aggressions nor anticipated ones. Old sectional and party divisions, always sharp in Alabama, intensified feelings, and the new lines followed the old in a general way with enough of variation, however, to add new fuel to old fires. Secessionists dominated in southern and central counties; co-operationists, in the northern part of the state. The thoroughgoing Unionists were to be found as a rule in the area adjacent to and dependent upon Tennessee.

Appeals for support were the same as in Mississippi. The secessionists insisted that the issue was "the Union, with white slavery

[32] Rainwater, *Mississippi, Storm Center of Secession,* 177–97; Natchez *Mississippi Free Trader,* December 28, 1860; *Official Proceedings of the Convention of 1861* (Jackson, 1861); Thomas H. Woods, "A Sketch of the Mississippi Secession Convention of 1861—Its Membership and Works," in Mississippi Historical Society *Publications,* VI (1902), 94.

[33] Denman, *Secession Movement in Alabama,* 90–92.

and amalgamation in their most monstrous and revolting forms, or secession, with Negro slavery as the basis of a grand Southern Confederacy in which the white race shall be placed upon the most elevated level of equality and civilization of which the history of the world affords an example." The North had the will and the power to "exterminate negro slavery and to enslave the white people of the South in the Union." It had grown fat with wealth and impudent with power. The Constitution was no longer a protection. The Union was gone; only the forms of a democratic system remained. The Republican intentions were clear. It was "the Union without slavery, or slavery without the Union." [34]

Co-operationists begged for forbearance, delay, and a Southern convention. No step should be taken which imperiled the lives, property, and liberty of all the people without giving them time to consider the issues, and without listening to their suggestions and finding out if there was not some remedy other than secession. If revolution was the only remedy, then it should be made "effectual and safe" by unity. Precipitate action was "no less to be dreaded than quiet submission." Nothing could be lost by delay. Time should be given the North to recede, for the wise and good men of the nation to try their hands, for Southern men to council together. At least there should be a chance to "reach the popular ears." [35]

The vote for delegates was light, only about three fourths of that in the November election. The secessionists won fifty-four seats; the co-operationists forty-six. Yet the vote was close, and the *Southern Advocate* insisted that if there had not been bad management in two counties, the co-operationists would have had a majority in the convention. News of South Carolina's action and the appointment of commissioners to confer with other states both worked to the advantage of the secessionists as did a growing feeling that peaceful secession was possible. The seizure of Federal forts in Alabama without resistance in the days just preceding the convention gave added assurance and encouraged quick action.[36]

[34] Montgomery *Weekly Advertiser,* December 12, 1860; Greensboro (N.C.) *Beacon,* December 21, 1860.

[35] Huntsville *Southern Advocate,* December 19, 1860; Tuscumbia *North Alabamian,* December 21, 1860; Jeremiah Clemens to Crittenden, quoted in Denman, *Secession Movement in Alabama,* 105.

[36] Denman, *Secession Movement in Alabama,* 119–22.

The Alabama convention afforded further evidence of the drive toward secession which was being generated at the South. Conservatives were yielding before an emotional tide that carried the sands from beneath their feet. Radicals were recovering lost ground. When Yancey was brought forward as a nominee to the convention, the Montgomery *Confederation* protested bitterly. "He has neither prudence, nor deliberation, nor reason in an exigency like this," it cried, "but is ruled entirely and wholly by his passions and his ungovernable prejudices." Yet Yancey was elected and was on hand ready to drive forward the radical program of immediate secession.[37]

Co-operationists received few favors at the hands of the majority and were able to delay action only to a slight degree. Yancey would have made all members pledge nonsubmission to Lincoln's inauguration and administration and would have declared resistance to any ordinance of secession "treason against the state." Cooler heads, however, checked such extreme measures but supported solidly the report of his committee recommending immediate secession and an invitation to the other slaveholding states to meet in convention at Montgomery on February 4 "for the purpose of consulting with each other as to the most effectual mode of securing concerted and harmonious action in whatever measures may be deemed most desirable for our common peace and security."

The co-operationist minority on the committee attempted to secure delay by submitting a proposal for a Southern convention held *before* secession, with suggestions to an Alabama delegation for seeking a settlement of all sectional difficulties. Failing in this, they proposed a delay in the inauguration of secession and finally the submission of the ordinance to the people for ratification. On each measure they were defeated by a strict party vote, and on Yancey's motion the ordinance was taken up and adopted 61 to 39. The crowd surged into the convention hall; a state flag made by the ladies of Montgomery was raised over the capital. A member from north Alabama viewed it against the Southern sky and wrote: "Here I sit & from my window see the nasty little thing flaunting in the breeze which has taken the place of that glorious banner which

[37] Montgomery *Confederation*, November 23, 1860.

has been the pride of millions of Americans and the boast of free-men the wide world over." [38]

The day before Alabama acted, the Florida convention had passed its ordinance of secession. In his message to the legislature in 1859, Governor Perry had recommended that Florida declare herself in favor of withdrawal from the Union in case of Republican success in the coming election, and in October, 1860, he had assured Governor Gist of South Carolina that Florida would follow the lead of any single Cotton State that might secede. Acting on this advice, the legislature had authorized the governor, in such a contingency, to work with any or all of the other slaveholding states for the preservation of their rights, and to convene the legislature in extraordinary session. Florida Democrats had, in the meantime, followed the lead of the radicals both at Charleston and at Richmond and now, with Lincoln's election, took a quick stand for immediate secession. Some urged the governor to make use of the power granted the previous year, but since the legislature was to meet the last week of November in regular session, this was soon dropped.[39]

Up until this time both of Florida's United States Senators, David L. Yulee and Stephen R. Mallory, had been definitely conservative. Mallory still held his ground, hoping for consideration, but when the legislators met they found a letter from Yulee saying that he would promptly and joyously return home to support the state at any time it might secede before the expiration of his term on March 4. That letter, reinforced by Governor Perry's fiery message asking for immediate secession, brought quick action. A bill calling for a convention to meet on January 3 was pushed through without an adverse vote.

Opinion, however, was not entirely unanimous on all matters. Efforts to delay the meeting and to require popular ratification of the convention's work did muster enough votes to indicate that at least one third of the members were conservatively inclined. Con-

[38] William R. Smith, *The History and Debates of the Convention of the People of Alabama . . . in which is preserved the Speeches of the Secret Sessions and Many Valuable State Papers* (Atlanta, 1861), 76–77, 77–80, 90–92, 118; L. R. Davis to John McClelland, January 13, 1861, quoted in Denman, *Secession Movement in Alabama,* 151.

[39] John G. Nicolay and John Hay, *Abraham Lincoln, A History* (New York, 1890), II, 313; Dodd, "Secession Movement in Florida," *loc. cit.,* 51–52.

sidering the fact that the press of the state and the political machinery for action were, and had been since the death of the Whig party, largely in the hands of the radical element, this was a remarkable showing. It indicated that a strong minority, if not a majority of the people, still had strong misgivings regarding the wisdom of breaking up the Union.[40]

The election of delegates to the convention showed the same divided opinion. In spite of the encouragement provided by South Carolina's secession just two days before the election, the Florida radicals carried the state by rather close majorities. Estimates of co-operationist strength range from 36 to 43 per cent—a proportion that under normal conditions could prove decidedly troublesome. Conditions, however, were anything but normal when the convention assembled on January 3 at Tallahassee. Commissioners from Alabama, Edmund Ruffin from Virginia, and Leonidas W. Spratt of the Charleston *Daily Standard* were on hand to observe and to lobby. Even the clergy, as it had done in Mississippi, threw its weight on the side of immediate secession. The excitement was intense.[41]

The final break, however, was not achieved without a struggle. A resolution asserting the right of secession and the justification for such action was carried only after an effort to delay proceedings had been rejected by a vote of 43 to 24. Even after a committee had submitted a secession ordinance with a report favoring immediate action, an amendment to suspend its operation until Georgia and Alabama had seceded was lost by a narrow margin. A change of only five votes would have carried the measure. The effort to require popular ratification of secession, however, was beaten by a substantial vote, and the final ordinance was passed with only seven members refusing to yield. The opposition had simply melted away before an impulse whose increasing momentum rendered resistance seemingly useless.[42]

Many expected Georgia to do as she had done in 1850—take a more or less conservative stand and check the mad drive toward disunion. There were good reasons for such hopes. The state had

[40] Dodd, "Secession Movement in Florida," *loc. cit.*, 52–54.
[41] *Ibid.*, 55–59; Ruffin Diary, January 3–10, 1861.
[42] Dodd, "Secession Movement in Florida," *loc. cit.*, 60–66.

a deserved reputation for solid, conservative development; its spokesmen in Washington had generally been moderates; and in the recent election the combined vote of Douglas and Bell had exceeded that of Breckinridge by more than 2,500. True, both Toombs and Cobb were now in the secession camp. The John Brown raid had set Toombs off on a radical course, and Cobb had resigned from the Cabinet when he realized that his influence both over Buchanan and over the Georgia Democrats was weakening. They were now back home preaching disunion. Neither, however, could wield as much influence as he had in 1850. The States Rights Democrats had never forgiven them for their part in the party disruptions in that year, and the influence for Union now exercised by Stephens and Herschel Johnson more than balanced their opposition. The real decision in Georgia would be made by Governor Joseph E. Brown and his followers, who were in control of the Democratic machine.[43]

Already the wily governor in his message to the legislature had recommended secession in case of Lincoln's election. The news of Republican success, therefore, brought a demand for immediate action and the suggestion that the legislature "resolve the State of Georgia out of the Union" without waiting for direct action by the people. Uncertain as to its course, the legislature invited prominent leaders to give their views on successive nights between its daily sessions. The most important of these were given by Thomas R. R. Cobb, younger brother of Howell Cobb, Robert Toombs, and Alexander H. Stephens. Cobb was for immediate secession by the legislature, which was better able to decide upon the policy to be adopted by the state than were the people. He was unwilling "to wait to hear from the crossroads and the groceries." Toombs was in agreement. He told of the wrongs which the South had long endured, of the even greater wrongs to follow after the fourth of March; and he urged the legislature to withdraw the state from

43 J. Henly Smith to Stephens, August 18, 1860, in Stephens Papers (Division of Manuscripts, Library of Congress); Linton Stephens to Alexander H. Stephens, November 9, 1860, in Stephens Papers (Manhattan College of the Sacred Heart, New York); Nichols, *Disruption of American Democracy*, 378–91; Cobb to the People of Georgia, December 6, 1860, in Phillips (ed.), *Correspondence of Toombs, Stephens, and Cobb*, 505–16; Greene, "Politics in Georgia, 1853–54: The Ordeal of Howell Cobb," *loc. cit.*, 185–211; Flippin, *Herschel V. Johnson*, 161.

such a confederacy as a right and as a duty. He was "afraid of conventions." Stephens spoke for a more moderate course. He insisted that the election of no man constitutionally chosen to the presidency was "sufficient cause to justify any State to separate from the Union." Lincoln could do no harm. The House and the Senate were both against him, and he would be pledged to uphold the Constitution. This government with all its defects came nearer the objects of all good governments than any other on the face of the earth. And up to now there had been no abuse which justified its destruction. Under American institutions even Georgia had more than doubled her wealth in a decade. Her people might well pause before striking them down.

There were evils, he admitted. The South had reasons for complaint. The remedy, however, was not secession but action within the Union. What was needed was a convention of the people of Georgia. The legislature did not have the power to act. The people alone were sovereign. If that sovereign spoke and determined to go out of the Union, he, Stephens, would bow to its will. If the Northern states refused Southern rights, then as a last resort he would accept disunion.[44]

The appeal was not entirely lost. The legislature acted only to authorize a convention and to require the governor to order an election on January 2, 1861, of delegates who were to assemble on January 16 at the state capital. It also authorized the issue of state bonds to the amount of one million dollars to provide a military fund.

Appeals during the brief campaign followed the pattern already established in other states and need not be repeated. A few felt Georgia's peculiar responsibility to the rest of the South, and there seems to have been considerably more thought about what might lie ahead beyond secession. Toombs disturbed the radicals by advising the citizens of a neighboring town to ask Congress for amendments which would secure their rights and to postpone action until the Northern states had been given time to ratify or refuse. But soon after his return to Congress he saw the hopelessness of securing

[44] Augusta *Chronicle and Sentinel*, November 14, 25, 1860; Phillips, *Life of Robert Toombs*, 200–201; Stephens, *Constitutional View of the Late War Between the States*, II, 279–300.

concessions and telegraphed his constituents to thunder from the ballot box the unanimous vote of Georgia for secession by the fourth of March.[45]

Governor Brown's letter of advice to electors of delegates, aimed to be an answer to Stephens' speech, and Howell Cobb's letter from Washington, denouncing the Republicans and advising "independence out of the Union," both did much to aid the radical cause. The argument of T. R. R. Cobb that "We can make better terms out of the Union than in it," may have been, as Stephens said, the most powerful argument in the campaign. Stephens attempted to organize the opposition, but the move ended, as it had elsewhere, only in a vague request for co-operation with the other states. Such an appeal failed again to rally the true Union strength, and the secessionists were victorious by a vote of 50,243 to 37,123.[46]

The struggle, however, was not quite over. When the convention met on January 16 the majority resolution asking for an ordinance of secession was answered by a minority proposal for a convention of all the states south of Pennsylvania. That produced a bitter debate, ended only by a call for the previous question and the passage of the majority resolution by a vote of 166 to 130. The reporting of the ordinance brought further strife, but in the end resulted in its passage by a vote of 208 to 89. Only six members refused to take part in the final signing of the document. Even these pledged their lives to defend the state from hostile attack.[47]

The shift from a conservative vote in early November to secession by a large majority in January is difficult to explain. One editor probably did as well as can be done when he wrote: "We have heard a great deal about rights, wrongs, remedies—but all this talk is mere delusion. Georgia today would not give a penny-whistle for the Fugitive Slave Law of 1850, or all the fugitive slave laws Congress could pass. She cares absolutely nothing at all about the Personal Liberty Bills of the North, considered as an interest. . . . Neither is it Lincoln that Georgia would resist. . . . Our opposition is to the animus of the North, as exhibited in the passage of

[45] Sandersville *Central Georgian,* December 19, 1860; Savannah *Republican,* December 20, 1860; Augusta *Chronicle and Sentinel,* December 8, 22, 1860; Phillips, *Life of Robert Toombs,* 204–209.

[46] Milledgeville *Federal Union,* April 10, 1861.

[47] Phillips, *Georgia and State Rights,* 202–10.

the Liberty Bills, and finally in the election of an irrepressible conflict representative, as the Chief Executive of these States." [48]

The secession of Louisiana is even more difficult to explain. The Bell and Douglas vote in November had exceeded that of Breckinridge by more than five thousand. Disunion sentiment had been conspicuously weak in 1850, and the Mississippi River highway was as important to the interests of those on its lower reaches as it was to those above. The planters and merchants alike had long been Whig in politics; a protective tariff was as valuable to sugar as it was to industry. John Slidell, the most powerful politician in the state, was close enough to the Buchanan administration to share its national purposes. [49]

Yet Lincoln's election had frightened the large slaveholders, and the hitherto moderate Slidell suddenly saw secession as the only remedy. "The hateful tyranny of Section is about to be consummated," said the Opelousas *Courier,* "and a government organized upon principles of hostility to the vested rights of a portion of the country, is to be made a government for the whole country." Governor Thomas O. Moore, who had answered Governor Gist's appeal for co-operation by saying, "I shall not advise the secession of my State and I will add that I do not think the people of Louisiana will ultimately decide in favor of that course," now called a special session of the General Assembly and demanded the immediate election of a convention to remove the state from the Union. [50]

There was an unusually large amount of outright Union sentiment in Louisiana, but division in the short campaign for the election of convention delegates followed the established pattern of secession versus co-operation. Moderates deplored the calling of a special session of the legislature when the regular session was only a few weeks off. They asked if Louisiana was "prepared to abandon

---

[48] Augusta *Chronicle and Sentinel,* December 12, 1860.

[49] Shugg, *Origins of Class Struggle in Louisiana,* 160; Alexandria *Louisiana Democrat,* November 5, 1860.

[50] Alexandria *Louisiana Democrat,* October 24, 1860; New Orleans *Weekly Delta,* October 6, 1860 ("There was a time, and that, too, not very remote, fellow-citizens, when the word 'disunion' fell upon my ears with powerful dissonance. . . . My views on that subject have since been undergoing a gradual change until by slow degrees, I have reluctantly arrived at the conviction that . . . we cannot with safety and honor continue the connection much longer"); Opelousas (La.) *Courier,* November 17, 1860; New Orleans *Daily True Delta,* November 20, 1860.

373

at once all duties upon foreign sugar." What about the river trade? Could cotton or sugar or rice or fruit be shipped with the custom-house closed and no arrangements for trade upriver or abroad? Interest, if nothing else, called for "coolness and calmness in thought and action." It might be well also to face the fact that up to date the national government had "not passed *one single law*" of which Louisiana could complain or violated the Constitution in a single instance. The appeal was to fears, not to "prudence, . . . good sense and humanity." [51]

The secessionist campaign was notable only for the unusual part played by the clergy. Benjamin M. Palmer, William T. Leacock, and J. J. Henderson were the most prominent and outspoken, but there were numerous lesser preachers who were "decided in their recommendations of resistance . . . and their advocacy of Southern rights." The Reverend Benjamin M. Palmer, pastor of the First Presbyterian Church of New Orleans, broke the clerical silence on political issues November 29, 1860, with a sermon on "Slavery a Divine Trust" and followed it with other sermons advocating secession. He held slavery a divine trust committed to the South, whose duty it was "to conserve and to perpetuate" it for the sake of "self-preservation," for the good of "the slaves themselves," and for the advancement of "the civilized world." As a Southerner, he believed that nothing was now left but secession. Honor demanded it. The defense of Southern rights required it. "I am willing, at the call of my honor and my liberty to die a freeman," he cried; "I'll never, no never, live a slave; and the alternative now presented by our enemies is secession or slavery. Let it be liberty or death."

The radical press rang with his praise. His words "rose far above the conventional forms and phrases of an ordinary sermon." It was "above compliment." From the office of the New Orleans *Daily Delta* alone more than thirty thousand copies were distributed. A contemporary later declared that Dr. Palmer had done more than "any other non-combatant in the South to promote rebellion." [52]

Henderson and Leacock were equally ardent for secession and

---

[51] New Orleans *Daily True Delta*, November 20, 1860; New Orleans *Picayune*, December 8, 1860; "Jefferson Papers," in New Orleans *Daily True Delta*, December 14, 1860.

[52] *Fast Day Sermons* (New York, 1861), 57–80; New Orleans *Daily Delta*, December 4, 1860.

the latter declared that an independent South would be in a position to dominate the rest of the Americas. They and their kind gave to the movement something of a crusading quality which was hard to resist. "All that could be done by moderate, dispassionate, political and experienced men," wrote one editor, "was to go with the current, endeavoring to subdue its boiling and seething energies." "Things have come to a pretty pass," wrote another, "when the decent people of the state are unable to speak out for fear of compromising their future." [53]

The election was a victory for secession by a reported vote of two to one. Yet the official election returns were suppressed, and gossip had it that the co-operationists had actually carried the state. The vote again was light—in New Orleans less than half the names which were registered. The slaveholding districts went heavy for secession; the small-farming areas were co-operationist.

The convention, with nearly two thirds of its members secessionists, made short work of the feeble efforts to secure a Southern convention and to refer the question of secession to it. Efforts to submit the action of the convention to the people for ratification were equally futile. The ordinance of secession was, therefore, quickly passed, and conservatives, without admitting that the move was either "necessary or wise," bowed to what was called "the will of the majority." [54]

The secession of Texas completed the movement in the Lower South. Here the matter of Southern rights was badly tangled with the problem of frontier protection from Indian raids. Party differences in early days had not been based on interest. Men brought their party affiliations with them. Western settlers were mainly Democrats, while the eastern slaveholding planters were Whigs. Many of the latter turned Know-Nothing when their party disintegrated and that had the effect of driving the Germans and Mexicans, strong in a few corners, into the Democratic ranks. When the Know-Nothing party, in turn, went to pieces, its members also be-

[53] Mrs. L. J. Stanton to Governor Thomas O. Moore, December 14, 1860, in Thomas O. Moore Papers (in private possession); Greer, "Louisiana Politics, 1845–1861," *loc. cit.*, 617–50; New Orleans *Bee*, December 17, 1860; John S. Simmerlin to Governor Moore, December 5, 1860, in Moore Papers.

[54] New Orleans *Daily Picayune*, January 11, 19, 25, 1861; Shugg, *Origins of Class Struggle in Louisiana*, 161–70.

came Democrats, creating two factions, the one national in its outlook, the other more and more Southern.[55]

The national group backed Senator Sam Houston in his opposition to the Kansas-Nebraska Bill, but state-rights sentiment was strong enough to defeat him for the governorship in 1857. Talk of annexing Cuba and reopening the African slave trade brought a reaction and gave Houston success in 1859. The balance, however, was so close that the John Brown raid, coupled with the failure of the United States government to give adequate protection against a whole series of Indian raids on the frontier, produced a second reaction which sent Louis T. Wigfall, the most rabid fire-eater in the state, to the Senate.

From that point forward Texas was with the radical South—at Charleston and at Richmond. As Captain J. S. Ford, fresh from the scenes of Indian ravages, wrote: "The citizens of this state are entitled to protection and they ought to have it. . . . [If the United States refuse it] let Texas assume high ground. Protection and allegiance go hand in hand. There is no principle better established than that when a Government fails or refuses to protect its citizens, the ties of allegiance are dissolved and they have a perfect right to take care of themselves. In my opinion Texas has already had ample cause to sever her connection with the Union on this very head." "The bloody knife which has reached the hearts of our people may have been held in the hand of the reckless savage," wrote another, "but the general government stood by listlessly when the deed was done." [56]

Houston had been as unable to secure Federal assistance in the defense of the West as had his rivals. He was therefore in no position to check the sharp reaction which followed Lincoln's election. He had taken a firm stand against disunion sentiment and had hoped for the Constitutional Union nomination at Baltimore. Disappointed, he had waged something of an independent campaign well into the summer before withdrawing. Slave disturbances and rumors of insurrections in the towns of northern Texas added to his troubles, and a belief that Kansas free-soil emissaries were back of horse-

[55] Charles W. Ramsdell, "The Frontier and Secession," in *Studies in Southern History and Politics Inscribed to William Archibald Dunning* (New York, 1914), 63–79.
[56] Austin *Texas State Gazette*, May 21, 1859.

stealings and Negro plots rendered him impotent against the rising tide of secession sentiment. He called its leaders "traitors" and insisted that secession was an unconstitutional and revolutionary measure, unjustified until the Federal government had begun aggressions upon the South. He stubbornly refused to assemble the legislature and despite the demands of mass meetings, editorials, threats, and entreaties, held firm.[57]

Not to be foiled, a group of secession leaders met in Austin on December 3, 1860, and drew up an address suggesting that the people of each district hold an election on January 8 to elect delegates to a convention to be held in Austin three weeks later. This action provoked Houston into calling the legislature to meet one week before the proposed convention. When it met he maintained in his message that Southern rights could best be preserved within the Union and intimated that the approaching convention was an illegal body. The legislature, however, recognized its authority to act but insisted that its action be ratified by the people. Houston was forced to yield. The convention with little delay repealed the ordinance of annexation of 1845, revoked the powers delegated by Texas to the Federal government, and declared Texas "a sovereign state," whose people were absolved from allegiance to the United States.[58]

Two attitudes, as a kind of background in men's thinking, had persisted throughout the period in which the Cotton States were seceding. The first was the hope of many and the fear of others that some kind of compromise or adjustment of sectional differences might still be possible; the second was the impression, held by all but a few in South Carolina, that the seceding states would ultimately be united under a common government. Some Southerners had accepted secession because they thought their state would be in a better bargaining position out of the Union than in it. Border State men viewed themselves as mediators between two extremes. Both wanted peace. Other Southerners, however, had accepted separate state action because co-operation would be a necessity thereafter. They had long dreamed of a Southern con-

[57] Charles W. Ramsdell, *Reconstruction in Texas* (New York, 1910), 11–17.
[58] *Journal of the Secession Convention of Texas, 1861* (Austin, 1861), 36.

377

federacy. Secession was but the first step in that direction. The idea that reconciliation was possible would, unfortunately, only add to the confusion in the last days of Buchanan's administration, turn the disillusioned Border States southward, and help push the Lincoln administration into civil war. The idea of Southern unity would, on the other hand, produce the Confederate States of America.

Hope for compromise, of course, lay with the Border States and Northern Democrats. The Congress which met in December would give them their opportunity. Southerners, with a few exceptions, had retained their seats, and those in the Cabinet had remained at their posts. Their objectives varied. Some would seek justice; some would work for delay to enable the seceding states to prepare for whatever lay ahead; some would use their positions to frustrate attempts at coercion. Little, however, was actually accomplished along any of these lines. Cobb, Thompson, and Floyd, in the Cabinet, did for a time influence Buchanan toward moderation in dealing with the problem of Federal property in the seceded states and in his Constitutional views on secession. They served as a medium through which the agents of South Carolina reached the President, and they did supply inside information to their Southern friends. Yet Floyd's lax business methods soon produced a scandal and rendered him a liability, while Cobb, unable to check the growing influence of Jeremiah S. Black and Edwin M. Stanton, resigned and left Washington. Thompson remained until the sending of the *Star of the West* with supplies for Fort Sumter without his knowledge brought an angry resignation. The total effect was to weaken the Southern cause in the public mind and to stiffen the administration in its attitudes.[59]

Senators and Representatives, meanwhile, in their committees of thirteen and thirty-three, demonstrated the complete futility of compromise as proposed by earnest men mainly from the "Borderland." They had received little encouragement from President Buchanan's message, in which he admitted Southern grievances but denied any right of secession or excuse for rebellion. He had thrown the whole problem into their laps by insisting that he had no power to wage war on the people of the state, and that without Federal officials in the seceded states he was helpless to enforce the law.

[59] Nichols, *Disruption of American Democracy*, 377–91, 423–35.

Congress accepted the responsibility without enthusiasm. Compromise measures of various kinds were quickly introduced in the House, but Republican opposition in the committee checked action. Only a resolution recommending that the states repeal their personal-liberty laws and one asserting that Lincoln's election did not justify secession could muster a majority. In the Senate early attempts at compromise fared little better, but they did produce the Crittenden proposal, which became the basis of most future efforts. He would extend the Missouri Compromise line to the Pacific, prohibit slavery to the north of it, but permit it and protect it on the south. New states were to decide the slavery issue for themselves; the Fugitive Slave Law was to be improved and fugitives paid for; the foreign slave trade was to be suppressed; and Congress would be forbidden to abolish slavery in the states and in the District of Columbia.

The Senate committee, however, followed Seward's lead as dictated by Lincoln. The items in Crittenden's proposal were rejected one by one as were others made by Toombs and Douglas and Joseph Lane. Such action hastened the secession movement in the South and strengthened South Carolina's determination to be rid of Federal troops in Fort Sumter. While Southern Senators and Representatives telegraphed their constituents that hope was dead and urged quick secession, South Carolina commissioners, pressing their claims, discovered the new temper in the Cabinet behind Buchanan and the fact that Sumter would not be yielded. Instead, plans for its relief were well under way. Things in Washington were beginning to assume their final form. The Republicans had already begun to have their way. And as Wade told his colleagues, "It would be humiliating and dishonorable to us if we were to listen to a compromise by which he, who has the verdict of the people in his pocket, should make his way to the presidential chair." [60]

The situation at the opening of the new year seemed hopeless. Crittenden and Douglas, however, were not ready to yield. They now came forward with a revised version of Crittenden's proposal only to have its introduction refused. R. M. T. Hunter followed with a plan for reconstructing the Union along lines once suggested

[60] David M. Potter, *Lincoln and His Party in the Secession Crisis* (New Haven, 1942), 100–11, 156–87; *Cong. Globe*, 36 Cong., 2 Sess., 99–104.

by Calhoun. That too was rejected. Men seemed to be willing to see the Union go to pieces. Only the stubborn loyalty of the Border States gave encouragement. They still held firmly to the Union, yet continued pressure for an adjustment.

The situation, however, was becoming more difficult and positive attitudes necessary. Governor Thomas H. Hicks of Maryland denied that either secession or the co-operation of the states with each other was Constitutional. He flatly refused to summon the legislature and stood firm against a small but active group who pressed for a convention. Elsewhere governors were not so stubborn, but public sentiment was firm. Governor Beriah Magoffin of Kentucky was thoroughly conscious of the strong Union sentiment in his state but equally aware of the danger which "sectional animosity," as he called it, carried to his people. He had, on December 9, asked the Southern governors to meet in convention and unite on a program of safeguards to be submitted to the North before any drastic steps were taken. This had come to nothing, and he was now thoroughly discouraged. The visit of commissioners from Mississippi and Alabama and the failure of the Crittenden Compromise moved him to call an extra session of the legislature for January 17. This call brought immediate protest and the organization of Union forces for opposition. A committee of ten, working through the state, made sure that secession would not be attempted. The legislature, therefore, refused to call a state convention but approved the Crittenden measures and requested Congress to call a convention of the states to propose amendments to the Constitution. They did, however, recognize the principle of secession and let it be known that any attempt to coerce the seceded states would meet with resistance "to the last extremity." [61]

Governor Isham Harris of Tennessee had also become discouraged by the failure of Republicans to offer proposals for Southern security or to support such measures in Congress. The majority of the people, however, were definitely Union in feeling and little

[61] George L. P. Radcliffe, *Governor Thomas H. Hicks of Maryland and the Civil War,* in Johns Hopkins University *Studies in Historical and Political Science,* Ser. XIX, Nos. 11–12 (Baltimore, *c.* 1902), 21–42; E. Merton Coulter, *The Civil War and Readjustment in Kentucky* (Chapel Hill, 1926), 25–34, 36–37; Dumond, *Secession Movement,* 224–25; Edward C. Smith, *The Borderland in the Civil War* (New York, 1927), 101–103.

disturbed by Lincoln's election. Secession was far from their minds. "Let every man put his foot on secession," said the Memphis *Enquirer;* "it is no remedy for Southern wrong, or it is only a madman's remedy." East Tennessee, however, was less satisfied, and Harris, now definitely in a secession mood, decided to act. On December 7 he issued a call for an extra session of the legislature for January 7, 1861, "to consider the present condition of the country." In his address to this body he stressed Southern abuses and the threat of further aggression and asked it to call a convention to consider the matter of Federal relations. The legislature, however, referred this to the people in a special election to be held February 9, when they should decide whether to hold a convention and, at the same time, elect delegates in case the move should carry. The vote was 68,282 to 59,449 against holding the convention, and 91,-803 to 24,749 in favor of Union delegates.[62]

Arkansas proved to be another interesting example of radical politicians attempting to crowd a reluctant people toward secession. Local affairs, including the struggle to break the political dominance of the Johnson family, had occupied the state's attention almost to the exclusion of national affairs. Five thousand more men voted in the August state election of 1860 than in the national election of that year. Sectional differences also added something to the political confusion with the plantation areas supporting Bell and the mountain section going to Breckinridge more from party habit than anything else. The question as to what should be done in case of Lincoln's election had scarcely been raised.

Now, however, Governor Henry M. Rector, backed by Senator Robert W. Johnson and Representative Thomas C. Hindman in Washington, came out flatly for secession in a special message to the legislature. Commissioners from Alabama and Louisiana added their pressure. Haste was the word. The legislature, however, hesitated, as letters and petitions in favor of the Union began to arrive from the interior. Not until January 15 was an act passed to submit to the people the question of calling a convention. The date

[62] Memphis *Enquirer,* November 13, 1860; Nashville *Republican Banner,* November 13, 1860; Knoxville *Whig,* June 9, November 17, 1860; James W. Patton, *Unionism and Reconstruction in Tennessee, 1860–1869* (Chapel Hill, 1934), 10–14; Parks, *John Bell of Tennessee,* 393.

was set for February 18, and the voters were not only to pass on the convention issue but to choose delegates as well. The politicians were jubilant. Encouraged, the governor seized the arsenal in Little Rock.[63]

The secessionists, however, had rejoiced too soon. The convention carried by more than ten thousand votes, but a majority of the delegates elected were Union men. The vote was comparatively light, and the best guess seemed to be that a large majority of the absent voters were Union men. There could be no doubt as to Arkansas' position.

Beaten at the polls, the secessionists tried every possible means of controlling the convention. They first attempted to stampede it into action. They argued that it had been elected only to pass an ordinance of secession. They sought commitment on the right to secede and to recognize the seceding states. The radical press tried ridicule, and the governor delivered a fiery speech in an effort to instill fear and invoke local pride. Even bribery and threats of violence were reported. In the end the conservatives had their way and provision was made for co-operation with the other "Border Slaves States," and the question of secession or co-operation was left to the people in an election to be held in August. The convention then adjourned to reassemble when the results were known.[64]

Sentiment in Missouri was also definitely moderate. Douglas had carried the state in 1860, and the retiring governor in his last message had taken middle ground, condemning the extremists of both North and South and suggesting armed neutrality in case of a sectional clash. The new governor, Claiborne F. Jackson, on the other hand, urged the people to take their stand with the South. Honor and interests both lay in that direction. Under his influence bills for the calling of a convention, for the reorganization of the militia, and for the appointment of a board to control the police of St. Louis were quickly introduced. This alarmed the Union forces and shifted the center of activity to St. Louis with its government arsenal and subtreasury. There both groups organized secret military bodies,

---

[63] Lewis, "From Nationalism to Disunion," 359; Little Rock *Arkansas State Gazette*, March 9, 1861; David Y. Thomas, *Arkansas in War and Reconstruction* (Little Rock, 1936), 56, 69–72.

[64] *Journal of the Called Convention* (Little Rock, 1861), 10–49.

and Federal troops were dispatched to defend public property. Southern "minute men" drilled and made ready to seize the arsenal. Republican Wide-Awakes, under the leadership of Francis Preston Blair, Jr., prepared to resist them. Civil strife seemed imminent. Angered by developments the legislature pushed through a measure to take control of the St. Louis police force and, on January 21, passed the bill calling a state convention and providing for the election of delegates.[65]

More alarmed than ever, Blair redoubled his efforts and soon found an ally in Captain Nathaniel Lyon, who had been sent with additional government troops. Together they planned to hold the arsenal and check secession. Their fears, however, were not justified. The election resulted in an overwhelming Unionist victory. Every delegate elected had already expressed himself in favor of preserving the Union, and the popular majority exceeded eighty thousand. The legislature immediately dropped all plans for arming the state, agreed to change the meeting place of the convention to St. Louis, and set its date at March 4. Missouri was safe for the present.[66]

North Carolina, too, had remained calm and unmoved by the fury about her. Lincoln's election had caused considerable dismay in the state, and some secession sentiment had developed in the eastern planting counties. The overwhelming majority of the people, however, saw no reason for alarm. A united South could still have security within the Union. They were willing to wait. Governor John W. Ellis, on the other hand, believed that the state could not remain inactive. He belonged to the radical element and when the legislature assembled on November 19, 1860, recommended a conference of all the Southern states and the calling of a state convention. The committee to which his message was referred rejected the suggestions and announced bluntly that the Constitution was not a compact between sovereign states, that secession was rebellion, and that the election of Lincoln was no cause for disunion.[67]

Debate continued to the end of the year with little agreement.

[65] Dumond, *Secession Movement*, 218–19; Walter H. Pyle, *Missouri, Union or Secession* (Nashville, 1931), 210, 220 ff.

[66] Smith, *Borderland in the Civil War*, 120–32.

[67] Sitterson, *Secession Movement in North Carolina*, 177–210; Wilmington (N.C.) *Daily Journal*, December 17, 1860; Raleigh *North Carolina Standard*, December 11, 1860; C. B. Harrison to Branch, December 2, 1860, in Branch Papers.

Efforts to secure a convention failed, but conservatives were conscious of the fact that the drift of events and the failure of Congress to secure compromise were weakening their position. The radicals sensed this also and redoubled their propaganda efforts. The seizure of Fort Caswell on the Cape Fear River by a group of Wilmington citizens and the approval of a convention by all but two of the Congressional delegation marked a new stage in developments. When the legislature reassembled on January 7, it was generally understood that the secession question would have to be faced. The struggle was a bitter one, and not until January 29 was a bill passed permitting the people to vote for or against a convention and to elect delegates. The election date was set for February 28, and the convention, if approved, was to assemble at the governor's call not earlier than March 11. Its actions had to be ratified by the people. In the meantime, the state was ready for co-operation with other states in the interest of "peace, honor and safety." [68]

In spite of the apparent defeat of compromise on every hand and the inclination of Congress to push tariff, homestead, and Pacific railroad measures favorable to the North but distasteful to the South, the convention in North Carolina was defeated by a vote of 47,323 to 46,672. Of the delegates chosen, forty-two were secessionists and seventy-eight Unionists of one kind or another. North Carolina was with the Border States.[69]

Virginia's course in the crisis period was a matter of intense interest not only to the other Border States but to the whole South as well. A new nation without Virginia would lack a genuine Southern quality. A movement without her approval and support could never be quite satisfactory. She was, after all, the founder and keeper of "the Southern tradition."

Here as elsewhere in the borderland during November and December, radical opinion had made some headway against a rather solid Union sentiment. At the time of Lincoln's election few dared suggest secession. By January 7, when the legislature met, many had become discouraged and uncertain as to the sound course to pursue.

[68] H. W. Miller to William A. Graham, December 29, 1860, in William A. Graham Papers (Historical Commission of North Carolina); W. S. Pettigrew to J. J. Pettigrew, December 29, 1860, in Pettigrew Papers.
[69] Raleigh *North Carolina Standard*, March 20, 1861.

Sectional lines of opinion had appeared. Secession sentiment was on the increase in the eastern and southern parts of the state. Some spoke of it as "irresistible." The failure of compromise and the success of disunion in the Cotton States was having its effect.

Governor Letcher in his message to the legislature took middle ground, denouncing extremists on both sides and declaring that he did not believe the calling of a convention was either necessary or wise. He would instead send a commission to the North to ask the repeal of the personal-liberty laws and to the South to discover the grounds on which they would return to the Union. He did, however, accept the right of secession and denounced coercion.[70]

This message did not meet with universal approval, and the legislature acted only on the suggestion to oppose coercion. It followed this with a blunt statement that if all efforts at redress failed, Virginia would go with the South. Yet members were not for disunion, and a move to foster a national peace conference, and to send commissioners to both Buchanan and the Southern states urging delay until a united effort to settle differences had been made, received the support of both houses. Delegates were appointed, and former President John Tyler started off to Washington to see the President, and Judge John Robertson went southward. Neither accomplished much, but plans for the conference went ahead anyway.[71]

Meanwhile, the legislature debated the question of a state convention. Division came largely over the issues of leaving the matter to the people and referring its decisions to them. The need for haste triumphed, and the act as passed provided for the election of delegates on February 4 and the convocation of the convention on February 13.[72]

The appeals in the campaign which followed ran according to the usual pattern. The outcome was even more favorable to Union than had been predicted. The secessionists elected only 30 out of 152 delegates, and out of 145,697 votes only 45,161 were cast in opposition to referring the convention's action to the people. With this backing the great Peace Conference in Washington which the

[70] Shanks, *Secession Movement in Virginia*, 142–44; Richmond *Daily Dispatch*, January 8, 1861.

[71] Richmond *Enquirer*, January 21, 1861; Virginia *Acts*, 1861, extra sess., 337–39.

[72] Richmond *Whig*, January 4, 1861; Richmond *Examiner*, January 5, 1861; Virginia *Acts*, 1861, pp. 24–26.

Virginia call had brought into being, and to which all the other Border States had given enthusiastic support, began its efforts on February 4.[73]

Like all other efforts at securing Republican co-operation for compromise, it was to fail. The very effort at avoiding strife was interpreted in the North as a sign of weakness. The recent elections in Virginia and Tennessee had been widely hailed as "Union" victories, and as indicating that firmness was all that was required. Many Northern delegations had, therefore, come to Washington under instructions that would prevent concessions or for the purpose of securing an adjournment until the Republicans were well established in control of the government. Some even charged that, with the exception of Rhode Island, the New England delegations had come to make certain that the convention would fail.

The seceding Southern states sent no delegates; neither did Texas or Arkansas. Michigan, Wisconsin, Minnesota, Oregon, and California were not represented. Combined with the fact that any action taken would have to be approved by the legislatures in many states, this robbed the convention of needed authority from the very beginning. Sharp disagreement on measures added to its troubles. Proposed Constitutional amendments touching slavery in the territories, fugitive slaves, and guarantees to the Southern states met bitter opposition and as submitted to Congress received scant attention.

The conference had failed—failed largely because the Republicans were determined to make no concessions. Perhaps they could not do so and hope to retain anything of party unity. Lincoln had already stated "that no good would come" of the conference. He had understood correctly. The delegates would return home as John Tyler said, with "a poor rickety, and disconnected affair, not worthy of your acceptance." [74]

Many Southerners had raised the question of what lay beyond separate state secession from the Union. Most of them seemed to

---

[73] Shanks, *Secession Movement in Virginia*, 153.

[74] Of the Peace Conference Potter, *Lincoln and His Party in the Secession Crisis*, 307, says: "The activities of the Peace Convention were so entirely ineffectual that it is useless to discuss them here." See also Dumond, *Secession Movement*, 239–65; Shanks, *Secession Movement in Virginia*, 170–72; Richmond *Examiner*, March 1, 1861.

take it for granted that some kind of new central government would
be formed to take the place of the old. The idea of Southern nationality was present in the radical's promise of a glorious future
as well as in the conservative's constant demand for co-operation.
The sending of commissioners from state to state and the demand
for Southern conventions revealed the need as well as the feeling
of unity, and the threat of civil war reinforced both. Actual steps
toward the formation of the new confederacy, therefore, appropri-
ately began at the South Carolina seceding convention when it
voted to invite the other states to send deputies to a conference
and authorized commissioners to carry the invitation and to encourage secession. These agents decided on Montgomery, Alabama,
as the place of meeting and February 4, 1861, as the date. This, it
will be noticed, was the date set also for Virginia's Peace Conference in Washington. The commissioners did their work well, and
after some hesitation on the part of Mississippi, all agreed to the
plan.[75]

The delegates chosen by the six seceding states—Texas had not
yet passed her ordinance—were a good cross section of the South.
Some, like those in the Georgia group, were national figures; others
were just local politicians. They were not quite certain when they
reached the little Alabama capital whether they had come to construct some kind of makeshift government or a more permanent
one. They were, however, experienced politicians and, like most
Southerners, were well versed in political theory and practice. Besides, they had never asked for anything but the United States Constitution "properly interpreted" and "strictly obeyed."

With all the zeal of "founding fathers" they settled down at their
task in the proud little city on the banks of the muddy Alabama.
It could boast only eight thousand inhabitants; its streets were un-
paved and its hotel accommodations inadequate. But its homes were
spacious, its gardens well up to the high Southern standard, and its
stores, warehouses, and churches things to boast about. Its river
trade was brisk, and Charles Pollard was making it something of

[75] Armand J. Gerson, "Inception of the Montgomery Convention," in American
Historical Association, *Annual Report*, 1910 (Washington, 1912), 179–87; *Journal of
the Convention of the People of South Carolina, Held in 1860, 1861 and 1862*, pp.
185–90, 349–53; *Journal of the* [Mississippi] *State Convention* (Jackson, 1861), 30–
35, 45–50.

a railroad center. At least its new capitol up on the hill with its six great pillars and its gleaming dome was worthy of being the cradle of a new nation.[76]

Cobb of Georgia was made president, and Stephens of the same state was appointed chairman of the committee on rules. The unit rule for voting was adopted, and then the Georgia suggestion of framing a provisional government and at the same time assuming the functions of a legislative body was approved. The plan was drastic, but the need was great. The matter of time was more important than a few details.

This much agreed upon, the convention then appointed a committee of two from each state to draft the provisional frame of government. The task was not too difficult, for the idea of adopting the Federal Constitution with only such changes as time and Southern experiences had shown desirable was widely accepted. Consequently, agreement was early reached with surprisingly few alterations in the original document. Interestingly enough, the slave trade was forbidden and Congress given the power to prohibit the importation of slaves from non-Confederation states; Congress was forbidden to appropriate money except at the request and estimate of the President or a Cabinet member, and the President might veto items in such appropriations. Then to meet the immediate situation, the President and Vice-President were to be chosen by the convention, which, in turn, would become a unicameral provisional Congress. The Supreme Court was to be composed of the district judges, and the provisional system was to last for but one year.[77]

To make such slight changes in a frame of government that many a Southerner in recent weeks had called the best ever designed by man, took little time and the convention accepted the work after one day's discussion. The really important task was to elect a president and vice-president. This problem was more difficult. If leadership in the moves that had brought the states to this point were to have force, Rhett or Yancey deserved consideration. Few, however, gave them serious thought. What the new nation in the mak-

[76] Boyd, *Alabama in the Fifties*, 84–85, 91–95, 159.

[77] Stephens, *Constitutional View of the Late War Between the States*, II, 324–33; Cobb to Mrs. Cobb, February 3, 6, 1861, in Phillips (ed.), *Correspondence of Toombs, Stephens, and Cobb*, 536–37; Nichols, *Disruption of American Democracy*, 465–71; Charleston *Mercury*, February 6, 1861.

ing needed was not emotional drive, but sound, solid, conservative leadership. The Border States must be attracted; the respect of Northern and European peoples must be gained. Men of the quality sent from Georgia were needed. Some talked of Cobb; some favored Stephens; others preferred Toombs, who straightway weakened his chances by excessive drinking. Here the influence of outsiders in Washington and the Border States entered, and the name of Jefferson Davis began to be mentioned with increasing favor. The usual shifting of preferences and behind-the-scenes bargaining soon evolved the ticket of Davis for President and Stephens for Vice-President, and the convention gave its approval. The Confederate States of America had been successfully launched and was ready to handle domestic affairs and diplomatic problems with such foreign nations as the United States of America.[78]

The success achieved at Montgomery contrasted sharply with the failure of the Peace Conference in Washington, and the Border States could not miss the point. They would soon have to make a decision. More and more it seemed to be a choice between "submission" and "secession." Lincoln had given no new assurances; Douglas and Crittenden and Virginia were getting nowhere. Discouragement if nothing else was playing into the hands of their minorities. Some talked of a Border State confederacy that would stand between North and South; plans were being laid for another conference in Kentucky in May. Yet if things went on as they were going someone was bound to make the decision for them. South Carolina was pressing for the surrender of Fort Sumter, and plans for its relief and promises for its surrender were being made by responsible and irresponsible parties in the government.[79]

And so March 4 came and with it Lincoln's inaugural. Read from different angles, it said different things, and the Border States learned little to help them solve their problems. Lincoln's handling

[78] Jefferson Davis, *The Rise and Fall of the Confederate Government* (New York, 1881), I, 640, Appendix K, for Constitution of the Confederacy.

[79] Charles W. Ramsdell, "Lincoln and Fort Sumter," in *Journal of Southern History*, III (1937), 259–88; Richmond *Enquirer*, February 26, 1861. For statement of S. M. Moore in Virginia Convention favoring a Border State confederacy and refusal to favor any confederacy permitting the slave trade, see Shanks, *Secession Movement in Virginia*, 163–64; for Seward's conversations with James Barbour, see Nicolay and Hay, *Abraham Lincoln*, II, 31–32.

of Sumter and his dealings with the agents sent from Virginia and the Confederacy did, however, begin to clear the air.[80] The day of drift was ended. Decisions were being made at last. Regardless of who was at fault in the steps that led to the firing on Fort Sumter that fateful April morning, the effect was to force a decision from the slaveholding states that had remained in the Union. Lincoln's call for troops to subdue South Carolina's "rebellion" required the decision that the borderland had until now refused to make. The very bitterness with which it was made revealed the strength of ties both with the Union and with Southern values. Robert E. Lee, pacing the floor at Arlington in anguish, Wyndham Robertson, tossing on his sleepless bed while the youth of Virginia celebrated, Jonathan Worth, at his desk in North Carolina, dipping his pen in gall against those who had betrayed his hopes, were only isolated examples of disillusioned Union lovers who were being swept into revolution. One by one the governors of Virginia, North Carolina, Tennessee, and Arkansas refused the call for troops, and their conventions stepped across the secession line to join the Confederacy. Maryland, Kentucky, and Missouri paid the penalty of a literal "brothers' war" by divisions that ran too deep for conclusive measures.

Southern nationalism, long in the making, had become a reality —or was it a reality? Majorities had not always made decisions, and many decisions had not been made at all; men had been pushed into position by forces over which they had no control. At any rate, blood was being spilled, and that required action, not thought.

---

[80] On the conference between John B. Baldwin and Lincoln, held at Lincoln's request, see Shanks, *Secession Movement in Virginia,* 192–95.

CHAPTER XIV

SOME GENERALIZATIONS

THE secession of the Southern states and Lincoln's call for troops to crush "rebellion" completed the breakdown of the democratic process. Men ceased to tolerate differences, to discuss their problems, and to compromise their clashes. The rule of the majority was no longer accepted. Bullets took the place of ballots; soldiers, the place of statesmen.

The immediate occasion for Southern withdrawal from the Union had been the election of a President by the Republican party and his refusal to recognize the right of secession or to yield Federal property within the seceding states. These matters, however, were only the final stages in a situation that had long been developing. Back of present actions lay fears, distrust, hatred, jealousy, values, and interests. Southerners were acting because of an accumulation of things, not just from some immediate happening. They desired the breakup of the Union, or accepted it, because they had come to feel that such a step was necessary for the preservation of their property, their self-respect, their rights, and the regard of their neighbors. Lincoln's election signified the final reduction of the South to the status of a permanent minority, subject, as they thought, to the will of a numerical majority whose purpose was the alteration of their social structure. The alternatives were submission or secession.

Lincoln's attitude and actions were also the product of certain great changes that were gradually transforming his part of the nation. A new interdependent age was dawning there—an age in which national unity was essential to social-economic welfare and in which the enslavement of human beings could not co-exist with the labor requirements of free enterprise or the ethical standards of a competitive society. For the realization of the American democratic ideals, the Union had to be preserved, and slavery had to be put on the road to ultimate extinction. There was no other choice.

Few men in either North or South, however, could have given a complete and correct reason for their immediate feelings and actions. Few were certain, until events pushed them into positions, as to exactly what they thought or what they were willing to do. The few who did know, or at least thought they did, were thus enabled to create situations in which action, not thinking, was required. Then events took charge, and individual wills counted for little.

The quarrel between the sections had developed largely around slavery—slavery as a thing in itself and then as a symbol of all differences and conflicts. As William H. Seward said: "Every question, political, civil, or ecclesiastical, however foreign to the subject of slavery, brings up slavery as an incident, and the incident supplants the principal question. We hear of nothing but slavery, and we can talk of nothing but slavery."

This was a situation that had developed largely in the lifetime of the last generation. At an earlier time slavery had existed in the North as well as in the South, and only a few groups, such as the Quakers, had offered solid resistance. Most of these groups, as a matter of fact, had been in the South. Then with the great changes which came with commerce and industry to the North and with cotton to the South, slavery gradually disappeared in the one, as it had earlier done across the Atlantic, but gained added strength in the other. Slavery thus became a Southern institution, and that section gained the dubious distinction of being one of the last spots in the whole western world where the institution kept a foothold.

Then in the 1830's there had come great changes. Whether or not the powerful democratic-humanitarian impulses that had already swept Europe and which now burned through the northeastern corner of the United States were the product of the Industrial Revolution does not matter. The important thing is that in the years from 1830 to 1860 there developed, in that part of the nation where factories and great merchants dominated, an intense antislavery sentiment that was soon as localized as slavery itself. It was part of a movement that aimed at creating a genuine democracy and a working Christianity in the nation. It took firm hold in evangelical churches and enlisted heavy support from the clergy. It thus had a moral quality and one that might also become political.

The great improvements in the means of communication, represented by the steam press, the telegraph, and the railroads, now made possible a degree of organization for propaganda and action in reform that had never before existed. Local, state, and national efforts were now possible through the spoken and printed word. Reforming could become a profession.

All this, coming as it did at a time when sectional rivalry over tariff, land, and internal-improvement policies was becoming intense, produced a movement of crusading proportions in one corner of the nation aimed at an evil existing in another corner. Interests and morals thus combined to create an emotional drive against slavery more violent and unrelenting than it had ever faced before.

For the South this meant a blow at an economic interest to be measured in millions of dollars. It threatened the destruction of a laboring system employed on the section's largest and most efficient economic units, and the crippling of an industry that had expanded widely to meet the needs of hungry machines both in Europe and in the United States. It promised to force a race question upon a people whose social philosophy, based on inherited European patterns, had long accepted social stratification as justified and productive of high values. It endangered the whole social structure in which the lives of two races were so hopelessly entwined that only chaos and ruin could follow quick changes.

The threat was bad enough. The inferences and open charges that went with it were even worse. Excited reformers, Southerners charged, pictured things not as they were but as "twisted minds" imagined them to be under what they believed was open wickedness. They imputed bad motives. They talked of sin and sinners to a people who made an unusually ardent profession of religion. They called them unpatriotic, a people who were holding the nation back, and denied them rights that the Constitution had guaranteed. In the end, they refused them an equal share in the territories and thus magnified an already growing inequality in political strength. The threats of permanent colonial status and of political impotency were thus added to distortion. The South was no longer an equal partner and her way of life was threatened not only by superior numbers but by a steady encroachment on her legal defenses. The nation was undergoing consolidation, regardless of the Constitution. It would henceforth be ruled by a numerical majority that lived in one section and represented a set of social-economic values completely at variance with all that the South now held. And what was just as offensive, it was all being done in the name of "right" and "manifest destiny."

Against such dangers, real and apprehended, Southern defenses had steadily weakened. The effort to keep antislavery out of Congress and out of politics had failed. Friends like Stephen A. Douglas had given way; the Whig party had split and died over the issue; and then the last political stronghold, the Democracy, had fallen. Only the Constitution promised protection, but now even politicians were talking of a "higher law" that rendered the Constitution worthless. Where once only the "fanatic" denounced slavery as an evil, now it seemed, as one editor said, that the whole western world was against it. The South was no longer respected. Men pitied her and her misfortune. To economic and political inferiority was added the charge of immorality and social backwardness.

Such a situation produced not only fear but resentment as well. Men talked of the "insults . . . deliberately tendered our people." Judah P. Benjamin declared that it was not so much what the Republicans and Abolitionists had done or might do, as "the things they said." It was the assumption made by that "pestiferous breed" —the "fools and knaves of New England"—that "the Earth belongs to the Saints and they were the Saints of the Lord," that rankled. There was sarcasm and anger as well as resentment and fear in Jefferson Davis' remarks to a New York audience: "You have among you politicians of a philosophic turn who preach a high morality; a system of which they are the discoverers. . . . They say, it is true that the Constitution dictates this, the Bible inculcates that; but there is a higher law than these, and they call upon you to obey that higher law of which they are the inspired givers. Men who are *traitors* to the compact of their fathers—*men who have perjured the oaths they have themselves taken* . . . these are the moral law-givers who proclaim a higher law than the Bible, the Constitution, and the laws of the land. . . . *These higher law preachers should be tarred and feathered, and whipped by those*

394

they have thus instigated. . . . The man who . . . preaches treason to the Constitution and the dictates of all human society, is a fit object for a Lynch law that would be higher than any he could urge."

The old friendship between the sections was ending. Enmity was taking its place. "We are enemies as much as if we were hostile States," declared Alfred Iverson of Georgia. "I believe that the northern people hate the South worse than even the English people hated France; and I can tell my brethren over there that there is no love lost upon the part of the South."

To make matters worse, Southern writers had woven a defense of Southern society, based on slavery, that found authority in the Bible, in history, and in science. It had at length become an assertion of the superiority of Southern ways and institutions. The South was exempt from labor troubles, depressions, and class struggles. And the reason for this "exemption" was that "the bondsmen, as a lower class, as the substratum of society, constitute[d] an always reliable, never-wavering foundation, whereon the social fabric rest[ed] securely rooted and grounded in stability, and entirely beyond the reach of agitation by such causes as shake other communities to their center." The South had no reason to apologize. Her institutions did not breed crackpots and unrest. Her people were not always interfering with the affairs of others. The condition of her slaves, compared to that of free Northern laborers, did not call for a guilty conscience.

Thus, at the North, slavery justified the appeal to a "higher law" than that which protected slavery and, at the South, it became the one and only reason for the values in Southern life. To the one it provided the clues to Southern resistance to eastern tariffs, western homesteads, and internal improvements, and to the free admission of foreign immigrants. To the other it explained the stable society which escaped isms and disorders and developed personal integrity in men and refinement in women. In fact, slavery had gradually become the symbol of all the differences and all the conflicts between the sections. It had taken on virtues and vices none of which were its own. It was bearing a nation's unrest.

How tangled men's thinking had become can be seen in the statements of the good Dr. James H. Thornwell when he attempted to explain the difficulty: "The real cause of the intense excitement of the South," he said in 1861, ". . . is the profound conviction that the Constitution, in its relation to slavery, has been virtually repealed; that the Government has assumed a new and dangerous attitude upon this subject; that we have, in short, new terms of union submitted to our acceptance or rejection." Yet he had just announced that the South was fighting to preserve a government that acknowledged God, that reverenced right, and that made the law supreme. That it was, in fact, fighting for "the salvation of the whole continent," fighting against "despotism" and for "the hopes of mankind." Theodore Parker himself could not have done better.

It was in fact this reduction of the struggle to the simple terms of "right" versus "rights" that placed issues beyond the abilities of the democratic process and rendered the great masses of men, North and South, helpless before the drift into war. Lincoln had revealed the "irrepressible" character of the conflict in Northern eyes when he wrote Alexander H. Stephens giving assurance that he would not "directly or indirectly, interfere with the slaves" of the South, but adding: "I suppose, however, this does not meet the case. You think slavery is *right* and ought to be extended, while we think it *wrong* and ought to be restricted. That I suppose is the rub. It certainly is the only substantial difference between us."

Stephens, in turn, revealed its "irrepressible" character in Southern eyes by insisting on the Constitutional right of slavery to exist and expand without regard to private opinions. He would go down with the Constitution. He would yield the Union before he would yield his section's rights.

Under such conditions, could the break have been avoided? Not unless either the North or the South had been willing to yield its position on an issue that involved the matters of "right" and "rights" and the fundamental structure of society.

If the South had not considered free access to the territories, with slaves, a Constitutional and moral right; had been willing to see slavery put on the road to ultimate extinction because it was a "sin"; and had accepted willingly the status of a political minority and an economic colony, that would have made an end to conflict. Since Southerners would ultimately do that after bloody defeat, why did they not do it in 1861? A new day was dawning, the day of financial-industrial domination. Why could they not see that slavery had no place in such an order and that agricultural groups could not hope to control its course?

Or why did the North not leave slavery alone and live up to the Constitution in regard to it? Why could Northerners not agree that Negro slaves were property and, as such, might enter the territories and have protection? If they had done so, a civil war might have been avoided and all the ills of reconstruction prevented. Furthermore, slavery may have already reached its limits. Some have so argued. Perhaps if passions had not been stirred, slavery might have been viewed, even in the South, for what it was—a rather inefficient, expensive system—and not have been exalted into the cornerstone of a superior civilization. Then why could the North not wait and let nature solve the problems?

The answers to these questions are simple. Neither the North nor the South could yield its position because *slavery had come to symbolize values in each of their social-economic structures for which men fight and die but which they do not give up or compromise.* These values had been emphasized and reinforced by two decades of emotional strife, name-calling, and self-justification. Right and wrong, justice and injustice were in conflict. The destiny of mankind was at stake.

These larger notions of the nature of the sectional struggle had emerged out of the conflicts over concrete issues such as expansion, lands, and tariffs. A power struggle had developed which encouraged the glorification of selfish and unselfish attitudes toward positions and gradually lifted them into the defense of principles. Abstractions had become more important than concrete things, and symbols had been substituted for them. The concrete issues had remained, but more and more they represented some higher abstraction, some principle which could not be yielded.

The North, throughout the period, was vaguely conscious of the necessity for nationalism in an age of growing interdependence. It was equally conscious of the fact that an agricultural interest, restricted by slavery to certain economic and political policies, was hindering the fullest development of the new financial-industrial capitalism which was sweeping the whole western world. It was more and more certain that slavery had no place in a nation that professed Christianity and democracy. Progress was being checked by slavery. The South was attempting to make the nation stand still. It had launched "a deliberate sectional movement . . . for political power," charged Benjamin Wade. It was attempting to control the nation's policies in the interest of slavery and backwardness. "If we are to have . . . [nothing but] conservative legislation," cried Joshua Giddings, "let us tear down the telegraphic wires, break up our galvanic batteries, and imprison Morse, and stop all agitation upon the subject of your 'magnetic railroads of thought.' Lay up your steamboats, place fetters upon your locomotives, convert your railroads into cultivated fields, and erase the name of Fulton from our history. Go to yonder institute; drive Page from his laboratory, break in pieces his galvanic engines, and unchain the imprisoned lightning which is there pent up; then pass an act of Congress prohibiting all agitation on these subjects." That was the only way, for freedom and progress went together.

Such attitudes lifted the economic programs and policies of the North to high moral levels and linked them with the nation's manifest destiny. They became a part of the great fight for human rights. The financial and industrial policies of the Northeast and those of the growing, expanding Northwest were planks in freedom's platform. "Our tariff," Giddings had said, "is as much an anti-slavery measure as the rejection of Texas. So is the subject of internal improvements and the distribution of the proceeds of the public lands." From this it was only a step to Lincoln's declaration that the conflict between North and South was "part of the eternal conflict between right and wrong."

Under such circumstances, tolerance, compromise, or even rational discussion was soon out of the question. Men who attempted to keep the democratic process going were called "doughfaces" and "traitors." Opponents rapidly became enemies. Only force could deal with problems.

The South even more quickly followed the same pattern. She had possessed a Calhoun to whom principles and abstractions, as he told Benton, made up the most of life. He had quickly supplied the doctrines—Constitutional and ethical—by which a minority, possessing slaves, might be protected. In his hands problems never dropped to the level of interests; they always had to do with clearly demonstrable rights. He had no compromises to offer. He never asked more or less than "justice." And to the defense of the system which he was so ably supporting came Fitzhugh, Holmes, Nott, and others, to prove its superiority, its tie with true progress. The "stable society" was as worthy of Southern devotion as was "progress" at the North.

Furthermore, the growing, expanding character of the young nation would not allow these basic differences and the conflicts they produced to remain long quiescent. Crowding, pressing events, one after the other, brought strife and added to the mounting belief that principles, not just mundane interests, were at stake. Tempers grew shorter; distrust deepened. Reactions became stereotyped and lost their true relation to events. The institutions and agencies by which the nation governed itself and kept things moving began to weaken. Parties split and went to pieces; legislative bodies ceased to function. Men unfit for the political game of give and take came into office, and a feeling of anger or helplessness spread across the nation. Men were discovering that the democratic process does not work when moral issues and those dealing with the fundamental structure of society are crowded forward. Edward Everett saw it this way in January, 1861: "Mr. Andrews chosen Governor of Massachusetts last November was a politician known only as an extreme abolitionist. He was brought forward mainly for having presided at the John Brown meeting. Is it to be wondered at, that things like this influenced the South? . . . It will be found out too late, I fear, that a confederacy of States cannot subsist if parties are made to turn upon irritating moral questions, which divided its members geographically." A short time afterward he added this comment: "There is absolutely no material interest at stake; but the politicians each side of the line, for selfish purposes, will keep up the war on abstractions."

The old notion that a few aggressive leaders tricked the South into secession or that Southerners felt a loyalty only to their states does not stand up as explanation for the Southern action in 1860–1861. True, a few men early reached the conclusion that the South must inevitably be reduced to an inferior place in national life if matters went on as they were going. They did preach secession and work for it, but they never led until the very end, when the masses had become numb and helpless before the onrush of events. There were far more Southerners who loved the nation and gloried in its achievements but who saw their section losing its comparative strength, felt the sting of Northern charges, true and false, and feared the growing tendency to make slavery and its restriction the basis for denying their section an equality or a chance for equality in national life. They were as much at fault in permitting slavery to be magnified into the "cornerstone of Southern society" as were the abolitionists, but to them the consequences were, as one of them said, "a daily crucifixion" on the race question. This great body of Southerners gradually accepted secession as the only way out. Seemingly the radical element in the North was gaining control. The Western alliance was gone. The Republican party was gaining strength. The spirit of tolerance and co-operation was ending. It was a case of submission or secession, and they made their choice. The rest were dragged into secession. The pressure of public opinion, the loss of hope because of the actions of Northern conservatives, the growing stubbornness and open hostility of increasing numbers at the North, the breakup of the Democratic party and Lincoln's election—these things forced conservative men to choose between the North, which was seemingly indifferent, and the South, of which they were a part in many ways. They made their choice in sorrow that easily turned to bitterness and hatred. They understood it to be a case of "fighting or running."

Was the war inevitable? That depends on the time of which one is speaking, and on whether one believes that democracy ought to be able to solve its problems peacefully. Was the cause of strife simply and solely Negro slavery? That depends on whether one is talking about the institution as a more or less decadent labor system or as the exaggerated symbol of all Southern ways and interests and of all Northern aggression. Both had a part, but not an equal part or the same kind, in producing conflict.

Wars do not have simple causes, and differences have to be emotionalized before they get beyond the ability of the democratic process to handle them. Times also change, and the modern world, in 1860, was crowding into the United States with values all its own. No one can question the fact that the kind of "slavery" the South had and the agricultural values it held were not those which the new age demanded. Perhaps the American tragedy lies in the way in which attitudes were allowed to develop and in the fearful cost which the nation paid to get itself into the modern world.

CRITICAL ESSAY ON AUTHORITIES

SINCE the period from 1848 to 1861 is one in which a civil war was in the making, the development of attitudes on issues is the important thing. Materials for an understanding of such a period must, therefore, come largely from the personal papers of individuals, from their biographies, and from contemporary newspapers. The controversial nature of the period gives added importance to the monograph, which treats in detail some particular phase of developments or presents a definite point of view. Recent changes in emphasis and the revision of old points of view stress the significance of shorter articles appearing in scholarly periodicals.

Materials of the kind mentioned are abundant but rather widely scattered. The most important manuscript collections are to be found in the Library of Congress, the Southern Collection at the University of North Carolina, the university libraries of Duke, Louisiana, and Texas, and in the various university and state historical society collections. These institutions also contain newspaper files, but they must also be sought in county courthouses, local libraries, and in the plants of present-day publishing concerns. Official documents often remain in state archives, and much valuable material of different kinds is still held in private hands.

MANUSCRIPTS

The quantity of manuscript material available for scholarly use has increased enormously during the past generation. Systematic efforts have been made in nearly every Southern state to gather and preserve the letters both of prominent and of obscure persons. The scholar's problem is now more one of selection than one of searching. Yet in the attempt to follow the development of public opinion, abundance has had its advantages. Some collections have yielded much; some, little that would justify even a footnote. The majority, however, have helped to confirm or disprove some opinion and to show the danger of dogmatic assertions and sweeping statements. Letters from the South in the

Stephen A. Douglas Papers at the University of Chicago give one point of view, favorable or critical; those in the Alexander H. Stephens Papers at the Library of Congress and at Manhattanville College of the Sacred Heart, New York, quite another. The Diary of Edmund Ruffin, Library of Congress, and many of the letters in the William Porcher Miles Papers, University of North Carolina, present a radical opinion to be contrasted with that in the Benjamin F. Perry Papers, Alabama State Department of Archives and History, or the immensely valuable John J. Crittenden Papers in the Library of Congress. The same contrast appears in the papers of Wyndham Robertson (a Virginia Whig) at the University of Chicago and those of Whitemarsh B. Seabrook (the Democratic governor of South Carolina) in the Library of Congress. It is interesting to follow the changing opinion from radical to semiconservative in the James H. Hammond Papers at the Library of Congress, the University of South Carolina, and the University of North Carolina; and to wavering, uncertain attitudes revealed in the letters of Governor Thomas O. Moore of Louisiana, in private possession. The Francis Lieber Papers in the Huntington Library show what an outsider residing in the South thought about things, and the William A. Graham Papers in the North Carolina Historical Commission, the John Bell Papers in the Library of Congress, and the Edward Stanly Papers at the University of North Carolina give the pathetic story of loyal men forced into secession.

These are but a few samples from dozens of collections that are reluctantly singled out. One feels guilty for not mentioning the delightful bits in the papers of the Pettigrew family at the University of North Carolina, of Clement C. Clay at Duke University, and of Benjamin L. C. Wailes, also at Duke University, that have yielded so much.

A few collections of value to the specialist are: the L. O'B. Branch Papers, some of which are at Duke University and some at the University of North Carolina; the Lawrence Keitt Papers and the John A. Bryan Papers at Duke University; the William T. Lenoir Papers and the Christopher G. Memminger Papers at the University of North Carolina; the Calvin H. Wiley Papers at the North Carolina Historical Commission; the Martin Van Buren Papers, the Francis Preston Blair Papers, the Giddings-Julian Papers, the George F. Holmes Papers, the John Floyd Papers, and the Alexander H. H. Stuart Papers at the Library of Congress; and the James D. Davidson Papers in the McCormick Collection at the State Historical Society of Wisconsin, Madison.

OFFICIAL DOCUMENTS

The official documents needed for a study of this period call for little comment. They are the obvious ones: The *Congressional Globe*, 1833–1873, 46 vols. (Washington, 1834–1873); House, Senate, and Executive documents of various kinds; the journals of the different state seceding conventions, such as *Journal of the Convention of the People of North Carolina, Held on the 20th Day of May, A. D. 1861* (Raleigh, 1862); and the reports of debates and proceedings of various kinds of Southern conventions. *A Report of the Debates and Proceedings in the Secret Sessions of the Conference Convention . . . Held at Washington D.C. in February, A. D. 1861* (New York, 1864), or the *Proceedings of the Southern and Western Commercial Convention at Memphis, Tennessee* (New Orleans, 1853), will serve to illustrate. In this connection Herman V. Ames, *State Documents on Federal Relations: The States and the United States* (Philadelphia, 1906), is always serviceable.

The journals of the state conventions held in 1860 and 1861 are important for showing the conflict between radicals and conservatives and the reasons given for the action taken. For this purpose, the *Journal of the Public Proceedings of the Convention of the People of South Carolina, Held 1860–'61. Together with the Ordinances Adopted* (Charleston, 1860), and the *Journal of the Acts and Proceedings of a general Convention of the State of Virginia, assembled at Richmond, on the thirteenth day of February, 1861* (Richmond, 1861), are particularly interesting. Now and then the proceedings of a political convention is of importance. The *Official Proceedings of the Democratic National Convention, Held in 1860, at Charleston and Baltimore* (Cleveland, 1860), and the *Proceedings of the Democratic State Convention* [of Alabama] *held in the City of Montgomery, commencing Wednesday, January 11, 1860* (Montgomery, 1860), are cases in point because of their relations to the events which followed. The *Resolutions and address, adopted by the Southern convention. Held at Nashville, Tennessee, June 3d to 12th inclusive, in the Year 1850* (Nashville, 1850), together with the *Condensed proceedings of the Southern convention, held at Nashville, Tennessee, June, 1850* (Jackson, Miss., 1850), are important documents for that episode. The *Minutes and Proceedings of the Memphis Convention, assembled Oct. 23, 1849* (Memphis, 1850), combined with John C. Calhoun's report of the special committee on "the memorial of the Memphis Convention," in *Senate Documents,* 29 Cong., 1 Sess., No. 410 (Washington, 1846), are the most valuable sources for this meeting. Murat Halstead, *Caucuses of 1860. A History of the National Political Conventions of the Current Presidential Campaign* (Columbus, 1860), is a handy aid for that campaign.

PUBLISHED LETTERS AND PAPERS

Fortunately for those who cannot travel from Washington to Texas in search of materials, much of a personal type is in print. Ulrich B. Phillips (ed.), *The Correspondence of Robert Toombs, Alexander H. Stephens, and Howell Cobb,* in American Historical Association, *Annual Report,* 1911, II (Washington, 1913), contains a goodly collection of letters to and from these Georgia statesmen. In the same category belong Charles H. Ambler (ed.), *The Correspondence of Robert M. T. Hunter, ibid.,* 1916, II (Washington, 1918); J. Franklin Jameson (ed.), *Correspondence of John C. Calhoun, ibid.,* 1899, II (Washington, 1900); and Chauncey S. Boucher and Robert P. Brooks (eds.), *Correspondence Addressed to John C. Calhoun, 1837–1849, ibid.,* 1929 (Washington, 1930). These with Richard K. Crallé (ed.), *The Works of John C. Calhoun,* 6 vols. (New York, 1851–1856), offer a rather well-rounded body of material dealing with the grim old South Carolinian. Dunbar Rowland edited *Jefferson Davis, Constitutionalist, His Letters, Papers and Speeches,* 10 vols. (Jackson, Miss., 1923).

Even more valuable is Milo M. Quaife (ed.), *The Diary of James K. Polk,* 4 vols. (Chicago, 1910). Its day-by-day entries afford intimate glimpses at what was going on and, on more than one occasion, deal with friend and foe without gloves. The *Life and Correspondence of John A. Quitman,* 2 vols. (New York, 1860), by J. F. H. Claiborne, provides enough of correspondence to enable the scholar to draw his own conclusions, sometimes quite at variance with those of the author; and the letters in Benjamin M. Palmer, *The Life and Letters of James Henley Thornwell* (Richmond, 1875), tell much more about the man than the good clergyman intended. These, with personal letters scattered through such biographies as James D. Waddell (ed.), *Biographical Sketch of Linton Stephens . . . Containing a Selection of His Letters, Speeches, State Papers . . .* (Atlanta, 1877); M. W. Cluskey, *Speeches, Messages and other Writings of the Hon. Albert G. Brown* (Philadelphia, 1859); and Percy S. Flippin, *Herschel V. Johnson of Georgia, State Rights Unionist* (Richmond, 1931), enable those denied access to the originals to make use of source material. While not exactly to be classed with such works as listed above, Thomas Hart Benton, *Thirty Years' View; or, A History of the Working of the American Government for Thirty Years, from 1820 to 1850,* 2 vols. (New York, 1854–1856), has a contemporary quality and contains enough of quotation to permit its inclusion here or to be given a classification all its own. It has much of the character of the "Old Bison" in it that is to be found nowhere else. Howard K. Beale (ed.), *The Diary of Edward Bates, 1859–1866,* in American Historical Association, *Annual Report,* 1930, IV (Washington, 1933), is valuable for the light it throws on both local and national affairs. *The Diary and Correspondence of Salmon P. Chase, ibid.,* 1902, II (Washington, 1903), while that of a Northern man, is valuable for revealing outside forces which greatly affected Southern opinion.

CONTEMPORARY BOOKS AND PAMPHLETS

The materials in this category are so abundant that only a few of the most important items can be mentioned. Contemporary works usually had something to do with slavery and the sectional struggle. One of the tragedies of the South was that most of her talents, literary as well as political, were ultimately drafted into this service. A public address or even a sermon that touched the question might be published and scattered in pamphlet form. The "Hon. John Townsend," for instance, spoke to a public meeting of the citizens of St. John's Colleton on the subject, *The South Alone, Should Govern the South. And African Slavery Should be Controlled by Those Only, who are Friendly to it* (Charleston, 1860). At the conclusion it was "Resolved, That Mr. Townsend be requested to have his address published in the public print." The result was a pamphlet issued as *Tract No. 1* in a series published by the Southern Rights Association to be "read" and sent "to your neighbor." *Tract No. 2,* by William D. Porter, was entitled *State Sovereignty and the Doctrine of Coercion . . . together with a Letter from Hon. J. K. Paulding,* [and] *The Right to Secede, by "States"* (Charleston, 1860). Others, with equally suggestive titles, flowed from the pens of such ardent Southerners as Edmund Ruffin, George Fitzhugh, and Thornton Stringfellow. All had the same purpose, with titles complete enough to make reading of the whole unnecessary. An excellent illustration is Stringfellow's *Slavery: Its Origin, Nature and History. Its Relations to Society, to Government, and to True Religion . . . to Human Happiness and Divine Glory. Considered in the Light of Bible Teachings, Moral Justice, and Political Wisdom* (Alexandria, 1860). Ruffin's three pamphlets, *The Political Economy of Slavery* (Washington, 1857), *Slavery and Free Labor Described and Compared* (Washington, 1860), and *African Colonization Unveiled* (Washington, 1859), not only were distributed by the Southern Rights Association but were sent out under the franking privilege of his Congressman as well.

The fast-day sermon of Reverend Benjamin M. Palmer, on *Slavery a Divine Trust, Duty of the South to Preserve and Perpetuate it* (New York, 1861), preached in the First Presbyterian Church of New Orleans, was also "requested and published." More than thirty thousand copies were distributed from one newspaper office alone. J. H. Thornton's sermon on *Our National Sins* (New York, 1861) met a like fate and perhaps deserved it from such blunt assertions as "slavery is a school of virtue," and "We do not hold our slaves in bondage from remorseless considerations of interest."

An Interesting and Important Correspondence between Opposition Members of the Legislature of Virginia and Hon. John Minor Botts, January 17, 1860 (Washington, 1860), gives the conservative view, as does the *Speech of Hon. A. H. Stephens, delivered in the Hall of the House of Representatives of Georgia, November 14, 1860* (Augusta, 1860), which in pamphlet form had a wide circulation.

Of the contemporary books Hinton R. Helper, *The Impending Crisis of the South: How to Meet It* (New York, 1857), received most attention. As the work of a Southern white, denouncing slavery, it was eagerly read and used in the North for political purposes and denounced as bitterly at the South. Its statistics, it must be said, were not always reliable nor its arguments sound. For propaganda purposes these things, however, were not necessary. George Fitzhugh, *Sociology for the South; or, The Failure of Free Society* (Richmond, 1854), and his *Cannibals All! or, Slaves Without Masters* (Richmond, 1857), had also a propaganda purpose lifting the proslavery argument to a new plane by comparing free and slave societies to the benefit of the latter. How widely either Helper or Fitzhugh was read in the South is a question. Their effects were probably greater on Northern thinking than on Southern. Thomas P. Kettell, *Southern Wealth and Northern Profits* (New York, 1860), which argued that the North was destroying its source of profits for a trivial pretense, came late but gave some aid to Southern opinion. A more pretentious work was that of Josiah C. Nott and George R. Gliddon, *Types of Mankind: or, Ethnological Researches* (Philadelphia, 1854). Its purpose was to refute the idea of a single creation and to place the Negro in a late and inferior one. It brought at least three answers from the clergy. Some significant essays of Chancellor William Harper, Governor James H. Hammond, William Gilmore Simms, and Professor Thomas R. Dew were brought together in a single volume called *The Pro-Slavery Argument* (Charleston, 1852), and in the same year John Fletcher published his *Studies on Slavery, in Easy Lessons* (Natchez, 1852), as a kind of high-water mark in Bible proof of

407

slavery's justification. The Reverend George D. Armstrong, *The Christian Doctrine of Slavery* (New York, 1857), and the Reverend Samuel Seabury, *American Slavery Distinguished from the Slavery of English Theorists, and Justified by the Law of Nature* (New York, 1861), are good examples of the many supports for slavery that the clergy of the South supplied.

Three answers to Harriet Beecher Stowe, *Uncle Tom's Cabin; or, Life among the Lowly* (Boston, 1852), will suffice: William L. G. Smith, *Life at the South: or, "Uncle Tom's Cabin" As It Is* (Buffalo, 1852); John W. Page, *Uncle Robin, in His Cabin in Virginia, and Tom without One in Boston* (Richmond, 1853); and *The Planter, or Thirteen Years in the South* (Philadelphia, 1853), by a Northern man (David Brown). Each gave a rosy picture of slavery to contrast with Mrs. Stowe's "distortion" and made an effort to point to Northern labor weaknesses. None of these or the dozen or so others that were written for the same purpose had any literary merit.

Daniel R. Hundley, *Social Relations in Our Southern States* (New York, 1860), is in something of a class by itself. It described Southern classes and clearly distinguished between the yeoman farmers and the "poor whites." Hundley found a "middle class" there and offered sharp correctives to the antislavery discussions. He was probably little read much before 1900.

NEWSPAPERS

Heavy reliance has been placed in this study on the newspaper. It was, throughout the period, both an expression and a molder of public opinion. It was, in almost all cases, a strictly party organ, either strongly Democratic or strongly Whig, American or Constitutional Union. It varied in quality with the editor, and its influence was usually confined to a neighborhood and only occasionally, as in the case of the Richmond *Enquirer* (1804–1877), the Augusta *Chronicle and Sentinel* (1785–), or the Charleston *Mercury* (1822–1868), did it reach a wider audience. Local papers, however, quoted heavily from each other, and something of party and sectional unity was thereby achieved. A good deal of independence, nevertheless, existed, and any wide reading of newspapers in different corners of the South will destroy the old idea that all Southerners agreed on all subjects.

On the Democratic side the Richmond *Enquirer*, edited by William Olds, was probably the most influential and most widely quoted paper in the South. It was not extreme, but gradually took a Southern rights position and in the end supported secession. The Charleston *Mercury*, edited by the Rhetts, was more extreme and in some ways more brilliant than the *Enquirer*. It was always well in advance in support of Southern rights. The Nashville *Union and American* (1835–1875), edited by Leon Trousdale and John C. Burch, and the Raleigh *Standard* (1834–1870), edited by William W. Holden, upheld the Democracy in their states and, in 1860, supported John C. Breckinridge. Holden, strangely enough, later became a conservative Union man. The New Orleans *Delta* (1845–1863), the Louisville *Courier* (1843–1868), and the Jackson *Mississippian* (1832–1865) were the most important Breckinridge supporters in their areas, while the Augusta *Constitutionalist* (1823–1877), the New Orleans *True Delta* (?–1866), the Mobile *Register* (1821–), and the Montgomery *Confederation* (1858?–1861) gave their support to Stephen A. Douglas. Of these, the Mobile *Register,* under John Forsyth, was decidedly the best edited and, in some ways, the equal of any paper in the South. A few of the lesser Democratic papers useful in this study were the Huntsville *Southern Advocate* (1825–), the Columbia *South Carolinian* (1849–1865), the Walhalla (S.C.) *Keowee Courier* (?), the Macon *Georgia Telegraph* (1826–1906), the Louisville *Democrat* (1843–1868), the Montgomery *Mail* (1854?–1871), the Jacksonville (Ala.) *Republican* (1837–1894), the Cahawba (Ala.) *Dallas Gazette* (1843–1859), the Wilmington *Journal* (1844–1895), and the Memphis *Enquirer* (1837–). There is, however, no particular reason for listing these over a dozen or more other files consulted.

The opposition press had a rather difficult time keeping its balance as the Whigs weakened, the Know-Nothings rose and declined, and the Constitutional Union movement came into being. Some shifted from one to the other in succession, and a few tried to assume an independent course. It was always necessary, however, to oppose the Democrats. In Richmond, the *Whig* (1824–1888) carried on the national-conservative traditions of John Hampden Pleasants, its founder, and in the secession period the *Examiner* vigorously joined it in opposing hasty action. North Carolina had the Raleigh *Register and North Carolina Gazette* (1799–), the Charlotte *North Carolina Whig* (1852–?), and the Fayetteville *Observer* (1851–1865). In Charleston, the *Courier* (1803–), still under Richard Yeadon, opposed the *Mercury* but drifted along with public opinion in defense of Southern rights and secession. Georgia had in the Augusta *Chronicle and Sentinel* one of the best papers in the section. Stanchly Whig in the beginning, it turned mildly Know-Nothing and then Constitutional Union in a bitter fight against disunion sentiment. In the end, however, like the other conservative papers, it gave up in despair and accepted secession. The Milledgeville

Southern Recorder (1819–1873), the Columbus *Enquirer* (1855–), and the Savannah *Republican* (1802–1873) followed a like course, while the Savannah *News* (1850–) considered itself independent at all times. New Orleans had three opposition papers that spoke kindly both of Douglas and of John Bell. The *Crescent* (1848–1869) , however, backed Douglas, and the *Bee* (1827–1917) and the *Picayune* (1837–1914) backed Bell. George Wilkins Kendall, of the *Picayune,* was considered one of the great editors of the day, but most of the editorials in the late period were from the pen of Alva M. Holbrook. All three papers were vigorous and well run and played no small part in keeping the city of New Orleans in a conservative mood.

The Mobile *Advertiser* (1823–1861) and the Montgomery *Journal* (1821–) were the most powerful Union papers in Alabama, with strong backing from the Montgomery *Post* (1860–1861) in the Constitutional Union period. The Vicksburg *Whig* (1839–1863) and the Natchez *Mississippi Free Trader* (1835–1861?) spoke for the conservatives in Mississippi, and William G. Brownlow's Knoxville *Whig* (1839–1883), the Nashville *Patriot* (1855–1862), and the Nashville *Republican Banner* (1837–1875) carried the Constitutional Union fight in Tennessee. To the north, in Kentucky, was the Louisville *Journal* (1830–1868) under the editorship of the talented George D. Prentice. An ardent supporter of Bell in 1860, he remained an unconditional unionist to the end. Strangely enough, he opposed the Washington Peace Conference but favored Kentucky neutrality so that she might serve as a mediator between the sections. To him, Kentucky constituted "the forlorn hope of the Union."

CONTEMPORARY PERIODICALS

Contemporary periodicals, especially *De Bow's Review* (New Orleans, 1846–1880), the *Southern Literary Messenger* (Richmond, 1834–1864), the *Southern Quarterly Review* (New Orleans, Charleston, 1842–1857), and *Russell's Magazine* (Charleston, 1857–1860), contain many articles dealing with local Southern problems and the sectional conflict. A significant article by Stephen A. Douglas, "Popular Sovereignty in the Territories," appeared in *Harper's New Monthly Magazine* (New York) , XIX (1859), 519–37. Now and then church publications such as the *Quarterly Review of the Methodist Episcopal Church, South* (Louisville, 1847–1850), or the *Southern Presbyterian Review* (Columbia, 1847–1908), are important not only because they throw light on church affairs but also because of articles revealing sectional attitudes. Agricultural periodicals are invaluable for securing a picture of practices and conditions in that field. The following were found of value: *American Farmer* (Baltimore, 1819–1897); the *Southern Planter* (Richmond, 1841–); the *Southern Cultivator* (Augusta, Athens, Atlanta, 1843–1935); and the *American Cotton Planter* (Montgomery, 1853–1856, combined with the *Soil of the South,* 1857–1861).

BIOGRAPHY

The important figures of this period have attracted competent biographers. For John C. Calhoun there is the older but still serviceable volume, *John C. Calhoun* (Philadelphia, 1908), by Gaillard Hunt; the well-written *John C. Calhoun, American Portrait* (Boston, 1950), by Margaret L. Coit; and the larger, more detailed study in three volumes by Charles M. Wiltse, the third of which, *John C. Calhoun, Sectionalist, 1840–1850* (Indianapolis, 1951), is of particular interest in these years. There are two excellent biographies of Stephen A. Douglas, both of which contain much period history as well as biography. The first is *Stephen A. Douglas; A Study in American Politics* (New York, 1908), by Allen Johnson; the second, *Eve of Conflict; Stephen A. Douglas and the Needless War* (New York, 1934), by George F. Milton. Both are more friendly to Douglas than earlier writers. Thomas Hart Benton has been less fortunate. William M. Meigs, *The Life of Thomas Hart Benton* (Philadelphia, 1904), is friendly but inadequate. A better balanced study is E. B. Smith, "Thomas Hart Benton, 1843–1850" (Ph.D. dissertation, University of Chicago, 1949). Glyndon G. Van Deusen has written the best of the recent biographies of Henry Clay. His *The Life of Henry Clay* (Boston, 1937) is scholarly and unusually well written. It treats the period as well as the man himself and as a result is in places quite general. George R. Poage, *Henry Clay and the Whig Party* (Chapel Hill, 1936), on the other hand, though limited in scope, is an unusually penetrating study of political events.

Mrs. Chapman Coleman, *The Life of John J. Crittenden, with Selections from his Correspondence and Speeches,* 2 vols. (Philadelphia, 1871), is serviceable largely because of the letters it contains and the fact that there is nothing else. A good biography of this important Whig is badly needed. Robert Toombs is well handled in Ulrich B. Phillips, *The Life of Robert Toombs* (New York, 1913), but much new material is now available and he, too, deserves to be restudied. His friend Alexander H. Stephens is the object of two valuable recent works. Rudolph R. Von Abele, *Alexander H. Stephens, A Biography* (New York, 1946), is an attempt to understand Stephens as a man, physically inferior, who tried to excel in other lines as compensation. The attempt is not entirely

411

successful but is, nevertheless, interesting. A far better biography is that by James Rabun, "Alexander H. Stephens, 1812-61" (Ph.D. dissertation, University of Chicago, 1948). It is a bit unfriendly to Stephens but soundly constructed.

The three good Southern Unionists, John Bell, Benjamin F. Perry, and Herschel V. Johnson, all have satisfactory biographies. Joseph H. Parks, *John Bell of Tennessee* (Baton Rouge, 1950), and Lillian A. Kibler, *Benjamin F. Perry, South Carolina Unionist* (Durham, 1946), are well above the average in soundness and presentation. Both rest on the use of abundant source materials, and both are written by authors who have a firm grasp of the period as well as of the personality. Percy S. Flippin, *Herschel V. Johnson of Georgia, State Rights Unionist* (Richmond, 1931), is not so well done. Johnson does not emerge as a clear-cut personality, and his contribution to his day is not well stated. Haywood J. Pearce, Jr., *Benjamin H. Hill, Secession and Reconstruction* (Chicago, 1928), is an inadequate biography of a badly underestimated Southern man.

Southern radicals, too, have had their dues. Laura A. White, *Robert Barnwell Rhett; Father of Secession* (New York, 1931), is a classic. Few figures of the period are so fairly handled or so soundly evaluated. John W. Du Bose, *The Life and Times of William Lowndes Yancey,* 2 vols. (New York, 1942), first published at Birmingham in 1892, is an older work, too friendly to Yancey and lacking in background. It is, however, serviceable because of the amount of source materials it contains. James B. Ranck, *Albert Gallatin Brown, Radical Southern Nationalist* (New York, 1937), and Avery Craven, *Edmund Ruffin, Southerner; A Study in Secession* (New York, 1932), deal with two other radicals in sympathetic fashion.

There is no outstanding biography of Jefferson Davis. William E. Dodd, *Jefferson Davis* (Philadelphia, 1907), is an early work by that writer which is scholarly enough but lacks distinction. H. J. Eckenrode, *Jefferson Davis, President of the South* (New York, 1923), written to support a Nordic thesis, is badly off balance. The two-volume work by Robert M. McElroy, *Jefferson Davis; The Unreal and the Real* (New York, 1937), is a more pretentious effort, but somehow it fails to catch the personality of the man or to penetrate the meaning of the events with which he was connected. Davis is still best found in his own writings and speeches.

Elizabeth Merritt, *James Henry Hammond, 1807–1864* (Baltimore, 1923), written as a doctoral dissertation, is good as far as it goes but does not catch the significance of this rather unusual man. Much material is now available that she did not use. A full study of the man, the political figure, and the agriculturist is badly needed.

Two splendid biographies remain to be mentioned: Harvey Wish, *George Fitzhugh, Propagandist of the Old South* (Baton Rouge, 1943), and Broadus Mitchell, *William Gregg, Factory Master of the Old South* (Chapel Hill, 1928). Both are the work of mature scholars, well grounded in their fields and masters of their subject matter. Wish sees Fitzhugh not only as the defender of slavery but as a sociologist of some merit. Mitchell treats Gregg as the man who brought the cotton mill to the South and made it stay and pay.

GENERAL AND SPECIAL HISTORIES

Any discussion of more recent works on this period must begin with Volumes I and II of James Ford Rhodes, *History of the United States, 1850–1896*, 8 vols. (New York, 1893–1919). His point of view was more balanced than that of his predecessors and the South received a larger and fairer treatment than before. His inclination to find patterns and plots, however, has weakened his reputation in recent years, and Volume VI of Edward Channing, *A History of the United States*, 6 vols. (New York, 1905–1925), is in many ways a sounder general treatment.

The most recent general work covering the decade before the Civil War is Allan Nevins' four volumes grouped under the titles *Ordeal of the Union*, 2 vols. (New York, 1947), and *The Emergence of Lincoln*, 2 vols. (New York, 1950). The canvas here is much broader than that of either Rhodes or Channing and far better balanced as far as coverage is concerned. Economic and social materials are included to a larger degree, and the style is superior to anything in the field. The point of view, however, is still decidedly Northern, and little gain in objectivity is shown over Rhodes or Channing. Civil War historiography makes little advance with Nevins.

Avery Craven, *The Coming of the Civil War* (New York, 1942), also covers the general period but makes no effort to study the causes of the coming struggle. His interest is entirely on the problem of how issues developed beyond the ability of the democratic process to handle them.

It is not necessary, however, to discuss the treatment accorded the problem of changing interpretations of the causes of the Civil War because that has been done thoroughly by Howard K. Beale in an article, "What Historians have said about the Causes of the Civil War," in *Theory and Practice in Historical Study: A Report of the Committee on Historiography, Bulletin 54, 1946, Social Science Research Council* (New York, 1946). Of more importance are the special monographs

413

dealing with specific phases or areas and the biographies of the men involved. Henry H. Simms in his *A Decade of Sectional Controversy, 1851–1861* (Chapel Hill, 1942), briefly summarizes the important events but offers little of interpretation. Roy F. Nichols in his *The Disruption of American Democracy* (New York, 1948), does more than tell the story of the break-up of the last great national party. He offers a sound analysis of the Kansas situation, a thorough discussion of the James Buchanan administration, and a thoughtful interpretation of the political side of the nation's difficulties. Robert R. Russel, *Economic Aspects of Southern Sectionalism, 1840–1861,* University of Illinois *Studies in the Social Sciences,* XI, Nos. 1–2 (Urbana, 1924), is a mine of information well organized and interpreted. Other important background books are Arthur C. Cole, *The Whig Party in the South* (Washington, 1913), and Fletcher M. Green, *Constitutional Development in the South Atlantic States, 1776–1860* (Chapel Hill, 1930). Cole's volume is invaluable for the political story, while Green's work shows that there was considerably more democracy in the South than has usually been supposed. Clement Eaton, *Freedom of Thought in the Old South* (Durham, 1940), on the other hand, reveals the underlying reactionary tendencies. W. Darrell Overdyke, *The Know-Nothing Party in the South* (Baton Rouge, 1950), is the first study of that party that has appeared. It fills a rather serious gap in the party history of the section. For educational materials Edgar W. Knight, *Public Education in the South* (Boston, 1922), is the best general survey of the subject; and Thomas C. Johnson, *Scientific Interests in the Old South* (New York, 1936), is a good introduction to that field. There are, however, monographic studies of education for each of the states, and the various histories of Southern universities provide considerable material on teachers and the scientific work being done there. E. Merton Coulter, *College Life in the Old South* (New York, 1928), is the most complete and entertaining among the college histories.

William S. Jenkins, *Pro-Slavery Thought in the Old South* (Chapel Hill, 1935), is the best general discussion in its field but needs to be supplemented by contemporary writings and by Arthur M. Lloyd, *The Slavery Controversy, 1831–1860* (Chapel Hill, 1939), which takes a slightly different approach.

Outstanding in scholarship and importance to any understanding of the period is James C. Malin, *John Brown and the Legend of Fifty-Six* (Philadelphia, 1942). Malin has studied the Kansas situation more thoroughly than any other and shows remarkable balance in dealing with John Brown and the troubled Kansas scene. His volume is a "must" for any grasp of the period. P. Orman Ray, *The Repeal of the Missouri Compromise* (Cleveland, 1909), is another volume dealing with Kansas that must be noted. His thesis is that the Missouri political situation involving David R. Atchison and Benton lay back of the repeal feature of Douglas' bill.

There is much good social history in Minnie C. Boyd, *Alabama in the Fifties; A Social Study* (New York, 1931); Gerald M. Capers, *The Biography of a River Town; Memphis: Its Heroic Age* (Chapel Hill, 1939); F. Garvin Davenport, *Cultural Life in Nashville on the Eve of the Civil War* (Chapel Hill, 1941); and Rosser H. Taylor, *Ante-Bellum South Carolina: A Social and Cultural History* (Chapel Hill, 1942).

Transportation has not yet been adequately studied. Ulrich B. Phillips, *A History of Transportation in the Eastern Cotton Belt to 1860* (New York, 1908), and Thomas D. Clark, *The Beginning of the L & N; . . . 1836–1860* (Louisville, 1933), are useful for the limited areas covered.

For the secession period itself, Dwight L. Dumond, *The Secession Movement, 1860–1861* (New York, 1931), remains a standard source for both information and analysis, and *Southern Editorials on Secession* (New York, 1931), of which he is the editor, makes available much badly scattered source material. Howard C. Perkins (ed.), *Northern Editorials on Secession*, 2 vols. (New York, 1942), serves the same purpose in bringing together a wide variety of Northern newspaper sources. *Lincoln and His Party in the Secession Crisis* (New Haven, 1942), by David M. Potter, discusses the failure of Northern leaders to understand the seriousness of the situation as it had developed in 1861 and shows the serious damage done by Lincoln's refusal to speak out in the crisis, and by William H. Seward's handling of the Border States. *The Slave States in the Presidential Election of 1860* (Baltimore, 1945), by Ollinger Crenshaw, is a thorough discussion of the campaign in each of the Southern states, with adequate treatment of the appeals made to voters and an analysis of the outcome. Jesse T. Carpenter, *The South as a Conscious Minority, 1789–1861; A Study in Political Thought* (New York, 1930), is useful in following out the development of the various defenses which the South offered to the growing Northern strength. His analysis of Calhoun's contribution is particularly good. Edward C. Smith, *The Borderland in the Civil War* (New York, 1927), while sketchy in many ways, is valuable for general information on developments in the last states to secede and in those which remained divided to the very end.

The details of the secession movement must be sought in the monographs that have been written for the different states. Here we are fortunate indeed. Splendid scholarly works exist for nearly every state and sound articles cover the remainder. For Virginia, Henry T. Shanks, *The Secession Movement in Virginia, 1847–1861* (Richmond, 1934), is a model of thoroughness and scholarly handling. The older and more general work, Charles H. Ambler, *Sectionalism in Virginia from 1776 to 1861* (Chicago, 1910), should serve as a background for Shanks's study and will provide much information essential to his work. J. Carlyle Sitterson, *The Secession Movement in North Carolina* (Chapel Hill, 1939), does for his state what Shanks has done for Virginia. It is both scholarly and readable. Georgia is covered more than adequately by Richard H. Shryock, *Georgia and the Union in 1850* (Durham, 1926); Ulrich B. Phillips, *Georgia and State Rights,* American Historical Association, *Annual Report,* 1901, II (Washington, 1902); Horace Montgomery, *Cracker Parties* (Baton Rouge, 1950); and Helen I. Greene, "Politics in Georgia, 1830–1854" (Ph.D. dissertation, University of Chicago, 1945). Two monographs are available for Alabama: Clarence P. Denman, *The Secession Movement in Alabama* (Montgomery, 1933), and Lewy Dorman, *Party Politics in Alabama from 1850 through 1860* (Wetumpka, 1935). Cleo C. Hearon, *Mississippi and the Compromise of 1850* (Oxford, Miss., 1913), and Percy L. Rainwater, *Mississippi, Storm Center of Secession, 1856–1861* (Baton Rouge, 1938), are both works of a superior quality. Roger W. Shugg, *Origins of Class Struggle in Louisiana . . . 1840–1875* (University, La., 1939), combined with James K. Greer, "Louisiana Politics, 1845–1861," in *Louisiana Historical Quarterly* (New Orleans), XII (1929), 381–425, 555–610; XIII (1930), 67–116, 257–303, 444–83, 617–54; and Willie M. Caskey, *Secession and Restoration of Louisiana* (Baton Rouge, 1938), unravel the complex story of Louisiana for the period. For Arkansas, Elsie M. Lewis, "From Nationalism to Disunion: A Study of the Secession Movement in Arkansas, 1850–1861" (Ph.D. dissertation, University of Chicago, 1946), covers the period adequately, but there is no good study for Kentucky. Mary Scrugham, *The Peaceable Americans of 1860–1861* (New York, 1921), and E. Merton Coulter, *The Civil War and Readjustment in Kentucky* (Chapel Hill, 1926), are helpful, but main reliance must be placed on newspapers and biographies. For Tennessee, James W. Patton, *Unionism and Reconstruction in Tennessee, 1860–1869* (Chapel Hill, 1934), and James W. Fertig, *The Secession and Reconstruction of Tennessee* (Chicago, 1898), are serviceable but give considerably more attention to Reconstruction than to secession. Again the newspapers and the biographies are most important.

The important South Carolina story has been the subject of several good monographs. Harold S. Schultz in his *Nationalism and Sectionalism in South Carolina, 1852–1860* (Durham, 1950) follows developments from the Compromise of 1850 through secession and shows that opinion in the state was considerably more divided than has often been supposed. Chauncey S. Boucher has written two scholarly monographs on different phases of the period which are of major importance. The first, "The Secession and Co-operation Movement in South Carolina, 1848 to 1852," was published in the Washington University *Studies* (St. Louis), V, No. 2 (1918), 65–138, and the second, "South Carolina and the South on the Eve of Secession, 1852 to 1860," appeared *ibid., Humanistic Series,* VI, No. 2 (1919), 79–144. Philip M. Hamer, *The Secession Movement in South Carolina, 1847–1852* (Allentown, Pa., 1918), is valuable for the early period culminating in the Compromise of 1850.

Kenneth M. Stampp, *And the War Came* (Baton Rouge, 1950), is an unusually well-balanced study of the secession crisis. Better than most scholars, he has understood the complexity of forces at work and the importance of public opinion in shaping events.

ARTICLES IN PERIODICALS AND PUBLICATIONS

Present-day periodicals require no comment. Most of the articles here listed are from scholarly publications and are the work of specialists in the fields covered. Only a few of the many dealing with the period can be given. Of an economic nature the following have proved of unusual value: James C. Bonner, "Genesis of Agricultural Reform in the Cotton Belt," in *Journal of Southern History* (Baton Rouge, Lexington), IX (1943), 475–500; James C. Bonner, "The Plantation Overseer and Southern Nationalism As Revealed in the Career of Garland D. Harmon," in *Agricultural History* (Chicago, Baltimore), XIX (1945), 1–11; Robert S. Cotterill, "The Beginnings of Railroads in the Southwest," in *Mississippi Valley Historical Review* (Cedar Rapids), VIII (1921–1922), 318–26; Philip G. Davidson, "Industrialism in the Ante-Bellum South," in *South Atlantic Quarterly* (Durham), XXVII (1928), 405–25; Henry G. Ellis, "The Influence of Industrial and Educational Leaders on the Secession of Virginia," *ibid.,* IX (1910), 372–76; Alfred H. Stone, "The Cotton Factorage System of the Southern States," in *American Historical Review* (New York), XX (1914–1915), 557–65.

Good social materials are contained in the following articles, whose titles suggest the subject matter: David R. Barbee, "Hinton Rowan Helper," in *Tyler's Quarterly Historical and Genealogical Magazine* (Richmond), XV (1933–1934), 144–72; David R. Barbee, "Hinton

Rowan Helper's Mendacity," *ibid.*, 228–31; Wilfred Carsel, "The Slave-holders' Indictment of Northern Wage Slavery," in *Journal of Southern History*, VI (1940), 504–20; Clement Eaton, "Henry A. Wise, A Liberal of the Old South," *ibid.*, VII (1941), 482–94; William O. Lynch, "The Westward Flow of Southern Colonists before 1861," *ibid.*, IX (1943), 303–27; Frank L. Owsley and Harriet C. Owsley, "The Economic Basis of Society in the Late Ante-Bellum South," *ibid.*, VI (1940), 24–45; Frank L. Owsley, "The Pattern of Migration and Settlement on the Southern Frontier," *ibid.*, XI (1945), 147–76; Clement Eaton, "Henry A. Wise and the Virginia Fire Eaters of 1856," in *Mississippi Valley Historical Review*, XXI (1934–1935), 495–512; Jay B. Hubbell, "Literary Nationalism in the Old South," in David K. Jackson (ed.), *American Studies in Honor of William Kenneth Boyd* (Durham, 1940), 175–220.

Articles dealing with political matters are even more abundant than those in other fields. Only those which make some contribution not to be found elsewhere are listed here. Among the most useful are the following: William K. Boyd, "North Carolina on the Eve of Secession," in American Historical Association, *Annual Report*, 1910 (Washington, 1912), 165–77; St. George L. Sioussat, "Tennessee and National Political Parties, 1850–1860," *ibid.*, 1914, I (Washington, 1916), 245–58; Charles E. Cauthen, "South Carolina's Decision to Lead the Secession Movement," in *North Carolina Historical Review* (Raleigh), XVIII (1941), 360–72; Arthur C. Cole, "The South and the Right of Secession in the Early Fifties," in *Mississippi Valley Historical Review*, I (1914–1915), 376–99; Frank H. Hodder, "The Railroad Background of the Kansas-Nebraska Act," *ibid.*, XII (1925–1926), 3–22; James G. Randall, "The Blundering Generation," *ibid.*, XXVII (1940–1941), 3–28; Ollinger Crenshaw, "Christopher G. Memminger's Mission to Virginia, 1860," in *Journal of Southern History*, VIII (1942), 334–49; Fletcher M. Green, "Democracy in the Old South," *ibid.*, XII (1946), 3–23; Kenneth M. Stampp, "Letters from the Washington Peace Conference of 1861," *ibid.*, IX (1943), 394–403; James G. Randall, "The Civil War Restudied," *ibid.*, VI (1940), 439–57; Avery Craven, "Coming of the War Between the States: An Interpretation," *ibid.*, II (1936), 303–22; Austin L. Venable, "The Conflict Between the Douglas and Yancey Forces in the Charleston Convention," *ibid.*, VIII (1942), 226–41; Charles W. Ramsdell, "Lincoln and Fort Sumter," *ibid.*, III (1937), 259–88; Charles W. Ramsdell, "The Changing Interpretation of the Civil War," *ibid.*, 3–27; Dorothy Dodd, "The Secession Movement in Florida, 1850–1861," in *Florida Historical Quarterly* (Jacksonville, Gainesville, Tallahassee), XII (1933–1934), 3–24, 45–66; James C. Malin, "The Motives of Stephen A. Douglas in the Organization of Nebraska Territory: A Letter December 17, 1853," in *Kansas Historical Quarterly* (Topeka), XIX (1951), 321–53; Laura A. White, "The National Democrats in South Carolina, 1852 to 1860," in *South Atlantic Quarterly*, XXVIII (1929), 370–89; Helen I. Greene, "Politics in Georgia, 1853–54; The Ordeal of Howell Cobb," in *Georgia Historical Quarterly* (Savannah), XXX (1946), 185–211; James K. Greer, "Louisiana Politics, 1845–1861," in *Louisiana Historical Quarterly* (New Orleans), XIII (1930), 270–80, 444–83, 617–54; James G. Randall, "When War Came in 1861," in *Abraham Lincoln Quarterly* (Springfield), I (1940–1941), 3–42; Avery Craven, "The Civil War and the Democratic Process," *ibid.,* IV (1946–1947), 269–92.

INDEX

431

433